THE
Naval
Officer's
Guide

THE
Naval
Officer's
Guide

TENTH EDITION

WILLIAM P. MACK
VICE ADMIRAL, U.S. NAVY (RETIRED)
with
THOMAS D. PAULSEN
REAR ADMIRAL, U.S. NAVY

Naval Institute Press
Annapolis, Maryland

Copyright © 1960, 1964, 1967, 1970, 1983
by the United States Naval Institute
Annapolis, Maryland
Published 1943, tenth edition 1991

Library of Congress Cataloging-in-Publication Data

Mack, William P., 1915–
    The naval officer's guide / William P. Mack with Thomas D.
Paulsen.—10th ed.
      p. cm.
    Includes bibliographical references and index.
    ISBN 0-87021-296-6 (alk. paper)
    1. United States. Navy—Officers' handbooks. I. Paulsen, Thomas
D. II. Title.
V133.M28   1991
359'.00973—dc20   90-22820

Printed in the United States of America on acid-free paper ∞

10 9 8 7 6 5 4

Cover photo: courtesy Michael Poche

CONTENTS

PREFACE

The Naval Officer's Guide is a collection of information and advice for officers of the U.S. Navy, to be used from the period of their preparation for commissioning through their years as junior officers. It can be a handy reference work for many additional years of service as well. This book provides the essential information for officers who are preparing themselves for their initial assignments, and it advises officers from each procurement source on how to round out their professional and school education. Counsel is given for those officers serving in billets at sea on all sizes of ships. Also included is information about serving in first shore and overseas billets and in a first staff billet. Officers serving in head-of-department billets in large ships and as executive officers of small ships should refer to *Command at Sea*, published by the Naval Institute Press, for advice on preparing for command.

The Naval Officer's Guide also contains information on such subjects as the organization of the Defense Department and the military services, military law, the code of conduct, and other topics of interest to officers of all ranks.

Every young officer should read The Naval Officer's Guide from start to finish early in his or her career. As a reference work, the book can also provide ready and practical answers to many problems that would otherwise be found only by searching the ship's library of official publications.

Frequent reference is made to other Naval Institute Press publications, which cover the entire field of the naval profession. All of the books mentioned should be part of the ship's library. They are listed in the bibliography.

Contained within these covers is over 50 percent of the information needed to meet the professional competency objectives set by the CNO for all line officers. The remaining 50 percent of

Preface

needed information can be obtained from textbooks and practical observation at sea.

Every attempt has been made to preserve the wisdom of the past while covering the experience of the present generation of naval officers. Past authorities have been appropriately acknowledged. Epigraphs in chapter heads, where not otherwise noted, were delivered in the presence of, and recorded by, the authors.

Since the publication of the ninth edition of The Naval Officer's Guide in 1983, organizational changes in the Defense Department, administrative document revisions, and technological advances have been made. This edition, therefore, is almost entirely new, except for the dissemination of wisdom, tradition, and certain time-honored values.

The original Naval Officer's Guide was written by Rear Admiral Arthur Ageton. Few of the words of the original book or of its later editions remain in this one, but the inspiration, wisdom, and experience of Admiral Ageton have been preserved.

It is appropriate that Rear Admiral Thomas D. Paulsen, who coauthored this edition, last served as head of the Department of Professional Development at the U.S. Naval Academy. The department is charged with, among other responsibilities, preparing midshipmen for entry into the Navy and for their subsequent careers, and so he took a personal interest in making sure that we included all the information needed by the young naval officer.

We would like to acknowledge the help of the public affairs offices of the services that furnished us with up-to-date materials and, at the Naval Institute, the personal concern and guidance of editor Carol Swartz and photo librarian Patty Maddocks.

THE
Naval
Officer's
Guide

I

THE IMPORTANCE OF OUR NAVY

SEA POWER HAS BEEN ONE OF THE MAIN STRENGTHS
OF OUR COUNTRY SINCE ITS INDEPENDENCE. WE HAVE
USED SEA POWER TO EXTEND OUR INFLUENCE
IN THE PACIFIC AND ATLANTIC OCEANS AND FROM THE
ARCTIC TO THE ANTARCTIC. NOW WE WILL NEED IT
TO PROTECT OUR POLITICAL, ECONOMIC, AND
MILITARY INTERESTS IN THE MIDDLE EAST
AND THE INDIAN OCEAN.

—Admiral John S. McCain

OUR NAVY MUST BE LED BY AN OFFICER CORPS WHICH
RECOGNIZES THE IMPORTANCE OF SEA POWER TO OUR
COUNTRY AND THE KEY ROLE OF THE NAVY IN
PROVIDING THE CUTTING EDGE OF THAT POWER.

—Admiral Robert L. Dennison

Officers in the U.S. Navy have served the American people with distinction and pride for more than two hundred years. During no other period in the history of our nation has a strong and ready peacetime Navy been as important as it has been since World War II. The Navy, Marine Corps, Army, Air Force, and Coast Guard have acted as the principal guardians of our way of life during a time of continuing challenge. Despite the hopes of many, an era of enduring good will and peace did not follow the end of hostilities in 1945. In the words of President John F. Kennedy, "We have been engaged in a long, twilight struggle" with the forces of communism.

Every naval officer—indeed every American—should know how this struggle threatens the ideals and principles that so many of us take for granted. As a member of the officer corps of one of our nation's leading military forces, you should be familiar with Soviet and American institutions, both military and political. With this knowledge you will be equipped to help the Navy solve our country's problems.

The Defense Department publishes at frequent intervals an unclassified document titled *Soviet Military Power: An Assessment of the Threat.* This is an excellent summary of the Soviet Union's military strength and should be studied closely by every naval officer.

Similarly the Navy Department publishes an unclassified document titled *Understanding Soviet Naval Developments.* This document treats the naval threat in greater depth than the DOD document. It, too, should be studied carefully.

Glasnost and *perestroika* may be new policies, or they may be smoke screens for continuing present policies. It is the duty of every naval officer to observe carefully and to be prepared for the worst case. In intelligence parlance, the military must be prepared for capabilities, not intentions.

Naval officers should be reminded of the following points: the surface of the earth is approximately seven-eighths water; sea power is essential to any country seeking to dominate the world or to prevent its control by other powers; the Soviet Union has recently strengthened its sea power; the United States is a strong sea power and has the resources to increase its power; the Navy is the key element in the sea power of the United States; one of the principal strengths of our Navy is its officer corps; and your contributions to the officer corps are important to its success.

Sea Power

Although sea power has been understood and exploited since the time of the ancient Greeks, who used navies and merchant shipping, the first real analyst of sea power was Admiral Alfred Thayer Mahan. Every naval officer should know something of his achievements and a lot about his philosophy. One of his most notable works was the trilogy composed of *The Influence of Sea Power on History, 1660–1783* (1890), *The Influence of Sea Power upon the French Revolution and Empire, 1793–1812* (1892), and *The Life of Nelson* (1897). He wrote *The Interest of America in*

Sea Power, Present and Future (1897), and about thirty other volumes as well.

Admiral Mahan summarized what was known of sea power up to his time and did his best to predict the trends of the future. Since Mahan, many more experts have written on sea power, but none has emerged as a preeminent spokesman. Two of the most knowledgeable writers were Admirals McCain and Dennison, quoted at the beginning of this chapter. You will find the best of current literature on modern sea power listed in the appendixes. As a young naval officer, you may well be one of the new experts if you excel at your profession, observe well, and learn the art of written expression. The study of sea power is not a static discipline, even though certain general principles we have in mind when we regard sea power remain unchanged. New theories about, and additions to the basic principles of, the functioning of sea power may provide us with the insights we need to gain the margin of victory in future years.

Definition of Sea Power.   Sea power is the sum of all physical, demographic, geographic, economic, and military resources of a country that are derived from or related to the sea and that are used by that nation to advance its political, economic, and security interests. As you study the subject, your research will reveal a dozen other definitions by as many experts. However, all agree that sea power cannot survive without the following:

1. A strong, ready navy, capable of projecting its power across the sea and ashore with combinations of surface, submarine, and amphibious forces, and carrier- and shore-based air forces, and capable of maintaining a sea-based strategic deterrent system.

2. A merchant marine that can carry overseas trade, enable us to import strategic materials, and promote the balance of trade. The ships of the merchant marine should be capable of assisting the navy in time of war and some should be capable of rapid conversion to navy auxiliary vessels.

3. A shipbuilding industry capable of producing superior naval vessels and merchant ships in peacetime and of being expanded in wartime to meet the nation's naval and maritime needs.

4. Ports, harbors, and bases to serve and support a Navy and merchant marine in peace and in war.

5. Adequate inland transportation systems from manufacturing centers to ports and harbors.

6. A population with the seagoing temperament, fighting ability, and patriotism to man a navy and merchant marine.

7. Surrounding seas that provide both protection from possible enemies and avenues of access to those enemies and to allies and areas where strategic materials may be obtained.

The Sea Power of the United States. We have set forth the essentials of sea power. Now we can point out how the United States meets these criteria.

1. The United States has a strong, ready Navy. Opinions differ as to whether it is adequate in size or in readiness. It does have the ability to project power across the sea and ashore by virtue of its surface and subsurface forces, carrier air power, and its Navy–Marine Corps amphibious teams, and to protect the sea-lanes with its air, surface, and submarine forces. Further, its missile-equipped submarine strategic-deterrent force is adequate, capable, and virtually invulnerable.

2. Our merchant marine is sadly deficient in size, capability, and readiness. We have a few good ships, but not enough to meet even the minimum export or import requirements. This is a glaring weakness in our sea power.

3. Our shipbuilding industry is inadequate. In order to reach and maintain a navy large enough to project our presence to the far reaches of the world, honor our commitments to friends and allies, and protect our own strategic interests, we must have a corresponding industrial-shipyard capacity. We do not have enough shipyards qualified to build nuclear-powered ships and submarines, and we do not have the number of shipyards capable of building enough conventional warships and merchant ships.

4. We are blessed with natural harbors and have many well-developed and -equipped ports, all of adequate size and location.

5. We do have an excellent internal transportation system made up of superb highways and trucking systems, railways and railroad systems, and airports and airlines.

6. We have a population capable of manning almost any size navy and merchant marine. Our countrymen have lived by the sea, sailed and fought on it, and understood it. We love it, we use it, and we excel on it. We are truly a seagoing nation.

7. We are protected by adjacent seas from potential enemies. Any enemy must pass through large ocean areas dotted with shore

The fleet ballistic-missile submarine *West Virginia* (SSBN 736) under construction and the *Pennsylvania* (SSBN 735) at launch. They will strengthen and modernize our strategic-deterrent force, a key component of U.S. sea power.

and air bases in order to reach our shores. Conversely, we can approach and reach potential enemies under the protection of these same bases.

In summary, we are the greatest sea power on earth, as we were during World War II, but we must guard against deficiencies in naval forces, and shipbuilding and merchant marine capabilities.

The Maritime Strategy. In the years just prior to 1986, various civilian leaders and officers within the Navy Department made an attempt to articulate a single, cohesive maritime strategy. In a supplement to the U.S. Naval Institute *Proceedings* issue of January 1986, Admiral James D. Watkins, then chief of naval operations, announced such a policy. Its goal was to use maritime

A demonstration of the use of a helicopter to unload a container ship. Container ships are important to U.S. sea power, but there are not many of them.

power, in combination with the efforts of our sister services and the forces of our allies, to bring about war termination on favorable terms. Although the strategy changes subtly with the rapid changes occurring in East-West relations, its basic premises should survive in succeeding Navy Department administrations for many years.

The Sea Power of Our Probable Adversaries. Our most likely adversaries are less fortunate. The sea power of the Soviet Union can be summarized as follows:

1. The Soviet Union has a growing navy. Its ships are new and are extending their operations to the far reaches of the world. Its amphibious capability and carrier-based air power continues to improve as new classes of ships are introduced, including the

A major component of U.S. sea power is the carrier battle group. The United States has fifteen of them, built around carriers such as the *Dwight D. Eisenhower* (CVN 69). Indications are, however, that reductions in the size of the U.S. Navy will result in a force of twelve.

first in a series of full-deck carriers. Its shore-based air power and surface and submarine combatant forces are strong and significant. Its navy, ship for ship, currently exceeds ours in numbers and in firepower. Its submarine-based deterrent forces are growing rapidly. Improvement in Soviet technology and in tactical employment of forces in recent years is impressive. The Soviet naval officer is well trained and highly disciplined—a formidable foe.

2. The Soviet merchant marine is adequate for a large power. Its merchant ships are numerous, well constructed, and manned by naval reservists who operate with the Soviet Navy on short notice. The Soviet fishing fleet, the largest in the world, provides the USSR with an immediate auxiliary naval force, capable of electronic and acoustic surveillance and electronic countermeasures; the fishing fleet can target U.S. forces throughout the world.

3. The Soviet shipbuilding industry, aided by the industries of its satellites, is adequate to support the merchant marine and meet the requirements of an expanding navy.

4. The USSR has only marginally capable harbors and ports. Some of them are frequently ice-bound.

5. The USSR's internal transportation is inadequate. Highway

U.S. ability to project sea power inland lies mainly with the Navy–Marine Corps amphibious teams.

and rail systems are in bad condition. However, its canal and river transport systems, where existing, are superb. The military-transport system is modern and growing, but the civilian air-transport system is poor.

6. The Soviet Union is made up of peoples who, over the years, have exhibited less than the average ability to use the seas. It does not have that last, indefinable component of sea power, an historical love for the sea and an understanding of it.

7. The seas bordering on the Soviet Union are very restrictive. To the east, the Kurile Island channels squeeze both naval forces and shipping into easily observed passages between islands. Ice on the northern coasts of the Soviet Union restricts passage during most of the year, and exit from the Baltic ports is controlled by the narrow strait between Sweden, Norway, and Denmark. After leaving the Baltic, ships and submarines must traverse the Greenland–Iceland–United Kingdom gap; when approaching the United States, they can come under further surveillance. The Black Sea

exit to the Mediterranean is also narrow and controlled. Geographically, the Soviet Union is handicapped as a major power.

In summary, although the Soviet Union's geographical set-up is a disadvantage, the USSR is a first-rate sea power.

Communist China is another potential adversary. At present it is deficient in all aspects of sea power, but it has the potential to develop a powerful navy in the next fifty years.

None of our other possible enemies has sea-power potential. Countries with significant sea-power capabilities or potential are, fortunately, either allies or uncommitted nations.

The Threat

Before setting a national policy or planning a military attack, it is customary to examine the nature of any opposition that might arise in relation to such issues. In planner's parlance this process is known as examining the "threat." A planner wants to be sure that his scheme provides enough forces to overcome the most likely opposition or threat; at the same time he does not want to waste forces or effort, a crucial consideration in an era of economic constraint.

Our government has a procedure for such an exchange of views. In January and February the Senate and House Armed Services Committees hold "authorization" or "posture" hearings. The two committees examine our military posture and then authorize the building and procurement of ships, tanks, aircraft, and major weapons systems. The appropriations committees of both houses later pass bills providing funds to buy these items and meet any remaining requirements of the services. At the posture hearings the secretary of defense, the chairman of the Joint Chiefs of Staff, the secretaries of the services, and the military chiefs of the services present statements giving their perspectives on the nature of the threat, the condition and status of our forces, and the necessary additions to those forces for the coming year. The secretary of defense and the chairman of the Joint Chiefs cover the entire spectrum of the Defense Department. Each service secretary and chief then covers each military branch, with the secretary of the Navy including the Marine Corps. All statements are presented in a classified version in closed session, and a declassified version is later released to the public. The declassified statements are published in various service magazines, such as the *Army Times*, the *Air Force Times*, and the *Navy Times*. These posture statements are the public's main source of information on the military threat.

For more detailed information, you should consult the biennially published book *Combat Fleets of the World*, which contains authentic information on the ships, submarines, and aircraft of all nations and is now found on the bridge of all Navy ships. Just as thorough is *Jane's Fighting Ships*, published in the United Kingdom. This can be found in your ship's library or combat information center (CIC).

Another book is *Weyer's Warships of the World*, compiled by Gerhard Albrecht. It is considerably cheaper and much more manageable in size.

The Soviet Military Threat.   Our main military threat comes from the Soviet Union and its allies. The USSR's forces alone have been increased and improved to the point where they exceed ours in numbers and capabilities. In addition, they have spread their influence and arms throughout South and Central America, Africa, Europe, and the Middle East, either directly or through Cuba and other third parties.

As of 1989 Soviet bloc capabilities included the following:

1. An annual devotion to defense of 15 to 17 percent of the gross national product.

2. The operation of 150 major military industrial plants.

3. SS-N-21 sea-launched cruise missiles now operational.

4. A large number of intercontinental missiles in place and a growing submarine-based intercontinental-missile capability, including the SS-24 rail-mobile ICBM.

5. 4.8 million men under arms, including 211 army divisions.

6. 80,000 tanks and 75,000 artillery pieces.

7. 10,000 modern T-64 and T-72 tanks.

8. Substantial chemical warfare capability.

9. 8 classes of submarines and 8 classes of warships being built each year.

10. 20 surface ships, 70 submarines, and 300 aircraft armed with antiship cruise missiles.

11. 308 submarines, mostly nuclear-powered.

12. New 25,000-ton Typhoon missile-firing submarines.

13. 5 V/STOL carriers in use and a large (65,000-ton) conventional carrier.

14. 5,000 Soviet and allied bloc fighters and fighter bombers based in Eastern Europe alone. More than 1,000 fighter types produced annually. A Soviet helicopter fleet of over 5,000.

15. 301 Backfire intermediate-range bombers deployed and 30 more being built each year. 160 Bear bombers, 272 Badger bombers, and 135 Blinder bombers in commission.

16. The addition of 30 modern units to the merchant marine each year.

17. A merchant marine of hundreds of conversion-capable ships manned by naval reservists.

Although the foregoing is only a quick overview of Soviet military assets in 1989, it does indicate the magnitude of the military threat. You will do well to follow changes that occur in future years; unfortunately, they will probably all be additions to Soviet military capabilities, in spite of the scrapping of older ships, tanks, and aircraft.

The Soviet Political Threat. To some students of history communism has a certain idealistic appeal, but we must recognize that the Soviet Union has gained military and political strength at the expense of its citizens, who are the victims of repressive power. The intentions of the USSR on the global level must also be questioned, for if its leaders play politics according to the rules of the *Communist Manifesto*, then they are indeed dedicated to spreading communism by what Karl Marx called the "forcible overthrow of all existing social conditions."

The changes in political leadership in Soviet bloc countries, and the increasing failure of communism in the Soviet Union and the Soviet bloc countries are encouraging to Western countries. The cold war may be nearing its end, but economic failures in the Soviet Union may bring back military and Communist leadership. Those who are responsible for the defense of our country must be appropriately cautious.

The Navy and National Security: Prospects for the Future

Since the United States became a country, our Navy has been a leading contributor to our national security and our military victories. More importantly, since World War II it has been devoted to preventing wars and keeping the peace. The Navy has always been the first force to be called upon in times of crisis and the quickest to respond. We must preserve and strengthen this vital service.

The posture statements made annually before the Senate and House Armed Services Committees by civilian and military leaders of the armed forces are informative opinions on the readiness of our military and, of course, on the ability of our Navy to help maintain national security.

Our Present Naval Posture. In preceding pages the function of the annual posture was discussed. In the latest posture statement made by former Chief of Naval Operations Admiral Trost, he testified:

> The American imperative for maritime power begins as a fundamental requirement for an island nation, dependent on world commerce, to have free use of the world's oceans. It is compounded by the emergence of the United States as a world power, with worldwide interests and alliance commitments to nations which are themselves islands or located in strategically exposed positions. To such a nation and to such an alliance, freedom of the seas is a prerequisite for economic and political survival.
>
> Freedom of the seas is not a gift, nor is it built into any international Bill of Rights. This crucial freedom is won largely through naval presence or engagements. In a perfect world based on the rule of law, the Western Alliance could rest assured that this freedom, once secured, would be inviolable. In a turbulent international arena, however, we must be ready, with resolve, to enforce claims for free movement on the world's seas and oceans with capable naval power applied where needed.

Then, with regard to national security strategy, he said:

> These inescapable geopolitical realities underlie a U.S. national security strategy supported by maritime strategy, which is, in essence, a professional judgement of how maritime power can best support national interests. Key elements of national military strategy—deterrence, forward defense, and alliance solidarity—each require maritime power.

Further, with regard to the threat:

America's location, global interests and interdependent economy would demand that the United States attain maritime superiority irrespective of the name or nature of the likely antagonist. However, our national military strategy clearly identifies the Soviet Union as the principal global adversary. For years this huge continental power has been amassing military forces far out of proportion to what we would consider reasonable for self-defense. Largely self-contained, it operates on interior lines of communications which minimize the need for intercourse with other countries. Soviet influence is not based on its economy or ability to produce goods, nor does it provide a marketplace for the world. Consequently, it does not need a navy to be secure within its borders, but it nonetheless continues to build a large and capable navy and power-projection forces.

Admiral Trost then stated that:

Several Soviet naval developments are particularly challenging to U.S. maritime superiority:
The mammoth force of Soviet attack submarines now includes several classes of nuclear ships which represent major gains to acoustic quieting and combat system sophistication.
The Soviets have recognized the need to improve their own ASW capability, and have embarked on an aggressive program to close the gap in submarine superiority.
The Soviet Union has developed a virtual copy of the United States' *Tomahawk* cruise missile.
The Soviet land-based air force is designed to counter United States forward defenses and will soon introduce a new Soviet-type AWACS.
Leonid Brezhnev [now named *Tbilisi*], the first Soviet large-deck aircraft carrier, has been launched.

Admiral Trost then went on to detail the international environment in which the U.S. Navy would have to operate, including the need to combat terrorism and drug trafficking. Then he gave the state of readiness of the U.S. Navy:

Today's Navy is the strong, capable instrument of maritime power the United States requires, more ready than ever to do what is asked of us in peace, crisis, or war. The nation's investment in the Navy has produced concrete results and substantial improvements in all aspects of naval capability, as evident by a variety of indicators. One such indicator is the extraordinarily positive personal observations of those with firsthand experience with today's fleet, ranging from uniformed naval leadership to a host of outside observers. A more quantifiable set of indicators is the measurement of the basic components or inputs of total military capability: high unit readiness levels; increasing sustainability indices; a force structure with new, more sophisticated ships and airplanes; and continuing modernization of existing forces. A third and perhaps most telling indicator is the sustained operational performance of naval forces worldwide in routine deployments, exercises, and crises. Taken together, these various measures of excellence point to a Navy today which is an impressive force in readiness: underway and on a steady course of quality and professionalism.

Marine Corps Posture. It is important that each naval officer know and understand the basic elements of the current posture of the Marine Corps. The former commandant of the Marine Corps, General P. X. Kelley, testified that:

> Our effectiveness is the result of three basic factors: our organization for combat; our ability to project power—rapidly and decisively; and the esprit of our Marines.
>
> We stand ready to deploy expeditionary forces which are organized from existing combat-ready units. These task-organized entities, generically referred to as Marine Air-Ground Task Forces, consist of aviation combat, ground combat, and combat service support elements that are formed under a single command element. This unity of command at the tactical level allows the commander absolute control of his subordinate elements, which is vital for success in combat.

In summary, the readiness of the Navy–Marine Corps team has reached a new high. You, as naval officers, will have the responsibility of maintaining that position, guarding it against "all enemies, foreign and domestic."

The Officer's Role

Each naval officer has an opportunity to serve his or her country and at the same time to pursue an interesting and rewarding career. There is a one-in-four chance that a CNO will be chosen from amongst those entering the service in any one year. Each year group will provide two four-star flag officers, eight vice admirals, and as many as thirty rear admirals. Many who do not reach flag rank will serve in important billets in command at sea, on staffs, and in various headquarters ashore. All officers of all ranks can make important contributions.

Nevertheless, opportunity is not given to you; it must be earned. When you report to your first station you may think that your education is complete, your training finished, your future assured. You will soon find that your education and training have just begun.

For the first time no one will prepare lesson plans and study guides for you. You must find out what you should know and then you must set about learning it. The many manuals aboard each ship and submarine and at each aviation squadron describe the machinery and equipment on your vessel or craft. Other books set forth Navy doctrine. Competent petty officers are repositories of practical knowledge. It will be your job to find all of these sources. No one will push you; push yourself. You will have a busy four years ahead of you.

Before serving in their first ship, almost all surface line officers will attend Surface Warfare Officer's School (SWOS) and Leadership Management and Education Training School (LMET). These schools, plus the professional education given you by your commissioning source, should qualify you for most junior officer billets in a surface ship in deck, engineering, and operations. Either en route to your first ship or at a later date, you will be ordered to attend specialty schools to learn such skills as emergency shiphandling or damage control. As a junior officer you will be placed in a department to qualify as a junior division officer and as a watch officer.

Some officers, as soon as they qualify, want to take in the slack. This is the worst thing you can do at this stage of your career. If it is not practicable for you to be rotated to other departments, you should voluntarily qualify in as many departments as you can. The extra qualification and training you achieve as a junior officer will be of use to you during your entire career. Many a Promotion Selection Board member has voted for an officer because his fitness report contained a notation to the effect that he had qualified as an officer of the deck (OOD) even though he had served in the engineering department. The point is, your education and training never stop. Successful qualification should be your inspiration to pass on to the next challenge.

Aviation warfare officers will be sent to flight training in Pensacola, Florida, as soon as possible. There is not sufficient room there to train all of a year group at the same time, so many will be sent to ships or air bases awaiting a vacancy in the training schedule. Like surface warfare officers, you should seize this opportunity to qualify as an OOD or as an engineering officer of the watch. Again, such qualification has been the deciding point in selection for promotion or for carrier command. After you arrive in Pensacola you will compete for and be assigned to various types of aviation training. Your first squadron tour, if in a ship, is another opportunity to broaden your professional training. Remember that you are a naval officer first and an aviation warfare officer second. There will come a time when you will return to general naval duties. Be ready.

Newly selected submarine warfare officers (either newly commissioned or later selected) have somewhat the same problem as aviation warfare officers: all must attend nuclear power school and serve at a nuclear prototype facility, and some may have to be assigned to a ship or station while awaiting a vacancy. The same recommendation pertains to these officers—every opportunity should be taken to qualify and to learn in other fields.

Officers of the restricted line and staff corps may become members of these communities either by transfer from the unrestricted line or by accession. Those fortunate enough to have served some time as line officers will bring to their career a background in general line duties.

Women officers of all categories will follow as nearly as possible the paths of other officers of their categories with one important exception. The law presently prohibits women from serving in the Navy in combat billets at sea or in combat aircraft in areas where fighting might break out. This has been interpreted to mean that women can serve in certain designated ships such as tenders and can fly all types of aircraft (including combat types) except in areas of possible combat. It is a fact that this prohibition prevents women officers from enjoying the full range of career opportunity. Until the law is changed or repealed, women officers should do their best to achieve all possible qualifications and to carry out all of their assigned duties in an outstanding manner.

Such performance will lead to successive promotions and to steadily increasing opportunities to make important contributions to our Navy.

The first four years, then, are devoted to attaining professional qualifications, first in your warfare specialty and, as time permits, in other specialties.

You will have an opportunity to contribute to the Navy during the first phase by standing good watches, administering your division well, and completing your education.

The second phase of your career is designed to prepare you for command of a small ship and for duty on small staffs and ashore. You will serve in billets that will give you the opportunity to obtain the experience necessary to command at sea. Chapter 19 will describe the experience, but a complete source of guidance is *Command at Sea*. Your early experience will enable you to serve on a small naval staff; at the Armed Forces Staff College you will qualify to serve on a joint staff.

Opportunities for participation will increase during this phase. You will find that you can begin to institute improvements in shipboard procedures and in tactical doctrines when in command. Ashore and on staffs possibilities are unlimited.

In the third phase of your career, you will command large ships and units of ships, and serve on large naval staffs, joint staffs, and in Washington on headquarters staffs. Again, your expanding experience and attendance at senior war colleges will prepare you for this duty.

The third phase offers unlimited opportunities for you to make use of your talents. A well-commanded aircraft carrier, cruiser, submarine, squadron, or fleet is itself a great contribution to the Navy. Further, you can initiate many improvements in tactical doctrines, you can propose changes in the use of sea power, and you can participate at the highest levels in Defense Department planning and political processes.

Count yourself fortunate if you are ordered to a war college, but do not give up if you are not. Apply for, and take, naval war college correspondence courses. You will learn a lot, which may influence a subsequent war college selection board to pick you. Similarly, try to attend postgraduate school. If you are not selected, go to night school at your first shore-duty location and try to earn a master's degree.

The point being made here is that your education is up to

you, and it is the key to your success in a very complicated and technical profession. Contrary to what you might expect, this extra effort on your part will not limit the time required for your assigned duties. You will find that the more you do, the more you can do. The more you can do, the more contributions you will be able to make to your Navy. After all, promoting the success of your Navy, whether by making out an improved version of the watch, quarter, and station bill as an ensign or formulating a new tactical doctrine as an admiral, is what your profession is all about.

2

THE NAVAL OFFICER

HE BECAME AN OFFICER AND A GENTLEMAN, WHICH IS
AN ENVIABLE THING.

—*Rudyard Kipling*, Only a Subaltern

IN EVERY MILITARY SYSTEM WHICH HAS TRIUMPHED IN
MODERN WAR THE OFFICERS HAVE BEEN RECOGNIZED
AS THE BRAIN OF THE ARMY, AND TO PREPARE THEM
FOR THEIR TRUST, GOVERNMENTS HAVE SPARED
NO PAINS TO GIVE THEM SPECIAL EDUCATION
AND TRAINING.

—*Emory Upton*, The Military Policy of the United States

The Navy, prior to World War II, was officered completely by
graduates of the Naval Academy and warrant officers. Shortly
before the war increasing numbers of reserve officers, mostly graduates of NROTC programs, were brought to active duty. During
the war, officers were procured from many sources, ranging from
the Naval Academy to direct procurement. In the postwar period
most reserve officers were released to inactive duty, but many
stayed on active duty and were later integrated (augmented) into
the Regular Navy.

In the years since World War II, the Navy officer corps has
been built around a group of regular officers from the Naval Academy, the NROTC scholarship program, lateral transfers, direct
procurement and other programs for the staff corps, and some
augmentation of the Reserve. The Reserve has been procured from
the NROTC Contract Program, Officer Candidate School (OCS),
Nuclear Power Candidate (NUPOC) program, Aviation Officer
Candidate (AOC) program, and the Enlisted Commissioning Program (ECP). Many reserve officers from these programs have
served required periods of duty and then become members of the

Regular Navy. Limited duty officers (LDOs) and warrant officers have continued to add their strengths to the officer corps.

This chapter will describe the procurement of each group of officers and analyze their educational background and training skills. Recommendations will be given for correcting areas of weakness. The summary should assist senior officers in analyzing and guiding their juniors. The result of their efforts should be a corps of officers equally proficient and educated.

Qualifications of a Naval Officer

Each line officer, regardless of his warfare specialty, must start with certain basic qualifications. These can be grouped into three general areas: professional competency, general education, and personal characteristics.

Professional Competency. All line officers must attain a certain level of professional competency. They must know, for instance, the fundamentals of navigation, whether surface, air, or subsurface. They must be familiar with the essentials of seamanship, naval law, naval administration, international law, and naval history and strategy.

Professional competency can be quantified. This has been done by the faculty of the Naval Academy, and the results are listed in appendix A. All Naval Academy midshipmen must pass a comprehensive examination in these areas before graduating. All officers from other institutions (aside from staff corps) should be able to pass those parts of the examination required of them and should be able to pass a self-administered examination of the entire area at the end of three years of service.

General Education. General education means a solid grounding in the liberal arts. Officers from major colleges and universities have a head start in this area. Others should read extensively in the first three years of commissioned service to broaden their education. Appendix C gives a suggested reading list.

Personal Development. Each officer should seek to acquire the qualities of a naval officer as set forth by John Paul Jones in a letter attributed to him. Some historians claim that he did not write a single letter containing a description of all of these qualities, and that the so-called letter is only a composite of several of his letters. Whatever the case is, the excellence of his challenge is uncontested. Jones is reported to have written the following:

It is by no means enough that an officer of the Navy should be a capable mariner. He must be that, of course, but also a great deal more. He should be as well a gentleman of liberal education, refined manners, punctilious courtesy, and the nicest sense of personal honor.

Coming now to view the naval officer aboard ship, and in relation to those under his command, he should be the soul of tact, patience, justice, firmness, and charity. No meritorious act of a subordinate should escape his attention or be left to pass without its reward, even if the reward be only one word of approval. Conversely, he should not be blind to a single fault in any subordinate, though at the same time he should be quick and unfailing to distinguish error from malice, thoughtlessness from incompetency, and well-meant shortcoming from heedless or stupid blunder. As he should be universal and impartial in his rewards and approval of merit, so should he be judicial and unbending in his punishment or reproof of misconduct.*

Each officer brings to the Navy a condensation of years of moral training, starting in the home and continuing with religious education, secondary school, and undergraduate study. An officer's moral and ethical standards have become ingrained upon joining the Navy. No two persons will necessarily have the same standards or moral positions. Each, however, must adapt to the Navy's requirements for moral leadership. Many of these are written in the Navy's moral leadership program, but most are understood in the light of the Naval Academy's honor system, which declares that no person should lie, cheat, or steal, and no one should tolerate another who does. Many naval officers will attend universities that have essentially similar codes. To this foundation are added the traditional requirements laid down by John Paul Jones and other naval officers.

Vice Admiral William P. Lawrence, when commander of the Third Fleet in Pearl Harbor, addressed a group of submarine officers. He outlined the common qualities of good leaders and ranked one particular quality at the top of the list:

> First is moral courage—to know right from wrong, to do what is right regardless of the consequences and to maintain standards even though at the time it might be unpopular. In

*L. H. Bolander, "Two Notes on John Paul Jones," Naval Institute *Proceedings*, July 1928, pp. 548–50.

our profession there simply has to be a high degree of truth and honesty or we won't function properly. Without it lives can be lost, battles can be lost, and the security of the country placed in jeopardy. I've never known a fine military leader who didn't possess a high standard of ethics and personal integrity.

Sources of Procurement

Naval Academy

The U.S. Naval Academy has been the primary source of regular officer procurement for many decades. Because its size is fixed, the Academy does not produce the largest number of officers, but it spends the most time, energy, and money per officer on procurement.

Entrance requirements for the Naval Academy are very stringent, and the equal of any university. The Academy is listed among the top fifty universities in the United States in academic excellence and among the top three in engineering. After four years of intensive study and training, midshipmen are commissioned ensign, Regular Navy, with a six- to eight-year obligation, depending upon the warfare specialty chosen.

Professional Training. From entrance in early July to graduation in late May almost four years later, the Naval Academy midshipman is engaged in some form of professional training. Formal professional courses with academic credit include leadership, naval history, shiphandling, engineering, weapons systems, navigation, electrical engineering, law, and naval administration.

Each midshipman completes four summers of professional training. This starts with indoctrination, infantry drill, and rifle and pistol training in the first summer. During summer cruises third- and first-class midshipmen are taught and perform the duties of enlisted men and junior officers. Second-class midshipmen obtain basic surface ship tactical training, using simulator trainers and yard patrol craft, and spend a week each undergoing flight, surface, submarine, and Marine Corps indoctrination.

In addition, each midshipman progresses upward through the brigade command organization in positions of increasing responsibility and leadership, starting as a fourth-class squad member and ending with a position as a brigade officer during first-class year.

Professional training is tested in every year when midshipmen are required to take and pass a comprehensive test in professional competency covering objectives applicable to that year. A professional examination given each year covers all of the preceding years. Each midshipman must pass the examination or take a remedial program in the summer.

Education. To graduate, a midshipman must complete 140 credit hours with a cumulative quality-point rating of 2.0 (C average). All eight bachelor of science degrees awarded lean heavily toward engineering, although eighteen credit hours, exclusive of required English courses, must be devoted to humanities and social sciences. With the heavy emphasis on engineering, it is not generally possible for the average Academy graduate to attain the level of liberal arts education a naval officer should ideally have.

Personal Development. Part of the threefold objective of the Academy is to give midshipmen a moral education. The Naval Academy has an excellent honor system, conceived and administered by the midshipmen and monitored by the administration. Midshipmen agree not to lie, cheat, or steal and not to tolerate anyone who does. Only in the first year will occasional minor indiscretions sometimes be tolerated and corrected, under the theory that this is a learning experience for the fourth class and a teaching experience for the upper classes.

NROTC Scholarship Program

The NROTC scholarship program produces many Regular Navy officers. For the past few years the number has been approximately equal to the number graduated from the Naval Academy. The program is conducted in sixty colleges and universities by professors of naval science aided by staffs of naval and Marine Corps officers. Entrance requirements are stringent and selection is competitive. On graduation, midshipmen are commissioned ensign, Regular Navy, with a six- to eight-year service obligation, depending upon their warfare specialty.

Professional Training. Midshipmen must major in an engineering or science field and complete courses in American military affairs, national security policy, calculus, physics, and two courses in approved technical areas. In addition, courses must be taken in naval ships' systems (engineering and weapons), sea-power and maritime affairs, navigation and naval operations, and leadership and management.

Three summer training periods of four to six weeks are conducted. The first and third are like the Naval Academy cruises, although they are not as demanding. The third is a series of indoctrinations in surface, air, submarine, and Marine Corps warfare. Additional indoctrination and training are given during weekly drills and in classes.

The total of professional training is the maximum that can be given in a university without interfering with its academic requirements. Professional competency objectives are being developed and midshipmen will soon be tested under a program similar to that used at the Naval Academy.

Education. Midshipmen enrolled in the NROTC scholarship program take courses leading to engineering and science degrees. They are, therefore, not completely familiar with the liberal arts, but they are more so than most of their Naval Academy counterparts.

Personal Development. NROTC midshipmen are exposed to a variety of honor systems, depending upon the practices of the universities they attend. There is some opportunity for teaching morals and ethics in leadership courses and for indoctrination during personal contacts with NROTC faculty and staff and on cruises. Such experience will vary widely from one midshipman to the next.

NROTC Contract Program

The Navy also conducts a nonsubsidized NROTC program as part of the activities of each individual unit. Entrants are chosen by the professor of naval science of each unit, and may enter two-, three-, or four-year programs. Graduates are commissioned ensign in the Naval Reserve.

Professional Training. Four-year college program students generally receive about the same professional training as scholarship students. Those who take the three- or two-year programs receive correspondingly less training. Should they decide to shift to the Regular Navy (augment) in later years, they will have to study further in professional areas.

Education. Midshipmen in the program will have a wide

variety of educational achievements. Those who chose liberal arts majors will have a head start in that direction, while those who decided on engineering will be ahead in that area. Additional study for each group will be required.

Personal Development. Midshipmen in this program will have widely varying sets of values, since they come from a variety of backgrounds.

Officer Candidate School

The OCS program provides an opportunity for enlisted men and women who have a bachelor's degree, if they are eligible and selected, to attend OCS for sixteen weeks. Graduates are commissioned ensign in the Reserve.

Those with previous college credit but no degree may, under the Enlisted Commissioning Program (ECP), be granted an opportunity to complete the requirements for a bachelor's degree and then join the OCS program. They receive full pay and allowances while attending school, but must pay the costs.

Professional Training. In sixteen weeks OCS provides the maximum amount of professional training possible. However, at the end of this time, not many graduates can pass a test in the professional competency objectives. This means continued study in professional areas after commissioning.

Education. The liberal arts education of OCS graduates will depend upon the majors pursued in their undergraduate programs. They will most likely have to expand their education by reading and study.

Personal Development. OCS graduates come from a variety of backgrounds that have influenced them in different ways. Some may have to work at developing the sort of qualities desirable in a member of the U.S. Navy.

Aviation Officer Candidate Program

Civilian and enlisted members selected for this program will serve eventually as naval aviators, naval flight officers, and aviation maintenance duty officers. They follow the same initial program as OCS candidates but must pass a more rigorous physical examination and the Aviation Selection Test (AST) battery. After graduation from OCS, they proceed to flight or naval flight officer training. Those selected for the intelligence program undergo further training in intelligence.

Professional, Education, and Personal Development. AOC officers have the same limits and strengths as other OCS graduates and should take the same steps after commissioning to improve their general qualifications.

Nuclear Propulsion Officer Candidate Program

The NUPOC program is designed to attract exceptional students in technical disciplines to the Navy's nuclear-power training program. To qualify for the program, the applicant must be at least 19 and not more than $27\frac{1}{2}$ years of age at the time of commissioning. The applicant can enter in either junior or senior year or just before the last year of a master's degree program. Juniors must be in a technical major and maintain a grade average of 3.0 on a 4.0 scale. Seniors and master's degree candidates are not required to be enrolled in a technical field but must have completed calculus and calculus-based physics. Senior applicants with an average below 3.0 may ask for consideration. Each applicant must meet the basic qualifications for commissioning and must continue with a 2.0 average.

Professional Training. Candidates do not receive any professional training while in school. After being graduated they attend OCS. They have an obligated period of service of four years, which includes nuclear-power training. Their professional training level will be low upon commissioning, and they will have to take the steps that other OCS graduates must to raise it.

Education. Candidates will have a wide variety of educational backgrounds, but almost all will be technical majors and therefore should expand their education in the liberal arts area.

Other Means of Procurement

Health Programs. Many programs are open to those who wish to enter the medical, dental, and nurse corps, and the Medical Service Corps (MSC). Those interested in the details should consult the nearest office of naval officer procurement. Programs range from attendance at the Uniformed Services University of the Health Sciences to direct procurement of experienced personnel in ranks as high as lieutenant commander.

Obviously men and women procured under such diverse programs will vary greatly in experience, education, and ability. Each officer will have to assess his or her own situation and take action to broaden education and promote professionalism.

Staff Corps. Staff corps other than the health-oriented groups, including legal, chaplain, and supply corps, procure by lateral transfer and by direct procurement.

Restricted Line. Restricted line officers are procured by lateral transfer.

Warrant and Limited Duty Officers. Warrant and limited duty officers are procured in enlisted-to-officer programs designed to meet the need for middle-grade technological skills and management expertise. In this way enlisted persons are given a professional development path. These officers do not need a college degree to acquire excellent technical capabilities in restricted areas.

Improvement Programs for Officers

Naval Academy Graduates. We have pointed out that Naval Academy graduates have an adequate professional background. Nevertheless, in the years after graduation they need to broaden their professional education, becoming expert in one warfare specialty and knowledgeable in all the others. They must also begin to study higher strategy. In educational development they are behind those from universities, and they should complete a reading program like that outlined in appendix C in order to further it.

NROTC Scholarship Program Graduates. These officers have a good start in professional training, but need to enlarge it. They should complete the professional reading program outlined in appendix B, and like others, seek to master one warfare specialty and become familiar with all others. Their efforts should be continued until they can pass the professional competency objectives. Then the NROTC graduate should commence the study of higher strategy.

NROTC Contract Program Graduates. Officers from this source start with handicaps in both professional training and educational development. If they are planning eventual augmentation into the Regular Navy, they will have to study in both areas, probably for more than three years, to become proficient professionally, educationally, and in their warfare specialties.

OCS and AOC Graduates. AOC and graduates of OCS also start with a handicap professionally and educationally. They will have to work hard in both areas. Most do bring to their careers technical knowledge, experience, and maturity, which seem to be producing officers of high caliber with above-average motivation.

Health Program Graduates and Members of Other Staff Corps. Officers from these programs vary so much in background, education, and career potential that no purpose is served in attempting an analysis. Each doctor, dentist, MSC officer, nurse, etc., will have to assess his or her position and goals and take appropriate action.

Restricted Line Officers. These officers join by lateral transfer, so their professional training and education depend upon their schooling and experience at the time of transfer. Each will have to analyze his or her past experience and education and compare or contrast them with the levels required for the professional paths they choose to pursue.

Warrant and Limited Duty Officers. These officers, if young enough, may train themselves without restriction. There have been many enlisted men who have completed their college education and gone on to fine careers.

3
FIRST STATION

THE DISTANCE IS NOTHING; IT IS ONLY THE FIRST STEP
WHICH COUNTS.

—*Madame du Deffand, letter to d'Alembert*

WHEN YOU JOIN YOUR FIRST SHIP YOU MUST NOT LET
ANYTHING DETRACT FROM YOUR DETERMINATION TO
GIVE IT YOUR FULL EFFORT AND ATTENTION, BUT IF
YOU ARE WORTH YOUR SALT THERE WILL ALWAYS BE IN
THE BACK OF YOUR MIND THE UNVOICED THOUGHT
THAT YOU WILL COMMAND SUCH A SHIP SOME DAY.

—*Vice Admiral Alexander Sharp*

You are about to become a naval officer, having attained that status through one of the programs described in the previous chapter. Now you are ready to meet the challenges of your new career.

Receipt of Orders

Receipt and Delivery of Orders.   Some months prior to commissioning you will receive your orders to first station. They will arrive with a "delivered" endorsement. If you are already commissioned, receipt of your orders to next station may occur anywhere from one to six months before detachment. Detailers aim for four months but do not always make it.

Now that you know what type of ship or station you are going to and its approximate location, employment, or mission, you must start procuring what you will need in the way of uniforms. A letter to your new executive officer will result in more exact information.

Letter to the Executive Officer.   As soon as you have your orders in hand, you should write a letter to the executive officer of your new ship or station. He or she will have a copy of your orders, but it is wise to enclose another copy anyway and to say exactly when and where you expect to report. Mention your background and career aspirations and request assignment to the department that best fits those goals. A formal but unofficial letter might read as follows:

> Dear Commander:
> I have just had the pleasure of receiving orders to report to the USS *Ship*. They permit delay in reporting until 1 September 1991. From the information I have, the ship will be in San Diego that day. I will proceed to that port in time to be on board about 1000.
> I am a graduate of the Naval Academy, where I majored in electrical engineering. As you can see from my orders, after completion of basic Surface Warfare Officer's School, I am going to attend Damage Control Assistant School before reporting. I plan to concentrate on gunnery and missilery and hope to be assigned eventually to a billet in those specialties.
> I have a full set of regular uniforms, but may need additional uniforms for watches and special occasions. Any information you could furnish that would allow me to procure required uniforms prior to arrival would be appreciated.
> I look forward to my service in the USS *Ship* and hope that I can contribute to her success.
>
> Very respectfully,
> J. R. Mahan
> Ensign, U.S. Navy

You should receive a reply in a short time, which will either confirm that you are reporting to the right place or give you a better location. If your ship is to be at sea, you will be directed to report to your type commander (for example, COMNAV-SURFPAC in San Diego), one of his subordinate commanders, or the senior officer present afloat (SOPA). If you are to do so, make sure your orders are endorsed by the receiving command showing the date, time, and location of your reporting. Because of short-notice demands on Navy ships, don't be surprised at schedule changes that move your ship at the last minute. Be aggressive, however, in trying to locate your ship and in getting on board. Check with the operations officer of the command you report in to and keep your ship informed of your whereabouts and intentions.

Uniforms

Between the receipt of your orders and your departure you should have time to acquire needed uniforms. Past editions of this book presented extensive lists of uniform items that it was thought each officer should have. The number of these items has been drastically reduced.

We recommend that you go to your first station with as little as a raincoat, one uniform cap, two suits of blue service, two suits of white service, three tropical white long, four white shirts, four work khaki uniforms, and one pair each of black and white shoes. Inspection shoes, gloves, ties, and personal items should be added as desired. V-neck undershirts are required to be worn with open-collar shirts. Sword and sword belt are optional for lieutenant and below and required for other ranks. It you have a sword, bring it. The uniforms you procure initially should be the best you can afford and should be carefully tailored.

If you have been unable to obtain sufficient information concerning uniform requirements before your arrival, you can assess your uniform needs more accurately after arrival. They will vary with climate, your particular billet, your ship's type and employment, and the laundry and cleaning facilities available. This is also true if you are at a shore station. In either event you can obtain the additional uniform items you feel you will need from the nearest exchange. Uniform procurement is more difficult and costly overseas.

Many initial assignments begin in the summer. In this case you can send cold-weather items in your personal-effects shipment and determine your cold-weather needs at a later time. If you are planning to stay in the Navy past your initial obligation, an overcoat is a must. You will be required to get one, and you will be glad on many occasions that you have it. One often overlooked item is a set of thermal underwear, a must since junior officers spend a lot of time topside in miserable weather. Do not go to sea without long johns.

One difficulty in outfitting yourself is rigging your sword with its knot. See the facing photo for the proper appearance. *Uniform Regulations* outline the rigging in more detail.

Uniform Care. The new materials used for uniforms have simplified their care. Blues retain their pressed appearance for prolonged periods and need only routine cleaning and pressing. A white plastic cap cover can be worn on most ships, at least for daily use. These can be washed clean of stack soot and other dirt without being removed. Some ships insist on cloth covers for watches and inspection. A cap stretcher is needed for these. Wash-and-wear white shirts and white summer (tropical) shirts are easily taken care of. Shoes should be of good quality and should be stored with shoe trees.

When your ship goes to sea, make sure the uniforms hanging in your closet are on good, wooden hangers and are covered with plastic or cloth. They should be secured so that the motion of the ship will not wear holes or cause abrasions in them. Many closets have clothes clamps for this purpose. If your doesn't, rig a substitute.

Uniform Designations. If you are not familiar with the commonly designated uniforms or with dress uniforms worn less often, consult a copy of *Uniform Regulations* in your ship's office or station personnel office.

Uniforms and Insignia of the Armed Forces. After you leave your commissioning source or indoctrination school, you will enter a much more sophisticated military world, where people wear the uniforms and insignia of all the services, not just the Navy. You will be wise to utilize some of your spare time reviewing them.

Uniforms have been used for centuries to identify military persons as to country, service, group, and place in the chain of command. Generally, all members of each service wear uniforms similar enough to permit identification by service, but also distinct enough to show membership by group in a given service.

Insignia are small marks of identification added to uniforms to identify each group, show position in the chain of command, and indicate group and individual qualifications.

The uniforms of the armed services of the United States should be familiar enough to the average person to permit identification by service. Some of the recently authorized summer uniform variants might present minor difficulty.

After identifying service, you should look for the rank or rate

The proper installation of the sword knot.

insignia. It is worn variously on the sleeve, arm, shirt collar, shoulder, and headgear. Figure 3-1 shows the comparative insignia of all services.

In the Navy, the next distinguishing feature is the headgear, which differs for flag officers, senior officers, junior officers, midshipmen, women, chief petty officers, and other enlisted men. Figure 3-2 shows the headgear worn by these groups. Enlisted men below the rank of chief petty officer wear the traditional white hat.

Unrestricted line officers and restricted line officers wear the star. Officers of the various corps wear the distinguishing mark of their corps. Figure 3-3 shows these marks. It is impossible to distinguish between restricted and unrestricted line officers in a boat. If you are an unrestricted line officer yourself, it is important to identify the senior unrestricted line officer in the boat, since that person is in charge. You can do so by discreet questioning of the officers present. The safety of the boat is the responsibility of the senior unrestricted line officer and he should clearly acknowledge his position to you, the boat officer if present, and the coxswain.

Warrant officers display a large variety of insignia, depending upon their specialty. Figure 3-4 shows the most common.

Both officers and enlisted men wear breast insignia, as shown in figure 3-5, to indicate warfare and other specialties.

Enlisted personnel wear a large variety of rating marks, which are shown in figure 3-6, to identify their specialties. They also wear distinguishing marks, as shown in figure 3-7.

Identification badges showing that an officer or enlisted person is serving or has served in various organizations are shown in figure 3-8.

All persons of all services wear medals (with full dress) and ribbons (with service dress). You need not be familiar with these in detail initially, but at some later date you will need to know enough to supervise the wearing of medals and ribbons by those under your control or command.

Interpretation of Orders

Your orders will be written by the commander of the Naval Military Personnel Command (NMPC) and signed by the chief of naval personnel (the same officer).

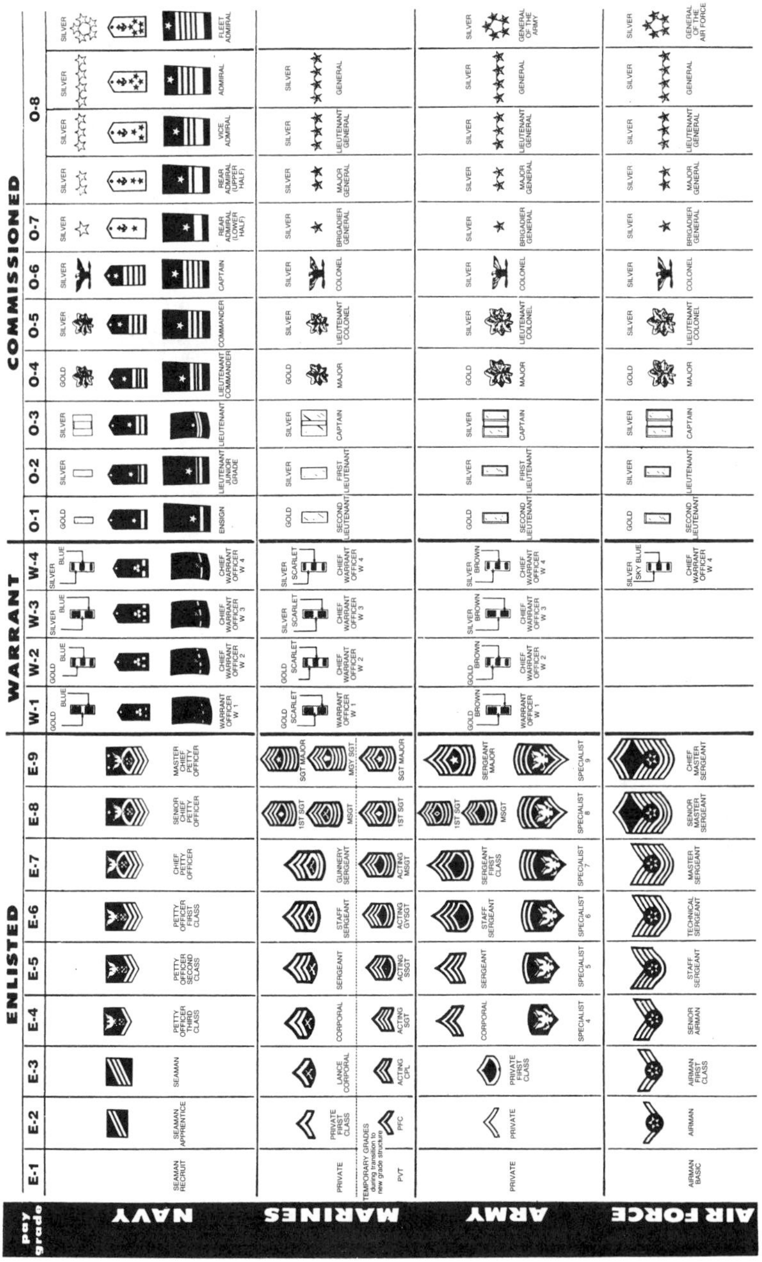

Figure 3-1. Comparative insignia of the U.S. armed forces by pay grades.

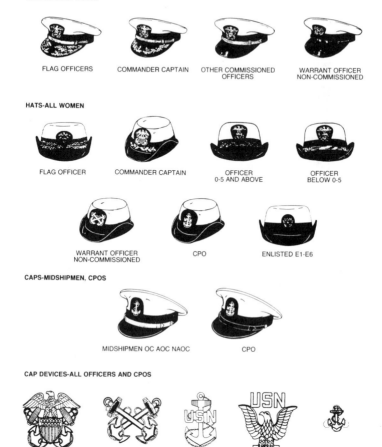

Figure 3-2. Headgear for all men and women. Cap devices are the same for men and women in the same ranks or rates, except that enlisted women below chief wear a device as shown. A midshipman's cap is also worn by all officer candidates. For the chief petty officer device, one, two, or three stars are added above the stock to indicate senior chief, master chief, or master chief petty officer of the Navy.

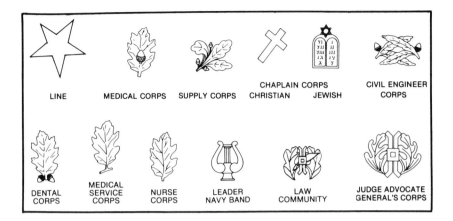

Figure 3-3. Distinguishing marks of the different corps.

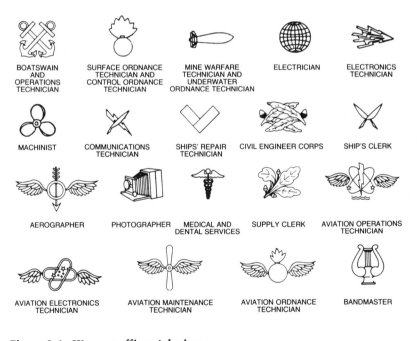

Figure 3-4. Warrant officers' devices.

NAVAL ASTRONAUT

NAVAL ASTRONAUT (NFO)

NAVAL AVIATOR

NAVAL AVIATION OBSERVER AND
FLIGHT METEOROLOGIST

NAVAL FLIGHT OFFICER

NAVAL AVIATION SUPPLY CORPS

FLIGHT SURGEON

NAVAL AVIATION EXPERIMENTAL
PSYCHOLOGIST
NAVAL AVIATION PHYSIOLOGIST

FLIGHT NURSE

SURFACE WARFARE OFFICER

ENLISTED SURFACE WARFARE

SURFACE SUPPLY CORPS

AVIATION WARFARE SPECIALIST

AIRCREW

SUBMARINE MEDICAL

SUBMARINE

SUBMARINE COMBAT PATROL

NAVAL RESERVE
MERCHANT MARINE

SUBMARINE SUPPLY

SUBMARINE ENGINEER DUTY

SSBN DETERRENT PATROL

COMMAND AT SEA (Gold)

DEEP SUBMERGENCE (Gold)
ENLISTED (Silver)

SPECIAL OPERATIONS

SPECIAL WARFARE (SEAL) (UDT)

SMALL CRAFT

CRAFTMASTER

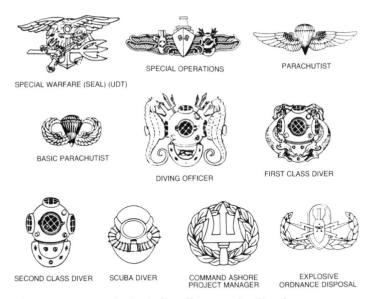

SPECIAL WARFARE (SEAL) (UDT)

SPECIAL OPERATIONS

PARACHUTIST

BASIC PARACHUTIST

DIVING OFFICER

FIRST CLASS DIVER

SECOND CLASS DIVER

SCUBA DIVER

COMMAND ASHORE
PROJECT MANAGER

EXPLOSIVE
ORDNANCE DISPOSAL

Figure 3-5. Breast insignia for officers and enlisted persons.

Guard the original copy of your orders with your life. When you travel, keep the original and a few copies on your person. A large number of copies will be provided, but even these may not be enough. Thirty copies is a reasonable number.

Some material that arrives with your orders will explain proceed time, leave time, and travel time. The back of your original orders will contain blocks of additional instructions, some of which will be referred to by means of numbers on the front of the orders.

Study your orders carefully. To help you, a sample set of orders has been included. (The NMPC is shifting to a computer-generated system; your orders may look quite different.)

R 061243Z MAR 89
FM CHNAVPERS WASHINGTON DC
TO PERSUPPDET ANNAPOLIS MD
USNA ANNAPOLIS MD
PERSUPPDET NEWPORT RI
SWOSCOLCOM NEWPORT RI
INFO USS SHIP
BT
UNCLAS//N01324//

(continued)

Figure 3-6. Navy enlisted rating badges.

AIRCREWMAN

ASSAULT BOAT
COXSWAIN

EXPERT LOOKOUT

FIRE FIGHTER
ASSISTANT

DIVER

NAVY "E"

Figure 3-7. Marks indicating special qualifications other than those required for a particular rating. They are worn on the right arm and only for the period of qualification. Such marks are embroidered in white on blue and blue on white, except for the Navy *E* indicating five or more awards, which will be in gold.

BUPERS ORDER 0764 045-65-1076/1150
SUBJ: NEW APPOINTMENT ORDER FOR
ENS JAMES R MAHAN, USN
USNA, ANNAPOLIS, MD; PADUCAH, KY
UPON GRADUATION AND WHEN DIRECTED REPORT AS DIRECTED
    BELOW:
ULTIMATE. NAME: STU SWOSCOLCOM
EDA: 2 JUL 89 EDD: 23 DEC 89 D-DESIG: 1110
COURSE: SWO BASIC CONV: 3 JUL 89 GRAD: 29 OCT 89
COURSE: DC ASSISTANT CONV: 2 NOV 89 GRAD: 22 DEC 89
PERMANENT DUTY STATION: NEWPORT, RI
REPORT FOR DUTY UNDER INSTRUCTION OVER TWENTY WEEKS
(Here will follow extensive advisory data concerning leave, travel, and housing availability)
FOLLOW ON ORDERS WILL ASSIGN YOU TO USS SHIP
BT

The group of numbers on line 17 is your designator, which shows you to be an unrestricted line officer of the Regular Navy. Each kind of officer has a different designator. A "5" as the fourth digit would have indicated a reserve officer. A complete listing may be found in the *Register of Commissioned and Warrant Officers of the Navy*, NMPC 15018.

The body of the orders tells you what to do, when to do it, and where to do it.

Figure 3-8. Identification badges. Those identifying persons performing presidential or vice presidential service, or assigned to the Office of the Secretary of Defense (*top row, left to right*) or JCS, may be worn by members of all military services.

Vice presidential service—worn by personnel detailed to the Office of the Vice President, during and after the period of detail, and on upper right pocket.

Office of the Secretary of Defense—worn by personnel during detail to that office (and may be worn afterwards if one year of service on the joint staff was performed), and on upper left pocket.

JCS—worn by personnel during detail to that office (and may be worn afterwards if one year of service on the joint staff was performed), and on upper left pocket.

Recruiting Service—worn by all personnel assigned to duty with the Recruiting Service, and on upper left pocket.

The accounting data is for internal NMPC use.

The abbreviations used are supposed to be self-evident. Any that are not can be found in the NMPC Instruction 2340.1 series.

You will be given a detaching endorsement on the date of detachment. Some commands give you the endorsement earlier, but it is dated according to the day of detachment. Sometimes both endorsements are combined. The commanding officer (CO) should detach the officer within twenty-four hours after the orders are received.

Detached When Directed On or About. The CO has a discretionary period of ten days on either side of the date given in which to detach the officer.

Detached When Directed. Orders should ordinarily be endorsed to detach the officer within ten days after the arrival of orders.

Detached When Relieved. Officer should be detached within ten days after the relieving officer has reported. The command may designate an officer already on board as a relief, if appropriate.

Detached in Time to Proceed and Report on a Certain Date. The latest, or limiting, date of detachment will normally be four days' proceed (if traveling by auto, but one day if traveling by air) plus travel time in advance of the specified reporting date.

Upon Discharge from Treatment. Orders will be endorsed by the CO of the hospital when the officer is physically qualified for discharge from treatment.

Proceed. Report not later than 2400 following the date of detachment, exclusive of travel time and proceed.

Proceed without Delay. Report within forty-eight hours, exclusive of travel time, subsequent to detachment.

Proceed Immediately. Report within twelve hours, exclusive of travel time, subsequent to travel.

Proceed On or About. Travel should be commenced within a discretionary period of ten days on either side of the date given in the orders. This phrase is used only in temporary duty orders.

Proceed Time. Proceed time is explained in Art. 1810300 of the NMPC manual. It is authorized only upon permanent change of station to or from ships or mobile units, or to or from an unaccompanied tour overseas, whether designated sea or shore duty. Proceed time is for making necessary personal arrangements and, unless otherwise designated, is four days. If ordered to intermediate stations, proceed time may be taken any time before final reporting. Proceed time is not authorized en route to the first permanent change of station for newly commissioned officers.

Travel Time. Authorized travel time by auto is computed in whole days on the basis of a usually traveled route by a facility offering through service. Travel is computed on the basis of 350 miles per day and one day for each fraction over 175 miles. Air travel is normally one day.

Leave. Delay authorized in permanent change of station orders in excess of proceed time and travel time is leave. Leave, proceed time, and travel time are charged in that order following the date of detachment. If you report early you will be charged only for the amount of leave you take. The date of detachment is a day of duty and the day of reporting is a day of travel. You will therefore want to leave as early as the detaching command will permit and to report as late as possible on the date of reporting. Commands are very flexible—in most cases the officer detached can call in to the OOD to report detachment rather than appear in person. This procedure should not be abused. It is used to allow the person detached to get a good rest before starting a trip.

Table 3-1, taken from NAVEDTRA 10802-AC, summarizes travel, proceed, and leave time for officers from each source. In connection with these tables, POC means "privately owned conveyance" and includes both auto and aircraft. The same number of mileage days is authorized for both bus and train. No travel time is authorized between points in a metropolitan area. If areas are separated by more than local transportation (as the distance from Annapolis to Washington is), one day is allowed. Official highway mileages are contained in the *Official Table of Distances*, NAVSO P-2471.

Exceptions. If you are an aviation reserve officer candidate (AVROC) or NROTC graduate who did not immediately report to active duty upon graduation, or if you are a reserve officer appointed to your first duty, your orders will tell you to report to a certain command on a certain date. Since you are in a nonpay status when you receive your orders, you will not be authorized leave or proceed time. If you arrive a few days late, you simply are not paid for those days. (You may be disciplined if the delay is not excused.) When you report, you are placed in a pay status

Table 3-1. Travel, Proceed, and Leave Time

Officers	Travel Time	Proceed Time	Leave
All	Time computed on distances is determined from official mileage tables, otherwise from shortest usually traveled routes as shown in commercial carrier or automobile guides. Time is counted in whole days, 24 hours; i.e., the whole 24 hours or nothing.	A period of time (not chargeable as leave, delay, or allowed travel time) which is granted for the purpose of facilitating necessary personal arrangements inherent in certain permanent change of station orders.	See BUPERS Manual, Art. 3020050 for complete explanation of the various types of leave: annual, earned convalescent, advance, excess, etc.
Naval Academy graduates*	Same as for NAVOIS below. Orders to USNA graduates usually specify a definite date to report, thus eliminating travel time. Travel time allowable to first duty station is computed on the basis of the official distance and the mode of travel authorized.	Not entitled to proceed time.	Graduates of USNA may be given up to 30 days' graduation leave which must be taken after graduation in connection with first orders as an officer and must be completed within 3 months of date of graduation. Such leave cannot be saved and used later. Present Navy practice is to allow some delay to count as graduation leave. This varies according to individual circumstances.
NAVOIS AOC (including	Air (government or commercial): 1 day for anywhere in continental U.S. Time can be extended	NESEP graduates are entitled to proceed time unless other-	Any leave earned in enlisted status will be carried over to commissioned status. Hence, any

Table 3-1. *Continued*

Officers	Travel Time	Proceed Time	Leave
NESEP and integrated students)	if delay is necessary owing to mode of travel; personal convenience does not count. If travel is part by air and part by other means, time is computed by combination of methods. Travel time is computed on the following standards: Commercial air—1 hour for each 500 miles. Commercial surface—1 hour for 40 miles Note: Commercial transportation implies 1 day travel time for each 18 hours or fraction of 18 hours travel is performed. POC: 1 day/350 miles and 1 day/ each fraction of 350 miles (more than 150 miles).	wise indicated in orders. NAVOIS/AOC are not entitled to first permanent duty station.	leave granted for delay en route will be charged as annual leave. An officer reporting earlier than required will save the leave for a later date. Present practice is to authorize 10 days' delay charged as annual leave.
NROTC regulars and reserves	Air (government or commercial): 1 day anywhere in continental U.S. Privately owned conveyance (POC): 1 day/350 miles and 1 day/fraction of 350 miles (more than 175 miles). Commercial surface name as for NAVOIS. NROTC graduates	Not entitled to proceed time.	Any delay is charged to advance leave and deducted from leave earned during the coming year. For USNR officers: leave, pay, and allowances will be computed based on the officer's reporting date specified in orders, adjusted for required travel

	appointed to USNR and *not* immediately ordered to duty (i.e., after acceptance of appointment, they return home and remain there for several days/weeks before commencing travel to first duty station): travel time via POC is computed at the rate of 350 miles/day with an additional day allowed for each fraction of 350 miles (more than 175 miles).		time. Early reporting does not provide advantage for pay or leave purposes.
USN officers appointed from civil life	Air (government or commercial): 1 day anywhere in continental U.S. POC: 1 day/350 miles and 1 day/each fraction of 350 miles (more than 175 miles). Commercial surface time same as for NAVOIS.	Not entitled to proceed time.	Any delay is charged to advance leave and is deducted from leave earned during the coming year.
Staff Corps officers graduating from OIS	Same as for NAVOIS.	Not entitled to proceed time to first permanent duty station.	Normally, no standard number of days' leave allowed; however, 5 days leave is generally indicated in the majority of cases, dependent both on amount of leave accrued and the degree of need for the officer at the new duty station.

*Because of graduation leave, travel time of Annapolis graduates does not affect pay or leave accumulation; however, it does affect the effective dates of orders, which can be of interest to those about to be married.

and are entitled to pay for the days of travel from your home of record to your duty station.

NROTC regulars are commissioned USN and therefore are placed immediately in a duty status with pay. Accordingly, any delay incurred in reporting in excess of actual travel time via commercial transportation or the 350-miles-per-day allowance for auto travel will be charged as leave.

Travel

Authorities. Table 3-2, taken from NAVEDTRA 10802 AC, gives the usual travel and transportation allowances. These examples cover most cases. If you have a complicated case involving repeated travel, ask the nearest transportation or supply officer for help and consult *Joint Travel Regulations (JTR)*. It is best to know the technicalities of your case so that you do not lose compensation.

Location of Your Ship or Station. If your local station cannot find out where your ship is located, call the NMPC traffic branch or Navy passenger transportation officer in Norfolk for Atlantic ships and in San Francisco for Pacific ships. If still in doubt, call the office of your type commander.

Compensation. The Navy will reimburse you for travel in one of two ways. If you furnish or choose your own method of transportation, you will receive an allowance of fifteen cents per mile. You will also receive a per diem allowance of fifty dollars. For government-furnished transportation a variable per diem allowance is paid after deduction for meals prior to the start of travel. Taxi fares and baggage-handling tips will be reimbursed. Retain receipts and keep a log of your expenses. Figure 3-9 shows a handy way of recording travel expenses.

Many first ships and stations will be outside the continental United States. You will then make your way to an overseas departure point, either McGuire Air Force Base in New Jersey or Travis Air Force Base in California. Your orders will generally specify your transportation from these points, and you will receive a per diem allowance for travel time.

Routes. You are not required to follow any fixed or direct route in executing your travel. However, your compensation is limited to that of a direct route. The distance Naval Academy graduates travel must not exceed the official distance from their

Table 3-2. Travel and Transportation Allowances on First Orders to a Permanent Station

	Naval Academy	NAVOIS, NESEP Officer Training Program	NROTC (Reserves and Regulars) and Officers Appointed From Civil Life
Personal Expenses 15 cents a mile or transportation in kind or transportation request(s) plus $50 a day determined at the current per diem rate.	May receive reimbursement either from Annapolis or from home to first duty station. That is, an academy graduate who lives in San Francisco and who is ordered to N.Y. can go (at own expense) to S.F. and then at end of leave go to N.Y. at gov't expense. This privilege is given only to Annapolis graduates on the occasion of their first orders to duty as ensigns and then only if so specified in orders.	Entitled to travel expenses from place stated in orders to first permanent duty station. That is, a NAVOIS graduate ordered from Newport to N.Y. will be entitled to claim only expenses from Newport to N.Y.—any other travel will be at own expense.	NROTC graduates appointed USN officers are entitled to travel expenses from place stated in orders (usually NROTC unit where appointed) to first permanent duty station. NROTC graduates appointed USNR officers and officers appointed from civil life are entitled to travel expenses from place stated in orders (usually home) to first permanent duty station.
Household Goods: Entitled to shipment of 9,500 lb household goods. Does not include automobiles,	May elect to ship from Annapolis to home or from Annapolis and/or home to first permanent duty station. This is a privilege permitted only to academy graduates and only upon the occasion of their first orders	From last permanent duty station or from home to new duty station.	From last permanent duty station or from home to new duty station.

Table 3-2. *Continued*

NAVAL ACADEMY	NAVOIS, NESEP OFFICER TRAINING PROGRAM	NROTC (RESERVES AND REGULARS) AND OFFICERS APPOINTED FROM CIVIL LIFE
to a permanent station as ensigns.		
Entitled to travel expense for travel actually performed not exceeding the distance from Annapolis or home (irrespective of point designated in orders) to first duty station, and dependency must exist on or before effective date of orders.	Entitled to travel expenses for travel actually performed not exceeding the distance from home address in orders to place of first permanent duty. Dependency must exist on or before effective date of orders.	Entitled to travel expenses for travel actually performed not exceeding distance from place addressed in orders to place of first permanent duty. Dependency must exist on or before effective date of orders.
NOTE: LACK OF SPACE PREVENTS MORE THAN A LIMITED TREATMENT HERE. CONSULT *JTR* AND YOUR DISBURSING OFFICER IN ALL CASES.	If marriage takes place after detachment but prior to the effective date of orders, entitlement will be from the place where the dependent is acquired (place of marriage) to the new duty station, not to exceed the distance from the old to the new duty station.	

baggage carried free on tickets, liquors, or articles for sale. TRs, government vehicle, and so forth, may be substituted for above without regard to the number of dependents.

TRAVEL EXPENSE RECORD

EXPENSES OF TRAVEL	DATE	DATE	DATE	DATE	DATE	EXPENSE TOTALS
	AMOUNT	AMOUNT	AMOUNT	AMOUNT	AMOUNT	
TRANSPORTATION COSTS						
PLANE FARES						
TRAIN & BUS FARES						
TAXI FARES						
RENTAL CARS						
OTHER						
AUTO MILEAGE						
AUTO EXPENSES						
GAS & OIL						
PARTS & REPAIRS						
WASH & LUB JOBS						
PARKING & TOLLS						
OTHER						
MEALS & TIPS						
LODGING						
OTHER EXPENSES						
BAGGAGE FEES						
LAUNDRY & CLEANING						
PASSPORT FEES						
POSTAGE & TELEPHONE						
MAID FEES						
REGISTRATION FEES						
TIPS						
OTHER						
TOTALS						

NOTE: This Travel Expense Record form may be reproduced for your convenience in keeping track of TDY & TAD expenses during 1979. Take a copy on each trip and record your expenses daily. After your travel voucher is paid, file this record with your copy of the voucher.

REIMBURSEMENTS RECEIVED	
MILEAGE ALLOWANCE	
PER DIEM	
TRAVEL ALLOWANCE	
OTHER (EXPLAIN)	
TOTAL REIMBURSEMENTS	

Figure 3-9. Travel expense record.

home or from Annapolis, as may be designated in their orders (first duty station only).

Dependents. If you have one or more dependents, be sure to see the disbursing officer or transportation officer before making travel plans. When moving dependents, Naval Academy graduates have certain entitlements in addition to those given to other newly commissioned officers.

Some general points about dependents and travel are:

1. For you to be entitled to reimbursement for dependents' travel, they must move to a permanent residence incident to permanent change of station orders and not just be visiting a new station. You must sign the application for your dependents' transportation—they are not allowed to. For exceptions to this rule see your transportation officer.

2. You may obtain a payment for transportation before you travel. Your dependents may also be provided with government conveyance upon receipt of orders.

3. In most cases, traveling done before the receipt of orders or before the official notification that orders are forthcoming will not be paid by the government. It is possible to move in advance of orders if authorized. However, in general, you will only be entitled to one move on any one set of travel orders.

4. Only the official distance traveled between any two authorized points will count for transportation in kind or for reimbursement. Graduates of officer training programs other than the Naval Academy's will have transportation for dependents authorized from old station (or in certain cases from home) to new station.

Joint Travel Regulations (JTR) M 7064 states the following in regard to Naval Academy graduates:

> When commissioned and ordered to active duty, a graduate of a service academy is entitled to transportation of dependents at government expense for travel performed by dependents incident to such orders, not to exceed entitlement from the further point, home of record or service academy, to the permanent station, irrespective of the point designated in the orders [service academy or home of record], from which the officer's travel is directed to be performed. When dependents are acquired subsequent to the date of an officer's departure [detachment] from a service academy incident to active duty orders but on or before the effective date of the orders, the officer will be entitled to transportation of dependents at government expense for travel performed by such dependents to the member's new duty station from one of the following:
> a. Home of record
> b. The service academy
> c. The place where the dependents are acquired, not to exceed entitlement from the further point, home of record, or service academy, to the officer's new permanent station, provided that in the event the dependents' travel from the place acquired to the home of record or service academy prior to the effective date of active duty orders, the place named in (a) or (b), as appropriate, will apply. Such entitlement is without regard to whether temporary duty is directed or performed en route.

(If, after wading through the foregoing legalese, you are tempted to cancel your marriage plans, don't—some clever yeoman in the disbursing office of your new station will figure it all out to your best advantage.)

5. Transportation in kind will be provided for dependents. Monetary allowances in lieu of transportation in kind may be substituted in varying amounts per mile, made payable upon the submission of a claim after the completion of travel, provided it commenced after the receipt of orders. When dependents travel on travel requests (TRs) or by government conveyance, certain miscellaneous expenses are reimbursable, such as taxi fares, tips for baggage handling at terminals, etc. For entitlement where the modification or cancellation of orders occurs after the commencement of travel, see the *JTR*.

6. Per diem allowances are paid for dependents traveling by automobile at the rate of $37.50 for those over twelve years of age and $25.00 for those twelve years and under.

7. The dependent must have been acquired before or on the effective date of the orders directing a permanent change of station. This is an important point to remember for those ensigns who plan to be married while on leave after graduation.

8. The dependents of an officer ordered to sea duty are entitled to transportation that must not exceed the cost of travel from the last permanent duty station to the home port of the vessel to which that officer is ordered.

9. An officer whose dependents are entitled to transportation on a first assignment to a permanent station is not entitled to a dislocation allowance in connection with this first assignment. (The dislocation allowance is two months' basic allowance for quarters [BAQ] authorized to defray moving expenses.)

Movement of Personal Effects

We have now reviewed the time allowed for travel and the various methods of travel available to you. The executive officer of your new ship should reply to your letter and confirm the place and time of reporting. He may also tell you that he has appointed a sponsor for you and your family, who will correspond with you, advising you on all aspects of your move and particularly on housing and other housekeeping matters in your new home port. If you are single, your sponsor will probably also be single.

Having in mind the advice of your executive officer and your sponsor, and having made your travel arrangements, with your passport, shot card, orders, health record, and pay accounts in hand, you are ready to travel. One last chore remains. You must have your personal effects moved.

Personal Effects. Officers already commissioned and making second and subsequent moves should have little trouble planning the movement of their personal effects. The newly commissioned officer might have a problem. If you have an automobile of decent size and can drive directly to home port or station, you won't have any trouble. If you have to go overseas, you should divide your effects into two groups. The first group will be the uniforms, equipment, and personal items that you will carry with you. If you are flying you may have to confine yourself to two Valpack suitcases and an overnight bag. Plan their contents carefully. You will need uniforms to last you until the rest of your belongings arrive. Don't take a lot of tropical uniforms to a cold area and vice versa. The remainder of your effects should be shipped to your new ship or station as soon as possible, so that they can be on hand when you get there or soon thereafter.

Your sword will be a problem. Some airlines will insist on placing it in custody. If you are going through Japan, ship it and explain to your executive officer that if you had carried it, the Japanese would have confiscated it and its release might have taken months.

Household Effects. The shipment of household effects is a complicated affair. You do not have to take the mover proposed to you, but you will probably not have enough information to find a better one. Most of your moves will be made to or from areas served by large supply depots, where you will find expert help. When you apply for movement, they will supply you with pamphlets and detailed information.

Movement of household effects overseas requires longer transit periods. You will have to be prepared to housekeep at your destination for several weeks without your effects. Most stations have pools of houseware that you can draw from to tide you over.

Travel Uniform. If you are traveling commercially, or by automobile, you can travel in civilian clothes. When you connect with the Military Airlift Command you will have to shift into uniform. Have a presentable uniform on hand to wear when reporting.

First Papers

The legal act that makes you a naval officer is your swearing in and the acceptance of your commission. You must complete your acceptance and oath of office form (NMPC 339) and send it to the NMPC. If you are commissioned at a large station, the forms will be forwarded by that command. With the form you will also be required to send a beneficiary form, a change-of-address card (OPNAV 2700-s), and an application for Naval Reserve correspondence courses if you are a reserve officer. Each form contains adequate, detailed instructions for completion.

After commissioning, you will depart, secure in the knowledge that you have calculated your proceed, travel, and leave time correctly, that your personal effects are safely en route or packed, and that your travel arrangements are in order. Enjoy your leave, for you will soon be hard at work.

Reporting Aboard

If possible, arrive at your ship's home port or at the place she will be on the day before you are to report. If you arrive a day early, you will have time to rest, clean your uniforms, confirm that your ship is or will be in that port, and find out the uniform of the day. If you are reporting to your first station, the same advice holds. Old hands do not need this extra time.

Transportation to Ship. Most ships will be moored at a naval station pier. Occasionally some ships will be anchored out. If you are fortunate enough to be reporting to a ship at a pier, take a taxi in mid-morning or mid-afternoon to avoid busy periods in the ship's routine or meal hours. If the boat schedule does not fit this plan, board as you can before 2400. If at a pier, leave your baggage at the end of the brow. If boarding by boat, leave your baggage in the boat. Remember the correct procedures for boarding set forth in the chapter on honors and ceremonies.

After you arrive on the quarterdeck, salute the colors if it is between 0800 and sunset; otherwise salute the quarterdeck. Turn to the OOD, salute, and say, "Sir, I request permission to come aboard." (Do not be surprised on a small ship if you are greeted by a petty officer of the watch. The procedure is the same.) After he says, "Permission granted," say, "Ensign W. T. Door reporting for duty, sir."

You should have your orders, pay accounts, and health record in your left hand. The OOD will ask to see your orders and take a copy to log you in.

The following sequence of events is difficult to predict. The approved and normal procedure would be for the OOD to welcome you and ask if you have baggage. He should send the messenger to retrieve it, either from the pier side or the boat, and then send you and it with a messenger to your quarters. He should tell you what your duty assignment is, if he knows, and he should direct you to report to your division officer or other immediate superior. There will be many variations in this procedure. Just remember that you have certain tasks to perform as soon as possible. They are to find your quarters; determine your assignment; report to your superior; arrange for a call on your head of department, executive officer, and CO; find and join the wardroom mess; and turn in your orders, health record, and pay accounts. All of these tasks should be performed or at least initiated the first day. Sometimes in a small and busy ship protocol gives way to expediency. Be patient, pleasant, and observant.

Subsequent Events. After your first day aboard (and it will be a memorable one) you will settle down to tackle the job ahead. This will include familiarizing yourself with the responsibilities and duties of your assigned billet, the watches to be stood, and the duties on boards and bills. Calls, protocol, social usage, wardroom etiquette, plans, education, training, and a host of other subjects that you will need to be familiar with are covered elsewhere in this book.

Shore Station. If you are going to a shore station, either as a first duty, for school, for indoctrination, or for rotational duty, the mechanics of reporting will differ. Proceed to the duty office, and then (depending on circumstances) to the executive officer's office or the aide to the CO. The exact title of the officer you are to report to may have to be determined on the spot by following signs or asking questions. Shore stations differ slightly in their administration. In any event, someone will take your orders and direct your subsequent movements, probably by means of a check-in list. If several of you are reporting at the same time, you will probably be made part of a group to be escorted to various offices. If you are alone, you will have to make your own arrangements.

4

PERSONAL
ADMINISTRATION

YOUR PERSONAL RECORDS ARE YOU, AS FAR AS THE
NAVY IS CONCERNED, UNTIL YOU HAVE HAD TIME
TO CREATE A SERVICE REPUTATION. THEREFORE,
MAKE SURE YOUR RECORDS ARE COMPLETE, ACCURATE,
AND INCLUDE ALL OF YOUR QUALIFICATIONS
AND ACHIEVEMENTS.

—*Admiral Chester Nimitz*

A FEW MOMENTS SPENT TAKING CARE OF YOUR
DEPENDENTS' AFFAIRS WILL GIVE YOU PEACE OF MIND
AND YOUR LOVED ONES A SETTLED FUTURE.

—*Vice Admiral Charles Melson*

It is wise to start your career off right by establishing your own personal administration on a sound basis. Once this is done, you can concentrate on your daily performance of duty, secure in the knowledge that what you do will be properly recorded and that your family will be taken care of. These two aspects of your personal administration are of the utmost importance.

Official Records

Records in the NMPC. The records of most importance to you are maintained in the NMPC. They are now maintained in a microfilm process known as microfiche (literally, "small cards"). A microfilm is a single film frame carrying data. The frame can be reduced in size to assist in storage. A microfiche is a series of microfilms making up a record on a particular subject.

57

Each officer has five such microfiche files and a sixth if he or she has been an enlisted person. They are:

Fiche No. 1—Fitness and Awards
1. Assignment officer code
2. Latest photograph
3. Fitness reports and attachments
4. Medals/awards/citations; commendatory data (received prior to 30 September 73)

Fiche No. 2—Professional History
1. Educational data
2. Qualifications/classification/designation data
3. Appointments/promotions/commissions
4. Reserve status
5. Service determination/separation/retirement
6. Miscellaneous professional history

Fiche No. 3—Personal Data
1. Security investigations, clearances, personal history statement
2. Record of emergency data
3. Record changes
4. Personal background data (citizenship/casualty/death/biography)
5. Miscellaneous personal data

Fiche No. 4—Orders

Fiche No. 5—Privileged Information. This microfiche is prepared on individual officers only if there is correspondence derogatory in nature or reflecting various board decisions.
1. Adverse information (Navy regulations establish that adverse matter shall not be placed in an officer's record without the knowledge of the officer. In all cases, the officer reported on may make an official statement in response. If the officer reported on chooses not to make a statement, that intention shall be made in writing. The commander, NMPC, will determine what is adverse matter.
2. Statements of the officer in reply to adverse matter.
3. Extracts from the findings and recommendations of courts and boards concerning the officer. These include statements of disciplinary action and court-martial orders or promulgating letters of general courts-martial where there has been a verdict of guilty. When trial

results in an acquittal of all charges and specifications, or in cases in which the final review of a conviction results in action tantamount to an acquittal of all charges and specifications, court-martial orders or the promulgating orders of courts-martial shall not be included in the officer's official record. No entry whatsoever regarding the acquittal shall appear in the officer's official record, neither the fact of having been tried nor any mention of the offense. Complete records of proceedings of court-martial inquiries, investigations, etc., are filed in the office of the judge advocate general.

4. Other information of a highly personal nature (for example, psychiatric examination)

Fiche No. 6—Enlisted Record. Prepared only for officers who have served an enlistment for two or more years and whose officer microfilm record was established during the initial conversion process from flat paper to microfiche format. Enlisted documents for officers who completed less than two years of enlisted service are distributed under appropriate subject matters on microfiches 1 through 5. A fiche no. 6 was not prepared during the conversion process for temporary officers who held concurrent enlisted status. In these cases, an enlisted microform record was prepared and filed with the officer microform record. This same practice is to be followed for each officer with prior enlisted service whose microform record is established subsequent to the conversion process.

The official officer record presented to selection boards is comprised of fiche nos. 1, 2, and if it exists, 5 for active duty officers, and fiche nos. 1, 2, 4, and if it exists, 5 for USNR (inactive) and temporary active reserve (TAR) officers. Fiche nos. 3 and 6 are normally maintained for administrative purposes only; however, fiche no. 3 may be provided to boards, upon their request, for determining medical status.

Record Availability. You may review your record personally in Washington, D.C., in the officer record review room, 3036 Navy Annex, or you may specifically authorize another person in writing to review your record for you. It normally takes about forty-five minutes for the receptionist to obtain your record, so you can save time if you call (202)694-2858 prior to your arrival and request that your record be drawn. Any officer may request that a copy of his microfiche be mailed to him or her by sending a request in writing to commander, NMPC (NMPC 312), Washington, D.C. 20370. There is no charge, and the microfiche record can be read on any microfiche reader.

Most of these records will be formed from letters and forms submitted without your taking the initiative. One that should get your personal attention is the record of emergency data (DD Form 93-1), which you should fill out carefully and change whenever appropriate. You will be the only one who will know when there has been a change. It includes the names of your beneficiaries and the names of the insurance companies and organizations that are to be notified in case of your death.

Your photograph will be seen by many persons involved with your selection for promotion and for assignment. Be sure that it does you justice and is a full-length photo. Navy photo labs will take the photographs for you, but many officers have used commercial photographers to ensure best results.

Corrections. After you review your record, you may find incorrect entries or feel that some of those made are unjust. Obvious errors in filing (such as another person's entry in your file) may be brought to the attention of the records section by filling out a form provided by the receptionist.

Serious errors or injustices may be corrected by writing an official letter to the commander, NMPC, setting forth the nature of the error and the correction desired. If such correction is not within the power of the commander, you will be advised to apply to the Board for the Correction of Naval Records (BCNR). Article 5040200 of the NMPC manual describes the board and its functions and powers. A booklet and application forms are available from the BCNR in room 4415 of the Arlington Annex.

Detailer Records. Your rank detailer maintains a small file containing detailing correspondence and your latest office preference and personal information card (NMPC 1301/1). He will give you access to this file if you request it when you visit him.

Records in the Bureau of Medicine and Surgery. Your master health record and dental record is maintained in the Bureau of Medicine and Surgery. The record you carry with you from station to station is a duplicate of the master record. Should it be lost or destroyed, a new copy can be obtained from the master.

Records in the Supply Systems Command. The original of your pay accounts is maintained in the Supply Systems Command. If the copy you carry with you from station to station is lost or destroyed, your supply officer will reconstruct your local records.

Records Kept by Your CO.   Your commanding officer will maintain your officer's qualification jacket, your health record, and your pay accounts. These records will be taken by you from station to station. You may need them while traveling or on leave. Guard them, for while they may be replaced, losing them is frowned upon.

The CO's office will also maintain a local correspondence file for you. The file remains with the ship when you leave and is usually destroyed.

Qualifications

NMPC File.   As stated in the preceding section, microfiche no. 2 contains a summation of your qualifications. These start with your source of commissioning and include designator, warfare specialty, formal education, technical and service-school attendance (but not short courses such as emergency shiphandling), awards, and subspecialty qualifications.

Officer's Qualification Jacket.   This record, which you will carry with you and leave with your CO, will contain all that is in your NMPC qualification file, but will also include information such as attendance at fleet short schools, watch qualifications, and qualifications peculiar to certain ships.

NATOPS Jacket.   If you are entering an aviation-training pipeline, you will soon acquire a NATOPS jacket that will outline all training you have received. You will carry this with you between duty stations.

Fitness Reports

Discussion in this section will be confined to the efforts required of the individual officer to maintain a complete and accurate fitness report file and to assist the reporting officer in making out fitness reports. The interpretation of fitness reports and their importance in career planning is covered in chapter 17.

Types of Fitness Reports.   There are three kinds of fitness reports: regular, concurrent, and special.

The regular report is submitted annually on the dates specified for each grade and also upon the detachment of the officer or that of his reporting senior. Reports of thirty days or less are usually marked so and not completely filled out.

Concurrent reports are made by a second reporting senior. Concurrent reports, for example, are made on an officer away at school on temporary additional duty or on a medical officer serving two commands.

Special reports are made for a specific event or period of time in which the officer's performance of duty warrants mention. The report may be either positive or negative.

Dates of Fitness Reports. Every day of an officer's career must be covered by a fitness report. When you report to a new station your first report must cover travel, leave, proceed time, and employment since the date of detachment from your last station.

Officer's Responsibilities with Regard to Fitness Reports. Each officer is required to fill out the upper section of his rough fitness report. Some ship's offices will carry this information over for you from your previous report, but you are still responsible for the accuracy of the data entered. This means checking the dates of the report and the accuracy of its information on the duties you have performed. You should also check the smooth copy of the report when it is shown to you.

Reviewing the content of a report is described briefly in the chapter on career planning. Reviewing a succession of reports is described fully in the *Unrestricted Line Officer Career Guidebook* (NMPC 15197A) Art. 210.

The fitness report is the most important record you will have. Learn early to keep personal track of your activities and master the manner of evaluating such reports.

Budgeting

Early in your career you should establish a budget. List all of your income, including pay, allowances, and investment income. Then list your expenses, such as your rent, mess bill, insurance premiums, and income tax. The difference should be available to you for uniforms, clothing, entertainment, and savings. When you marry, these items will change, but the necessity for budgeting will be even more important.

Estate Planning

Listing of Estate. A person's estate is the total of his or her material possessions, financial assets, liabilities, and future assured income. You may not feel the need for making out a list of your assets and liabilities, particularly in your early years, when they are not large. However, you must remember that your profession is dangerous and that you are likely to be separated from your parents, family, and executor if you are injured or killed. Even early in your career it is advisable to make out such a list as a starting point for estate planning. This exercise will help keep your financial situation in perspective and will be of great assistance to the person who may have to administer your estate after your death.

Simply list all assets in one area and all of your liabilities in another. Include the location, cost, and date of acquisition. Assets should include money, bank accounts, securities, real estate, automobiles, jewelry, furniture, insurance, death gratuity, accrued Social Security payments, and like items. The liability list should include loans, liens, mortgages, debts, credit cards, and similar items. Update annually or when major changes occur.

Place a copy of the list of your estate in your safe with a note asking that it be forwarded to your next of kin or executor in the event of your death.

Will. After listing your assets and liabilities, the next step is to make a will. Consult your station or ship legal officer (or if in a small ship, the nearest legal officer ashore) for advice. You will find that your first will can be quite simple (see the example on page 65) and can even be done in your own handwriting (holographic). If you are married, you will need a more complicated will and should seek legal assistance in preparing it.

Your spouse should also execute a will.

As you develop the need for a more complicated will you will also need to understand certain terms. A will is a legal instrument executed with the formalities of law whereby a person makes disposition of his property to take effect after death. A testator is a person who leaves a will in force after death. A codicil is an addition to, or a qualification of, a will. The codicil must be executed in the same fashion as the will. Probate is a legal process of presenting a will to the registrar of wills in the county where the deceased legally resided. A holographic will is one made in the testator's handwriting.

Method of Executing a Will. A will must be in writing. No particular form of expression is necessary in a legal will if it intelligently discloses the intent of the maker respecting the disposal of property after death; but the execution must be in strict compliance with the formalities required by the statutes of the state.

A will that bequeaths personal property must conform with the law of the testator's legal jurisdiction. One that devises real property must be in conformity with the law of the state in which the real property is situated. If both real and personal property are to be disposed of in different places, the law of both places must be met.

Nearly everywhere, a will must be attested and subscribed by witnesses. The number of witnesses required by law varies from zero to three. Assemble three reliable, disinterested witnesses. The testator then states, "This is my last will and testament. For its execution will you three please by my witnesses." The testator then signs the will in their presence, circles the word "seal," and inserts the date. If there is more than one page, the left-hand margin of each page should be signed.

Witnesses must be competent, that is, qualified to testify in court to the facts that they attest by signing the will. They should be of age, sober and sane, should not stand convicted of crime, should believe in the obligation of an oath, and should understand the testator's language. They must not be beneficiaries of any part of the estate. The witnesses should enter their places of residence under their signatures. Since the authenticity of the signatures must be proved in court at the time of the probating of the will, care should be exercised in selecting witnesses who will be available to complete this legal requirement. If witnesses die or move to remote places, a new will should be prepared with new witnesses.

Avoid duplicate signing. One original is enough. Typewritten copies, clearly labeled as such, may be prepared and not signed. If you send copies for safekeeping or other purposes to places such as the Navy Mutual Aid Association, indicate where the original is located.

Short Form of a Simple Will. The following short form of a simple holographic will is given as an example. It has been used by many officers.

> All my estate I devise and bequeath to my wife, Mary Doe, for her own use and benefit forever, and I hereby appoint her my executrix, without bond, with full power to sell, mortgage, lease, or in any other manner dispose of the whole or any part of my estate.

Richard Doe   [Seal]

Dated 1 June 1991

> Subscribed, sealed, published, and declared by Richard Doe, testator above named, as and for his last will in the presence of each of us, who at his request and in his presence, and in the presence of each other, at the same time, have hereto subscribed our names as witnesses this first day of July, 1991, aboard the USS *Stoddert*, San Diego, California.
> [Signatures and addresses of three witnesses]

If you have a will as an unmarried person, you should immediately make out a new one upon marriage.

Probating a Will. A will made in any part of the world, if executed according to the laws of the testator's domicile, will be there admitted to probate without question.

A will should be offered for probate in the county in which the deceased had his legal residence at the time of his death. The probate of a will simply establishes its due execution by the testator. Wills may be presented for admission to probate by the executor, a legatee, a devisee, a creditor, or other person interested in the estate. The will is probated in a court having jurisdiction over such matters, called variously the register of wills, probate court, or surrogate court, or in an ordinary district court, the county court, common pleas acting as probate court, or orphan's court.

In some states, the testimony of witnesses to the signing of the will by the testator must be produced in court at the time of the probate. If, at the time of the testator's decease, one of the subscribing witnesses is dead or cannot be present for other reasons, proof of the handwriting of any such absent witness is admitted. It should be apparent that easily obtainable witnesses should be used and maintained.

Designation of an Executor. This is a problem that may trouble you. Asking a business friend or a close personal friend will impose a burden on that person. If your estate is small, it is wise to make your spouse executor and vice versa. Sometimes a relative is appropriate.

If your estate is large or your will complicated, give careful consideration to making your bank executor or coexecutor of your estate. The trust department of a bank is trained to handle large estates; it is financially responsible and its fees will not be more than a lawyer's.

Estate and Inheritance Taxes. Recent liberalization of gift and inheritance tax laws make it unlikely that you, as a naval officer, will have to be concerned about your survivors paying inheritance taxes. If you have outside income, you should seek legal advice about the possible use of gifts and trust agreements to minimize inheritance taxes.

Bank Accounts. If you have not already done so, establish one or more bank accounts. You will need one in the state or area in which you are stationed so that you can cash checks readily. Out-of-state checks are hard to cash in some areas. You should establish a second bank account, if you do not already have one, in your home town or state or in the Washington, D.C.-Virginia-Maryland area. You should maintain this account on a continuous basis for the purpose of establishing credit. You can make deposits by mail if necessary. The purpose of such banking is to build up a financial history so that when you apply for a mortgage or other credit you will have a bank that can be used as a reference.

Establish the kind of account that is most useful to you. Most banks have combination savings-checking accounts with automatic lines of credit that permit you to overdraw without penalty and to make small loans automatically.

Credit Unions. Federal credit unions are located at most large stations and at major overseas bases. These unions are chartered by the National Credit Union Administration (NCUA), an agency of the federal government. These accounts pay higher interest rates than savings accounts and make low-interest personal loans. The Navy Federal Credit Union in Washington has branches in most domestic and foreign bases. They have a type of no-charge checking service and automatic teller machines at nearly every Navy base (including those overseas), as well as a system of mail deposits and deposit by allotment.

Credit Cards. Apply for one or more service-station credit cards and one or more major credit cards (American Express, Visa,

MasterCard, etc.). They require a small annual fee, depending on state law. Use them occasionally, just to keep your credit rating active. Your bank will act as backup for your major credit card. Over the years you will then establish a credit rating that will increase as you use your credit successfully.

Use of Allotments. The Navy will automatically send payments to insurance companies, banks, and dependents by the allotment system. Ask the disbursing officer how to register allotments. If you use this system, you will not have to worry about making payments on time when you are at sea, and when you have dependents you will be sure your pay reaches your bank promptly and regularly. Under this system you should have a joint bank account.

If you are a prisoner of war or missing in action, allotments will be continued.

Planning Your Estate. With a will made out, bank accounts established, credit cards in hand, and a periodically updated listing of what you have in your estate now, you can plan for the future.

As a newly commissioned officer, you may need very little in the way of an estate if you do not have dependent parents or a spouse. The death gratuity will provide for your burial expenses, which will be over and above the death benefits described later. If you have a spouse and children, you will need to increase your estate to take care of them.

Insurance. Your first priority should be insurance. It comes in many varieties. You need be familiar with only a few.

The simplest form of insurance is straight term life. Under this coverage you pay a minimum premium for a fixed amount of insurance and the policy is in effect for a fixed "term" or number of years. This insurance is designed to provide maximum protection at minimum cost for your dependents for the period of their lives when protection is most needed. After your children are grown, the need for protection diminishes, and the term insurance can be allowed to expire.

An alternative form of straight (whole) life insurance is for the period of your life rather than for a limited term. This can be used to protect your spouse throughout your life. It is more expensive than term insurance.

Some annuities are complicated forms of insurance that provide for periodic payments to you or to your dependents after varying periods of time. Straight life insurance features can be combined with annuities. Naval officers have little need for annuities. Retired pay, social security, and the Survivor Benefit Plan provide better protection at lower rates.

When you progress to mid-career and your insurance needs multiply, you should consult a qualified insurance expert and establish a coordinated program.

Before taking any commercial insurance, you should consider the government or quasi-government programs described in the sections that follow.

Service Government Life Insurance (SGLI). Public Law 98-289 provides SGLI in the amount of $20,000 for every officer on active duty. Three dollars is automatically deducted from pay to cover a part of the total premium. The remaining portion is paid for by the service concerned. An officer may elect to submit VA Form 29-8286 requesting coverage only in the amount of $15,000, $10,000, or $5,000, or no coverage at all. Premiums will be reduced accordingly. This insurance is so low in cost that no officer can afford to be without it. This is the first insurance policy each naval officer should have.

Navy Mutual Aid. Navy Mutual Aid is a membership organization that provides varying death benefits, assists beneficiaries in filing claims for government benefits, and provides follow-up services as necessary. This is the second insurance a naval officer should have, and it should be acquired no later than the time of marriage.

Navy Mutual Aid provides members with safekeeping facilities for important papers and a computerized family financial planning statement service. It helps surviving dependents of members obtain all government benefits to which they are entitled. It will also provide group financial counseling, briefings on government benefits on request of commanding officers, and will make its computerized family financial planning statement service available to nonmembers at cost.

Armed Forces Relief and Benefit Association (AFRBA). This is one of several quasi-military associations that issue low-cost varieties of term insurance. Aviation policies are also included. This type of insurance should be considered before any commercial insurance is taken.

Commercial Insurance. If you feel the need for additional insurance after exhausting the foregoing sources, seek a reliable insurance broker representing a major insurance company. He or she should be able to service all your needs.

Premium Payment. While you are on active duty, all these forms of insurance, including commercial, may have their premiums paid by allotment. Using this convenience will spare you and your spouse the burden of making monthly payments.

Beneficiaries and Payout. All of these policies will require that you designate beneficiaries. Keep them up-to-date. Most policies have various methods of payment. Select the one that best fits the financial plan you have set up for your dependents.

Dependency and Indemnity Compensation (DIC). This is a system administered by the Veteran's Administration that makes payments to spouses, unmarried children, and dependent parents of those who die in active service. While not an insurance program, it is considered here because its benefits are the same as insurance benefits.

Compensation is paid at a monthly rate based on the service member's pay grade. Remarriage of the spouse stops the payments. Children under eighteen receive compensation at one rate if the spouse survives and at an increased rate if there is no surviving spouse. Payments terminate at age eighteen, but may continue until age twenty-three if the child is in school or has a certain kind of disability.

Survivor Benefits. The Survivor Benefits plan, formed in 1972, complements Social Security and is a program for those retired. It is fully described in the chapter on retirement, but is included in summary form here because it should be part of your estate planning. Briefly, when you retire you may opt to have a portion of your retired pay set aside in exchange for one of several options that will provide payment to your spouse and/or children for the life of your spouse and for shorter periods for your children. The amount may be as much as 55 percent of your pay. It will be difficult to predict the rank in which you will retire or the rate of pay at that time, but you can estimate the effect such an option would have on how much of an estate you will need and what your insurance needs will be.

Social Security. Every officer is automatically enrolled in the Social Security program, and payments are deducted from monthly pay. The amount of Social Security benefits payable to you or your survivors should be considered a part of your estate.

The benefits will depend upon the average monthly wage earned by you and the amount of inflation over the years. Amounts due to your survivors under the Survivor Benefit plan are reduced by the amount of Social Security they receive. (See chapter 20 for further information.) Social Security will provide a supplement to your retired pay beginning at age sixty-two, or later if you so choose (in an increased amount); in the event of your death it will provide a monthly income for your spouse, children under eighteen (until twenty-three if unmarried and students), and dependent parents if there are no dependent children. Some of these payments may be phased out soon.

Real Estate. The most likely addition to your estate will be real estate. It is generally felt that real estate is a good hedge against inflation. It is, if you acquire a house and then sell and buy one each time you move so that you have more or less continuous ownership. Obviously, the costs of buying and selling, the rate of inflation, and mortgage rates are factors relevant to the success of your investment. Generally, if a piece of real estate is held long enough to compensate for depreciation and closing costs, buying a house will be considered financially profitable. Remember that a house appreciates and depreciates in value according to the prevailing real estate market, and that it also depreciates in condition and in the eyes of the Internal Revenue Service if you use it for business or for rental. The volatility of the real estate market and the national economy requires that each officer understand basic economics and the changes in real estate investment that have occurred and may potentially occur in the years ahead.

Security Investments. When your insurance and real estate needs have been met, and if you are fortunate enough to have additional funds left over, you may want to turn to security investments.

When considering security investments, always take into account the amount of liquidity. Liquidity simply means the speed and sureness with which you can get your money back in case you have a sudden need for it or wish to change your investment program. Generally the greater the liquidity the lower the return.

Another aspect to consider is risk. Some investments are low risk and others may be very high. Risk usually varies directly with the rate of return.

Bank savings accounts are the simplest forms of investment,

although they are not really a security. They return very little, but they are high in liquidity. Some have a thirty-day withdrawal clause, but this is seldom enforced for modest accounts. Keep as much in bank savings accounts as you think you will need for contingencies and emergencies.

The next step up the investment ladder is the savings and loan account. It is usually insured by the government and therefore virtually risk-free in the amounts you will have invested. You will receive a slightly higher return than from a bank, but may find that there is some delay in withdrawals.

If you desire a greater return with liquidity preserved, there is a growing variety of investments available. The most popular is the money market fund. For an initial deposit of about $500 you will be able to open an account that will give you a return of about the same rate as that of short-term government treasuries. Return can be reinvested and compounded daily. Some accounts have checking systems that allow you to write checks. Liquidity is excellent and the accounts are government-insured to certain amounts.

Mutual funds specializing in various categories of securities such as income stocks, growth stocks, tax-exempt bonds, and other classes of income are available. Liquidity is good, but you will be paying a small fee for management.

Treasury bills, certificates of deposit, and other similar investment instruments provide excellent returns for varying periods. There are liquidity restraints and penalties for early withdrawal of funds in a certificate of deposit. Moreover, you will also have to spend time and effort managing them. All of the foregoing investments may be procured directly or through a broker or bank.

Stocks and Bonds. At some time in your career you may want to establish a securities account with a brokerage firm in order to facilitate the buying and selling of securities. It is true that you can go to a bank and have them purchase securities for you and then hold them personally, but this is wasted effort. You can open an account with a brokerage firm for a modest amount of about $5,000. Select a firm that has offices country-wide so that you can continue with the same firm when you are transferred. Visit the nearest office and ask to speak to the manager. Tell him what you want to do and he will assign a broker to you who will be your adviser as long as you want to continue the arrangement. There is no direct charge for his services. He makes his money from the fees charged for securities transactions, so he naturally wants to see as many transactions as possible. As long as you monitor this one aspect of brokerage, you should be well protected. He will make available to you all the advice of specialists in the firm. Your account will be rendered to you monthly in a statement recording all transactions of the past month and summarizing the current state of your account. All of the stocks you buy can be kept by the firm and all dividends collected by them and credited to you. Or you can hold your own stocks and have the dividends sent to you. Establish a margin account so that you can borrow against your stock as a convenience and for ease in managing your account. If you are transferred, the firm will allow you to keep the same broker and to deal with him by telephone, or you may shift your account to an office near your new station and change to a local broker.

The buying and selling of stocks and bonds is not for amateurs. Many naval officers become quite knowledgeable over the years. If you decide to open an account, make plans to study the market process before getting too deeply involved in it.

Briefly, bonds offer a fixed return for a specified period, but the value of the bond fluctuates with the bond market. If the bond can be held to maturity, the full value can be realized, but if earlier liquidation is necessary, losses may result.

Common stocks vary in value daily with the market. Some stocks, such as utilities, are relatively stable and pay good dividends. At the other end of the spectrum are so-called growth stocks, which "grow" in value as the company matures and prospers and which pay modest dividends. In between are combination growth-and-dividend stocks, with the general average of total return about 15 percent. Obviously many stocks increase at a faster pace, and just as many decrease radically.

Preferred stocks pay fixed dividends regardless of the success of the company (unless it makes less than the amount of the preferred dividend), but the price of the stock is relatively fixed.

There are many other forms of securities, such as put-and-call options and commodities. Commodities are not suitable for the naval officer unless he studies the market daily.

Savings bonds, obtained on monthly or quarterly allotment, do not pay large returns, but for the less daring are a safe way of establishing monthly savings.

Taxes. One of your earliest financial chores will be making out your income tax returns. Any naval officer should be able to make out all returns correctly and honestly and at the same time protect personal interests by assuring that no more is paid than the minimum amount due. If, in later life, tax returns become more complicated, there are many tax manuals available for assistance.

The first occasion on which you will be able to take advantage of other than routine income tax deductions will be when you purchase real estate. Real estate taxes and mortgage interest are deductible, and when you rent your home to others, the expenses of renting and repairs as well as depreciation will be deductible. These deductions can be quite substantial.

State income taxes vary from zero to quite large amounts. If you have a choice, establish your home in an area that gives you the best tax advantage. Other taxes to consider when choosing a home of record are automobile registration and personal property taxes.

Pay System and Records

General. Prompt rendering of pay and correct pay records are important to each individual. The Navy does a superb job of managing individual pay records. They keep track of allotments, federal and state withholding taxes, social security payments, and all of the types of pay and allowances you may be eligible for. Your pay record will also keep track of your leave balance. Nevertheless, each officer must carefully monitor *every* aspect of his leave and pay accounting, for, unfortunately, mistakes often occur.

Navy Pay Record System. The Navy pay record system is centralized and computerized at the Navy Finance Center in Cleveland, Ohio. The system is known as the Joint Uniform Military Pay System (JUMPS). Your master monthly pay account is automatically updated by computer. Each person receives a monthly leave and earnings statement (LES). This is your individual pay account for the period shown. Check the blocks for correctness. Once you have learned the meaning of each block indicating the monthly payments, earnings, and leave, this should take only a few minutes. Bring errors to the attention of the disbursing officer. Maintain at least one year's worth of records.

One block needs some explanation. Block 8 shows the pay

entry base date (PEBD). Pay is calculated by grade and starts with PEBD. This date is the actual or constructive date of entry into service. It is the actual date of your commissioning, but if you have active or reserve service prior to commissioning, your PEBD will show an earlier date that includes this service.

When Paid. You will be paid twice each month and between pay days if need be. When traveling, you may present your pay accounts to any disbursing officer for pay. When you are transferred, you may draw three months' advance pay less allowances (a "dead horse") and repay it interest free over a period of six months. Needless to say, it requires a great deal of discipline for an officer to draw this advance.

Types of Pay. Every officer is entitled to base pay and subsistence allowance. Base pay is calculated by grade starting with your PEBD. The pay scale is graduated within each grade, so you will receive pay increases as your service time lengthens. You will also receive an increase in pay with each promotion. An annual pay raise is provided (usually in January) by Congress for both military and government employees. It is based on the consumer price index, but can vary according to the dictates of the Congress and the Defense Department.

Hazardous Duty and Special Duty Pays. Officers performing certain hazardous or special duties are entitled to additional pay. Examples are incentive pay for flying or submarine duty and special pay for diving duty. Amounts vary from time to time. Officers serving in nuclear submarines receive large bonuses.

Combat Pay. In time of war or in an emergency declared by Congress, combat pay of one hundred and ten dollars per month is paid.

Responsibility Pay. Officers serving in billets of high responsibility receive extra pay.

Special/Variable Incentive Pay for Medical Officers. Medical, dental, veterinary, and optometry officers are entitled to incentive pay, and some qualify for additional specialty pay in substantial amounts.

Career Sea Pay. NAVOP 209/80 placed in effect the sea pay provisions of the Military Pay and Allowance Benefits Act of 1980. Naval officers in pay grades W-1 through W-4, O-1E through O-3, and O-3 through O-6 are entitled to career sea pay. Officers must provide personnel support detachments with certain information to establish a base for the amount of pay. NAVOP 209/ 80 provides information necessary for this purpose.

Basic Allowance for Quarters (BAQ), Variable Housing Allowance (VHA), and Off-Station Housing Allowance (OHA). These are provided for officers living off base. VHA varies with the cost-of-living index for various areas in the United States. OHA is provided for high-cost areas overseas.

Death and Burial

In the event of your death many benefits will be available. Some are automatically provided, and others must be requested by your survivors.

Notification and Arrangements. When death occurs near a Navy shore station or in a hospital, the local supply officer takes charge and arranges for local burial or, in the case of an active officer, shipment of the body at government expense. The commanding officer makes the required reports.

When death occurs at a place remote from a Navy station or from the person's command, and the officer is on leave or shore leave, the spouse or nearest relative should radio or telegraph (1) the commanding officer and state all details and ask for instructions, and (2) the Bureau of Medicine and Surgery and give the deceased's full name, rank, and branch of service; date, place, and cause of death, and cemetery where burial is desired; and request instructions as to burial arrangements. In most circumstances the Navy will send a casualty assistance control officer (CACO) to assist in making all arrangements.

Burial. You are entitled to be buried in a national cemetery. Some, such as Arlington, have restrictions because of size, but most are available. If you are to be buried in the Washington, D.C., area, a special section of the NMPC will handle the local arrangements.

Honors. When burial is in a cemetery in the immediate vicinity of a naval station, military honors will be provided if practicable and if requested by the next of kin. However, it is not always possible for the Navy to provide honors at cemeteries not close to naval stations. Sometimes a local reserve group or a veteran's organization can provide minimum honors.

Certificate of Death. The surviving spouse should obtain

from the Bureau of Medicine and Surgery certified copies of the official certificate of death. A copy of this certificate must accompany claims, including settlement of commercial insurance policies. The surviving spouse should ask two officers or friends who knew the deceased well to identify the remains before the coffin is closed. They will be prepared to furnish the affidavit sometimes required by commercial insurance companies to be filed with claim for insurance due. Five or six copies are desirable.

Burial Expenses. If burial is in a national cemetery, there is no charge for the burial expenses. If burial is not in a national cemetery, a $2,140 basic burial allowance is available. When burial is in a national cemetery, a headstone or grave marker is provided without request. Markers for private cemeteries are shipped free, but the survivor is responsible for transportation to the cemetery and for the cost of placement. If a marker is purchased from a private supplier, $76 is available to help defray the cost.

Transportation. Transportation from the place dependents were located upon notification of death to a point where they want to make their home will be furnished for dependents at government expense, upon application by the senior dependent.

Personal property of the deceased and dependents will be moved at government expense from the location at time of death to the selected home if the move is made within one year.

Survivor Benefits

Financial Benefits. In the event of your death, your survivors will receive assistance in various ways. The burial assistance described above will be available immediately. Payment of the death gratuity and back pay will be prompt. The Navy Mutual Aid will immediately forward a sizeable initial payment. Proceeds of insurance policies may not be available for several months. Social Security payments must be applied for; this process will take several months. Other parts of your estate will be available after probate of your will; this process may take some time.

In addition to the various financial benefits described above, your dependents will be entitled to certain other privileges, descriptions of which follow.

Educational Benefits. Various kinds of scholarships from more than twenty Navy-affiliated organizations are available.

These are summarized in a pamphlet published annually by the NMPC (NMPC 15003 series).

The Navy Relief Society conducts a guaranteed student loan program. Loans up to $2,500 per year ($7,500 total) are provided for undergraduate study or vocational training. Graduate study loans can be made up to $5,000 per year ($15,000 total, or a maximum of $15,000 if undergraduate and graduate are combined).

Identification Card. Widow(er)s, dependent children age twenty-one or under (twenty-three if attending an institution of higher learning full time), and dependent parents and parents-in-law are entitled to an identification card that may be used to obtain the privileges described in the following sections.

Exchange, Commissary, and Theater. Those entitled to have an ID card are entitled to use the base exchanges, commissaries, and theaters of all services. The ID card must be displayed for admission.

Medical Care. Widow(er)s and dependents are entitled to medical care under the Unified Services Health Benefit Program and the Civilian Health and Medical Program of the Unified Services (CHAMPUS). After the age of sixty-five Medicare is available.

Navy Relief Assistance. Temporary financial assistance may be obtained from the Navy Relief Association.

Carl Vinson Hall. Carl Vinson Hall is a residence for sea-service widows. When space is available, couples are accepted. Entry is by application and payment of an entry fee that varies with the number of rooms in the desired apartment. No age limit is set, but the applicant must pass a physical examination and screening process to determine if he or she is suited for residence in a retirement home. Some medical assistance is available, but when residents are no longer able to live in Vinson Hall, the government will move them to a nursing facility or other medical institution.

Legal Assistance. There are more than two hundred legal assistance offices located at various commands. Navy legal officers cannot represent your dependents in a court, but they can provide assistance and advice on all legal matters.

Miscellaneous Benefits. Unremarried widow(er)s are entitled to civil service employment preference in connection with examinations, ratings, appointments, and reinstatements for civil service positions. Unremarried widow(er)s may also be eligible for GI Bill home loans when death is service-connected.

Service academy appointments are available to a limited number of children of deceased officers who died of war injuries. The president makes some of these appointments.

Many states provide benefits of various kinds for dependents of officers. State-maintained veterans offices can provide exact information.

The income of an officer who dies of wounds, disease, or injury sustained in a combat zone is exempt from federal income tax for the year in which death occurs.

The Navy will continue to look after your dependents in every possible way if you are unable to do so. The Navy is a very large family, and there are members of it who will continue to make your dependents feel at home. Do your best to provide for them by wise financial and estate planning. The Navy will do the rest.

5

MILITARY COURTESY, HONORS, AND CEREMONIES

HOW SWEET AND GRACIOUS, EVEN IN COMMON SPEECH,
IS THAT FINE SENSE WHICH MEN CALL COURTESY!

—*James Thomas Fields*

A NAVAL CEREMONY SHOULD FOLLOW THE LONG-
ESTABLISHED RULES FOR ITS EXECUTION CAREFULLY
AND EXACTLY. SUCH ATTENTION TO DETAIL HONORS
THOSE WHO, LONG BEFORE US, ESTABLISHED THE
RITUAL, AND ALL THOSE WHO, PAST, PRESENT, AND
FUTURE, TAKE PART IN THAT SAME CEREMONY.

—*Fleet Admiral Chester Nimitz*

Every naval officer should acquire, as early in his or her career as possible, a thorough understanding of military courtesy, honors, and ceremonies. Military behavior is a very important component of both your fitness report and your service reputation. Your knowledge of military honors, ceremonies, customs, and traditions and your personal demeanor will constitute a major portion of your military behavior grade. Do not be misled by the feeling that superior academic ability or technical qualifications can substitute for these qualities.

The moment you enter the quarterdeck area of your first assigned ship or station you will also enter the Navy world of honors and ceremonies. Therefore, you should know about them, preferably before reporting. You will have learned the rudiments of military behavior in your professional education and indoctrination; this chapter will give you a working knowledge of it. Further details can be gotten from *Naval Ceremonies, Customs, and Traditions*, which will give you the history and reasons behind the establishment of honors and ceremonies. *Navy Regulations* (1973) is the official guide and authority on honors and ceremonies, but you will not always have ready access to it.

Courtesy

Courtesy. Before discussing the details of rendering honors and ceremonies, it is important to understand that they are based on the societal principle of courtesy, which implies politeness and graceful and considerate behavior toward others. Some version of the golden rule exists in the basic tenets of every major religion or set of ethics. It can be found in the Christian command, "Do unto others as you would have others do unto you," in the Taoist, "As you deem yourself, so deem others," and in the Hindu, "This is the sum of duty, that you do nought to others which if done to you might cause you pain." This general philosophy, which should govern daily conduct, is the foundation of those special acts and ceremonial procedures that members of society observe according to custom and usage. In addition to the required formalities, there are many acts of civility and good breeding required of ladies and gentlemen both in civilian and military life.

Military Courtesy. Military courtesy is the extension of the system of civilian courtesy. The rules for military courtesy are soundly based on custom and tradition, and their strict observance is an important factor in the maintenance of discipline. Respect and courtesy are observed by all officers and enlisted persons of the naval service. Like loyalty, military courtesy operates from senior to junior as well as from junior to senior. Consideration and respect for the junior are necessary attributes of any senior.

Chain of Command. Recognition of the chain of command is long established in the Navy. The chain extends from the president to the most junior seaman recruit. Each officer must understand that this system is not only mandated by regulations, but is a form of naval courtesy. This means respecting and being prompt in response to orders from seniors, and being fair and compassionate toward juniors while still exacting obedience from them. Occasionally the best interests of the Navy may require violation of the chain of command, but each such occurrence should be reported as soon as possible to those in the chain.

The Salute. The most basic act of military courtesy is at a meeting of two military persons. Customarily a salute is exchanged. This form of courtesy has been handed down through the ages and is an integral part of military life. The person receiving the salute (the senior) is just as responsible for returning it as the junior is for rendering it. Learn to salute in a correct and military manner, but without exaggeration. A sloppy salute is more discourteous than a failure to salute. How punctiliously the various forms of military courtesy, particularly the salute, are observed measures the degree of discipline of the ship or station.

Navy Regulations Regarding Salutes. *Navy Regulations* Art. 1009 sets forth in a clear manner the requirements for hand salutes. The following summarizes these requirements and gives added information.

The hand salute is the long-established form of greeting and recognition between persons in the armed services. All persons in the naval service must be alert to render or return the salute as prescribed in the regulations. It must be made with the right hand, when practicable, otherwise with the left. With firearms in hand, the appropriate salute for type of arm must be made.

Juniors salute first. All salutes received when in uniform and covered must be returned; at other times salutes must be appropriately acknowledged. Persons uncovered must not salute,

Figure 5-1. The hand salute.

IN GENERAL

ENLISTED MEN SALUTE OFFICERS AND JUNIOR OFFICERS
SALUTE SENIOR WHEN MEETING, PASSING NEAR, WHEN ADDRESSING
OR BEING ADDRESSED

WHEN SEVERAL OFFICERS ARE
SALUTED, ALL SHALL RETURN IT

WHEN OVERTAKING A SENIOR,
THE SALUTE SHALL BE GIVEN WHEN
ABREAST, WITH "BY YOUR LEAVE, SIR."

OFFICERS AND ALL ENLISTED MEN NOT IN FORMATION SALUTE
DURING HONORS TO THE FLAG OR PLAYING OF NATIONAL ANTHEM

WHEN REPORTING (COVERED)

GUARDS SALUTE ALL OFFICERS
PASSING CLOSE ABOARD

(*Courtesy of* All Hands *Magazine*)

Figure 5-2A. When to salute.

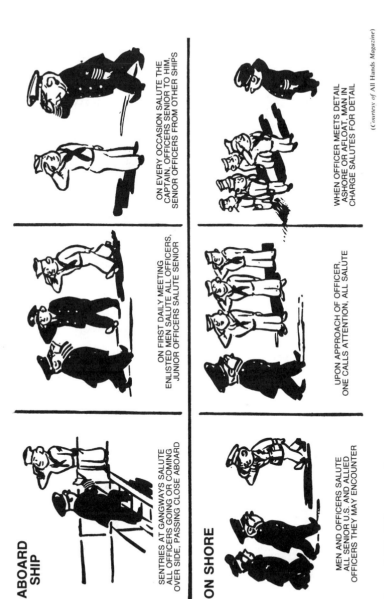

(Courtesy of All Hands Magazine)

Figure 5-2B. When to salute.

IN BOATS

WHEN OFFICER PASSES NEAR,
OFFICER OR PETTY OFFICER IN CHARGE
SALUTES, IF NONE PRESENT MEN DO

OFFICERS RISE AND SALUTE
WHEN A SENIOR ENTERS OR LEAVES

ENLISTED MEN RISE AND SALUTE
WHEN AN OFFICER ENTERS OR LEAVES

VEHICLES

PASSENGERS IN CARS RENDER
AND RETURN SALUTE (DRIVER:
NO, IF SAFETY IS INVOLVED)

WHEN COLORS ARE SOUNDED
MAN IN CHARGE OF DETAIL
SALUTES: OTHERS AT ATTENTION

RENDER SALUTES DUE THEM TO
ALL OFFICERS IN VEHICLES
(IF SAFETY PERMITS)

Figure 5-2C. When to salute.

Figure 5-2D. When not to salute.

except when failure to do so would cause embarrassment or misunderstanding.

Civilians may be saluted by persons in uniform when appropriate, but the uniform hat or cap must not be raised as a form of salutation.

A person in the naval service not in uniform must, in rendering salutes or exchanging greetings, comply with the rules and customs for civilians; except that, when saluting another person in the armed services, the hand salute must be used.

Navy Regulations Art. 1010, which sets forth the occasions on which salutes must be rendered, is given in the following paragraphs along with added information.

Salutes must be rendered by persons in the naval service to officers of the armed forces of the United States, the National Oceanic and Atmospheric Administration, the Public Health Service, and foreign armed services.

All persons in the naval service must salute all officers senior to themselves on each occasion of meeting or passing near or when addressed by or addressing such officers, except that:

1. On board ship salutes should be dispensed with after the first daily meeting, except for those rendered to the CO and those senior to him, to visiting officers, to officers making inspections, and to those officers when addressed or being addressed by them.

2. When such procedure does not conflict with the spirit of these regulations, at crowded gatherings, or in congested areas, salutes must be rendered only when addressing, or being addressed by, an officer who is senior to them.

3. Persons at work or engaged in games must salute only when addressed by an officer senior to them and then only if circumstances warrant. (Persons engaged as described in this or the previous rule will stand at attention when addressed or may be called to attention to clear a gangway for a senior officer.)

4. Persons in formation must salute only on specific command to the formation. Normally only the person in charge of a formation will salute during any evolution requiring the salute.

5. If addressed by a senior officer, a naval person should stand at attention until the conversation is finished or the officer gives the command "At ease" or "Carry on."

6. When boats pass each other with embarked officers or official in view, hand salutes must be rendered by the senior officer

and coxswain in each boat. Officers seated in boats must not rise when saluting; coxswains must rise unless dangerous or impracticable to do so. (It is customary for the senior officer in a boat to rise and salute when an officer senior to him or her enters or leaves the boat or when acknowledging a gun salute.)

General Notes on Salutes and Other Military Courtesies. Salutes are normally exchanged at a distance of six paces, but twenty-five paces is not excessive. The junior remains at the salute until his or her salute is returned or the senior is well past. Conversely, a senior should always be alert to see salutes extended to him or her from longer distances than the minimum. For juniors, it is always a good practice to accompany your salute with a greeting, such as, "Good morning, sir."

When overtaking a senior, the salute should be given when you are abreast the senior and you should ask, "By your leave, sir." Pass after he has returned your salute and answered, "Very well" or "Permission granted."

If escorting a civilian, on meeting another naval person, the customary exchange of salutes should be made. If seated, rise and salute.

If not wearing headdress, or both hands are burdened, you should greet your senior officer with, "Good morning, sir," or with some other appropriate remark. When your right hand is engaged and cannot be used, salute with your left hand.

The custom at Air Force and Army posts is to salute when uncovered as well as when covered. Follow their custom when at their bases.

A salute is rendered to a senior officer whenever he or she is recognized, whether covered or not, in uniform or in civilian clothes. Be zealous in recognizing your seniors. A junior, uncovered, stands at attention until a senior has passed. A senior, uncovered, usually bows to a junior, or speaks to him to acknowledge the salute.

When formally addressing, or being addressed by, a senior officer, stand at attention. If covered, salute when first addressed and again upon the conclusion of the instruction or conversation. If uncovered, stand at attention throughout the conversation, unless otherwise directed by the senior officer. While saluting and before entering upon a conversation, give your name, as "Ensign Joseph Doaks, sir."

Rise, uncover, and stand at attention when a senior visits your room or office.

The command "Gangway" should be given by anyone who observes an officer approaching an area where his or her passage is blocked. This courtesy should be extended to important civilians as well. Enlisted persons should not use this word to clear a passage for themselves or for other enlisteds, but should say, "Coming through" or something to that effect. When the command "Gangway" is given, the senior petty officer in the vicinity should see that it is carried out.

All military commands should be given firmly but impersonally. A pleasant tone affirms the respect to be rendered to the person passing.

Sir is a word always used after *yes* and *no* when conversing with senior officers and officers on duty. Many senior officers use it when addressing their juniors as a matter of courtesy downward. *Sir* is customarily added in such routine statements as "The watch is relieved, sir" and "I request permission to leave the ship, sir." *Ma'am* is used for a woman officer.

Women officers and women enlisted personnel in the Navy render to officers and other officials salutes in accordance with established customs and rules of military courtesy. Outdoors, when a woman officer or enlisted person is wearing a hat, she will always salute an officer senior to her. It should be noted that the rendering of official salutes takes precedence over the usual social customs established between men and women. The only exception is that women do not remove their hats indoors, as do men, and do not salute, even though covered, in an indoor area where men would remove their hats or caps.

Boat Etiquette. Figure 5-3 illustrates some of the more common rules of boat etiquette. You should master them thoroughly. As a junior officer you will be called upon frequently to act as a boat officer, and through the years you will make many trips both in command and as a passenger. The following rules will help you:

1. Juniors board boats first. Move forward as necessary to give following seniors room astern.

2. Rise when seniors embark.

3. Leave after seniors unless a senior gives an order to the contrary.

ENTERING BOAT, JUNIORS GO FIRST
LEAVING BOAT, SENIORS GO FIRST

ALWAYS STAND WHEN A SENIOR
ENTERS OR LEAVES A BOAT

SENIORS ARE ACCORDED THE
MOST DESIRABLE SEATS

ALWAYS OFFER A
SEAT TO A SENIOR

IF BOAT IS TOO CROWDED AND YOU
ARE JUNIOR, CATCH NEXT BOAT

WHEN A SENIOR OFFICER IS
PRESENT, DO NOT SIT IN STERN
SHEETS UNLESS ASKED TO DO SO

DON'T CROSS BOWS, CROWD, OR IGNORE
PRESENCE OF A SENIOR

DON'T MAKE LAST-MINUTE DASH
GET INTO BOATS BEFORE
LAST BOAT GONG

(*Courtesy of* All Hands *Magazine*)

Figure 5-3. Boat etiquette.

4. Keep your hands and arms inside the boat.

5. Step carefully on spaces provided and avoid walking on thwarts, decks, and other varnished areas.

6. Do not change a coxswain's orders except in an emergency, and if you do so be prepared to substantiate your decision to the OOD upon your return to the ship.

7. If you are senior to the boat officer and other officers and eligible for command at sea, identify yourself to the boat officer and coxswain. You are responsible for the safe and proper operation of the boat, but leave the normal operation to the boat officer unless it is necessary to intervene.

When you are in command of a boat, you should ensure that the coxswain is aware of and ready to enforce the following rules of etiquette and seamanship:

1. No junior should overhaul and pass a senior without permission.

2. Ensure that you and your coxswain salute passing seniors first. Return salutes promptly.

3. When approaching a ship or landing, give way to seniors.

4. Enlisted persons in boats with officers must maintain appropriate silence, particularly when approaching ships or landings.

5. The coxswain must haul clear of the ship or landing while waiting and not allow the crew to leave the boat.

6. The crew must not lounge in the boat while it is running.

7. Keep all members of the crew in the same uniform, which must be properly worn.

Boat Salutes. Boats salute in passing much the same as military men and women do. The junior salutes first. However, only the coxswain and the senior officer, if officers are embarked, render or return the salute. Others do not salute, but sit in the direction of their seats at attention. Those saluting do not rise, but face in the direction of the boat saluted if practicable. The coxswain rises if seated and if rising is not dangerous.

When the boat is not underway, rules are the same except that the coxswain salutes officers entering and leaving the boat, if it is safe to do so.

During colors the boat lies to and the senior officer, boat

officer, or coxswain stands at attention and salutes. Others remain seated at attention.

During gun salutes, boats not carrying the person saluted observe the same courtesy for colors. The boat carrying the person saluted stops, disengages clutch, and heads parallel to the saluting ship. Only the person honored rises.

Boat Appearance. A ship is known by the appearance of her boats. An alert, well-uniformed crew is the first step in this direction. A good crew will keep a good boat. Chrome and fancywork help, but they are not substitutes for cleanliness, preservation, and neatness. Boats should have a full allowance of flags and flag-staff devices. Coxswains should understand their use.

Boat Hails. In the days prior to World War II, large ships usually anchored or moored to buoys in Pearl Harbor, Long Beach, San Diego, and Norfolk. (Except for ships conducting visits to foreign ports, most ships today moor to piers.) Much boating was required, and it was necessary that the OOD have some system of determining the station of passengers in approaching boats. The custom of hailing boats provided this information. The procedure, which grew in sophistication over the years, is not found in regulations. It is still used today, particularly overseas, and you and your boat coxswains should be prepared to use it.

All boats approaching a ship at night should be hailed as soon as they are within hearing distance. The proper hail is "Boat ahoy!" The coxswain should answer to indicate the rank of the senior passenger as follows:

Rank or Rate	Coxswain's Reply
President or vice-president of the United States	"United States"
Secretary of defense, deputy or assistant secretary of defense	"Defense"
Secretary, under secretary, or assistant secretary of the Navy	"Navy"
Chief of naval operations, vice chief of naval operations	"Naval Operations"
Fleet or force commander	"Fleet," or abbreviation of administrative title
General officer	"General officer"

Chief of staff	"Staff"
Flotilla commander	"(Type) Flot (number)"
Squadron commander	"(Type) Ron (number)"
Division commander	"(Type) Div (number)"
Marine officer commanding a brigade	"Brigade commander"
Commanding officer of a ship	(Name of ship)
Marine officer commanding a regiment	"Regimental commander"
Other commissioned officer	"Aye, aye"
Noncommissioned officer	"No, no"
Enlisted personnel	"Hello"
Boat not intending to come alongside, regardless of rank or rate of senior passenger	"Passing"

During hours when honors are rendered, the OOD or the quartermaster of the watch should challenge the coxswain by raising his arm with fist closed in the direction of the approaching boat. The coxswain should answer by raising his hand and extending the number of fingers as indicated from the following:

Passenger	Number of Fingers Held Up
President of the United States	8
Secretary of the Navy	7
Assistant secretary of the Navy	6
Admiral	6
Vice admiral	6
Other flag officers	4
General officer	4
Commanding officer, chief of staff, or unit commander	3
Marine officer commanding a brigade or regiment	3
Other commissioned officers	2
All others	1

A clenched fist indicates no passengers. As soon as the boat is within hearing distance, the boat should be hailed and the proper reply given by the coxswain.

Boat Flags and Pennants. A boat should display the personal flag or pennant of an officer entitled to the boat or when he is officially embarked for some other reason. The ensign is also displayed. If he is embarked in uniform but not officially (not en route to or from an official visit or call), the ensign only is displayed. If he is in civilian clothes, a miniature personal flag or pennant is displayed in the cockpit.

Flag Staff Insignia. Boats should display, on both staffs, insignia appropriate to the rank and position of the occupant. These are:

President	Spread eagle perched on ball
Cabinet and flag officer	Halberd head mounted on ball
Captain	Ball
Commander	Five-pointed star
Below	Flat truck

They are shown in figure 5-4.

Boat Markings. Over the years systems of identification, markings, insignia, and colors have been developed. Letter and numeral groups are carried on both bows; they are raised for of-

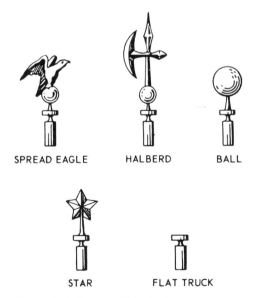

SPREAD EAGLE   HALBERD   BALL

STAR   FLAT TRUCK

Figure 5-4. Boat staff insignia.

ficers' boats and painted for other boats. Officers' boats have transom markings. Amphibious force boats have large markings on ramps for identification from beaches.

Flag officers' barges are marked as follows:

1. Chrome stars on bows are arranged as in flags.
2. The abbreviated title is carried on the transom in gold.
3. Hulls are painted black; waterlines are green.

Unit commanders' gigs are marked as follows:

1. Broad or burgee command pennants in miniature are carried on the bows with unit numbers superimposed.
2. The abbreviated title is carried on the transom in gold.

The gigs of chiefs of staff, not of flag rank, are marked as follows:

1. Insignia are carried on the bows consisting of the official title of the command in chrome letters with an arrow running through the letters.
2. The abbreviated title of the command with an arrow running through the letters and in gold is carried on the transom.

CO's gigs are marked as follows:

1. The ship's name in chrome with an arrow running through the letters is carried on both bows.
2. The ship's name with an arrow running through it is painted in black on the transom.
3. The waterline is painted blue.

Other boats are marked as follows:

1. The ship's type designation and hull number, such as DD 946-1 or CV 65-2, are carried on each bow. The last number is the number of the boat of that ship. Numbers are black.
2. The same marks appear on the transom except for whaleboats.

Amphibious landing craft are marked as follows:

1. All boats use two- or three-letter abbreviations, indicating the ship type, followed by boat numbers assigned by the individual ships. Examples are:

LCC	CC
LPA	PA
LKA	KA
LHA	LHA
LSD	LSD
LST	LST
LPH	LPH

2. When used as barges or gigs, landing craft use standard markings appropriate to the occupants.

Shore-station boats are marked as follows:

1. Barges and gigs are marked as for other boats afloat.
2. Other boats are given consecutive numbers within the naval district, such as 5ND 50, etc.
3. Some shore-station boats are marked with the abbreviation of their station followed by the boat number.

Boat Gongs. The thoughtful senior always informs his junior about a visit to his ship. Proper honors can then be prepared and the CO can be ready and on deck. When officers arrive unexpectedly and the proper officers of the ship and embarked staff have not been notified, boat gongs are usually sounded, with the number of gongs corresponding to the number of side boys rated by the arriving officer. The arriving officer's organization, determined from the answer to a boat hail, is then announced. In some ships this procedure is extended to every arrival and departure, but best opinion holds that this is an unnecessary burden on those who have to listen to the announcing system and is not a substitute for proper and alert watchstanding.

Boat gongs are also used to announce the impending departure of scheduled boats. Three gongs are used for ten minutes to departure, two gongs for five minutes, and one gong for one minute.

The National Anthem. The national anthem of the United States of America is the "Star-Spangled Banner." When played by a naval band, it is played through without repetition of any part, except for those measures repeated to accommodate the words when the anthem is sung.

The playing of the national anthem of the United States or of any other country as part of a medley is prohibited.

Whenever the national anthem of the United States is played, persons in the naval service must stand at attention and face the music, except at colors, when they must face the ensign. When covered, they must come to the salute at the first note of the anthem and must remain at the salute until the last note of the anthem. Persons in ranks come to the salute together, by command. Persons in vehicles or in boats must remain seated or standing. Only the senior officer, boat officer, and coxswain stand and salute.

The same marks of respect prescribed during the playing of the national anthem of the United States are shown during the playing of a foreign national anthem. When both a foreign national anthem and that of the United States are played during honors, the latter is played last. At morning colors, when foreign warships are present, the national anthem of the United States is played first. (These rules come from *Navy Regulations* Arts. 1004, 1005.)

When uncovered, in uniform, you should stand at attention during the playing of any national anthem. If you are in civilian clothes and covered, remove the hat with your right hand and place it over your left breast. If you are uncovered, place your right hand over your left breast.

Navy Regulations on Other Marks of Respect. Juniors should show deference to seniors at all times by recognizing their presence and by employing a courteous and respectful bearing and mode of speech toward them.

Juniors stand at attention when addressed by a senior or when an officer enters the room, compartment, or space where they may be. If impracticable or inappropriate they may remain seated.

Juniors walk or ride on the left of seniors they are accompanying.

Officers shall enter boats and automobiles in inverse order of rank and shall leave them in order of rank, unless the senior indicates he desires other arrangements. Seniors shall be given the most desirable seats.

Subject to the rules for preventing collisions, junior boats must avoid crowding or embarrassing senior boats.

Visiting Men-of-War. A member of the naval service wishing to visit a man-of-war anchored out should obtain permission at the landing to embark in one of her boats. He should ask the senior officer in the boat or the coxswain if he may have permission to go off to the ship in that boat.

On large ships the starboard accommodation ladder is used by officers. On flagships a second ladder is rigged for the flag officer and his staff. The port ladder is used by all others. On small ships often only one ladder is rigged on either side and is used by all hands.

Observe proper boat etiquette.

Do not embark or disembark across another boat without permission. Ordinarily such permission should not be requested.

All officers and enlisted persons, when reaching the quarterdeck of a man-of-war from a boat, from another ship, from the shore, or from another part of the ship, must salute the national ensign. In the event the ensign is not hoisted, this salute is rendered only when coming aboard. It is entirely distinct from the salute to the OOD.

In summary, when boarding a man-of-war, stop at the top of the accommodation ladder or the inboard end of the brow (the gangway is the aperture in the side through which you will pass), face the colors, and salute. Then turn to face the OOD, salute him, and say, "Sir, I request permission to come aboard." If you are attached to the ship you say, "Sir, I report my return aboard." It is then customary to state your reason for visiting, so that the OOD can assist you.

When leaving a man-of-war, salute the OOD and say, "Sir, I request permission to leave the ship." If you are attached to the ship you say, "Sir, I have permission to leave the ship." Then proceed to the top of the accommodation ladder or the inboard end of the brow, face the colors, if hoisted, and salute. After saluting, depart.

Honors, Official Visits, and Calls

Honors, official visits, and calls are an important part of military courtesy. They must be carried out meticulously. As an OOD or other officer engaged in preparing for them, you should carefully review all regulations concerning the events to take place. More will be said about this later. The CO, executive officer, and navigator will all be concerned with planning and preparing for these events and should be consulted by the OOD if there is doubt about anything. But it is the OOD who will execute the required honors, and he must master all the details.

The OOD must be entirely familiar with any situation concerning the rendition of honors, and therefore must also be prepared to render honors without advance notice or preparation.

Although wartime requirements eliminate many of the honors and ceremonies carried out in peacetime, even during war there will be occasions where knowledge of honors procedures will be necessary.

In most ships a copy of the honors tables is generally posted near the quarterdeck for quick reference. The tables in this chapter include honors tables for your personal use and study.

Constant vigilance is required of the entire watch. The signal bridge must be alert to note flag officers leaving and returning from adjacent ships and should report the movement of barges and gigs headed at or near your ship. The deck watch should supplement the efforts of the signal watch.

If your ship is a flagship, maintain close liaison with the flag lieutenant. Know where the admiral, chief of staff, and flag lieutenant are at all times, and tell them promptly when you have been informed of a pending visit.

Make all preparations in advance. Make sure the bandmaster or bugler and the officer in charge of the guard know exactly what their duties are. Instruct the boatswain's mate and the quartermaster of the watch in their duties and inspect and rehearse the side boys. If time permits, conduct a complete rehearsal. Be above reproach in appearance and manner. The OOD represents the CO and the entire ship and must set an example. (These rules come from *Navy Regulations* Arts. 1034–52, 1054, 1055.)

Passing Honors. Passing honors are those honors other than gun salutes, rendered on occasions when ships or boats with embarked officials or officers pass, or are passed, close aboard. "Close aboard" means passing within 600 yards for ships and within 400 yards for boats. These rules are interpreted liberally to ensure that appropriate honors are rendered. Passing honors between ships of the Navy and the Coast Guard consist of sounding "Attention" and rendering the hand salute by all persons in view on deck and not in ranks. The junior ship initiates the honors.

Passing honors are not rendered after sunset or before 0800, except when international courtesy requires.

Manning the rail for the passage of the king and queen of Greece.

Passing honors are not exchanged between ships of the Navy engaged in tactical evolutions outside port.

The senior officer present may direct that passing honors be dispensed with in whole or in part. They are usually suspended in time of war, bad weather, or low visibility.

The passing honors to be rendered to officials and officers embarked in boats are given in table 5-1.

Passing honors to be rendered to a ship of the Navy passing close aboard are given in table 5-2.

A foreign president, sovereign, or member of a reigning royal family is given the same honors as are listed in the above tables for the president of the United States, except that the foreign national anthem is played in lieu of the national anthem of the United States.

Similar passing honors are exchanged between foreign warships passing close aboard. Honors consist of parading the guard of the day, sounding "Attention," rendering the salute by all persons in view on deck, and playing the foreign national anthem.

Table 5-1. Passing Honors to Officials and Officers Embarked in Boats

Official	Ruffles and Flourishes	Music	Guard	Remarks
President	4	National anthem	Full	"Attention" sounded, and salute by all persons in view on deck. If directed by the senior officer present, man rail*
Secretary of state when special foreign representative of president	4	do	do	"Attention" sounded, and salute by all persons in view on deck
Vice president	4	"Hail Columbia"	do	do
Secretary of defense, deputy secretary of defense, secretary of the Navy, and assistant secretary of defense, under secretary, or an assistant secretary of the Navy	4	Admiral's march	do	do
Other city official entitled to honors on official visit	—	—	—	do
Officer of an armed service	—	—	—	do

*Those who man the rail will salute on signal.

Table 5-2. Passing Honors Between Ships

Official	Uniform	Ruffles and Flourishes	Music	Guard	Remarks
President	As prescribed by senior officer present	4	National anthem	Full	Man rail, unless otherwise directed by senior officer present
Secretary of state when special foreign representative of the president	do	4	do	do	Crew at quarters
Vice president	Of the day	—	"Hail Columbia"	do	do
Secretary of defense, deputy secretary of defense, secretary of the Navy, or director of defense research and engineering	do	—	National anthem	do	do
An assistant secretary of defense, under secretary or an assistant secretary of the Navy	do	—	do	do	do

The crew is normally paraded at quarters entering or leaving port in daylight, so as to be prepared for passing honors.

Persons on the quarterdeck salute when a boat displaying a miniature of a personal flag or pennant passes close aboard.

The foregoing honors are initiated when the bow of one ship passes the bow or stern of the other ship and terminated when the honors have been rendered and acknowledged. Passing honors for a boat are initiated when the boat is abreast the quarterdeck.

Definitions of Official Visits and Calls.   An official visit is a formal visit of courtesy that requires special honors and ceremonies.

An official call is an official but informal visit of courtesy that requires no more than side honors. It is not to be confused with personal calls.

A full guard is not less than one Marine rifle platoon. Without Marines, one officer in charge and eighteen to twenty-four enlisted personnel are required.

A guard of the day is not less than one Marine rifle squad. Without Marines, one squad leader and eight to twelve enlisted personnel are required.

A guard of honor is a guard of not less than two Marine platoons on shore stations.

A compliment of the guard is expressed when an interior guard turns out and presents arms to an officer or dignitary visiting a shore station.

Shipboard compliments include honors by a guard and any of the following honors, which are not rendered ashore: manning the rail, crew at quarters, piping boats alongside and dignitary over the side, and side boys.

Preparations for Official Visits and Calls.   The flag lieutenant or aide makes arrangements for visits and calls. On ships and stations where there is no flag officer, the executive officer or the ship's secretary performs these functions. The navigator is responsible for the ship's arrangements. All but the smallest ships should have a permanent full guard and guard of the day, usually furnished by the weapons department. They should be designated and trained at all times.

If full honors are involved, close liaison should be maintained to coordinate the following details: the exact time and place of the visit; the uniform; transportation; the use of calling cards; refreshments; arrangements to break or haul down personal flags;

gun salutes; on shore, arrangements for the entrance to the station, and decisions regarding the use of a guard of honor and an escort from the gate to the ceremonial area.

When to Make Official Visits and Calls.   In the naval service official visits and calls are paid only by officers in command and are distinct from personal calls. Generally speaking, official visits are made more frequently by commanders afloat. Official calls are usually made on shore.

An officer assuming command should, at the first opportunity thereafter, make an official visit to the senior to whom he has reported for duty in command and to any successor of that senior; except that for shore commands a call should be made in lieu of such official visit.

Unless dispensed with by the senior, calls must be made by

1. The commander of an arriving unit upon his immediate superior in the chain of command, if present; and, when circumstances permit, upon the senior officer present.

2. An officer in command upon an immediate superior in the chain of command upon the arrival of the latter.

3. An officer who has been the senior officer present upon his successor.

4. The commander of a unit arriving at a naval base or station upon the commander of such base or station; except that when the former is senior the latter will call. (Call arrangements should normally be requested in a logistics requirements message prior to entering port.)

5. An officer reporting for duty upon his commanding officer. (When arrivals occur after 1600, or on Sunday or holidays, the required calls may be postponed until the next working day.)

Officers of other armed services should be called upon as arranged by the senior officer present.

Diplomatic and consular representatives accredited to the government of a port visited should be called upon as arranged by the senior officer present. A suitable boat should be arranged for the representatives, and advance notice of the time of arrival in port and probable duration of the visit must be given.

Officers of the naval service should make the first visit to the chief of a diplomatic mission of or above the rank of chargé d'affaires. In the exchange of visits with consular representatives, officers of the naval service must make or receive the first visit in accordance with their relative precedence as given in the following:

Official	*Takes Precedence*
Chief of a U.S. diplomatic mission, including a chargé d'affaires*	Over any officer of an armed service of the United States; and over any U.S. civil official, except the secretary of state, whose official salute is less than 21 guns
Career minister	With, but before, rear admiral or brigadier general
Counselor	
First secretary, when no counselor is assigned	
Consul general, or consul or vice consul or deputy consul general when in charge of a consulate general	With, but after, rear admiral or brigadier general
First secretary, when a counselor is assigned	
Consul or vice consul when in charge of a consulate	With, but after, captain in the Navy
Second secretary	
Vice consul	
Third secretary	With, but after, lieutenant in the Navy
Consular agent	

Calls and Visits on Foreign Officials and Officers. The senior officer present should make official visits to foreign officials and officers as custom and courtesy demand.

When in doubt about what foreign officials and officers are to be visited, saluted, or otherwise honored, about the rank of any official or officer, or about whether a gun salute should be returned, the senior officer present must send an officer to obtain the required information.

---

*An acting chief of a U.S. diplomatic mission when holding the title of chargé d'affaires takes precedence as specified but is accorded the honors specified for a chargé d'affaires on the occasion of an official visit.

The following rules, in which the maritime powers generally have concurred, must be observed by officers of the naval service, and their observance by foreign officers can be expected:

1. The senior officer present must, upon the arrival of foreign warships, send an officer to call upon the officer in command of the arriving ships to offer customary courtesies and to exchange information as appropriate; except that in a foreign port such call shall be made only if the officer of the arriving ship is the senior officer present of his nation. This call will be returned at once.

2. Within twenty-four hours after arrival, the senior officer in command of arriving ships must, if he is the senior officer present of his nation, make an official visit to the senior officer of each foreign nation who holds a grade equal to or superior to his; and the senior officer present of each foreign nation who holds a grade junior to his will make an official visit to him within the same time limit.

3. After the exchange of visits between the senior officers

Inspection of a Japanese full guard on the occasion of an official call ashore.

specified above, other flag officers in command and the COs of ships arriving must exchange official visits, when appropriate, with the flag officers and COs of ships present. An arriving officer must make the first visit to officers present who hold grades equal to or superior to his and must receive first visits from others.

4. It is customary for calls to be exchanged by committees of wardroom officers from the ships of different nations, in the order in which their respective COs have exchanged visits.

5. Should another officer become the senior officer present of a nation, he must exchange official visits with foreign senior officers present as prescribed here.

Procedure for Rendering Honors Afloat. Table 5-3 gives the honors to be rendered to foreign officials and officers. Table 5-4 gives the honors to be rendered to U.S. officials. Table 5-5 gives the honors to be rendered to U.S. officers. These honors are as follows:

1. When the rail is manned, men and women must be uniformly spaced at the rail on each weather deck, facing outboard.

2. "Attention" must be sounded as the visitor's boat or vehicle approaches the ship.

3. The boat or vehicle must be piped as it comes alongside.

4. The visitor must be piped over the side, and all persons on the quarterdeck must salute and the guard must present arms until the termination of the pipe, flourishes, music, or gun salute, whichever shall be the last rendered.

5. The prescribed flag or pennant must be broken as the visitor reaches the quarterdeck and salutes the colors.

6. The piping of the side, the ruffles and flourishes, the music, and the gun salute must be rendered in the order named. In the absence of a band, "To the Colors" must be sounded by the bugle in lieu of the national anthem when required.

7. The visitor, if entitled to eleven guns or more, will be invited to inspect the guard upon completion of the gun salute or of such honors as may be rendered.

Table 5-3. Honors Rendered to Foreign Officials and Officers

Official or Officer	Uniform	Gun Salute — Arrival	Gun Salute — Departure	Ruffles and Flourishes	Music	Guard	Side Boys*	Crew*	Flag — What	Flag — Where	Flag — During
President or sovereign	Full dress	21	21	4	Foreign national anthem	Full	8	Man rail	Foreign ensign	Main truck	Visit
Member of reigning royal family	do	21	21	4	do	do	8	do	do	do	Salute
Prime minister or other cabinet officer	do		19	4	Admiral's march	do	8		do	Fore truck	do
Officer of armed forces, diplomatic or consular representative in country to which accredited, or other distinguished official	Civil officials: Honors as for officials of the United States of comparable position. For example, foreign civil officials, occupying positions comparable to U.S. Department of Defense civil officials, shall receive equivalent honors. Officers of armed forces: Honors as for officer of the United States of the same grade, except that equivalent honors shall be rendered to foreign officers who occupy a position comparable to chairman JCS, CNO, chief of staff army, chief of staff air force, or CMC. Honors as prescribed by the senior officer present; such honors normally shall be those accorded the foreign official when visiting officially a ship of his own nation, but a gun salute, if prescribed, shall not exceed 19 guns.										

*Not appropriate on shore installations.

Table 5-4. Honors Rendered to U.S. Officials

Official	Uniform	Gun Salute Arrival	Gun Salute Departure	Ruffles and Flourishes	Music	Guard	Side Boys†	Crew†	Within What Limits	Flag What	Flag Where	Flag During
President	Full dress	21	21	4	National anthem	Full	8	Man rail		President's	Main truck	Visit
Former presidents	do		21	4	Admiral's march	do	8	Quarters		National	do	Salute
Vice president	do		19	4	"Hail Columbia"	do	8	Quarters		Vice president's	do	Visit
Governor of a state	do		19	4	Admiral's march	do	8		Area under his jurisdiction	National	Fore truck	Salute
Speaker of the House of Representatives	do		19	4	do	do	8			do	do	do
The chief justice of the United States	do		19	4	do	do	8			do	do	do
Ambassador, high commissioner, or special diplomatic representative whose credentials give him author-	do		19	4	National anthem	do	8		Nation or nations to which accredited	do	do	do

ity equal to or greater than that of an ambassador										
Secretary of state	do	19	4	do	do	8		do	do	do
U.S. Representative to the UN	do	19	4	Admiral's march	do	8		do	do	do
Associate justice of the Supreme Court	do	19	4	do	do	8		do	do	do
Secretary of defense	do	19	4	Honor's march	do	8	Quarters	Secretary's	Main truck	Visit
Cabinet officers (other than secretaries of state and defense)*	do	19	4	Admiral's march	do	8		National	Fore truck	Salute
President pro tempore of the Senate	do	19	4	do	do	8		do	do	do
Senators	do	19	4	do	do	8		do	do	do
Members of the House of Representatives	do	19	4	do	do	8		do	do	do
Deputy secretary of defense	do	19	4	Honor's march	do	8	Quarters	Deputy secretary's	Main truck	Visit
Secretary of the Army	do	19	4	do	do	8		National	Fore truck	Salute
Secretary of the Navy	do	19	4	do	do	8	Quarters	Secretary's	Main truck	Visit
Secretary of the Air Force	do	19	4	do	do	8		National	Fore truck	Salute
Director of defense, research, and engineering	do	19	4	do	do	8	Quarters	Director's	Main truck	Visit

Table 5-4. *Continued*

Official	Gun Salute				Music	Guard	Side Boys†	Crew†	Within What Limits	Flag		
	Uniform	Arrival	Departure	Ruffles and Flourishes						What	Where	During
Assistant secretaries of defense and general counsel of DOD	do	17	17	4	do	do	8	Quarters		Assistant secretary's	do	do
Under secretary of the Army	do	17	17	4	do	do	8			National	Fore truck	Salute
Under secretary of the Navy	do	17	17	4	do	do	8	Quarters		Under secretary's	Main truck	Visit
Under secretary of the Air Force	do	17	17	4	do	do	8			National	Fore truck	Salute
Assistant secretaries of the Army	do	17	17	4	do	do	8			do	do	do
Assistant secretaries of the Navy	do	17	17	4	Honor's march	do	8	Quarters		Assistant secretary's	Main truck	Visit
Assistant secretaries of the Air Force	do	17	17	4	do	do	8			National	Fore truck	Salute
Governor general or governor of a commonwealth or possession of the	do		17	4	Admiral's march	do	8		Area under his jurisdiction	do	do	do

Grade or title										
United States or area under U.S. jurisdiction	Of the day				do			do	do	do
Other under secretaries of cabinet, the deputy attorney general	do	17	4	do	do	8		do	do	do
Envoy extraordinary and minister plenipotentiary	do	15	3	do	do	8	Nation to which accredited	do	do	do
Minister resident	do	13	2	do	do	6	do	do	do	do
Chargé d'affaires	do	11	1	do	do	6	do	do	do	do
Career minister, or counselor of embassy or legation	do		1	do	do	6	do	do	do	do
Consul general, or consul or vice consul or deputy consul general when in charge of a consulate general	do	11	1	do	do	6	District to which assigned	do	do	do
First secretary of embassy or legation	Of the day				Of the day	4	Nation to which accredited			
Consul, or vice consul when in charge of a consulate	do	7		do	do	4	District to which assigned	do	do	do
Mayor of an incorporated city	do				do	4	Within limits of			

Table 5-4. Continued

Official	Uniform	Gun Salute Arrival	Gun Salute Departure	Ruffles and Flourishes	Music	Guard	Side Boys†	Crew†	Within What Limits	Flag What	Flag Where	Flag During
Second or third secretary of embassy or legation	do		5				2		mayorality Nation to which accredited			
Vice consul when only representative of the United States, and not in charge of a consulate general or consulate	Of the day					Of the day	2		District to which assigned	National	Fore truck	Salute
Consular agent when only representative of the United States	do						2	do				

*In order of precedence as follows:
secretary of state
secretary of the treasury
secretary of defense
attorney general
secretary of the interior
secretary of agriculture
secretary of commerce
secretary of labor
secretary of health and human services
secretary of housing and urban development
secretary of transportation
The secretaries of energy, education, and veterans affairs have not yet been added to this list.
†Not appropriate at shore installations.

Table 5-5. Honors Rendered to U.S. Officers

OFFICER*	UNIFORM	ARRIVAL GUN SALUTE	DEPARTURE GUN SALUTE	RUFFLES/ FLOURISHES	MUSIC	GUARD	SIDE BOYS
Chairman, Joint Chiefs of Staff†	Full dress	19	19	4	General's or Admiral's march	Full	8
Chief of staff, U.S. Army†	do	19	19	4	General's march	do	8
Chief of naval operations†	do	19	19	4	Admiral's march	do	8
Chief of staff, U.S. Air Force†	do	19	19	4	General's march	do	8
Commandant of the Marine Corps†	do	19	19	4	Admiral's march	do	8
Commandant of the Coast Guard†	do	19	19	4	Admiral's march	do	8
General of the Army†	do	19	19	4	General's march	do	8
Fleet admiral†	do	19	19	4	Admiral's march	do	8
General of the Air Force†	do	19	19	4	General's march	do	8
Generals‡	do	17	17	4	do‖	do	8
Admirals‡	do	17	17	4	Admiral's march	do	8
Naval or other military governor, commissioned as such by the president, within the area of his jurisdiction	do		17	4	General's or Admiral's march‖	do	8
Vice admiral or lieutenant general§	do	15	15	3	do‖	do	8
Rear admiral or major general	do	13	13	2	do‖	do	6
Commodore or brigadier general	do	11	11	1	do‖	do	6
Captain, commander, colonel, or lieutenant colonel	Of the day					Of the day	4
Other commissioned officers	do					do	2

*On official occasions, honors may be rendered to retired flag and general officers with their permission and at discretion of local commanders. Honors so rendered will be in accord with retired grade, except former chiefs of naval operations and former commandants of the Marine Corps will receive the honors prescribed for those officers.

†Takes precedence, in order shown, after secretary of the Air Force.

‡Take precedence after under secretary of the Air Force.

§Takes precedence after other under secretaries of cabinet.

‖Marine Corps general officers receive the Admiral's march.

The honors prescribed for an official visit must be rendered on departure as follows:

1. The rail must be manned, if required.
2. "Attention" must be sounded as the visitor arrives on the quarterdeck.
3. At the end of leave-taking, the guard must present arms, all persons on the quarterdeck must salute, and the ruffles and flourishes, followed by the music, must be rendered. As the visitor enters the line of side boys, he must be piped over the side. The salute and present arms must terminate with the pipe, and unless a gun salute is to be fired, the flag or pennant displayed in honor of the visitor must be hauled down.
4. If a gun salute is prescribed on departure, it must be fired when the visitor is clear of the side, and the flag or pennant displayed in honor of the visitor must be hauled down with the last gun of the salute. A more detailed description is contained in *Navy Regulations* Art. 1047.

Returning Official Visits or Calls.   An official visit shall be returned within twenty-four hours, when practicable.

A flag or general officer shall, circumstances permitting, return the official visit of officers of the grade of captain in the Navy or senior thereto and of officials of corresponding grade. He may send his chief of staff to return other official visits.

Officers other than flag or general officers shall personally return all official calls.

Flag and general officers may expect official visits to be returned in person by foreign governors, officers, and other high officials except chiefs of state. Other officers may expect such visits to be returned by suitable representatives.

Calls made by juniors upon seniors in the naval service shall be returned as courtesy requires and circumstances permit; calls made by persons not in the naval service shall be returned (*Navy Regulations* Art. 1048).

Side Honors, Side Boys, Guard, and Band.   On the arrival and departure of civil officials and foreign officers, and of U.S. officers when so directed by the senior officer present, the side must be piped and the appropriate number of side boys paraded.

Officers appropriate to the occasion must attend the side on the arrival and departure of officials and officers (*Navy Regulations* Art. 1049).

Side boys must not be paraded on Sunday, or on other days between sunset and 0800, or during meal hours of the crew, general drills and evolutions, and periods of overhaul, except in honor of civil officials and foreign officers, when they are paraded at any time during daylight. Side boys should be paraded only for scheduled visits.

Side boys must not be paraded in honor of an officer of the armed services in civilian clothes, unless such officer is at the time acting in an official civilian capacity.

The side must be piped when side boys are paraded, but not at other times.

When required, the guard should be paraded in the vicinity of the quarterdeck and the official honored should inspect it prior to leaving the quarterdeck. An area should be set aside for the remainder of the party during the inspection.

The guard and band must not be paraded in honor of the arrival and departure of an individual at times when side boys in his honor are dispensed with, except at naval shore installations. (*Navy Regulations* Art. 1050).

Musical Honors to the President. If, in the course of any ceremony, it is required that honors involving musical tribute to the president of the United States be performed more than one time, "Hail to the Chief" may be used interchangeably with the national anthem.

When specified by the president of the United States, the secretary of state, the chief of the Secret Service, or their authorized representatives, "Hail to the Chief" may be used as an opportunity for the president and his immediate party to move to and from their places while others stand fast.

Display of the National Ensign, Personal Flags, and Pennants

National Ensign and Union Jack Afloat. When not underway, the national ensign and union jack must be displayed from 0800 until sunset from the flagstaff and jackstaff, respectively. The union jack must be the size of the union in the national ensign.

A ship that enters port at night must, when appropriate, display the national ensign from the gaff at daylight for a time sufficient to establish her nationality; it is customary for other ships of war to display their national ensigns in return. The national ensign, union jack, and personal flags and pennants must be displayed from ships and craft of the Navy, in or out of service or commission in accordance with the rules laid down in *Navy Regulations* Art. 1059.

The national ensign must be displayed during daylight from the gaff of a ship underway under the following circumstances, unless otherwise directed by the senior officer present:

1. Getting underway and coming to anchor
2. Falling in with other ships
3. Cruising near land
4. During battle (*Navy Regulations* Art. 1059)

On board ship or at a command ashore, upon all occasions of hoisting, lowering, or half-masting the national ensign, the motions of the senior officer present must be followed, except as prescribed for answering a dip or firing a gun salute. It is customary for the senior present, at 0745, to make a preparatory signal, giving the size of the colors to be hoisted.

At Commands Ashore. The national ensign is displayed from 0800 to sunset near the headquarters of every command ashore, or at the headquarters of the senior commander when the proximity of headquarters of two or more commands makes the display of separate ensigns appropriate. When an outlying activity of a command is so located that its government character is not clearly indicated by the display of the national ensign as prescribed above, the national ensign shall also be displayed at that activity (*Navy Regulations* Art. 1060).

Figure 5-5 illustrates the correct method of displaying the ensign ashore and afloat.

In Boats. The national ensign is displayed from waterborne boats of the naval service as follows:

1. When underway during daylight in a foreign port.
2. When ships are required to be dressed or full dressed.
3. When going alongside a foreign vessel.
4. When an officer or official is embarked on an official occasion.

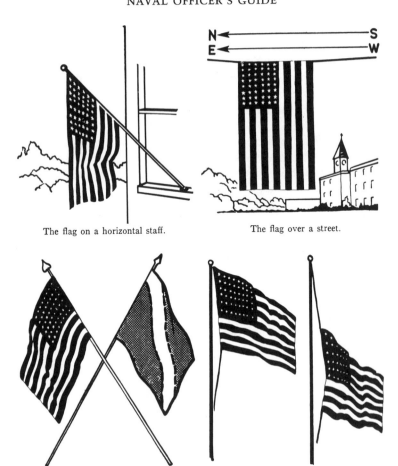

The flag on a horizontal staff.

The flag over a street.

The flag on a crossed staff.

The flag at half-mast.

Figure 5-5. Correct methods of displaying the national ensign.

5. When a flag or general officer, a unit commander, a CO, or a chief of staff, in uniform, is embarked in a boat of his command or in one assigned to his personal use. Appropriate staff insignia should be used.

6. When prescribed by the senior officer present afloat.

During Gun Salutes. A ship of the Navy displays the national ensign at the masthead while firing a salute in honor of a U.S. holiday or official as follows:

1. At the main during the national salute prescribed for 22 February and 4 July.

2. At the main during a twenty-one gun salute to a U.S. official, except by a ship displaying the personal flag of the official being saluted.

During a gun salute, the national ensign remains displayed from the gaff or the flagstaff, in addition to the display at the main or fore (*Navy Regulations* Art. 1061).

Dipping the National Ensign. When any vessel, under the U.S. registry or the registry of a nation formally recognized by the government of the United States, salutes a ship of the Navy by dipping her ensign, it is answered dip for dip. If not already being displayed, the national ensign must be hoisted for the purpose of answering the dip. An ensign being displayed at half mast is hoisted to the truck or peak before a dip is answered.

No ship of the Navy should dip the national ensign unless in return for such compliment.

Of the colors carried by a naval force on shore, only the battalion or regimental colors is dipped in rendering or acknowledging a salute (*Navy Regulations* Art. 1063).

Half-masting the National Ensign and the Union Jack. In half-masting the national ensign it must, if not previously hoisted, first be hoisted to the truck or peak and then lowered to half mast. Before lowering from half mast, the ensign is hoisted to the truck or peak and then lowered.

When the national ensign is half-masted, the union jack, if displayed from the jackstaff, is likewise half-masted.

Personal flags, command pennants, and commission pennants must not be displayed at half mast except as prescribed in the regulations for a deceased official or naval officer.

When directed by the president, the national ensign is flown at half mast at military facilities and on naval vessels and at stations abroad, whether or not the national ensign of another nation is flown full staff alongside that of the United States (*Navy Regulations* Art. 1064).

Morning and Evening Colors. Certain ceremonies are observed at colors on board ships in commission.

The guard of the day and band are present, if available. At morning colors, "Attention" is sounded on the bugle. This is followed by the playing of the national anthem by the band, at

Morning colors on a large ship.

the beginning of which the ensign is started up and hoisted smartly to peak or truck. All officers and men face the ensign and render the salute required, and the guard of the day and sentries under arms come to the position of present arms while the national anthem is being played. In the absence of a band, "To the Colors" is sounded on the bugle. In the absence of a bugle, "Attention" is sounded by another appropriate means and the procedure prescribed is followed during the raising or lowering of the ensign. Subsequent to "The Star-Spangled Banner," honors to foreign ensigns are rendered, at morning colors only, by the band playing the appropriate foreign national anthem. The salute and present arms terminate with the sounding of "Carry on."

The same ceremonies are observed at sunset, the ensign being started from the truck or peak at the beginning of the national anthem and the lowering so regulated as to be complete at the last note. In the absence of a band, "Retreat" is sounded on the bugle.

The same ceremonies are observed, insofar as may be practicable, at naval stations.

During colors a boat within sight or hearing of the ceremony must lie to or proceed at the slowest safe speed. The boat officer, or in his absence, the coxswain, must stand and salute, except when it is dangerous to do so. Others must remain seated and must not salute. Automobiles will be stopped. Persons riding must not salute.

Distinctive Mark of a Naval Vessel. The distinctive mark of a commissioned ship or craft of the Navy is a personal flag or command pennant of an officer of the Navy, or a commission pennant. The distinctive mark of a commissioned hospital ship of the Navy during war is the Red Cross flag. Not more than one distinctive mark should be displayed by a ship or craft at one time, nor should the commission pennant and the personal flag of a civil official be displayed at one time (*Navy Regulations* Art. 1059).

Personal Flags and Pennants Afloat. Except as otherwise prescribed in the regulations, a flag officer or a unit commander afloat must display his personal flag or command pennant from his flagship. At no time should he display it from more than one ship.

When a flag officer eligible for command at sea is embarked for passage in a ship of the Navy, his personal flag must be displayed from the ship, unless there is already displayed from the ship the flag of an officer his senior.

Flags and pennants of officers not eligible for command at sea must not be displayed from ships of the U.S. Navy.

When a civil official, in whose honor the display of a personal flag is prescribed during an official visit, is embarked for passage in a ship of the Navy, his personal flag must be displayed from that ship.

A personal flag or command pennant may be hauled down during battle or at any time when the officer concerned or the senior officer present considers it desirable to render a flagship less distinguishable. When hauled down, it must be replaced with a commission pennant.

For further information on the display of personal flags and pennants afloat, ashore, and in automobiles and boats, consult *Navy Regulations* Arts. 1066–75.

The foregoing descriptions of the display of the national ensign, personal flags, and pennants are taken almost verbatim from *Navy Regulations* (1973). Pertinent articles are noted. There are other articles covering the lesser-known aspects of the subject, and the reader should consult *Navy Regulations* for any information not contained in this section.

Senior Officer Present Afloat Pennant. If two or more ships of the Navy are together in port, this pennant must be displayed from the ship in which the senior officer present afloat is embarked, except when his personal flag clearly indicates his seniority. It is displayed from the inboard halyard of the starboard main yardarm (*Navy Regulations* Art. 1080).

Gun Salutes. Gun salutes are covered in *Navy Regulations* Arts. 1012–26. These articles should be referred to whenever the occasion calls for a gun salute. Only those ships and stations designated by the secretary of the Navy fire gun salutes. The number of guns to be fired and the occasions on which they are to be fired are given in the articles. Officers to be saluted should be notified in advance.

Guns will be fired at five-second intervals. During the gun salute, persons on the quarterdeck or in the ceremonial party, if ashore, must salute. Observers on deck or in the vicinity must stand at attention and salute. An officer being saluted shall salute, and if he is in a boat or vehicle, the conveyance must stop during

Burial at sea.

the salute. There are certain restrictions on gun salutes given in *Navy Regulations* Art. 1026.

Honors and Ceremonies at Death. Honors and ceremonies upon the death of a U.S. civil official are listed in table 5-6.

Honors and ceremonies on the death of a person in the military service are listed in table 5-7.

The national ensign is half-masted upon receipt of notification of death of one of the designated officials from any reliable source, including news media. Other less-used procedures are given in *Navy Regulations* Art. 1088.

Funerals. Navy Regulations Art. 1089 gives general provisions pertaining to funerals. Participation of a ship or station occurs so seldom and is so varied when it does happen that you should consult *Navy Regulations* Arts. 1089–94.

Ships Passing USS Arizona *Memorial.* When a ship of the Navy is passing the USS *Arizona* memorial, Pearl Harbor, Hawaii,

Table 5-6. Honors upon the Death of a U.S. Official

Official	National Ensign Half-Masted		Gun Salute	
	By	Period of Display	Fired by	How and When Fired
President, former president, or a president-elect	All ships and stations of the Department of the Navy	For 30 days from the day of death	(a) All saluting ships, not under-way, in ports under U.S. jurisdiction, and each naval station having a saluting battery (b) Senior saluting ship present in each port under U.S. jurisdiction, and each naval station having a saluting battery	1 gun every half hour from 0800 till sunset on day after receipt of notice of death; 21 minute-guns fired at noon on day of funeral
Vice president, chief justice or retired chief justice of the United States, or speaker of the House of Representatives	do	For 10 days from the day of death	(a) All saluting ships, not under-way, in ports under U.S. jurisdiction, and each naval station having a saluting battery (b) Senior saluting ship present, and	Minute-guns equal in number to official salute of deceased, fired at noon on day after receipt of notice of death

An associate justice of the Supreme Court, a member of the cabinet, a former vice president, the president pro tempore of the Senate, the majority leader of the Senate, the majority leader of the House of Representatives, the minority leader of the House of Representatives, the secretary of the Army, the secretary of the Navy, or the secretary of the Air Force	do	From the day of death until interment	naval station having saluting battery, in port where funeral occurs	do
Governor of a state, territory, commonwealth, or possession	All ships and stations in such state, territory, commonwealth, or possession	do	Ship and station as designated by senior officer present in port where funeral honors are directed to be rendered	do

Table 5-6. *Continued*

Official	National Ensign Half-Masted		Gun Salute	
	By	Period of Display	Fired By	How and When Fired
U.S. senator, representative, territorial delegate, or the resident commissioner from the Commonwealth of Puerto Rico	All ships and stations in the metropolitan area of the District of Columbia, and all ships and stations in the applicable state, congressional district, territory, or commonwealth	On the day of death and the following day / From the day of death until interment	do / do	do / do
Civil official not listed above, but entitled to gun salute on official visit	Ships and stations in the vicinity when directed by senior officer present or other competent authority to join in funeral honors	From 0800 until sunset on the day of funeral	Ship and station as designated by senior officer present in port where funeral honors are directed to be rendered	do

Table 5-7. Honors upon the Death of a Military Person

| DECEASED | NATIONAL ENSIGN HALF-MASTED | | PERSONAL FLAG OR COMMAND PENNANT OF DECEASED, COMMISSION PENNANT OF SHIP COMMANDED | GUN SALUTE | |
	BY	PERIOD OF DISPLAY		FIRED BY	HOW AND WHEN FIRED
Chairman or former chairman of the Joint Chiefs of Staff, U.S. military officer of 5-star rank, chief or former chief of naval operations, commandant or former commandant of the Marine Corps	All ships and stations of the Department of the Navy	From the time of death until sunset of the day of the funeral	Half-masted from time of death until sunset of the day of the funeral or removal of the body, and then hauled down	Flagship or station commanded; or as designated by senior officer present	Minute-guns equal in number to official salute of deceased, fired during funeral
Flag or general officer (Marine) in command	All ships present, not underway, and by naval stations in vicinity	From the time of death until sunset of the day of funeral or removal of the body	do	do	do

Table 5-7. *Continued*

| DECEASED | NATIONAL ENSIGN HALF-MASTED | | PERSONAL FLAG OR COMMAND PENNANT OF DECEASED, COMMISSION PENNANT OF SHIP COMMANDED | GUN SALUTE | |
	BY	PERIOD OF DISPLAY		FIRED BY	HOW AND WHEN FIRED
Flag or general officer (Marine) not in command	do	From the beginning of the funeral until sunset of that day		Ship or station designated by senior officer present	do
Unit commander not a flag officer; commanding officer	do	do	Half-masted from time of death until sunset of day of funeral or removal of the body, and then hauled down; except commission pennant rounded up	Flagship, or ship or station commanded; or as designated by senior officer present	7 minute-guns, fired during funeral
All other persons in the naval service	do	During funeral and for 1 hour thereafter			

between sunrise and sunset, passing honors must be executed by that ship by sounding "Attention" and having the hand salute rendered by all persons in view on deck.

Ships Passing Washington's Tomb. When a ship of the Navy is passing Washington's tomb, Mount Vernon, Virginia, between sunrise and sunset, the following ceremonies are observed insofar as they are practicable. The full guard and the band are paraded, the bell tolled, and the national ensign half-masted at the beginning of the tolling of the bell. When opposite Washington's tomb, the guard presents arms, persons on deck salute, facing in the direction of the tomb, and "Taps" is sounded. The national ensign is hoisted to the truck or peak and the tolling ceases at the last note of "Taps," after which the national anthem is played. Upon completion of the national anthem, "Carry on" is sounded.

National Holidays. National holidays to be observed are listed in *Navy Regulations* Art. 1082; ceremonies for these occasions followed in Art. 1083.

Foreign Participation in U.S. Solemnities. *Navy Regulations* Art. 1084 sets forth the details of such participation.

Observance of Foreign Solemnities. Requirements for observance are given in *Navy Regulations* Art. 1088.

Full Dressing and Dressing Ship. Full dressing and dressing ship are done so infrequently that they will not be covered in detail here. *Navy Regulations* Art. 1079 gives the procedure.

Ceremonies

A ceremony is a formal series of acts carried out in a manner prescribed by authority or custom. Most naval ceremonies are prescribed by authority. The details of formal ceremonies afloat are given in the *Navy Regulations*. Informal ceremonies are governed by custom and tradition. Ceremonies ashore follow the regulations for ceremonies afloat insofar as possible. Where not possible or not applicable, ceremonies follow the methods formalized by the Marine Corps.

Types of Ceremonies Ashore. The Navy and Marine Corps have eight military ceremonies in which an officer may become involved when serving at shore stations. These ceremonies are conducted in a manner described in appropriate articles of the *Landing Party Manual.* (See also *The Marine Officer's Guide*, paragraphs 1822–23.)

A review is a ceremony at which a command parades for inspection in honor of a senior officer other than its commander.

Presentation of awards follows, in part, the procedure prescribed for a review, except that the individuals being decorated receive the review.

A parade is the ceremony at which the CO of a battalion or larger unit forms and drills his entire command and then has them pass in review. The battalion parade is the most common form of ceremony on shore.

Escort of the national colors is known in the Marine Corps as "marching on (or off) the colors." When the colors are used in a ceremony, they are ceremonially received by an escort, taken from their place of safekeeping, and similarly returned.

Escort of honor is the ceremonial in which a senior officer or other dignitary is escorted during an official visit or upon arrival or departure.

A military funeral ceremony is probably the most ancient in the profession of arms.

Inspection of troops is a ceremony in which the general military appearance and condition of the individual uniforms and equipment of a command are determined.

Morning and evening colors have already been described.

Precedence in Parades or Ceremonies. Members of the armed forces of the United States take precedence in the following order during formations in which they participate:

Cadets, U.S. Military Academy
Midshipmen, U.S. Naval Academy
Cadets, U.S. Air Force Academy
Cadets, U.S. Coast Guard Academy
U.S. Army
U.S. Marine Corps
U.S. Navy
U.S. Air Force
U.S. Coast Guard
Army National Guard of the United States
Army Reserve
Marine Corps Reserve
Naval Reserve
Air National Guard of the United States
Air Force Reserve

Coast Guard Reserve

Other training organizations of the Army, Marine Corps, Navy, Air Force, and Coast Guard, in that order.

During any period when the U.S. Coast Guard is operating as part of the Navy, Coast Guard units take precedence after corresponding Navy units.

Veterans' and other patriotic organizations take place after the organizations listed above in the order prescribed by the grand marshal of the parade.

The place of honor is at the head of the column or the right of line.

When a ceremony is conducted by U.S. forces or on U.S. territory, foreign units should be assigned the post of honor in alphabetical order of nationalities ahead of U.S. forces.

Commissioning a Ship and Assuming Command. The ceremony for commissioning a ship is not prescribed specifically in *Navy Regulations*, but custom has established a uniform procedure that is formal and impressive. By the appointed time, the crew is assembled on the quarterdeck, stern, or other open area, usually in two ranks facing inboard. Officers are assembled in two ranks facing the ceremonial area. A band and Marine or seaman guard forms in an area on or near the quarterdeck. Distinguished guests and principal participants are seated in a position to observe but not to be between the ceremonial area and the crew. If space is limited, guests can be seated on an adjacent ship or on the pier. The first watch, including the OOD, is assembled on the quarterdeck. Quartermasters are stationed at national ensign, jack, and commission pennant or personal flag halyards.

The officer making the transfer (the naval district commandant if available) opens the ceremony by reading his orders for delivery of the ship. "Attention" is then sounded on the bugle, the national anthem is played, and the ensign, jack, and commission pennant or personal flag are hoisted simultaneously. The ship is officially commissioned with this act.

The commandant or other officer effecting the transfer delivers the ship to the CO by saying, "I hereby deliver the USS *Blake*." The officer ordered to command the ship reads his orders from the commander, NMPC, and states, "I hereby assume command of the USS *Blake*," and orders the executive officer to "set the watch." The executive officer in turn directs the OOD to set the watch, and the ship's boatswain (or chief boatswain's mate in small ships) pipes the watch. Then the OOD and the other members of the watch take stations.

The CO customarily makes a short speech touching on the work of the building yard, the name of the ship, the history of any previous ships of the same name, and other items of interest.

If the state, city, or sponsor has a presentation of silver or other gift to make, this portion of the ceremony then takes place, and the CO makes an additional speech of appreciation on behalf of the Navy Department, himself, and his or her officers and men. The ceremony is completed with a benediction by the ship or yard chaplain.

It is customary, particularly in peacetime, for the officers and crew to be provided with formal invitations, which they may use to invite family and friends to the ceremony. Some COs prefer to have the officers and crew submit lists of guests and then have the ship's office do the addressing and mailing. After the ceremony, a reception or lunch is usually held simultaneously in the wardroom, chief petty officer's (CPO's) mess, and crew's mess to entertain the guests.

The ceremony is impressive, a fitting way to enter the U.S. Navy.

Turnover of Command. Navy Regulations state that "a commanding officer about to be relieved of his command shall, at the time of turning over command, call all hands to muster. The officer about to be relieved shall read his orders of detachment and turn over the command to his successor, who shall read his orders and assume command."

This ceremony is always quite formal, even though in smaller ships the event may be relatively simple. The turnover of command is the formal passing of responsibility, authority, and accountability of command from one officer to another. The ceremony is rich in naval tradition, and has no counterpart in the other services.

All hands are called to quarters at the appointed hour. It is proper for an appropriate guard to be paraded and ready for inspection by the senior officer participating in the ceremony. The crew usually forms in ranks so placed that all can have an unobstructed view of the ceremonial area, preferably facing the lectern. Officers form in ranks in the same manner in an adjacent area. Chairs are placed for the principal participants behind the lectern.

Guests are seated where they can see, but their position should not preempt that of the officers and crew. The main purpose of the ceremony is the turnover of responsibility from one officer to another, followed by a chance for the relieved CO to say good-bye to his or her officers and enlisted personnel and for the new CO to greet the crew. COs should not forget this primary requirement. A lectern and public address system should be provided. A quartermaster mans a telephone in a location where he or she can observe the ceremony and still communicate with the signal bridge. The uniform should be full dress with swords for participants and service dress for military guests.

When the executive officer reports the crew at quarters and the ceremony ready, the retiring CO, the relieving officer, the chaplain if available, and any distinguished guests, proceed to the ceremonial area. The executive officer may act as master of ceremonies. An invocation is delivered by the chaplain. The retiring CO then delivers a speech, followed by the reading of his or her orders. (Some COs invite a guest to make remarks, which should be short, since the retiring CO's speech should be the focus of the ceremony.) The CO then steps back and says to his or her relief, "Sir/Ma'am, I am ready to be relieved." The new CO steps forward and reads his or her orders. He or she then faces the retiring CO, salutes, and says, "Sir/Ma'am, I relieve you." If the unit commander is present, he or she is saluted by the new CO, who says, "I report for duty." The new CO makes a few brief remarks, usually confined to wishing the departing CO well and stating that all orders of his or her predecessor remain in effect. At the time of relief, a new commission pennant is broken and the old one lowered and presented by the senior quartermaster or master chief of the command to the retiring CO. After a benediction, the new CO orders the executive officer to "pipe down." The ceremony is over, and the official party retires. Usually a reception is held simultaneously in the wardroom, CPO's mess, and crew's mess. If a more elaborate reception is planned ashore, care should be taken to include all officers, crew, and their guests. If separate receptions are held, either aboard or ashore, both COs should attend all events.

Presentation of Awards. For this ceremony the crew is usually formed in approximately the same manner as for a change of command. Those receiving awards form in a single rank in front of the lectern. The executive officer calls each recipient forward by announcing his or her name. The recipient then marches to a point one pace in front of the lectern and salutes. The CO reads the citation, makes a few personal remarks if he or she desires, and receives the medal, if there is one, from the executive officer. The CO pins the medal on the recipient's uniform, shakes his or her hand, and steps back one pace. The recipient salutes and the salute is returned, whereupon the recipient steps back one pace and re-enters the ranks.

On shore the awards ceremony is usually part of a parade ceremony, but it also may follow the format described above.

The presentation of an award is a dignified and meaningful occasion.

Other Ceremonies. There are many occasions for ceremonies of lesser importance and formality than those described in the foregoing sections. Their origins are explored in *Naval Ceremonies, Customs, and Traditions*. Some of the most common are those held when crossing the equator, crossing the International Date Line, crossing the Arctic and Antarctic circles, and reaching the North Pole. Appropriate certificates for these ceremonies may be obtained from the NMPC or the U.S. Naval Institute. The procedures for other ceremonies are not standard, and an innovative crew can make up its own.

6

TRADITIONS AND CUSTOMS OF THE NAVAL SERVICE

THE VALUE OF TRADITION TO THE SOCIAL BODY IS
IMMENSE. THE VENERATION FOR PRACTICES, OR FOR
AUTHORITY, CONSECRATED BY LONG ACCEPTANCE, HAS
A RESERVE OF STRENGTH WHICH CANNOT BE OBTAINED
BY ANY NOVEL DEVICE. RESPECT FOR THE OLD CUSTOMS
IS PLANTED DEEP IN THE HEARTS, AS WELL AS IN THE
INTELLIGENCE, OF ALL INHERITORS OF THE
ENGLISH-SPEAKING POLITY.

—*Rear Admiral Alfred Thayer Mahan,*
The Military Rule of Obedience

SINCE CUSTOM IS THE PRINCIPAL MAGNITUDE OF MEN'S
LIVES, LET MEN BY ALL MEANS OBTAIN GOOD CUSTOMS.

—*Francis Bacon,* Essay on Customs

In the preceding chapter, courtesy, honors, and ceremonies were
described. You, as a young officer beginning a career, should also
become familiar with many customs and traditions of the naval
service. Being piped aboard is an official honor and a custom of
many years' standing. So are many of the other customs you will
encounter in your first days in a ship.

As soon after reporting as possible and as part of the shaking-
down process, a young officer should attempt a thorough study
of all the traditions and customs of the naval service. The most
comprehensive treatment of this subject can be found in the book
Naval Ceremonies, Customs, and Traditions. The more common

customs that the young officer is required to know will be covered in this chapter.

Naval Customs and Traditions

Many think that tradition, having been established by people long gone, is stale. The more remote the origin of tradition, they feel, the more meaningless it is. This attitude does not do justice to naval tradition, which, rather than being the dead relic of an obsolete time, grows and expands as the body of customs comprising it adapts to changing circumstances.

A custom may be defined as a form or course of action characteristically repeated under like circumstances, or a whole body of usages, practices, or conventions regulating social life. A custom may be a long-established practice considered as unwritten law or a usage that has by long continuance acquired a legally binding force.

Much of our daily life is regulated by force of custom. Many customs are so firmly entrenched as to have become established as law. Custom and usage often have the force of law—they may be recognized by a court of law.

There are many customs in civilian life, as there are many peculiar to the naval service. The origin of many of these is obscure, but they have the power of full authority and are conscientiously observed. Many have been incorporated into regulations that have the force of law. Customs are less stringently enforced than tabus. The breach of some Navy customs merely brands the offender as ignorant, careless, or ill-bred, but the violation of a taboo will bring official censure or disciplinary action.

Naval Customs Afloat

The Quarterdeck. Navy Regulations require that the CO "clearly define the limits of the quarterdeck." The sanctity of the quarterdeck should be firmly enforced, and when on the quarterdeck every officer and enlisted person should take pride in observing proper etiquette. To the OOD and his assistants falls the duty of maintaining this discipline.

If you follow the rules listed on the next page, your quarterdeck etiquette will be good.

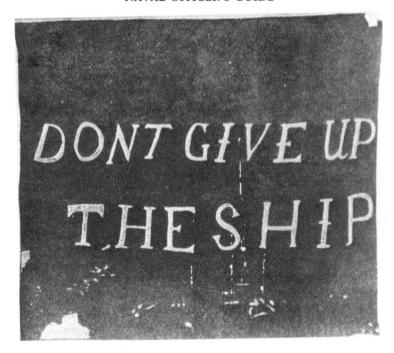

Lawrence's immortal words on Perry's battle flag.

1. Never appear on the quarterdeck unless in the uniform of the day, except in crossing to enter or leave a boat as your duties may require.

2. Never stand around the quarterdeck for any length of time in civilian clothes.

3. Salute the quarterdeck every time you come onto it. (This applies particularly to large ships that have a quarterdeck with defined limits.)

4. Never smoke on the quarterdeck.

5. Never engage in recreational athletics on the quarterdeck unless sanctioned by the captain, and then only after working hours.

6. Never walk on the starboard side of the quarterdeck or any other area reserved for the flag officer or CO unless on official business or on invitation of those officers.

7. Never stand on the quarterdeck with your hands in your pockets. This pose is unmilitary in any area, but even more so on the quarterdeck.

8. Refrain from horseplay and other unmilitary conduct on the quarterdeck.

Gangways.   The gangway is the aperture in the side of a ship through which passage is made. The ladders leading up to the gangway from the grating at the waterline are "accommodation ladders." Ships moored to each other or to piers are boarded by brows passing through gangways.

Normally the starboard gangway to the quarterdeck is used by all commissioned officers, warrant officers, and their visitors. Some large ships have an additional starboard gangway reserved for the embarked flag officer and the senior officers of his staff. The port gangway is used by all others. In heavy weather the lee gangway is used by all. Small ships usually have but one gangway, which may be rigged from either side.

Forms of Address and Introduction.   Choosing the proper form of address and introduction for very senior U.S. officials and foreign dignitaries can be quite complicated. Fortunately help can be obtained from the *Social Usage and Protocol Handbook,* OPNAVINST 1710.7. Chapter 12 of that book gives the correct forms of address for all foreign dignitaries, including such personages as the Queen of England.

Everyday forms of address and introduction are quite simple. Prior to 1973 this book required a complex table to present all possible variations in address and introduction just for naval personnel. In 1973 changes made in *Navy Regulations* simplified the task. However, many older officers still remember the older customs, and even though you use the present forms correctly, you may occasionally discern a raised eyebrow amongst the older hands who have not kept up with the current regulations. Hold your ground, but be discreet about it.

Navy Regulations Art. 0810 states that, except as provided in the succeeding paragraph, every officer in the naval service shall be designated and addressed in official communications by the title of grade preceding his or her name.

In official spoken communications, officers will be addressed by their grade (as distinct from the custom prior to 1973, when officers of the grade of commander and above were addressed by their grade and those below commander were called "mister"). Officers of the medical corps and the dental corps, and those officers of the MSC and the nurse corps having doctoral degrees, may be addressed as "doctor." Officers of the chaplain corps may be addressed as "chaplain." When addressing an officer whose grade includes a modifier, the modifier may be dropped.

In written communication, the name of the corps to which any staff officer belongs shall be indicated immediately after his or her name.

Additionally, by custom there is only one person in any ship or organization correctly addressed as "captain," the regularly assigned CO. Likewise, the regularly assigned executive officer is "the commander." Other captains attached to the ship or station should be addressed by rank and name, as "Captain Jones."

Women officers are addressed in the same way as men officers. When the word "sir" would be appropriate for a man, the word "ma'am" is used for a woman.

Officers are introduced using their title, the junior to the senior, men and women alike. Follow civilian custom when introducing military personnel to civilians.

All Marine Corps enlisted personnel are addressed by their titles, as in "Lance Corporal Smith."

Enlisted personnel, Navy and Marine Corps, are introduced in the same manner as officers. For Navy personnel, CPOs are customarily addressed and introduced as "Chief Smith" or "Master Chief Smith." Petty officers are introduced as "Petty Officer Second Class Smith" rather than "Radarman Second Class Smith." Nonrated persons are introduced as "Seaman (or Airman) Smith."

Relations with Other Officers.   When a junior reports to the office of a senior, he should announce himself through the orderly if one is stationed or by knocking on the door. In some cases the door will be open, and the officer is expected to enter without being told. Upon entering, he should hold his cap in his left hand, proceed directly to the officer, announce his rank and name, and state his business. If he knows the officer well, it is not necessary to announce his name.

When conducting business with a senior, maintain a military bearing. Do not lounge against his desk or otherwise relax unless asked to be seated.

Unless on watch, a junior officer always uncovers when he enters a room in which a senior is present. Such formality is not observed in the mess room, but it is good practice for all officers to uncover before entering the mess. When wearing side arms, an officer remains covered except during church services, in a chapel or a church, within hallowed shrines, and while indoors at a social occasion.

It is a custom in the naval service for a junior to supplement his salute on first meeting with a brief greeting, such as "Good morning, commander."

A junior should not be unduly obtrusive with this greeting. If the senior is engaged, as in conversation, salute and omit the greeting.

Juniors should avoid keeping seniors waiting. When told that a senior wants to see you, proceed immediately to his or her location. If the senior does not want to see you immediately, he or she will tell you to come back at your convenience or sometime that morning. Learn to use this same thoughtfulness when summoning your juniors.

When a senior says "I desire" or "I wish," remember that the expressed desires or wishes of a senior are, by tradition and custom, equivalent to an order.

A senior presents "compliments" to a junior when the former is transmitting a message to the latter by a third person, such as an orderly or messenger. A junior sends or pays his "respects" to a senior. In written correspondence a senior may "call" attention to certain matters, but the junior should "invite" attention. In writing a memorandum, a senior officer subscribes it "respectfully." A junior writing a memorandum subscribes it "very respectfully."

The signature of an officer is his or her bond. Signed to a check it means there is sufficient money in the bank to cover the check. Signed to a letter or memorandum it signifies that the ideas expressed are the signer's (unless stated otherwise).

The place of honor is on the right. Accordingly, when a junior walks, rides, or sits with a senior, the junior takes position alongside and to the left of the senior. A junior opens doors for seniors and then passes through last. When officers are walking in company, juniors keep in step with seniors. When pacing to and fro, positions are not exchanged on reversing direction, and the senior is accorded the outboard position. When passing a senior, pass to the left if possible, and as you draw abreast, salute and say, "By your leave, sir." After your salute is returned, proceed.

When you have been ordered to perform some task, report back promptly to the officer issuing the order upon its completion;

if it is not completed, report the reason why and state when it can be completed.

Learn to give complete, accurate, and pointed answers to questions. If you do not know or cannot give a complete or correct answer, be open and direct in your reply. A frank "I don't know, sir, but I will find out and let you know" is much better than an inconclusive or evasive reply. Chapter 9 will help you in your oral and written communication.

Officers must be open and direct in all their contacts with others. Command, duty, and watch must be considered prime responsibilities.

Phraseology. Certain standard forms of speech and address are in general use. The forms, "Captain, I report . . ." and "Sir, I request . . " are correct. Note that officers go on "shore leave." Enlisted personnel go on "liberty." When preparing to leave your own ship, address your head of department (the executive officer on a small ship) thus: "Sir, I request permission to leave the ship." On departure from your own ship, say to the OOD, "Sir, I have permission to leave the ship." On your return say, "Sir, I report my return."

If you are not attached to a ship you are boarding say, "Sir, I request permission to come aboard," and "Sir, I request permission to leave the ship."

When given an order, respond with "Aye, aye, sir," which means that you understand the order and will carry it out. "Very well" is used by a senior to acknowledge or approve a report from a junior—the reverse is never the case.

Tabus

Do not jump the chain of command by going "over the head" of your immediate superior without his or her authority. If it is necessary to confer with the CO or executive officer, the junior officer doing so must explain why to his or her immediate superior and obtain permission. Inform your immediate superior of any emergencies as soon as possible.

Excuses for failure or negligence are generally unacceptable. When you assume responsibility, you should freely accept the blame if the failure is yours.

Origin of Certain Customs and Phraseology

Much of our phraseology and many of our more common customs have been handed down from the days of sail. Many strictly military terms have come to us from the Royal Navy. The origin of many of these is obscure, but some of the more commonly accepted versions follow.

Anchor Watch. In days of sail, when hemp anchor cables and oil-burning anchor lights were in use, a ship at anchor needed an alert watch to trim the lamps and to observe the cables. Today the anchor watch is available to handle the ship's ground tackle if necessary, but it also performs other duties.

Aye, Aye. The word "aye" derives from Middle English and means "yes." Today the phrase *aye, aye* means "I understand your orders and will carry them out."

Binnacle List. Originally this was a list placed on the binnacle each morning by the ship's surgeon to indicate to the captain and to the watch which personnel were not available for full duty. Today it is a list of personnel not fit for full duty but not hospitalized.

Boatswain. Pronounced *bō'sun.* Our word *swain* derived ultimately from the Anglo Saxon word for servant or boy. A boatswain was, therefore, the servant of the entire ship. His pipe was originally used to call the stroke in a galley, but it is now his badge of office and is used to pipe the side or to direct hoisting and lowering maneuvers.

Chains. Chains were once used to brace the platform in the bows from which the leadsman heaved the lead. Now the area where the lead is heaved has retained this name.

Dipping the National Ensign. In the days of sail a merchant ship was supposed to heave to when approaching a warship on the high seas. This required clewing up most of her canvas with attendant delay. The custom of dipping her ensign as an indication of readiness to be searched developed during years of peace. The man-of-war gave permission to proceed by answering the dip. U.S. naval vessels answer dip for dip, but they never dip except in acknowledgment.

Dogwatch. This is probably a corrupted form of deck watch.

Eyes of the Ship. In ancient times mariners placed carved figures or figureheads on bows of ships. The forepart of the ship came to be known as "the eyes of the ship," from the eyes of the figure.

Forecastle. Pronounced *fōk's'l.* Early ships had tall, castle-like structures fore and aft; hence, forward castle, or forecastle.

Head. The ship's latrine in sailing days was located as far forward on the ship as possible, since wind was usually from aft or abeam.

Mast. The old location for the dispensation of justice was near the ship's mainmast.

Midshipmen. Midshipmen were originally young men serving as officer apprentices who were quartered amidships.

Piping the Side. Piping was originally done by the boatswain to control hoisting of the basket in which the visiting officer was brought aboard from a small boat. Side boys were assigned to assist the hoisting and to swing in the basket. The more senior officers were generally stouter and required more side boys. Necessity became custom and eventually regulation.

Gun Salute. First salutes were rendered by firing all the ship's batteries. Since considerable time was required to reload, firing a salute indicated an absence of hostile intent. The custom evolved into an honor. The origin of the use of an odd number of guns is unknown.

Wardroom. In the Royal Navy a common compartment near the officer's staterooms was used as storage for the officer's uniforms. Its name, *wardrobe*, was subsequently corrupted to *wardroom*. This compartment gradually came to be a room for meals and socializing.

Dead Horse. Shipping-on pay used to be given to members of a crew as an advance pay. When this was worked off, a stuffed canvas horse was burned to celebrate the event. The custom of paying a dead horse still exists in our Navy. It now means paying up to three months' base pay on change of station. The advance is paid back over a six-month period.

Drawing Sword in the Wardroom. In earlier days, swords were worn more often and drawn more frequently in anger. To preserve the decorum of the wardroom, dueling among officers was discouraged with stiff fines levied upon anyone who drew a sword within its confines. The custom has evolved into the modern practice of requiring an officer who unsheathes his sword in the wardroom to stand drinks or cigars for all officers present. The same custom applies to wearing a hat in the wardroom. Hats are worn only on watch and when making a report to an officer in the wardroom.

The Wardroom

Wardroom Mess. The term *mess* is applied to those in the Navy who, for convenience and sociability, eat together. It comes from the Latin word *mensa*, meaning table. *Navy Regulations* assigns compartments for officers' messes. Those officers entitled to the privileges of the wardroom are members of the wardroom mess. Junior officers are members of the junior officer's wardroom mess (the JO mess) in large ships having such a mess.

In large ships the CO has his own mess and the executive officer is the president of the wardroom mess. In small ships the CO is a member of the wardroom mess and is usually the president. *Navy Regulations* prescribes the seating arrangements. Officers are assigned permanent seats at the table; they alternate in the order of rank to the right and left of the presiding officer, except that the seat opposite the president is occupied by the mess treasurer. Common courtesy and respect require you to be in the mess prior to mealtime so that you may sit down when the president sits down. Etiquette also requires that officers remain at the table until he or she rises or until they are excused.

The officer's mess has a mess fund from which food and supplies are purchased. Each officer must contribute his or her share (the per-person value of the mess on the last day of the preceding month) and pay the mess bill (the anticipated cost of the current month) upon joining the mess. Custom dictates that officers pay their mess bills within twenty-four hours of joining and promptly at the beginning of each succeeding month. The fund is administered by the mess treasurer, who is elected monthly.

In general, the atmosphere of the JO mess is relatively informal. Members address each other by nicknames. In the wardroom, where the atmosphere is more formal, the normal courtesies of juniors toward seniors are observed. The seniors of the wardroom usually welcome junior officers and will soon treat them with warmth and welcome.

The wardroom is your home in your ship. Help to make it as pleasant a place to live as your own home. It is also your club, where you may gather with your shipmates for moments of relaxation, a discussion of daily problems, or a cup of coffee. Do not abuse this privilege during working hours by taking any but short breaks.

The wardroom country is out of bounds to enlisted personnel except in special circumstances. Some work can be done in your stateroom, but division and other business should be conducted in the division part of the ship.

The Wardroom during Peacetime. Do not enter the wardroom out of uniform. Some small ships have latitude in this matter, but be sure the CO approves. It is best to remove your hat at all times and by all means during meals.

Never sit down to meals before the president or senior member sits down. Most presidents allow the senior member present to sit down if the president is more than five minutes late. If you must leave before the meal is over, ask permission from the senior member at your table.

Always introduce your guests to the wardroom officers. In a large ship you may confine introductions to your table, but if possible, you should include the president of the mess.

All guests are guests of all wardroom officers. Be friendly and sociable to every guest.

Whenever an officer from another ship enters the wardroom, introduce yourself, extend him or her the welcome of the mess, and ask if you can be of assistance.

Never be late for meals. If you are, make your apologies to the senior member before sitting down.

Do not be unduly loud in the wardroom. Laughter and jesting are expected, but keep them within reasonable bounds.

Pay your mess and other bills promptly.

Be civil and just in your dealings with messmen. If you have a complaint, make it to the mess treasurer.

Do not abuse the use of the duty messman by sending him on long personal errands.

The Wardroom during Wartime. During a war or extended crisis, wardroom routine can be vastly different. Regular mealtimes must be altered, particularly when general quarters is prolonged. On some aircraft carriers meals are served continuously all day and night. Under these circumstances meals must be taken when opportunity permits and with speed and informality.

Seating arrangements usually go by the board, and some ships deliberately place high-ranking officers at different tables to prevent their simultaneous loss in the event of attack.

Shop talk must be the order of the day in wartime. Mealtime may be the only time you will have an opportunity to transact business with certain shipmates.

In short, wartime dictates some common sense changes in form, but not in principle.

The Wardroom Mess Treasurer and Caterer.   The position of mess treasurer is a very responsible one, particularly on long cruises and in wartime, for on his or her effectiveness depends the quality of the food served and, in a large measure, the contentment of the mess. In some ships both a mess treasurer and a mess caterer are elected, and the duties are divided. In some ships the mess treasurer is elected from among all the members of the mess, while the CO appoints the ship's supply officer, commissary officer, or medical officer as a semipermanent mess caterer.

Should you be elected or appointed to one of these positions, devote as much time and attention to it as you can spare from your regular duties.

The general duties of the mess treasurer are to:

1. Maintain the accounts of the mess using a standard form of double-entry bookeeping; obtain receipts for all expenditures by the wardroom steward; make entries in your books as they occur; keep books balanced; check the purchase of shore-bought supplies frequently to make sure full amounts are delivered; and check issues on a random basis in cases where purchases from the general mess are made.

2. Maintain an appropriate checking account if you are treasurer of a large mess.

3. Arrange a place of safekeeping for your cash account.

4. Close your books promptly at the end of the month, take an accurate inventory, and complete your monthly summary. Ask the auditing board to meet promptly in order to have the audit in the hands of the executive officer by the tenth of the month.

The general duties of the mess caterer are to:

1. Supervise the preparation of the menu, providing variety and proper nutrition.

2. Supervise the preparation and setting of the table and service.

3. Inspect the wardroom, pantry, and galley daily for cleanliness and check the condition of food.

4. Inspect messmen for cleanliness.

5. Supervise messmen in the cleaning and maintenance of officers' rooms.

Living with Others

The normal military courtesies expected of you were covered in this and the previous chapter. There are many other areas in which you can contribute to making life aboard your ship pleasant for yourself and others.

Avoid thoughtless offense and be considerate of those with whom you associate.

Avoid complaining. If there is something to complain about, do something to rectify the situation or keep quiet.

A cheery greeting and a smile will motivate your juniors and help your seniors get started with their day.

Gambling, drinking, and drug use afloat are general court-martial offenses. If you have to gamble or drink, do it in moderation and privacy ashore. Avoid drugs anywhere, anytime. This includes marijuana. Drug use by officers is not tolerated. If caught you will be dismissed from the service either by administrative discharge or by court-martial. If you refuse urinalysis you are subject to disciplinary action and court-martial. Possession is a federal offense, and you have sworn to uphold the Constitution and the laws deriving from it. The consequences of use are all out of proportion to the temporary pleasure you might get from drugs. If someone else is using a drug, leave. Report the incident to your CO as soon as possible. If you do not, and it comes to the attention of your CO by other means, you will be in trouble for failing to report a crime. Protect yourself by early reporting and do not be concerned about having made the report. The person who uses drugs in your presence has no concern for your welfare and deserves no consideration.

Navy Social Life

Social life in the Navy is kept as simple and informal as possible. You will entertain your friends, both naval and civilian, in your home or at the officer's club. About all that a young married couple can usually manage is having a few friends to cocktails or to an informal dinner. The single officer can entertain just as readily by using the officer's club or his or her apartment. You will find that your seniors, when you have the occasion to entertain them, prefer that you entertain simply. Regardless of your status, good manners dictate reciprocating in some way for invitations received from your shipmates, senior or junior. For more senior officers the scope of social occasions is wider. The following sections will give only a brief summary of the sort of affairs they can expect to attend.

Receptions and Cocktail Parties. A reception is a get-together in honor of someone or some special event, such as a change of command, a commissioning, or a ship visit. It is formal and may be held any time, but usually in the late afternoon or in the evening. It is ordinarily limited to about two hours' duration. Your stay should be about thirty minutes unless you have been asked to assist with the guests, in which case you should stay for the whole affair. Tea, coffee, and mixed drinks together with a light buffet may be served. A reception can vary in size from a few friends to a large number of guests. If given outside, it may be called a garden party. When a senior officer calls it an "at home," all calls are considered made and returned by attendance.

The cocktail party differs from the reception in that it is informal, there is no receiving line, usually no honored guest, cards are not left, and the time limit is not as strict. Usually the party lasts about two hours, but your attendance should be considerably shorter. In Washington thirty minutes is normal, but in other cities with less demanding social schedules it is acceptable to stay for an hour. Do not overstay the closing hour. The cocktail party is a useful affair for the young, low-salaried officer to use to entertain a large number of guests. You may serve a fruit punch or other low alcoholic content beverage to ease the financial strain and to avoid paying a bartender. A simple buffet may be served. Sometimes several members of the wardroom join together to give a common party. Some guests may be invited to stay on after the official end of the party, but do not do so unless your host and hostess insist.

Official Command Performance Functions. Many times in your career you will be called upon to represent your wardroom, ship, or unit at a social function honoring an official or a special event. Doing so is a social obligation you must accept as part of your duties. Ensure that you present the best wishes of the organization you represent to the guest of honor.

Another form of command performance is the unit function given by your organization in honor of a departing member or given in a port to repay the hospitality of persons in the port. You may be assigned to make some part of the arrangements for the function. The cost of such an affair is usually prorated equally among all members of the unit, although sometimes a higher charge is made for the senior officers. If the affair is to be given by your mess, you are one of the hosts and must do your best to welcome and entertain all of the guests. These affairs not only repay your social obligations—they can be a good way to meet and enjoy the guests, spouses, and friends of others.

Other less formal affairs are also given by messes, ships, units, and shore station groups. These run the gamut from group receptions to dinners, dances, bowling parties, and picnics. Some will be occasions that you will have the option to attend, and others you will be expected to attend. When in doubt, attend.

A common form of command performance is the receipt by your CO of an invitation from a shore or community organization to send a specified number of officers and spouses to a banquet, dinner, luncheon, or similar function. If the CO considers that it is in the best interests of the Navy to accept these invitations, you may be detailed to attend. You may also be invited to bring your spouse, who should accompany you if it is possible. If you have children and cannot find a sitter, explain the problem to the CO, who should appreciate the importance of child care and relieve you of your social obligation.

Balls and Dances. The function most frequently attended by young naval families is the officer's club dance. These affairs are inexpensive and informal. Ask your contemporaries what to wear. Other larger functions that are popular are the annual birthday balls and parties given by and for the various services and warfare specialties. Restricted line and staff corps groups also give such balls. These are usually formal but not very expensive and will give you an opportunity to meet a large group of officers and spouses who have interests similar to yours. In later years officers and their families will take part in more formal social activity at Washington embassies, the White House, and large charity affairs such as the Navy Relief Ball.

Dinners and Buffet Suppers. These may be as simple as the

family dinner or as elaborate as a formal dinner for thirty guests. For the young officer, the first experience at managing a formal dinner will probably be as a mess caterer for a shipboard mess dinner or as personal aide to a flag officer. The *Social Usage and Protocol Handbook* will give you all the information you need to carry it off.

Military Weddings. Many of your contemporaries will be getting married in your early years. Weddings differ in their degree of formality. Reply promptly to your invitation, choose a suitable present, and arrive in plenty of time to be seated.

Calls. Since World War II, and because of the minimum time spent in home port by most ships, the custom of calling has declined. Many commands do not require calling in any form. However, if your command should require it, the following guidelines generally apply. Upon reporting ask your executive officer what procedure the CO wants followed. He or she may prefer to

The culmination of Navy social life in Washington is the Navy Ball. Officers of all ranks are invited to attend.

have periodic at homes or ship's receptions, at which time all calls are considered made and returned. In any event, all officers should know all the details of the custom of calling, and they should follow accordingly.

Both civil and military customs require the exchange of social calls under certain circumstances. An earlier edition of *Navy Regulations* stated that "an officer joining a ship or station shall, in addition to reporting for duty, make a courtesy visit to his commanding officer or commandant within forty-eight hours after joining." As previously pointed out, this call is made on board ship in the captain's cabin. Ask the executive officer when it will be convenient for the captain to see you. The call is made even though you have previously reported to the captain. On large shore stations and on some large ships the at-home method of making and returning calls may be used. Social calls in wartime are usually discontinued. However, in peacetime, if required, the newly arrived officer should call in turn at the homes of the CO, the executive officer, and his or her own head of department. These calls should be made within two weeks of reporting.

If you are married, your spouse should accompany you. The usual calling hours are from 1600 to 1800, but you should arrange the time at the convenience of the senior officer. Although the use of calling cards has declined in late years, some COs expect you to observe the custom. Do so unless informed that cards are not required. Leave two cards. If your spouse accompanies you, leave one of your cards and a joint card. Stay about twenty minutes and then, at some convenient break in the conversation, rise and take your leave. Be careful to sense whether or not you have called at a bad time. If you think you have, leave earlier. If your hostess insists that you stay longer, do so, but do not overstay, particularly on a first call. You should find your call a pleasant experience. Relax and enjoy conversing. Older officers and their wives almost universally like to meet younger couples and will do their best to make your experience enjoyable.

You can expect your call to be returned within two weeks, unless you are a single officer, in which case the senior officers will probably respond by including you in their future social affairs. If you are a single officer living in civilian quarters, it is appropriate to invite seniors to call on you. Be relaxed as a host or hostess. Offer your callers a choice of soft drinks, mixed drinks, and fruit juice. They will stay a short time and will probably leave cards.

As for calls on other officers, it is up to the older hands, regardless of their rank, to call on you as a newer arrival. Return their calls within two weeks. After you have achieved the status of an "older hand" you should call on the newer arrivals.

Commissioned Officers' Messes Ashore. Bases or stations ashore may have two messes. The commissioned officer's mess open is often referred to as the officer's club. It is available for membership, not only to officers of the base, but to officers afloat and to reserve and retired officers. Nominal dues are required. Like any club, the mess is a private association operated for the convenience of its members. Privileges are generally extended to visiting officers and their families on a temporary basis. Open messes customarily serve meals and have bars; some operate recreational facilities such as swimming pools.

The few commissioned officers' messes closed, until phased out, are restricted in membership to bachelor officers and transients, and provide living accommodations for their members and their guests. Some messes can accommodate transient families. Members pay a proportionate amount of the cost of the service furnished in excess of that furnished by the government.

Bachelor Quarters. Most shore stations have quarters for bachelors, commonly known as the Bachelor Officers' Quarters (BOQ). Both transients and permanently assigned bachelor officers may use these or elect to live off base. Payment of housing allowance (BAQ) is a complicated and changing matter. Consult the personnel officer at the shore station regarding your alternatives. For meals you will have to use the officer's club, post exchange, or off-base facilities.

Private Clubs. In the various ports you visit, at home and abroad, you will be offered the facilities of private clubs. Accept these invitations and opportunities to meet the members. Enjoy the facilities, but be circumspect in your use of them. When extended the privileges of a club, leave a card for the secretary and write a short note of thanks upon leaving.

In addition to the several officer's clubs and messes in the Washington area, two outstanding private military clubs offer excellent services to members. The Army Navy Town Club, located on Farragut Square, provides all the facilities of a private club, including rooms for members. The Army Navy Country Club, in nearby Arlington, Virginia, is a family country club offering a wide variety of restaurant, bar, grill, and sports facilities.

Both clubs offer newly commissioned officers an opportunity to join at reduced entrance rates. In both clubs, the young officer in a nonresident status pays the equivalent of one month's dues per year and is able to use the club on visits to Washington. In view of annually increasing rates for entrance, the young officer is well advised to consider this offer, even though first duty in Washington may be some years away. Also, if the young officer joins one of the clubs just after commissioning, he or she has immediate access to membership upon arrival for duty in Washington. Otherwise the wait might be as long as three years.

Mess and Club Etiquette Ashore. The club or mess belongs to its members. Assume responsibility for your mess and support it. As a guest, observe the local rules and customs. Participate in meetings, campaigns, and elections. Be ready to assume responsibility if elected as an officer or board member.

At the club or mess, dress appropriately. Wear athletic dress only where authorized.

Pay your bills promptly and maintain bank balances to back up your checks.

Most clubs have rules against tipping, but you should encourage combined contributions for Christmas gifts to employees.

Washington Social Life. The White House is the center of Washington social life. Young unmarried officers on duty in the Washington area are sometimes detailed to additional duty as White House naval and marine aides, which gives them the opportunity to participate in White House social activities and eventually in Washington social life. The more senior officers may expect occasional invitations to the White House for various events.

A White House invitation is considered a presidential command, which takes precedence over all other commitments. If you have a question about uniforms or other matters, telephone the office of the military aide to the president.

White House aides and many other officers will be invited to official parties of the diplomatic corps. The invitation will indicate the dress. Active officers always wear appropriate and complete uniforms to these functions.

If you are on Washington duty, learn foreign badges, insignia of rank, and the national anthems of the countries represented. Be courteous and helpful at diplomatic parties. Your dignity and conduct as well as your uniform set you apart as a representative of the United States.

Washington Calling Etiquette. Calling etiquette varies with the character of the political administration in power. When you report for duty, ask what is customary in Washington at that time. If still in doubt, ask the aide or administrative assistant to your CO. At certain times the customs described in the following paragraphs may be in effect.

Make the customary call upon your reporting senior. Dress in civilian clothes. Flag officers do not require or expect calls, but many of them hold periodic at homes. If at homes are not held, the practice of leaving cards may be used. Unlike procedures outside of Washington, where it is considered discourteous to leave cards when the person called upon is not at home, leaving cards is designed to spare both the senior and you from the time-consuming process of calling. The large number of officers per command and the long distances between living areas would require a vast amount of time if all indicated calls were made and returned. Again, ask the aide or administrative assistant if and where you should drop the cards.

Officers of the grade of captain and above should leave cards at the White House. It is permissible to leave cards with the secretary of defense, and the secretary, under secretary, and assistant secretaries of the Navy. The practice of leaving cards with senior officials is dying out, so make a discreet inquiry before you take action.

Officers returning from foreign duty should call the social secretary of the embassy of the country in which they served and make arrangements to call on the naval attaché.

Social Customs and Etiquette. Etiquette is the body of forms prescribed by authority to express good breeding and good manners in social or official life. However, there is more to being well-bred than knowing table manners or rules of decorum. Good manners require an innate sense for saying and doing the right thing in any social or official situation. The essential ingredients of etiquette are consideration for others, kindliness, and courtesy. If you cultivate these qualities, you cannot go far wrong in any company.

The mechanics of etiquette can be obtained from several good books on the subject. Among them are *Service Etiquette* and *Welcome Aboard.* A summary of their contents appears in the following paragraphs. The advice may sound a little stilted in this age, but it is timeless nonetheless.

In all social situations, whether within the bounds of service society or among civilians, the naval officer is expected, on his own initiative, to observe the highest standards of conduct. Good manners arise from the innate qualities of the individual and from a knowledge and acceptance of social customs.

Be courteous to fellow guests at the dinner table, manifesting a kindly attitude toward all guests, and especially toward those in your near vicinity. Talk, but do not monopolize the conversation.

The social relations between men and women must be based upon individual dignity and mutual respect. If they are, the position of those who are both officers and women should not make relations awkward. Special consideration should always be extended to elderly men and women. In the presence of civilian women, men should rise, remove their hats (or salute if in uniform outdoors), offer their arm if necessary, and never keep them waiting.

An officer renders appropriate acknowledgment for every courtesy and kindness extended. It is rude to accept hospitality without expressing appreciation. It is selfish not to attempt to reciprocate social favors accepted. Persons of modest income are not expected to meet social obligations on the same scale as wealthy or senior friends, but within the limits of their resources, they should discharge their obligations.

If invited to dinner, you are not necessarily expected to remain all afternoon or evening. A visit of one half to one hour after the meal ends is sufficient. If a guest of honor is present, depart after that guest. If a senior officer is present, depart after him or her.

Correct and dignified speech, coupled with a capacity for interesting and intelligent conversation, is one of the finest assets a person can have. While a limited use of slang adds salt to American speech, overuse betrays a deficient vocabulary. One who swears or uses obscene words lacks the ability to employ proper language. Give attention to the tone of your voice and expression. It is well to remember the advice of Colonel J. G. D. Tucker, who wrote in his *Hints to Young Officers*, "Although all words of command should be given in an authoritative and firm tone, it does not follow that drill manners should accompany the officer into private society."*

Interesting conversation comes from wide reading and a familiarity with current events. Devote a part of each day to reading and study.

Be meticulous about your personal correspondence. Answer all letters promptly and invitations immediately. You can find the proper form for acknowledging formal invitations in the books mentioned at the beginning of this section.

As a house guest, an officer must be exceedingly thoughtful. Be punctual at meals and do nothing to upset the routine. Never stay longer than the period for which you are invited. On leaving after a visit of a week or longer, leave tips for the servants. If there are no servants in the house, do not hesitate to help by caring for your room and bath and helping with meals. Promptly after departure write a note of appreciation to your host or hostess. Send or leave an inexpensive present such as a book, flowers, or candy.

In making introductions, except when a man is an exceedingly important dignitary, men are introduced to women. Very young women are properly introduced to men of advancing years combined with high civilian or military rank. When introducing close relatives, give the relationship. Avoid the use of elaborate introductory phrases. When being introduced, a simple acknowledgment suffices. Women may or may not extend their hand. Men extend theirs to women, but never first. Some foreigners kiss the extended hand of a woman. Female officers are introduced in the same manner as male officers, the junior to the senior. If seated, men rise to acknowledge an introduction. Women officers rise when being introduced to senior officers.

If an unmarried officer accepts an invitation, he or she is obligated to make a call within two weeks. If the host or hostess has been exceptionally kind or the dinner was given in your honor, a small present is in order. A note is proper for any occasion.

If you leave port before you have had an opportunity to express your appreciation for hospitality received, either write an informal note or send PPC cards (PPC stands for *pour prendre congé*, which means "to take leave"). Also send such cards to clubs that have extended their privileges.

*Robert Heinl, *Dictionary of Military and Naval Quotations* (Annapolis: U.S. Naval Institute, 1966), p. 72.

Women officers who are married generally observe the same customs as men do. Their military titles are used on correspondence and invitations in similar fashion. They leave cards with men. They may choose to assume the role of spouse whenever they want to.

A card with "To inquire" penciled in may be left at the house of a friend who is too ill to receive calls. Only intimate friends should call at a home where death has occurred. You may leave a card on which is written "With deepest sympathy."

In a receiving line, the woman precedes the man through the line. Married women officers may take the lead if they desire. As they reach the head of the line, the man gives his wife's name to the aide or other person. After the aide has introduced the woman to the first person in the line, the man gives his name to the aide and is in turn introduced. If necessary, introduce yourself to the remaining persons in the line. If, as mentioned above, the married woman officer elects to go through the line first, she should introduce her spouse to the first person in the line and then precede him through the line. At White House and Air Force functions the man precedes the woman.

Do not worry if you are not familiar with the social activities already discussed. They may sound complicated and forbidding, but any observant person with a compassionate feeling for his fellows should have no trouble with social customs.

Social customs among young people of your association may be far different from those described here. If so, behave as you desire when in their company, but adhere to these rules when in the presence of other naval and civilian personnel.

Accommodation.   The new officer is expected to accept his or her fair burden of responsibility cheerfully and willingly. Life in the Navy will be new and strange. The problems you will encounter will present you with a succession of challenges.

There is a path of success for you if you can find it. How well you take advantage of your opportunities will depend upon how quickly you find your proper place in the organization and adapt to it. Remember, it is you and not the organization that must change. Learning to live with others might require that you change some of your behavior, but never your principles.

7

MILITARY DUTIES OF THE NAVAL OFFICER

AN ARMY FORMED OF GOOD OFFICERS MOVES
LIKE CLOCKWORK.

—*George Washington,* letter to the president of Congress

ON THE CONDUCT OF THE OFFICERS ALONE DEPENDS
THE RESTORATION OF GOOD ORDER, DISCIPLINE, AND
SUBORDINATION IN THE NAVY.

—*Lord St. Vincent,* letter to Admiral Dickson

Fixing responsibility has been a topic of interest in the military profession for hundreds of years. One of the best discourses on the subject came from Admiral Hyman G. Rickover, who said responsibility is

> a unique concept. It can only reside and inhere in a single individual. You may share it with others, but your portion is not diminished. You may delegate it, but it is still with you. You may disdain it, but you cannot divest yourself of it. Even if you do not recognize it or admit its presence, you cannot escape it. If responsibility is rightfully yours, no evasion, or ignorance, no passing the blame, can shift the burden to someone else. Unless you can point your finger at the man who is responsible when something goes wrong, then you never really had anyone responsible.

These strong words amplify that portion of chapter 1 on responsibility. The concept of responsibility is almost sacred in our Navy.

Basic Authority and Responsibility

The authority and responsibility of a naval officer begins the day he or she accepts a commission or warrant and takes the oath of office. The wording of the commission, that "special trust and confidence in the patriotism, fidelity, and abilities" repose in the person commissioned, is always an inspiration to the new officer. The acceptance of a commission is followed by an equally inspiring occasion of taking the oath of office, at which time the officer swears "to support and defend the Constitution of the United States against all enemies, foreign and domestic; to bear true faith and allegiance to same; to take that obligation freely and without any mental reservation or purpose of evasion; and to well and faithfully discharge the duties of the office on which he or she is about to enter." This is indeed a solemn oath, which should not be entered into lightly.

On the day a commission or warrant is accepted and the oath taken, one becomes a naval officer. Certain basic responsibilities are acquired by virtue of these actions. More responsibility and authority is given by *Navy Regulations* and other directives. These sources should be examined carefully by all officers so that they will know the extent and limits of their authority.

Authority and Responsibility Under *Navy Regulations*

Navy Regulations sets forth regulations concerning officers in chapter 2, entitled "Rights and Responsibilities of Persons in the Navy Department." Art. 1101 gives the duties of officers with regard to laws, orders, and regulations, and requires that every officer in the naval service acquaint himself with, obey, and so far as his authority extends, perform these duties to the best of his ability in conformance with his solemn profession of the oath of office. In the absence of instructions, he shall act in conformity with the policies and customs of the service to protect the public interest. The phrasing of Art. 1101 is broad and covers a multitude of possible situations in which an officer can and should take action. Every officer, then, upon acceptance of his or her commission or warrant and upon taking the oath, accepts the general duties of all officers.

Required Conduct.   Art. 1103, titled "Conduct of Persons in the Naval Service," requires that everyone in the naval service be a good example of subordination, courage, zeal, sobriety, neatness, and attention to duty. All persons, to the utmost of their ability and to the extent of their authority, are to maintain good order and discipline in all matters concerned with the efficiency of the command. The succeeding article requires everyone in the naval service to obey readily and strictly the lawful orders of superiors. This means avoiding the course that young Nelson took when he "put a blind eye to the telescope" and disobeyed flag hoist orders.

Exercise of Authority. Art. 0811, entitled "Exercise of Authority," states that everyone in the naval service is at all times subject to naval authority. This article is somewhat convoluted, but in essence it says that any naval officer, unless on the sick list, under custody or arrest, suspended from duty, under confinement, or otherwise incapable of discharging duties, *may* exercise authority over all persons who are subordinate to him. A person in the naval service on leave *may* exercise authority, as *may* a person in a naval ship, submarine, or aircraft when placed on duty by the CO or the aircraft commander. In addition, a person in the naval service *may* exercise authority in a ship or aircraft of the armed forces other than the Navy when a CO of naval personnel is embarked or when placed on duty by the CO. This article then specifically states that you *may* exercise authority if you are the senior officer at the scene of a riot or other emergency, or if you are placed on duty by another officer who is the senior officer exercising authority.

The senior officer reviewing an officer's conduct under this article would react badly if the latter said it was understood that he or she *might* exercise authority at the scene of a riot but had decided not to do so. Senior officers of the Navy not only *may* exercise authority when necessary—they *must* exercise it. Such action is a duty under custom, not a right. If, when on leave between assignments, an officer observes misconduct by a member of the naval service, he is bound by custom, if not by law, to take corrective action.

Amplifying Directives Concerning the Authority and Responsibilities of Officers

Authority from Organizational Position. While the basic authority for all officers comes from *Navy Regulations*, their organizational position invests them with additional authority and responsibilities, which are set forth in *Standard Organization and Regulations of the U.S. Navy (SORN)*.

SORN Art. 150 reminds us that authority falls into two categories: the general authority necessary to carry out duties and responsibilities held by all officers by virtue of their position in the Navy, and the organizational authority necessary to fulfill duties and responsibilities by virtue of the officer's assignment to a specific billet. The command organizational structure is maintained by command, department, division, and other instruction manuals, which set forth the positions, duties, and responsibilities of all persons in the structure.

Limits on Authority: Lawful Orders

Injurious or Capricious Conduct. Their broad authority notwithstanding, there are limits to what officers can do. Only lawful orders are to be given and obeyed. *Navy Regulations* prohibits persons in authority from abusing their subordinates with tyrannical or capricious conduct or with abusive language.

Limits on Organizational Authority. SORN Art. 150a3 points out that since authority is given only to fulfill duties and responsibilities, only so much organizational authority as may be considered necessary to fulfill responsibilities need be delegated. This is limitation of authority by command. It is a vague concept referring to a situation not often encountered but it should be noted.

Contradictory Orders. Navy Regulations Art. 0815 covers the subject of contradictory and conflicting orders. If an officer contradicts the orders issued to another by a superior, the officer who issues the contradictory orders must immediately report that fact, preferably in writing, to the superior whose orders have been contravened. If an officer receives a contradictory order, he or she must immediately exhibit his or her orders, unless otherwise instructed, and represent the facts in writing to the officer who has given the last order. If that officer insists upon the execution of his or her order, it must be obeyed and the circumstances should be reported to the officer issuing the original order.

Unlawful Imposition of Nonjudicial Punishment. What are lawful orders must be clearly understood by all officers. Most instances of doubt occur in the area of nonjudicial punishment. *SORN* discusses this in detail in Arts. 150a4 and 150b1, 2, and 3.

Article 150a4 states that no order may be given imposing punishment outside of the Uniform Code of Military Justice (UCMJ). It further states that UCMJ nonjudicial punishment is carefully reserved for certain commanders, COs, and officers-in-charge. What is not well understood, according to this article, is what measures may be taken by officers and petty officers to correct minor deficiencies not meriting punishment under UCMJ Art. 15, to correct deficiencies in a subordinate's performance of military duty, or to direct completion of work assignments that may extend beyond normal working hours.

Extra Military Instruction (EMI).   In an effort to clear up the foregoing uncertainty, *SORN* Art. 150b establishes policy guidance for EMI. This article was much-needed. More letters have been written to COs by parents, congressmen, and concerned citizens on this subject than on all others put together. Making sure your junior officers, leading petty officers, and enlisted people understand this subject will cut your administrative load and letter writing drastically.

SORN Art. 150b1a defines EMI as instruction in a phase of military duty in which an individual is deficient. This instruction, sanctioned by the *Manual for Courts-Martial (MCM)* para. 128c (1969), is a training device to improve the efficiency of a command or unit and must not be used for punitive action that should have been taken under UCMJ. *SORN* Art. 150b1b then describes how to implement this form of instruction and states that it will not be assigned for more than two hours a day, may be assigned at a reasonable time outside of working hours, will be no longer than necessary to correct the deficiency, and will not be assigned on a person's sabbath. Further, a person who is otherwise entitled to liberty may commence liberty upon completion of EMI.

EMI assignment during normal working hours may be made by any officer or petty officer. EMI after working hours should be assigned by the CO, whose authority in this matter may in turn be delegated to officers and petty officers. If it is so delegated, the CO must monitor the process. COs may delegate authority to CPOs, and in some cases where trustworthy leading petty officers are filling organizational billets normally filled by CPOs, they may delegate authority to such petty officers.

Withholding Privileges.   Certain privileges may be withheld temporarily, an act sanctioned by MCM 128c and 129. This procedure may be used to correct infractions of military regulations or performance deficiencies of a minor nature where stronger action is not required. Examples of privileges that may be withheld are special liberty, exchange of duty, special pay, special command programs, movies, libraries, and off-ship events on bases. The authority to use this procedure rests with the individual empowered to grant the privileges. Withholding privileges from personnel in a liberty status is the prerogative of the CO. This authority may be delegated, but it must not result in deprivation of liberty itself.

Additional Work Assignments. SORN Art. 150b3, an important article, is usually the cause of most of the misunderstanding about lawful or unlawful deprivation of liberty. It states that deprivation of liberty as a punishment, except under the UCMJ, is illegal; no officer or petty officer may deny liberty as a punishment for any offense or unsatisfactory performance of duty. This is clear enough. The next part of the article then goes on to state that it is necessary to the efficiency of the naval service that certain functions be performed and that certain work be accomplished in a timely manner, and it is therefore not a punishment when certain personnel are required to remain on board and perform work assignments *that should have been completed for additional essential work* or *for the currently required level of operational readiness. SORN* suggests that good leadership and management practices will cure any resultant problems. This means extending working hours for all hands or for certain selected personnel *only when absolutely necessary.* When you recommend to your seniors that they do so, you should make every effort to ensure that your personnel understand the necessity for such action. If they understand it, they will carry out their duty readily and well; if not, you can expect some additional letters to answer. The extension of individual work requirements is legitimate, for example, if the work is not done correctly the first time or if there is a short-notice operational or administrative commitment.

Ordering and Assignment of Officers

Officer Distribution. The commander of NMPC has responsibility for assigning qualified officers to authorized billets and for giving each officer assignments that allow him or her the opportunity for development of professional and personal capabilities. The officer distribution system, in implementing this responsibility, takes into account the needs of the service, the professional needs of the individual, the officer's record and qualifications, and where possible, the officer's preference as to billet, command type, and location.

The officer distribution system, as described in chapter 17, is organized so that a group of placement officers monitors ships and other organizations by types and another group takes care of officers by ranks. Together these officers are called detailers. The placement officer, several months in advance, posts his requirements for officers to relieve or fill the billets for his ships with the appropriate rank detailers, giving dates of expected rotation and qualifications for the billet. The rank detailer then attempts to fill the billet with an officer of appropriate rank and qualifications who is due to rotate at the proper time. The two officers then get together to work out details or orders to be issued. The placement officer usually informs the ship's CO of the results, and the rank detailer writes to the officer to be ordered, giving him advance notice and information. Officers should communicate only with their detailers.

Assignment to Specific Billets. Only certain officers are assigned to specific billets. COs and executive officers are always assigned specifically. The reactor and engineer officers of nuclear-powered ships and certain peculiarly qualified officers in submarines and in air departments are assigned by name. Supply, medical, dental, and legal officers and chaplains are not assigned specifically, but their qualifications leave no doubt as to what billets they are intended for. In larger ships officers with particular qualifications are ordered with the understanding that they will then be assigned by the CO to the billet for which the detailer feels they are best qualified, but this is not mandatory. For instance, the detailer will attempt to see that each ship has an officer assigned who is qualified for each department-head billet.

Nuclear-powered ships usually have an allotted number of officers of assigned ranks in the reactor and engineering departments. The remainder of the ship will be manned at the manning level for her type.

Junior officers are ordered by number rather than by name, so they are not assigned to specific billets.

Duties of Specific Assignments

When an officer arrives at a ship, squadron, or station and takes a position in the organization of that unit, the officer assumes with that position the authority and responsibility assigned to the billet by the ship's organization and regulations, which are described in chapter 10.

The Executive Officer and His Assistants. The executive officer is second in command of the unit and is the alter ego of the CO. The XO takes precedence over all other officers of the command and has responsibility for the organization, performance of duty, good order, and discipline of the command. XOs have certain administrative assistants who report directly to them.

Administrative Assistant. The administrative assistant is an aide to the executive officer, observing and reporting to the executive officer on the effectiveness of administrative policies, procedures, and regulations of the command. He or she carries out those duties assigned by the executive officer, which may include screening and routing of incoming correspondence, assignment of responsibility for replies, maintenance of the tickler file, review of outgoing correspondence, and preparation of the plan of the day. He or she may also act as budget officer for the division or division officer, or supervise the print shop.

Chaplain. The chaplain is responsible for all religious and related activities. He or she may conduct worship according to the manner of his or her own church, but must do everything possible to have other forms of worship performed, either by presiding, by using lay leaders, or by arranging for visiting chaplains. He or she should be available for counsel on all matters and should be the CO's liaison with the Navy Relief Society and the American Red Cross.

Command Career Counselor. The command career counselor is responsible for establishing a program that will disseminate career information and furnish career counseling.

Drug and Alcohol Program Advisor. The responsibility of this officer is to advise the command on how to set up a drug and alcohol abuse program and then establish and administer the program.

Educational Services Officer. This officer administers educational programs, acts as a member of the training board, and assists the training officer. He or she may be assigned other duties in the educational and training area and usually administers examinations and examining boards.

Legal Officer. The legal officer is an advisor and staff assistant to the CO and executive officer on all matters concerning the interpretation and application of UCMJ and other military laws and regulations.

Personnel Officer. The personnel officer is responsible for the placement of all enlisted personnel in accordance with the personnel assignment bill and for the administration and custody of all enlisted records.

Postal Officer. This officer supervises the postal functions of the command.

Public Affairs Assistant. This officer is charged with carrying out the public affairs program of the command.

Safety Officer. In ships other than aircraft carriers, this officer is assigned and given the responsibilities for carrying out a safety program. He or she distributes safety information, maintains safety records, and monitors the safety program. In aircraft carriers this billet belongs to a department head.

Ship's Secretary. The ship's secretary is responsible for administrating ship's correspondence and directives, officer personnel records, the preparation of the CO's personal correspondence, the preparation of officer's fitness reports, and the ship's nonclassified reference library.

Special Service Officer. This officer carries out the ship's special services program, which includes athletics, recreational programs, and entertainment. He or she is the custodian of the recreation fund and all special services equipment.

Training Officer. This officer is an advisor and assistant to the executive officer for training matters. He or she is a member of the training board and prepares and monitors training plans and schedules.

Coordinator of 3M. This officer is responsible for administering the ship's maintenance, material, and management (3M) system.

Security Manager. The security manager is responsible for all matters concerning the security of classified information. He or she prepares destruction bills, security procedures, clearance requests, and security classification plans.

Collateral Duties. Other duties are assigned on a collateral basis directly under the executive officer to officers and some-times to petty officers. Care must be taken to ensure that those assigned are qualified, there is no conflict of interest, and no individual is overburdened. These duties are performed by the following officers:

Senior watch officer
Athletic officer
Chief censor
Communication material security (CMS) custodian
Brig officer
Crypto-security officer
Library officer
Mess treasurer
Mess caterer
Movie officer
Naval warfare publications (NWP) control officer
Nuclear-handling supervisor
Nuclear safety officer
Photographic officer
Recreation fund custodian
Security officer
Top secret control officer (cannot be the same person as the NWP control officer or the CMS custodian)
Witnessing officer (for custodians)

Operations Officer. In addition to carrying out the duties of a head of department, the operations officer is responsible for the collection, evaluation, and dissemination of combat and operational information required by the mission of the ship. This covers the areas of air, surface, and subsurface search; control of aircraft; collection, display, analysis, and dissemination of intelligence; preparation of operating plans and schedules; meteorological information; and repair of electronic equipment.

The following officers report to the operations officer. In large ships they may be, where indicated, separate heads of departments; in small ships they are part of the operations department.

Administration and training assistant of the operations department
Air intelligence officer (supplied by the appropriate type commander)

Carrier air traffic control officer (supplied by the appropriate type commander)

Combat information center (CIC) officer

Communications officer (when not a department head)

Electronics material officer (EMO) (except when the ship has a combat systems department)

Electronics warfare (EW) officer

Intelligence officer

Meteorological officer

Photographic officer

Strike operations officer (supplied by appropriate type commander)

Computer programmer

First lieutenant (when the ship has a combat systems department but not a deck department)

Cryptologic officer (on ships that have a counter-electronics capability)

Navigator. The navigator is the head of the department of navigation. He is responsible under the CO for the safe navigation and piloting of the ship.

Communication Officer. In ships with a communication department, the communication officer acts as a head of department. He is responsible for visual and electronic exterior communication systems and the administration of the interior systems supporting them. Assistants to the communication officer include the radio officer, signal officer, custodian of CMS distributed material, crypto-security officer, and communication watch officer.

Weapons Officer. In ships that have a weapons department, this officer is the department head. He is also responsible for the ordnance equipment and equipment associated with deck seamanship that is not specifically assigned to another department. Assistants to the weapons officer, if billets are assigned, are as follows:

First lieutenant

Antisubmarine warfare (ASW) officer

Missile officer

Gunnery officer

Nuclear weapons officer

Ordnance officer

Marine detachment officer
Fire control officer

Combat Systems Officer. Ships that have a combat systems department will have a combat systems officer serving as head of the department. He will be responsible for the supervision and direction of the ship's combat systems, including ordnance equipment. The combat systems officer will have the following assistants if billets are assigned:

Department administrative assistant
ASW officer
Missile officer
Battery control officer
Fire control officer
Ordnance officer
Gunnery officer
Electronics readiness officer
Computer (NTDS) maintenance officer
Nuclear weapons officer
System test officer

Air Officer. In ships with an air department, the air officer is assigned as head of department. He or she is responsible for the supervision and direction of the launching and landing operations and for the servicing and handling of aircraft. The air officer is also responsible for salvage, fire fighting, aviation fuels, aviation lubricants, and safety precautions. His or her assistants will include an assistant air officer, catapult officer, arresting gear officer, aviation fuels officer, and training assistant (air).

Helicopter Capability. In ships without air departments where a Navy helicopter detachment is embarked, an aviation department is organized with an aviation officer as its head. He should have under him a qualified helicopter control officer.

Embarked Air Wing Commander. An air wing is commanded by an officer of the rank of captain. He has the status of a commanding officer and reports to the battle group commander and, when the air wing is embarked aboard the carrier, additionally to its commanding officer. He has responsibility for the readiness and tactical operation of the embarked air wing. The term "Senior CAG" or "Super CAG" is sometimes used to describe him, but he should be referred to as "CAG." A deputy CAG is subordinate to the senior CAG. His duties vary, depending upon the desires of the senior CAG, but he generally supervises the tactical training and indoctrination of the air wing and the co-ordination and supervision of the various squadrons and detach-ments of the wing.

First Lieutenant. In ships with a deck department, the first lieutenant is the department head. He or she is responsible for supervising the use of equipment associated with deck seaman-ship and, in ships without a weapons or combat systems depart-ment, of the ordnance equipment. His or her assistants, if billets exist, are the assistant repair officer, electrical assistant, hull as-sistant, machinery assistant, and others depending upon the class of the tender.

Engineering Officer. This officer heads the engineering de-partment. He or she is responsible for the operation, care, and maintenance of all propulsion and auxiliary machinery, the con-trol of damage, and upon the request of the head of department, the repairs beyond the capacity of other departments. The follow-ing are assistants to the engineering officer if billets are assigned: main propulsion assistant, reactor control assistant, damage con-trol assistant, electrical officer, and others as provided in nuclear-powered ships.

Submarine Ship's Diving Officer. This officer is assigned under provisions of the *Standard Submarine Operations and Reg-ulations Manual (SSORM).* This function may be a collateral duty handled by the chief engineer or by his damage control assistant, if he is so qualified.

The diving officer is listed here with officers of the engineering department, but he is not a part of that department. He reports directly to the CO in matters concerning the safe submerged operations of the ship and to the executive officer in matters concerning the administration and training of personnel. He keeps the engineering officer informed of technical matters concerning the submerged operation of the ship, but he is not otherwise under the control of the engineering officer.

Reactor Officer. In ships that have a reactor department, the reactor officer is the head of department. This officer will be ordered by name and be senior to all engineering watch officers and engineering and reactor division officers. He will be respon-sible for the operation, care, maintenance, and safety of the reactor plants and their auxiliaries. He will receive all orders concerning these responsibilities directly from the CO and make all corresponding reports directly to the CO. He reports to the CO for reactor matters and acts as his technical assistant. He reports to the executive officer for administrative matters.

There is special responsibility attached to the operation of reactor plants; the reactor officer and the engineer officer must cooperate closely in matters pertaining to the propulsion plant. The reactor officer and his assistants are responsible for some duties (prescribed by their specific duties) normally set aside for the engineer officer and his assistants in non-nuclear-powered ships without separate departments. Assistants to the reactor officer are the reactor control assistant, reactor mechanical assistant, and reactor watch officers. The reactor officer and his principal assistants will be qualified before arrival at the ship.

The reactor officer will be ordered by name to that specific billet. Specific responsibilities of the reactor control assistant and the reactor mechanical assistant are described in *SORN* Art. 325.

Research Officer.   In ships whose mission is research, this officer is assigned as head of department and carries out responsibilities regarding research.

Deep Submergence Officer.   In ships whose mission is deep submergence, this officer serves as head of department and carries out appropriate responsibilities.

Supply Officer.   In ships having a supply department, the head of department is designated as the supply officer. He or she will be responsible for procuring, receiving, storing, issuing, transferring, selling, accounting for, and maintaining, while in his or her custody, all stores and equipment of the ship.

In large ships and in most medium-sized ships an officer of the supply corps is ordered as supply officer. In very small ships the CO must designate an officer of the line to be supply officer. The supply officer of a large ship will have as assistants a commissary officer and a disbursing officer not in the supply corps.

Medical Officer.   The senior medical officer is the head of the medical department. He or she is responsible for maintaining the health of the personnel of the ship, making appropriate inspections, and advising the CO with respect to hygiene and sanitation.

Almost all major ships will have a medical officer. Small ships without medical officers will have a hospital corpsman qualified for independent duty who will function under the executive officer. Squadrons of small ships have a medical officer ordered to the squadron commander's staff. This medical officer serves all ships of the squadron.

Dental Officer.   The dental officer is the head of the dental department. He or she is responsible for preventing and controlling dental disease and supervising dental hygiene. Small ships without a dental officer have their dental affairs overseen by the leading hospitalman, who arranges periodic checkups and other care at nearby dental facilities.

Duties of Heads of Departments.   Officers assigned as specific heads of departments in a ship organization have duties as outlined in the past sections. They also have other duties by virtue of their designation as a department head.

Heads of departments may confer directly with the CO concerning matters within their department, if they believe such action necessary to the good of their department or the naval service. That right should be used carefully, and in any event, the executive officer should be brought up-to-date on any such matters as soon as possible.

Heads of departments are responsible for organizing and training their departments for battle, preparing and writing bills and orders for their departments, and assigning and administering all personnel of the department.

A detailed description of all duties and responsibilities of a department head is contained in *SORN* Art. 310.

The head of department in a large ship may have an assistant department head and an administrative assistant. In almost all ships he or she will have a department training officer and division officers.

Division Officers.   Division officers are assigned to major groupings of personnel within each ship's organization. They are responsible for the total performance of the personnel of their division. They train, supervise, and administer these personnel. They assign division personnel to watches, battle bills, other bills, and nonrecurring assignments. Their detailed responsibilities are outlined in *SORN* Art. 350. All division officers have other duties assigned collaterally and have assignments in the battle and other bills. Division officer billets are usually filled by very junior officers without specific qualifications.

In addition to *SORN*, the *Division Officer's Guide* is an excellent source of information, guidance, and advice for the division officer.

Watchstanding

Officers have duties related to specific billet assignments and to the administering organization. But your ship won't move very far or accomplish very much without a watch organization. Each officer has added authority and responsibilities assigned to him or her by the ship's watch organization.

Senior Watch Officer. A watch organization begins with a senior watch officer. Under the executive officer, he or she is responsible for the assignment and general supervision of all deck watch officers and enlisted watchstanders in port and under way. He or she maintains records concerning the qualifications of all deck watchstanders, coordinates their training, and prepares appropriate watch bills.

Deck Watchstanding. The *Watch Officer's Guide* is a good source of information and guidance on deck watchstanding. It covers the deck watch in general, log writing, shiphandling, rules of the road, and other safety-at-sea problems. It also covers the duties of the OOD in port.

CIC Watchstanding. The duties, responsibilities, and requirements of the CIC watch officer and his subordinates are set forth in the *Op's Officer Manual.* CIC is a vital part of the ship's operations.

Engineering Watch. The chief engineer is responsible to the CO for making out and administering the engineering watch bill and for qualifying all watchstanders. Cooperation between the engineering officers of the watch and the OOD is essential. In order to make sure that they understand the problems of the engineering plant and its watch officers, deck watch officers should refer to *Engineering for the Officer of the Deck.* This easily readable book describes what happens below and how you can use the full capabilities of the engineering plant.

Communication Watch. The communication watch is very important. With a good one, the ship will be able to disseminate orders received and make corresponding responses rapidly and accurately.

Small-Boat Duties

Another source of authority and responsibility for officers is the assignment to small-boat duties. There are two categories of duty.

In Charge of a Division Boat. Each boat is assigned to a division for operation and maintenance. As a division officer or junior division officer you will be responsible for the boats of your division. This means their cleanliness, preservation, safety, and smartness. You must select and instruct a crew that understands the importance of these components of maintenance, and you must inspect frequently and thoroughly to see that they are carried out.

The second part of responsibility for a division boat is to see that the selected boat crew is well uniformed, military in bearing, and well versed in boat customs. Last, but not least, is to assure that the boat coxswain knows the rules of the road, boat-handling, boat courtesy, boat safety, and the boat's capacity.

As a Boat Officer. Junior officers, including aviators assigned to squadrons embarked aboard carriers, can expect assignment in bad weather or in some foreign ports as a boat officer. This assignment carries with it the authority to command the boat, but also the responsibility for knowing the physical characteristics and limitations of the boat to which you are assigned, the navigational charts of the area together with expected hazards, weather, boat courtesy, rules of the road, and boat safety. Since you may be assigned to any of the ship's boats on short notice, you should be familiar with all of them. *The Boat Officer's Handbook* will provide all the information you will need.

Training Responsibilities

With your organizational assignment go certain responsibilities for training the personnel under your care.

Executive Officer. The executive officer is responsible, under the CO, for forming a training board and seeing that the board produces a training plan with necessary subsidiary plans. He or she is responsible for monitoring the execution of the training plan and testing its effectiveness by scheduling drills, exercises, inspections, and critiques.

Department Heads. Department heads are responsible for

executing that part of the training plan pertaining to their department and for the supervision of all division officers in their training efforts.

Division Officers. It is upon division officers that the heaviest burden for training falls. They must prepare the personnel of their division individually for the responsibilities relating to both their rating structure and their administrative assignments. They must also monitor their battle station and watch qualifications to ensure that their division can fill the battle bill, watch bill, and emergency bill assignments. Finally, they are responsible for the individual counseling, training, and education of their personnel.

Planning Board for Training. Every officer should know the functions of the planning board for training, more commonly called the training board, which is required by *SORN* Art. 0812. The executive officer is chairman, and the members are the heads of departments, the educational services officer, and the training officer. This board prepares the training plan and supervises its execution. The board normally meets weekly on board most ships and stations.

Training Program. *SORN* Art. 0812 sets forth in detail the requirements of a training program. A long-range program over the period of a year starts the process. A quarterly plan, a monthly plan, and a summary and record of type commander training are also required. Many other subsidiary programs, such as drug and alcohol abuse programs, career benefits counseling, and safe driving, are included.

Personal Qualification Standards (PQS). PQS is a method of qualifying officers and enlisted personnel for performing assigned duties, including watches. The duties are the everyday administrative ones expected of a rated person and the military ones required at drill, battle, and watch stations. A PQS card can be carried by each person, showing the duties for which he is in training and progress to date. Other summary forms are kept by the division officer.

Training Records. Each division officer, as part of his responsibilities, must keep comprehensive records of the training accomplished by his men, both as individuals and as members of bill teams. The PQS system takes care of portions of this task, and summary forms are available from the type commanders for the remainder.

Temporary Additional Duty

You may be assigned to temporary additional duty either during a period of instruction or for other purposes. Your orders should state whether you are relieved of your regular duties or whether these duties are in addition to your regular duties. If you are relieved of them, you must turn them over to a designated relief in proper fashion. You are not responsible for your organizational duties, having been relieved of them, but you retain the other general authority and responsibilities of an officer. If you are not relieved of your duties, you assume the additional responsibilities given to you in your orders.

Member of Court, Board, or Committee

You are assigned as a member of a court or board by written orders. The orders placing you on duty will specify whether or not you are relieved of all other duties. Normally only those assigned to general courts-martial and to out-of-town selection boards are so relieved. Orders will clarify this status and will direct travel. Orders to on-board courts and boards will usually direct this duty in addition to regular duties. However, when the court or board meets, it takes priority over all other duties.

Duty on minor boards and on committees is assigned in the monthly ship's roster. On some occasions such appointment is accompanied by a letter of appointment. This sort of duty is in addition to other duties and does not take precedence over them.

Assignment to selection boards and other important boards is by orders. The orders will specify the duty as temporary additional duty and will direct you to attend at a specific location and time and for an approximate duration. This duty has priority over all others.

Shore Patrol

Shore patrol duty is of two kinds. Permanent shore patrol officers are ordered for an extended period by the senior officer present afloat (SOPA) or other authority and are relieved of all other duties. Temporary shore patrol duty is a temporary additional duty. The responsibility of shore patrol is unique. You will need to know the limits of your authority regarding arrest, detention, and other actions you may be required to take. If in doubt, consult the nearest legal officer.

From the preceding discussion it is evident that an officer's authority and responsibility are broad—they start with the law and *Navy Regulations* and end with the authority given by ship's organization, regulations, and additional orders. Each officer should understand thoroughly his or her complete range of responsibilities in order to exercise authority properly.

8

LEADING THE AMERICAN BLUEJACKET

THE AMERICAN BLUEJACKET CAN DO ANYTHING,
ANYTIME, ANYWHERE, PROVIDED HE IS LED BY AN
EQUALLY CAPABLE OFFICER.

—*Fleet Admiral Chester Nimitz*

TO INSURE VICTORY, THE TROOPS MUST HAVE
CONFIDENCE IN THEMSELVES AS WELL AS IN
THEIR COMMANDERS.

—*Niccolò Machiavelli*, Discourse

The most important task entrusted to a naval officer is the safety of his ship. The next most important task, the one that occupies almost all of his time, is leading the American bluejacket. Before discussing the bluejacket and the theory and mechanics of leadership, we will trace the history of our Navy's changing patterns of leadership.

British Influence on Our Navy

Our early Navy adopted much of its professional expertise and many of its methods of operation from the British Navy. This was to be expected, since most of its officers were of British descent, the only gun-making foundries were British, and other key supplies and equipment were of British manufacture. However, the character of American navy personnel differed from that of their British counterparts.

The reasons for the divergence are simple. British officers were chosen for their political connections and aristocratic origins rather than for their skill, bravery, and leadership ability. Lord Nelson was a partial exception to this rule. The son of a clergyman who belonged to a class below the aristocracy, he spent many years at sea as a boy and man. He was a captain at twenty, but spent many years watching political appointees pass him by before being recognized as a superior naval leader and being rewarded with high command. He was not like the average British naval officer, who tended to be bullheaded and overbearing, which kept the lower-class enlisted man in a very subservient position.

The Americans who came to this country brought with them the seagoing traditions and abilities of Great Britain, but they rejected some of the British class system at sea. A few American naval officers were actually elected by the crew, although this system proved impractical when the first ships were built and manned by the early American government. Officers and captains were chosen for their professional skill and experience and not for political reasons. Enlisted men were capable mariners and a lot more, for they had a spirit of independence, initiative, and aggressiveness, the very qualities that prompted them to leave Great Britain and come to America. They were still, however, considered second-class citizens.

Tactics reflected the attributes of the relatively young, independent captains of the first American ships. Speed was considered the most important asset of a ship. John Paul Jones himself said, "I wish to have no connection with any ship that does not sail fast, for I intend to go in harm's way."* American captains used speed to place their vessels in advantageous positions and overcome larger and more powerful ships.

In general, our early Navy was manned by technically capable men who knew how to fight and sail. They were rough, ignorant, and argumentative. Even near the height of his success, John Paul Jones wrote of his officers and men, "Plunder rather than honor was the object of *Ranger*'s crew. . . . I ran every chance of being killed or thrown overboard."† Nonetheless, the competent sea-

---

*Letter to le Ray de Chaumont in Robert Heinl, *Dictionary of Naval and Military Quotations* (Annapolis: U.S. Naval Institute, 1966), p. 294.

†C. S. Alden and A. Wescott, *The United States Navy* (New York: Lippincott, 1943), pp. 34–35.

men and skilled fighters of the early American Navy generally were worthy ancestors of today's fighting men.

Demography of the Navy of the 1990s

The size of the Navy's enlisted ranks is fairly stable. Some small reduction is expected during this decade. A sampling from March 1988 showed the following:

Grade	Numbers
E-9	4,296
E-8	9,879
E-7	32,420
E-6	82,142
E-5	100,355
E-4	164,010
E-3	93,413
E-2	44,954
E-1	33,552
Total	565,021

Their ages range as follows:

102,664	21 and younger
189,548	21–25
105,580	26–30
60,269	31–35
37,296	36–40
13,573	41–45
3,481	46–50
1,315	over 50

These men and women (45,191, or 8.9 percent, were women) came from all states of the union. Seventy-five percent had high-school diplomas upon entrance into the Navy. The Navy worked hard to recruit them, and in recent years achieved 100 percent of its recruiting goals.

In 1987, 55 percent of first-term men and women reenlisted, and in the career category 77 percent reenlisted. Of the 1988 group, 77,580, or 15.2 percent, were black; 23,932, or 4.7 percent, were Hispanic; and 28,850, or 5.6 percent, were other minorities. Fifty-one percent had spouses.

The conclusion that can be drawn from the foregoing demographic data is that the Navy of today is young, not as well educated as it should be, short in middle-grade petty officers, and partially staffed by women who are limited by law from serving in combatant ships and aircraft.

Some of these factors can be changed in the future. The raises in Navy pay and the economic troubles of our country will increasingly influence better-educated men and women of the civilian community to enlist. The Navy can expect to attract some petty officers who left in recent years to return. The result may be an older, more experienced Navy. The percentage of minorities and women probably will not change much, nor will the numbers of dependents.

The Enlisted Person of the 1990s

We can draw some general conclusions regarding the general character of these men and women, but first we should remember that there is one key trait of American men and women that is at once a handicap and a great advantage, and that is the tendency of Americans to be individuals. Any one person will not be like any other person. A key point in leadership is to treat each person, where possible, as an individual.

The average bluejacket will be fairly well educated: about 75 percent will be high-school graduates. Many will want more education, but most will want vocational training. You will encounter many people with a quick, native intelligence and a mechanical bent, who will want to solve problems with their hands and avoid manuals and instructions. Positive leadership will be required to make many people under your command adhere to safety precautions and sign check-off lists.

They will need adequate explanation as to why a course of action is to be followed, but if the leader is respected, they will carry out orders promptly and wait for a later explanation.

Many will be strongly controlled by the welfare, interests, and feelings of their dependents, including parents, spouses, and children. Those who are married are often more easily led, since they have made a commitment to their families that requires that they succeed in order to provide support.

Some will be highly motivated and should be encouraged to achieve rating and commissioning. Many will see the Navy as a satisfying career, will put up with the hardships that come with it, and will go on to become the backbone of the Navy. Some, at the other end of the spectrum, will never do well; they should be marked early and discharged as soon as possible. Early discharge procedures and better recruiting now make this possible.

These men and women will represent Americans of many ethnic and social origins. They will be willing to accept deprivations and to work hard and long if they know why they are making these sacrifices, but they will resist dictatorial leadership. Many will be too independent to be driven or regimented, but given proper leadership, they will be the world's best. Rear Admiral Richard Fontaine, a service group commander, at a change-of-command ceremony for one of his COs, said, "Treat the American bluejacket well, for with proper leadership and guidance, there is nothing they can't or won't do for you, and they will do it well."

With these thoughts in mind, we will examine some of the leadership techniques that should succeed with your people.

Leadership in the 1990s

Self-Knowledge. All authorities on leadership agree that the first requirement of a naval leader is that he or she have a knowledge of self, profession, and ship.

The famous military historian Douglas Southall Freeman, in a classic lecture to the students of the Naval War College in 1949, summed up his advice on leadership in three simple phrases: "Know your stuff, be a man, and look out for your men." "Knowing your stuff" means that you must first assess yourself critically. Ask yourself the following questions:

Do you know your own strengths and weaknesses? Are you prepared to make use of your strengths and to compensate for your weaknesses? No naval officer is perfect. Even John Paul Jones had his faults, but he led in such a way that his strengths overcame his weaknesses.

Do you know your profession? For the unrestricted line officer this means knowing thoroughly all of the professional competency objectives listed in the appendixes. You can't maintain the respect of the personnel of your division if you don't know how to do your job or how each person under you is to do his or her job. You can learn after you are on the job, and you had better do it quickly if necessary, but you will do better if you know your profession before you are put to the test.

Finally, do you know your ship? In the old days officers newly arrived aboard ship were seldom granted shore leave until their heads of departments were sure they knew their part of the ship, and they were not granted much additional leave until they had mastered all of their ship. This is not usually the case today, but you will do well to restrict yourself until you have mastered your ship.

When you can answer these three questions to your own satisfaction, you are ready to lead others.

In the foregoing discussion, we have actually treated 90 percent of leadership. All of the writings of acknowledged experts on leadership make the points that we have. If you can master them, the remaining 10 percent is relatively easy.

When you have time for readings in leadership, look for the sources listed in the professional reading list. We have summarized in the following sections the most important points made by these authorities.

Leading Others to Self-Knowledge. If you have passed the test of self-knowledge, you are in a position to require that your personnel meet the same test. Convince your men and women of the importance of knowing their profession and their ship. The PQS system described earlier is designed to help you determine at any time the knowledge of each person concerning the requirements being made of him or her. The PQS record, together with the division officer's notebook and other records, should enable you to assess just what each person knows about his or her profession and ship. It is your job to oversee a training plan to increase this knowledge.

Moral Leadership. Much has been said in recent years about moral leadership. The phrase comes from a program set up by Admiral Burke in the early 1960s. The first principle of moral leadership requires that the leader set high personal standards for him- or herself. This leads to a feeling of personal worth, and the leader is then ready to impart values to those he or she leads. Someone with moral values and a feeling of self-worth is likely to treat subordinates as persons of worth. This point is particularly important in relations with minorities.

Self-Confidence. Self-confidence is relative. A new ensign should be confident that he or she can perform the normal duties required of that rank. He or she should not feel qualified to command a ship. A new or unusual experience should not deter a leader, who should be confident that old qualifications and skills can be adjusted to new situations.

Self-confidence can be sensed by those being led, who know the difference between false confidence and a quiet, sound feeling of knowing how to solve a problem. If you are confident, your followers will know it.

Courage. Courage comes in two forms, physical and moral. Physical courage is the overcoming of one's fears in order to carry out one's duties in time of danger. Moral courage is sometimes more difficult to exercise than physical courage. Moral courage means having the courage of one's convictions, calling situations as they are seen, admitting mistakes, and speaking up when a senior is thought to be in error. It means giving true quarterly marks and making out accurate fitness reports, so that the Navy is relieved of incompetents.

Ability to Communicate. Good decisions are worthless unless communicated to those who have to carry them out. Every leader has to find the best method he or she has of communicating. First, orders must be given clearly, completely, and firmly. An impersonal tone of voice must be cultivated, with a more personal and urgent approach reserved for emergencies or times when instant response is necessary. Chapter 9, on oral and written communication, goes into this subject at length.

Loyalty. It should go without saying that every leader must display a feeling of loyalty to country and should never tolerate any other feeling on the part of a subordinate. Loyalty to the Navy should be treated in a like manner, but with the understanding that occasional disagreement with Navy policy is not necessarily disloyalty. Expression of disagreement within the system is not disloyalty; expression of disagreement outside the system is disloyalty.

Loyalty to those above you is part of leadership. It means serving them efficiently and well. It means passing down orders expected to be unpopular in such a manner that they appear to be your own orders. It does not necessarily mean blind obedience, for if you feel an order is not in the best interest of the one who gave it, you have the duty to inform that person of your opinion. This, too, is part of loyalty.

Loyalty also means looking after your people, their interests,

DEPARTMENT OF DEFENSE

HUMAN GOALS

Our nation was founded on the principle that the individual has infinite dignity and worth. The Department of Defense, which exists to keep the Nation secure and at peace, must always be guided by this principle. In all that we do, we must show respect for the serviceman, the servicewoman and the civilian employee, recognizing their individual needs, aspirations and capabilities.

The defense of the Nation requires a well-trained force, military and civilian, regular and reserve. To provide such a force, we must increase the attractiveness of a career in Defense so that the service member and the civilian employee will feel the highest pride in themselves and their work, in the uniform and the military profession.

THE ATTAINMENT OF THESE GOALS REQUIRES THAT WE STRIVE...

To attract to the defense service people with ability, dedication, and capacity for growth;

To provide opportunity for everyone, military and civilian, to rise to as high a level of responsibility as possible, dependent only on individual talent and diligence;

To make military and civilian service in the Department of Defense a model of equal opportunity for all regardless of race, color, sex, religion or national origin, and to hold those

who do business with the Department to full compliance with the policy of equal employment opportunity;

To help each service member in leaving the service to readjust to civilian life; and

To contribute to the improvement of our society, including its disadvantaged members, by greater utilization of our human and physical resources while maintaining full effectiveness in the performance of our primary mission.

Harold Brown
Secretary of Defense

Charles W. Duncan
Deputy Secretary of Defense

David C. Jones
Chairman, Joint Chiefs of Staff

Clifford L. Alexander Jr.
Secretary of the Army

W. Graham Claytor
Secretary of the Navy

Secretary of the Air Force

September 13, 1978

Chief of Staff, U.S. Army

Thomas R. Hayward
Chief of Naval Operations

Chief of Staff, U.S. Air Force

Lewis H. Wilson
Commandant, U.S. Marine Corps

Figure 8-1. In their capacity as leaders, all naval officers should live up to the standards of the Department of Defense as set out in this document.

their welfare, and their careers. It does not mean accepting inferior performance or concealing malfeasance.

Common Sense. Common sense is the ability to make practical choices or decisions that are prudent, fair, and reasonable. Common sense is a trait that cannot be developed—it must be exercised. Education and experience transform common sense into judgment, and judgment is one of the most valuable attributes of any person exercising leadership.

Initiative. Initiative has several allied qualities: imagination, aggressiveness, and the ability to think ahead. A wise old seaman once said, "Initiative is the ability to do the right thing without being told." When you use initiative, your senior may not know what you have done. Inform your senior promptly if you have done something without his or her knowledge. Many a young officer has made a career out of sending messages to superiors saying something like, "Unless otherwise directed I intend to do so and so," and then doing it.

Decisiveness. There is a feeling among certain officers that decisiveness means voicing an instant and unchanging opinion on every subject. A better name for this is stupidity. A good decision-maker listens, asks questions, investigates, and assembles all possible information needed to make a decision. The wise decision-maker does not announce a decision until it is required, but at any time he or she will have in mind a tentative decision based on what is known at that moment. Be decisive, but do not be rushed. Once you have made your decision, be firm about seeing it carried out; if subsequent developments indicate that it should be changed, be prompt in doing so.

Compassion. Lastly, the men and women you will lead are human beings, supposedly dedicated to the same principles and goals that you are. While you must insist on loyalty, discipline, performance, and dedication, always remember that those under you may not have the rewards in sight that motivate you. As a young officer, you are headed toward higher rank and eventual command. You can work hard and loyally because you have this prospect before you. In most cases a young seaman has far less motivation. If he fails, remember to exercise more compassion than you would expect to get for your own failure.

Summary. You will observe many other qualities in those who lead you. For the last 10 percent of desirable qualities you may want to pick your own and concentrate on them, but remember the first 90 percent: knowing yourself, your profession, and your ship. These are vital tenets.

Leadership and Management Education and Training

The Navy has had many different forms of leadership training and has taught varied techniques. In 1976 it was decided to consolidate these diverse systems in LMET. In 1981, as part of the Admiral Hayward's Pride in Professionalism program, it was decided that all officers and petty officers would be taught in a uniform manner using LMET. The first step was to train all of the prospective instructors at a single school in Memphis. The program was then expanded to schools at fourteen different sites. As of now the two-week course will be attended by all officers and petty officers, at first while en route to duty stations, and then at a later date when they advance to a higher rank or rate.

The course emphasizes sixteen characteristics and skills (also called competencies) that are clustered into five major areas for instructional purposes. These are: concern for efficiency and effectiveness; management control; skillful use of influence; advising and counseling; and conceptual thinking. The course uses a fixed curriculum, but it also focuses on the personal experiences brought to the course by students.

9

ORAL AND WRITTEN COMMUNICATION

THE FIRST AND MOST IMPORTANT THING OF ALL, AT
LEAST FOR WRITERS TODAY, IS TO STRIP LANGUAGE
CLEAN, TO LAY IT BARE DOWN TO THE BONES.

—*Ernest Hemingway,* Paris Was Our Mistress

THE BEST MILITARY DECISION EVER MADE WILL BE
WORTHLESS UNLESS IT CAN BE TRANSMITTED—EITHER
IN WRITING OR IN SPEECH—RAPIDLY, ACCURATELY,
AND SUCCINCTLY, TO THE UNIT WHICH IS SUPPOSED TO
EXECUTE IT.

—*Secretary of the Navy William B. Franke*

From the moment you step onto the quarterdeck of your first ship and ask for permission to come aboard, to the day when you deliver your retirement speech, you will be communicating orally. You must master this art if you are to succeed as a naval officer. If you do not, your success will be modest and your upward mobility limited. Whether developing plans, executing orders, or administering details of the day, the more proficient you become in the art of communication the more successful you will be in carrying out any assignment.

The other part of the communication process is the written word. Mastering it is equally important, for you will be writing almost as much as you will be speaking.

The practice of both oral and written communication is an integral part of public affairs programs that you will be involved in, either directly or indirectly, for most of your career.

Oral Communication

Voice. The human voice has several qualities that distinguish it. The most important are pitch, projection, and a less definable attribute that we will call tension. You are born with these physical traits, and they cannot be changed much, but some can be improved upon or at least controlled.

Pitch is the average frequency of tones produced by the vocal cords. A low-pitched voice is more pleasing to the ear than a high-pitched voice, even though the latter carries farther. Pitch can be lowered several notes by breathing properly. Watch an opera singer closely. You will see that the singer's chest does not move appreciably. The singer uses the lower abdomen for breathing. This technique is, of course, contrary to athletic breathing techniques, so it may require some effort to learn. Try to speak using your diaphragm and lower abdomen muscles for breathing. At the same time consciously relax your chest muscles. You will find that you can learn to speak with minimum use of the muscles of your upper chest and that your throat and voice can be made to relax in the process. This will lower pitch and will increase resonance and projection. Most importantly, it will decrease the tension in your voice. We will return to this later.

Resonance is the ability of the voice-producing apparatus to resonate to the vibrations of the vocal cords and produce tones and overtones that make the voice sound pleasant. Fifteen violins sound richer (and more resonant) than one violin. Good resonance is a function of the internal cavities and shape of the throat, sinuses, and skull. You can improve resonance by the opera-singer breathing technique, which will give you a more effective resonance cavity.

Projection is the property of a voice system that helps carry it long distances. It is composed of pitch, resonance, and diction and is hard to define or to measure. Obviously, projection is desirable if you are speaking without an amplifying system to a large group or in a noisy atmosphere. Again, by using the opera-singer technique, keeping your mouth in the direction you wish to project, and opening it as wide as you can to project the sound waves you will get the maximum result. Strengthening the abdominal muscles and practicing will help, particularly if you will be speaking in noisy environments or giving orders to troops at parades or similar functions. The muscles of the larynx and the vocal cords themselves will respond to exercise just as other muscles of the body do.

The additional quality of the human voice, tension, is an important one. It is a combination of pitch and resonance. The tenseness of a high-pitched delivery will be detected by listeners, who will become antagonistic to the speaker. Audiences are much more receptive to a low-pitched, relaxed delivery.

Thus, you can improve the characteristics of your voice within certain limits. Work at it; results will pay dividends. Jason the Cyrene, in *Second Maccabees*, said, "A voice, finely framed, delighteth the ear."

Speech. The most vibrant, beautiful voice is of no use unless its owner can speak well. Speaking well means using appropriate diction, proper grammar, and good sentence structure, and avoiding obscure words, excessive accent, and idiosyncratic mannerisms.

Good diction comes with practice. Listen to and analyze the enunciation of good speakers. Most television news commentators pronounce each word completely by opening their mouths and not dropping their voices at the end of a phrase or sentence. You should learn to use good diction, which sounds natural and unexaggerated.

Good grammar and proper sentence structure are usually a reflection of education. Your secondary school and college education should have taught you proper phrase, sentence, and paragraph construction. If in doubt about usage, you can refer to many helpful style manuals. Grammar is just as important in oral communication as in written communication, but when speaking many more liberties can be taken with structure in order to emphasize thoughts or accommodate to the mood of the conversation.

Choosing words starts with your own acquired vocabulary, which is a product of your education and reading. You can expand and correct your vocabulary with a good dictionary and thesaurus.

Naval officers come from all parts of the country and bring with them a variety of accents, which reveal their individuality and place of origin. However, too pronounced an accent may do nothing but draw attention to itself. If your accent is too strong for the American norm, listening to a television commentator's English every day will help you standardize it.

Speechmaking. Publius Syrus, in his *Maxims*, said, "Speech is a mirror of the soul; as a man speaks, so is he." You will have many occasions to demonstrate the truth of this maxim. You will make a speech of some length almost every day of your career. Making an oral request of your executive officer, conducting a training session for your division, and addressing a Rotary Club luncheon are all forms of speechmaking. Each, no matter how small in scope, will need preparation, rehearsal, delivery, and a post-delivery critique.

Let us look at the preceding examples in order. First, in making a simple request, learn to be succinct and exact. Time permitting, formulate your request in your mind and practice it. If you come before your executive officer and say, "Commander, I'd like to bring my boat aboard and get it in shape for leaving port," you will waste several seconds of his time and leave several questions unanswered. If the executive officer wants to know which boat you want to hoist and exactly when you want to do so, he or she will have to ask you, and additional time will be wasted. It is much better to think first and then say, "Sir, I request permission to hoist in no. 1 motor launch at 0900 and secure it for sea." You will have been exact and succinct because you spent a few minutes of your time, not the officer's.

Secondly, you will be called upon frequently to instruct your division, a more complicated situation. You will need to prepare yourself fully ahead of time. This means determining what you are to teach and how much your division already knows about the subject; how you are going to present your information; and when and where you will make the presentation. Choose a time, if you have the option, when your personnel will not be tired or hungry. Find a quiet, comfortable area for your class. Break down the subject matter into easily handled units. Use the simplest words possible without seeming to talk down to your group. Be ready to repeat or emphasize important points. Prepare or procure visual aids, no matter how crude or simple. Some people remember the printed word better than the spoken phrase. Rehearse your presentation and its delivery, and after the event ask yourself or some of your students how the session could have been improved.

Later, you will graduate to more important instruction tasks and more sophisticated students and eventually to conducting briefings of senior officials and officers. Regardless of the sophistication or seniority of the audience, your own part in the process does not change much. You must master your material, use good voice and instructional techniques, and radiate sincerity, enthusiasm, confidence, and good humor.

As you progress, you will be able to increase the sophistication of your training aids. Simple sketches and blackboards will give way to movie projectors, television videotape systems, and public-address systems. You must be able to use them all. Movie projectors are handy in that they may be set up easily, and most are capable of being stopped on a single frame for discussion and of being reversed for review. Most ships are now equipped with internal television systems that can be used with videotapes or for live instruction. We will say more later about appearing personally on television and about the use of the public-address system.

The third most likely use of speech for you will be as an informal or formal speechmaker. As you advance in rank, there will be an increasing number of invitations for you to address audiences and groups of various sizes and varieties. The invitations in some cases may be assignments given out by higher authority.

Regardless of the size or importance of your audience, you should observe certain fundamentals of speechmaking. Get all the information you can regarding the event. Where is it? When is it? What uniform will you wear? What is the topic? How long do they want you to speak? Will others be on the same program? Will there be a question period? Will a lectern and a public-address system be provided? Who is responsible for setting it up and testing it? What will be the size and character of the audience? Some of these questions may seem trivial, but you would be surprised to know how many Navy speakers have arrived at the wrong place on the wrong date in the wrong uniform with a written speech and no lectern to put it on.

With the foregoing information in hand, you will know how to get there, what to wear, what your audience will be like, what speech aids you will have, and who, if required, is assisting. With these housekeeping details out of the way, you can concentrate on your speech.

Your first consideration is to determine what the audience wants to hear. You can't tell sea stories to a large, sophisticated audience that wants to know about Navy shipbuilding. If they have specified a topic, try to give it to them. If they haven't, decide what you want to tell them and choose your topic.

Speech arrangements are important. This flag officer's aide did not arrange for a lectern, which would have provided a resting place for the written speech.

The chief of information prepares speech kits that will give you "cleared" official positions on a variety of naval subjects. Use these if you are a beginner and do not feel qualified to strike out on your own. You can personalize excerpts from the speech kit and turn out an interesting speech on many topics.

The second element of speechmaking is organizing what you want to say. Even if you feel you are qualified to speak extemporaneously, you should prepare an outline and reduce it to notes. A small outline on index cards has saved many a speaker who suddenly lost his train of thought. A card outline is a minimum. You would do better to write out your speech and put it on large index cards. Go over it several times. By the time you speak you may not need it, but you should keep it on the lectern. If you must read your speech, take time to separate the phrases and to note words to be accented, using a marker pen. This will help you to simulate as much as possible natural speech when reading. Other techniques that will help you are reading slowly, lifting your glance frequently (while keeping your place with your finger), and making your delivery sound as if you were talking rather than reading.

Start your speech with acknowledgments, such as, "Mister Chairman, Senator Smith, distinguished guests, members of the Rotary Club," and then start slowly. Give your audience a chance to adjust to you and vice versa. A few topical remarks, an anecdote, or an amusing quotation will help. Once you are acclimated, proceed, but do so slowly. Be natural, sincere, and enthusiastic. If you know your subject and present it well, you will soon begin to enjoy speechmaking, for your audience will let you know they appreciate you and your message.

Use stories and quotations only if they are applicable and make a point. Robert William Chapman, in *Portrait of a Scholar*, gave this good advice: "A quotation, like a pun, should come unsought, and then be welcomed only for some propriety or felicity justifying the intrusion."

Finally, learn to use a public-address system. If you are offered one or can arrange for a lapel microphone, you are fortunate. With the latter, you can move about. With a fixed microphone, you must learn, whatever you do with your head, to keep your mouth a fixed distance from the microphone and positioned at all times so that it is pointed directly at the microphone. If you do not, you will produce annoying fluctuations in volume. This means that if you want to turn your head to scan your audience (and you should) you must do so by keeping your mouth in a fixed position and literally moving the back of your head. If you look down at your script, you must raise your head to compensate. This sounds complicated, but it is easily learned with a little practice.

Organize your speech so that you have an introductory section in which you tell your audience what you are going to say. Then put together a rational argument to make your point or points. Finish with a conclusion. Thank them for inviting you and sit down.

Be brief. Aim at fifteen minutes, with additional time for questions, unless you are invited to speak for a longer period. If you have done your preliminary work, you will know if there are other speakers. A long speech after other speakers and a full program of awards and introductions may put your audience to sleep.

It may be some years before you appear on television, even the shipboard variety of television. When you do, there are a few simple rules that will get you through a program. Think of the camera lens as your audience and maintain eye contact with it. If there is more than one camera, the transmitting camera will have a red light on it. Some camera systems show one red light for a camera that is ready but not transmitting and two red lights for the transmitting camera. Turn your head toward the transmitting camera. Television is very revealing, so remember to comb your hair and adjust your clothes before going on the air, and when you are on, keep hand gestures to an absolute minimum. They can be very distracting.

Finally, in all these various speeches, remember to use the best diction you are capable of, to cut down on idioms, to employ simple words, and to avoid excessive gestures and idiosyncratic mannerisms.

Clearance. Clearance means submitting your proposed speech or article for publication to the Office of the Assistant Secretary of Defense for Public Affairs (it goes via the Navy's chief of information) to determine whether it is in conformance with national policy and whether it presents unclassified information. You are not allowed to say or write anything that is classified. You do not have to submit your speech for clearance if you are sure that it does not contain classified information, but if you do not submit something that turns out to be controversial, you may well be in trouble. You should not have many occasions to request clearance in your early years. If you are in doubt, or if you know you should request clearance, consult the *Public Affairs Manual* for the procedure to be followed or see the nearest staff public affairs officer.

Written Communication

There are two schools of thought regarding the skill of writing. One holds that it is natural, springing somehow from the subconscious, and cannot be taught, only honed with a few lessons in punctuation and grammar. The other holds that any intelligent person can be taught to write, and that it is just a matter of education, training, and practice. Here education means wide reading, training means learning grammar, sentence construction, punctuation, spelling, and vocabulary, and practice means repeated writing. Few naval officers are natural, outstanding creative writers, although there have been some. Every naval officer should be able to learn to write and write well. Style need only be simple and straightforward to suffice for writing such official documents, letters, and dispatches as will be required. Succession to higher rank and responsibilities will require greater and more versatile skills in the use of the written word.

Most officers today have only a fair grounding in grammar, spelling, composition, and vocabulary. Most will need to continue to improve in these areas. A style manual such as Strunk and White's *Elements of Style* can be of immense value. In the meantime, following a few fundamental rules will produce satisfactory writing.

Organize and outline your composition before you start. Make sure it has a beginning, or introduction; a central development, setting forth your message; and a conclusion, covering the points you have made.

Write simply, using as few words as are necessary to convey the point of a sentence. Admiral Arleigh Burke allowed those preparing his official papers and proposed statements to use only two adjectives, *bad* and *good*. The finished products were simple and effective.

Choose the simplest word that will express what you want to say. On the other hand, do not hesitate to use a more complex word if it means exactly what you want to get across.

When you have finished your first draft, read it critically and remove superfluous words. Put it aside for a day or two, and read it again. You will be surprised to see how unclear you were just a few days ago.

Assemble all the reference books you can. Start with a good

dictionary, and add Roget's *Thesaurus*, Bartlett's *Familiar Quotations*, Fowler's *Modern English Usage*, and if you want to go further, Hayakawa's *Language in Action.*

These simple rules should enable you to construct the text of a letter, dispatch, war college study, JCS paper, or any other official written communication.

The Official Letter. The official letter must conform to a specific set of rules. These are simple and should be mastered early in your career. Although you will often be able to get help from yeomen and secretaries, do not depend upon them to put your letter in proper form. Give them a rough draft correctly composed and check the final draft for accuracy of form as well as content.

The following is a sample official letter:

DEPARTMENT OF THE NAVY
USS JOHN K. POLK (FF1334)
F.P.O. San Francisco, CA, 96601

WAF:rs
1340
Ser 234
15 Apr 1982

From: Commanding Officer
To: Commander Cruiser Destroyer Group FIVE
Via: Commander, Destroyer Squadron SEVENTEEN

Subj: Request for Personnel
Ref: (a) COMNAVSURFPAC NOTE 13 of 16 Feb 1980
(b) My ltr of 16 Dec 1980

Encl: (1) List of Personnel Deficiencies as of 1 Apr 1982

1. Enclosure (1) is a list of personnel deficiencies of this command.
2. It is requested that this ship be brought to the manning level for this type of ship as set forth in reference (a).

R.A. JOHNSON

WAF are your initials: *rs* are the initials of the yeoman. The file number, which comes from *Standard Subject Identification Codes* (SECNAVINST 5210.11d), is 1340. Ser 234 is the serial number assigned by the ship's office on the day the letter is to leave the ship. The date is similarly assigned.

Classified letters have a separate serial system preceded by the letters *C*, *S*, or *T*, depending upon the classification. If you think the letter should be classified, place the classification on your rough draft. The yeoman will type the word *secret* or the designation of some other classification two lines above the *from* line, stamp or type it in the upper right corner above the identification symbols, and stamp and type it in red in the lower right-hand corner.

The *from*, *to*, and *via* lines are self-explanatory. All letters go from the head of one organization to another. The current titles and mailing addresses of all activities are contained in the Standard Navy Distribution List (SNDL). Shore-station addresses require a geographic locator; ships do not. If there are two or more *via* addressees, they are numbered and listed in the order in which they will receive the letter.

The subject line contains a brief statement of the subject of the letter.

References, if any, are listed to help the recipient understand the text.

Enclosures are made if you think the recipient does not have them and will need them. Note the abbreviations used.

The text is, of course, where you give your message. It should be as concise and simple as possible. State your problem and what you would like to have done about it. Do not use abbreviations in the text. A common acronym may be used if its full title is given the first time it is used.

The last part of the letter is the signature. The letter is signed by the CO even if you write it. The name is used without title. Letters may be signed "by direction" if the authorization is in writing.

General Notes on Official Written Communication. Official correspondence between subordinate officers of ships or stations is forbidden. Therefore, any interoffice correspondence should be in the form of a memorandum. The form of a memorandum is similar to that of a letter except that the *from*, *to*, and *via* lines are omitted and replaced by the phrase "Memorandum for." In memorandum communications custom dictates that the junior subscribe himself, above his signature, "Very respectfully," while the senior addressing a junior uses "Respectfully." Abbreviations are commonly used.

When official business is conducted by telephone or orally,

the substance of the communication or order should be recorded in writing without delay.

All communications, orders, bills, requisitions, and papers that by law or regulation are to be signed, approved, or forwarded by an officer in command must actually be signed by such officer in that person's own handwriting or, in his or her absence, by the officer next in command at the time. The name of the officer should be typewritten under the signature.

An officer signing for another in whose absence he or she is in command or in charge, should have the word *acting* after the signature; in this case the title of the official from whom the communication emanates, indicated after the word *from* at the beginning of the letter, should not be modified.

In very large commands some officers in command will permit administrative officers to use a rubber stamp of their signature. This practice is somewhat risky and should be restricted. Normally the use of the stamp is limited to one officer or personal secretary and is used only on simple administrative communications within the command.

When an officer is writing on his or her own account, rank is indicated after the word *from* in the heading of the letter and his or her file number and numerical indicator are included after the name. Therefore, only a signature is necessary in conclusion. This, however, should include the typewritten name.

The only time an officer's rank appears after the signature is in letters addressed to officials and civilians who would not otherwise be familiar with it. These letters are prepared in regular business style.

Message Drafting.   You will be doing a lot of dispatch drafting during your career. Learn to do it right early on. By doing so you will avoid a lot of trips to the executive officer's stateroom.

Figure 9-1 is a sample unclassified message using DD form 173. You will make out the rough drafts of hundreds of such messages during your career. You will also use a somewhat simpler form at sea to draft tactical or time-sensitive messages, which are transmitted directly from the rough and written up later. Learn to make out both varieties quickly, accurately, and legibly.

For more complex messages of a classified nature more work is needed. Classification will have to be determined using the criteria and instructions in Naval Training Publication (NTP) 3

JOINT MESSAGEFORM						SECURITY CLASSIFICATION UNCLAS			
PAGE	DRAFTER OR RELEASER TIME	PRECEDENCE ACT | INFO	LMF	CLASS	CIC	FOR MESSAGE CENTER/ COMMUNICATIONS CENTER ONLY	DATE - TIME	MONTH	YR
1 of 1	0900R	D | D							
BOOK						MESSAGE HANDLING INSTRUCTIONS			

FROM: COMCRUDESGRU TWO

TO: COMNAVSURFLANT

INFO: CRUDESGRU TWO

XMT: USS GARCIA

UNCLAS //N12345//

TRAINING

A. COMNAVMILPERS WASHINGTON DC 201632Z AUG 80

B. COMCRUDESGRU TWO 201845Z JUL 80

1. REQUEST PROVIDE ONE OFFICER QUALIFIED SPANISH INTERPRETER

TO EACH INFO ADEE.

2. GARCIA HAS ONE QUALIFIED INTERPRETER.

DISTR:

DRAFTER TYPED NAME, TITLE, OFFICE SYMBOL, PHONE & DATE	SPECIAL INSTRUCTIONS	
ENS P. JONES, SHIPS SEC. 3467 1023-80		
TYPED NAME, TITLE, OFFICE SYMBOL AND PHONE D. Faragut Exec. Off. 3567		
RELEASER SIGNATURE	SECURITY CLASSIFICATION	DATE TIME GROUP

Figure 9-1. Sample unclassified message.

and OPNAVINST 5510.1, and the message and each paragraph will have to show proper classification. The last element of the text should show the specific date on which downgrading and declassification will occur.

Precedence is an important consideration. Just as you should never over-classify a message, you should never assign a higher precedence than necessary.

For further information on message drafting, refer to Allied Communication Publication (ACP) 21, NTP 3, and ACP 122.

Security of Oral and Written Communications. Security is the process of keeping classified information confined to channels where it belongs and preventing its dissemination to unauthorized persons. It means not talking to anyone except authorized officers and officials about publications, codes, ciphers, or classified information. *The Department of the Navy Security Manual for Classified Information* (OPNAVINST 5510.6) covers, in great detail, all aspects of security including classification, dissemination of information, custody and storage, security control, and personnel investigations and security clearances. Adequate security is vital to naval operations. Master the subject.

Other Forms of Written Communication. As you advance in rank, you will be required to prepare briefings, operation plans and orders, speeches for those of higher rank, instruction pamphlets, and other items. No specific guidance can be given for all of these forms of written communication, but if you search out successful examples of each type, you will have the means to improve your own. The general principles of good writing discussed previously will carry you through. You will find vocabularies unique to each field you enter. Master them, but do not carry bad habits out of their respective domains. It is true that some words do express exact meaning to those familiar with them, but it is better to use common, simple words. Don't *finalize* anything—*finish* it. Don't write *irregardless* when you mean *regardless*, or *utilize* when a simple *use* will suffice.

Public Affairs

Public affairs refers to the relations between the public and a commander and his command. It includes, but is not limited to, general visiting, calling upon public officials, speaking publicly, hosting social events, and conducting relations with the press.

Most methods of conducting public affairs involve supplying information directly to the public. Other methods are more indirect, but just as effective. An example of indirect public relations is to send uninformed, well-mannered officers and enlisted men and women out into the communities of our country and overseas. Another method is to plan events such as entertaining groups of orphans.

Public Relations. Those aspects of public affairs conducted through channels other than the media are usually called public relations. It is important that the public know about the Navy. The taxpayers are defended by the Navy and their taxes fund the armed forces. They elect the members of Congress who equip and pay the Navy. The taxpayers should know what kinds of ships, submarines, and aircraft the Navy has and should meet the men and women who man them. The taxpayers should know both the Navy's strengths and weaknesses so that they can make their desires known to their congressional representatives. You, as a naval officer, represent the public you also serve.

Public Information. The most direct way to educate the public is to disseminate information through various public communications media (television, radio, newspapers, and magazines). The methods available and the skills necessary to supply the public with information are fully described in the *Public Affairs Manual.*

Each Naval Academy graduate will have had a short course in public information. Officers from other sources will be able to catch up by studying the *Public Affairs Manual.*

Each officer must be able to communicate with reporters and writers when authorized to do so. Remember that public affairs is the personal responsibility of the CO, who is assisted by his public affairs officer. If you are the public affairs officer, or are designated to make contact with the media, be sure you know the CO's policy and what he or she wants told to, and withheld from, the media. Robert Smith, a philosopher of the seventeenth century, said, "Speech was given to the ordinary sort of men whereby to communicate their minds; but to wise men, thereby to conceal it." Sometimes you will have to be wise to keep information from reporters. Do so, but never lie or equivocate. Say simply that you cannot comment on that subject. Using correct oral and written communication techniques means you know both what to say and what not to say.

You may note how often we keep coming back to these simple techniques. If you can speak with good diction and voice projection, and use simple language, you can communicate orally on any occasion and with any audience. Similarly, good writing techniques make written communication easy. Work at developing your talents for both oral and written communication; the payoff will be lasting and well worth the effort.

IO

SHIP'S ORGANIZATION AND REGULATIONS

GENERALLY, MANAGEMENT OF THE MANY IS THE SAME
AS THE MANAGEMENT OF THE FEW. IT IS A MATTER
OF ORGANIZATION.

—*Sun Tzu,* The Art of War

ORGANIZATIONS AND REGULATIONS ARE NECESSARY TO
COVER NINETY PERCENT OF WHAT HAPPENS IN A SHIP.
IF THIS MUCH IS TAKEN CARE OF AUTOMATICALLY, THE
OTHER TEN PERCENT CAN BE GIVEN THE FULL
ATTENTION IT SHOULD HAVE.

—*Admiral Robert L. Dennison*

Each ship must be organized carefully and regulated properly, so that each person knows what his or her duties are, how they relate to the duties of others, and what can and cannot be done in the daily routine of living. A ship so organized is efficient and her crew happy. One lacking organization is lax and unsure and her crew is indifferent. Fortunately, almost all naval ships are properly organized and regulated, because they are required to adhere to a standard organization and to issue fairly standard regulations.

General Principles of Organization

Planning an Organization.   OPNAVINST 3120.32B *(SORN)* describes some of the basic principles of organization in chapters

206

NAVAL OFFICER'S GUIDE

3, 4, and 6. These should be read by every naval officer. In the following paragraphs most of the basic principles referred to in *SORN* will be covered, together with the personal opinions of many well-known naval officers who are experts in organization.

Funk and Wagnalls' *College Standard Dictionary* defines *organize* as follows: "to bring into systematic relation the parts of a whole." *SORN* defines organization as "the orderly arrangement of materials and personnel by functions." It states that sound organization is a requisite for good administration, that it is designed to carry out the objectives of command, and that it should be based on a division of activities and an assignment of responsibilities and authority to individuals within the organization. Further, to ensure optimum efficiency within the organization, all essential functions must be recognized and delineated as specific responsibilities of appropriate organizational units, and there must be a clear definition of individual duties, responsibilities, and authority.

Definitions.   *SORN* gives definitions of several basic terms that will be used repeatedly and should be known by every naval officer.

Accountability refers to the obligation of the individual to render an account of the discharge of his responsibilities. This account is made to the person to whom the individual reports. An individual assigned both authority and responsibility also accepts a commensurate accountability, which means that the individual must answer to his or her superiors for a success or failure in the execution of duties.

Authority means the right to make a decision in order to fulfill a responsibility, the right to discharge particular obligations, and the right to require action of others.

Delegating means a person in authority may send another person to act or transact business in the name of the originator. Authority may be delegated; responsibility may never be delegated.

Duties refer to the tasks that the individual is required to perform.

Responsibility means accountability for the performance of duty.

There is nothing new about these terms. They have been used since the beginning of our Navy, but they are not peculiar to it. You will find the same terms and the same elements of organization discussed in books on business organization and management.

Setting Up an Organization. Chapter 1 of *SORN* lists steps to be taken in establishing an organization. Your ship, unless newly commissioned, will already have one, but you may want to set up your own organization for your division. You will need to do the following:

1. Prepare a statement of objectives or of missions and tasks
2. Familiarize yourself with the principles of organization
3. Group functions logically so that they can be assigned to appropriate segments of the organization
4. Prepare manuals, charts, and functional guides
5. Establish policies and procedures
6. Inform key personnel of their individual and group responsibilities
7. Set up controls to ensure achievement of objectives.

Four Principles of Organization

There are four principles of organization discussed in *SORN*.

They are unity of command, homogeneity of assignment, span of control, and delegation of authority and assignment of responsibility.

Unity of Command. One person should report to only one superior. One person should have control over one segment of the organization. Lines of authority should be clear-cut, simple, and understood by all.

Homogeneity of Assignment. Functions should be grouped homogeneously, with individuals assigned to groups in accordance with their abilities.

Span of Control. A superior should be responsible for a group of individuals. Three to seven individuals is normally the span of control for inexperienced officers. The more senior the supervisor the greater the number of persons he or she is assigned. The span of control also depends on the type of work done, its complexity, the responsibility involved, and the supervisor's capability.

Delegation of Authority and Assignment of Responsibility. Authority delegated to a subordinate should be commensurate with his or her ability and should be delegated to the lowest level of competence.

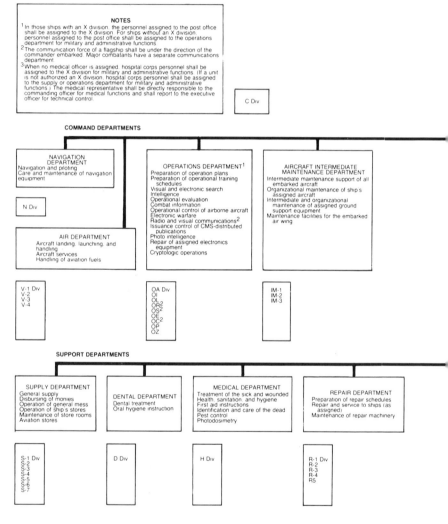

Figure 10-1. Shipboard organization.

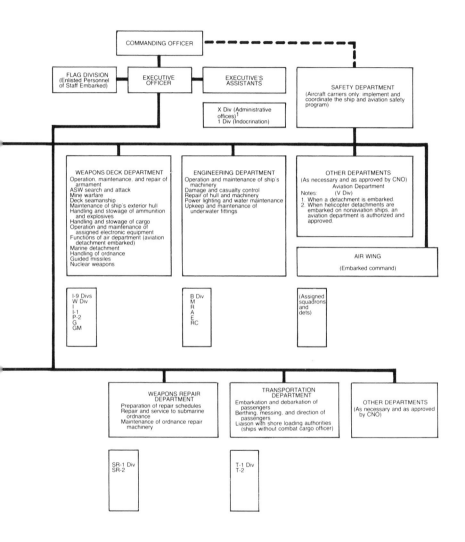

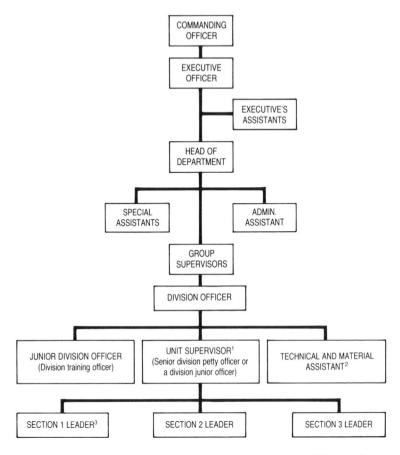

1. When a division has more than one function, such as deck and weapons responsibilities, it would have a supervisor for each of these functions.

2. Usually a warrant officer or limited duty officer assigned to supervise the maintenance and repair of certain material or equipment.

3. The number of sections in each division will depend on the number of watch sections in the individual unit.

Figure 10-2. Department organization.

Organizational Authority and Directives

Organizational Authority. *Navy Regulations* Arts. 0812 and 0829 are the source of authority for officers and petty officers. Exact limits and kinds of authority stem from guidance promulgated by ship, department, division, and other manuals and regulations accompanying the corresponding organization.

Organizational Directives. The basic directive for the organization of ships of the Navy is in *Navy Regulations.* Art. 0704 states that all commands are to be organized and administered in accordance with law (as set forth in *Navy Regulations*) and with the orders of competent authority, and that all orders and instructions of the CO are to adhere to these directives.

Art. 0725 states that a ship should never be left without an organized force that will be effective in an emergency and capable of ensuring satisfactory operation.

The next echelon of directive is *SORN*. This volume is inclusive, covering shipboard organization in detail. The development of each area is so complete that various sections can be adopted verbatim by most ships. The directives of italicized sections must be followed exactly; others may be modified by those in the chain of command.

The authority on organization is the type commander. Many type commanders promulgate a standard organization and regulations manual for each type of ship under their command. Some type commanders use *SORN* as the basic organization and issue modifying addenda at the back of the book. Others have written completely new organization manuals, but in all cases each organizational directive must conform with *SORN*.

Finally there is the ship's own organization. It must conform with the directives of *SORN* and the type commander's variation on those directives.

A newly commissioned ship has her own organizational directive, regulations, and standing orders; battle bill including a condition watch system; watch, quarter, and station bill; administrative, operational, and emergency bills; safety program; training program; and the necessary boards and committees. The *SORN* includes fifty bills and twenty-eight committees, but your ship will not need all of them.

Organization for Battle

A combat ship was built to fight, and a ship's allowance of officers and men is tailored to that task. Any man who does not have a place in the battle organization does not meet the ship's needs. A man's position in the battle organization should be a source of pride to him, and he should be honored for the qualifications required of him in such an important station. Many a ship's cook or barber has become a gun or mount captain or a key man in a missile-loading system.

Battle Bill. The chief directive for the formulation of a battle bill is NWIP 50-1, *Battle Control.* This confidential publication describes shipboard battle organization and conditions of readiness and is a guide for developing a ship's battle bill and battle organization manuals. It is supplemented by a type commander's standard battle bill for each type. Both bills will need to be adjusted to the individual ship because of the rapid changes in equipment and weaponry.

The battle bill, then, assigns men to stations according to the qualifications they possess or achieve and the requirements of the various weapons, equipment, and machinery of the ship. When possible, divisions or parts of divisions are assigned to station units as a group; the first division may be assigned, for example, to mount 51. This enables the feeling of working together on a daily basis to be carried over to the battle station.

Condition watch teams are formed from the battle organization (condition I). They provide for the manning of selected ship-control, communication, weapon, and engineering stations. A few "idlers," or nonwatchstanders, are left over to man commissary stations, key administrative jobs, and such supportive billets.

When war begins, there is a tendency for a ship to remain at general quarters for prolonged periods. As the novelty of war wears off, members of the crew discover that they need rest and food, that the ship still has to keep functioning, and that ship and personal cleanliness are required. Theoretically condition IE allows for some of this, but a well-prepared crew can shift down to condition II or III and still resume full readiness very quickly.

Ship Manning Document. A new manning system for some classes of ships is given in the Ship Manning Document (SMD). Tasks are related to the man-hours required by the 3M system.

Each ship under the SMD system is manned in accordance with the resulting SMD for that class. The system assumes four manpower requirements for a ship. They are as follows: operational manning, which includes personnel required for condition watchstanding and battle; maintenance, including preventive, corrective, and ship's force overhaul; the miscellaneous functions of administration and support; and utility tasks and evolution manning. The basic publication describing the SMD is *Guide to the Preparation of Ship Documents* (OPNAV 10 p-23).

Condition Watch Organization

Conditions of readiness are:

Condition I	General quarters
Condition II	Large ships only; halfway between general quarters and condition IV
Condition III	Wartime cruising with approximately one third of the crew on watch; armament manned to match threat
Condition IV	Normal peacetime cruising
Condition V	Peacetime watch in port; enough personnel on board to man emergency bills and to get ship under way
Condition VI	Variation of condition V
Condition IAA	Variation of condition I to meet AA threat
Condition IAS	Variation of condition I to meet ASW threat
Condition IE	Temporary relaxation of condition I to provide for rest and messing
Condition IM	Variation of condition I to take precautions against mines

Condition watches soon become very old. After eight hours of daily watch, not much of a person's productive time or inclination is left over for ship's work. Many ships allow some to sleep on station (depending on the station) or to work in the vicinity.

Administrative Organization

While the primary organization of a ship is its battle organization, it remains a fact that 95 percent of ship's time, even in war, is spent on administrative matters. Administration requires an organization of its own, known as the ship's organization plan. Chapters 2 and 3 of *SORN* describe in great detail the form of the standard organization of any ship. As has been pointed out, your ship will already have one when you report, or you will participate in the formulation of one if you help to commission a new ship. The exact organization will include the functions, duties, responsibilities, and authority of each officer and petty officer.

The normal progression of organization and authority (the chain of command) is from the CO, through the executive officer, heads of departments, division officers, and down to the section leaders and nonrated men and women.

Heads of Departments. In addition to the specific duties and responsibilities assigned to a head of department by virtue of his or her billet, each head of department has certain general duties. The head of department is a representative of the CO in all matters pertaining to the department and must conform to the policies and orders of the CO. All persons in the department are subordinate to its head. The head of department may confer directly with the CO concerning any matters relating to the department whenever he or she believes such action to be for the good of the department or the naval service. This right should be used sparingly, and in any event, the executive officer should be informed of such actions as soon as possible. The head of department should keep the CO informed about the general condition of the machinery and equipment of the department and particularly of any adverse condition affecting safety or operations. Machinery or equipment should not be disabled without the permission of the CO. The specific responsibilities of each head of department are listed in *SORN*.

Division Officers. Officers are assigned to command major divisions of each department. *SORN* lists specific duties of the division officer, who is assigned by junior division officers, enlisted section leaders, and other leading petty officers. The division officer is the final officer link between the CO and the enlisted personnel. The division officer's performance of duty is important because enlisted crew will react very strongly—either positively or negatively—to the officer's leadership. *The Division Officer's Guide* is an excellent handbook for division officers and describes their duties in great detail.

Boards and Committees. Many organizational functions lend themselves to administration by boards and committees.

One of many boards meets in the wardroom of a small ship.

SORN Art. 304 describes the composition and purpose of many such boards and committees. A board or committee is a group of persons organized under a president, chairman, or senior member to evaluate problems and make recommendations to proper authority for their solution. Boards and committees are generally policy-recommending groups; however, some have executive functions. Membership can include officers, petty officers, and nonrated men. On some boards technical expertise is required.

Watch Organization

SORN, chapter 4, covers in great detail the watch organization of ships in general, both in port and under way. Condition watches have already been described earlier in this chapter.

Development of a Watch Organization. The standard, required watch organizations are given in *SORN*. Eliminate those functions that do not apply to your ship. Written material will then have to be produced and included in the organization book to delineate the responsibilities of each watchstander. A corresponding system will have to be established for the qualification of personnel to meet these requirements.

Establishment of Watches. Once the organization is com-

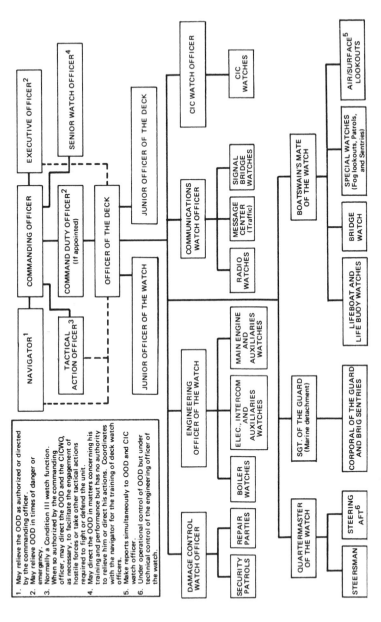

Figure 10-3. Watch organization under way.

1. May relieve the OOD as authorized or directed by the commanding officer.
2. May relieve OOD in times of danger or emergency.
3. Normally a Condition III watch function. When so authorized by the commanding officer, may direct the OOD and the CICWO, as necessary, to facilitate the engagement of hostile forces or take other tactical actions required to fight or defend the unit.
4. May direct the OOD in matters concerning his training and performance but has no authority to relieve him or direct his actions. Coordinates with the navigator for the training of deck watch officers.
5. Make reports simultaneously to OOD and CIC watch officer.
6. Under operational control of OOD but under technical control of the engineering officer of the watch.

plete, its requirements codified and published, and a system of qualifying watchstanders in place, the system is ready to be implemented. *SORN* requires the establishment of watches necessary for the safety and operation of the command. *SORN* also requires that the watches of the OOD and the engineering officer of the watch be continuous. Any officer of the command may stand any watch for which he is considered qualified. Marine officers below the grade of major may stand OOD watches in port and junior officer-of-the-deck (JOOD) watches at sea. In small ships, and in case of hardship, petty officers and noncommissioned officers may be used.

Watchstanders. The general duties of watchstanders are set forth in *SORN* Art. 410. The following articles cover orders to sentries, watchstanding principles, control of weapons firing by members of the watch, length of watches, performance of watch duty, setting the watch, relieving the watch, and special watches. These and subsequent articles give all the guidance necessary for manning a watch organization. For handy reference, the *Watch Officer's Guide* will be all your watchstanders will need.

Logs. The two main logs to be kept are the deck log and the engineering log. Other important records are the magnetic compass record, the quartermaster's log, the bearing book, the engineer's bell book, and the CIC log.

Unit Bills

A unit bill sets forth policy and directions for assigning personnel to duties or stations for specific purposes or functions. *SORN* requires that a bill have a preface stating its purpose, assigning responsibility for maintenance of the bill, and giving background information. A bill should also set forth a procedure to interpret the responsibilities of each person with regard to the functions discussed in the bill.

Chapter 6 of *SORN* contains bills for every conceivable type of ship for every possible contingency or evolution. They are intended to be a guide for type commanders and COs. Bills are of three general kinds: administrative, operational, and emergency.

Watch, Quarter, and Station Bill

The watch, quarter, and station bill is the division officer's summary of the allocation of personnel to duties and assignments

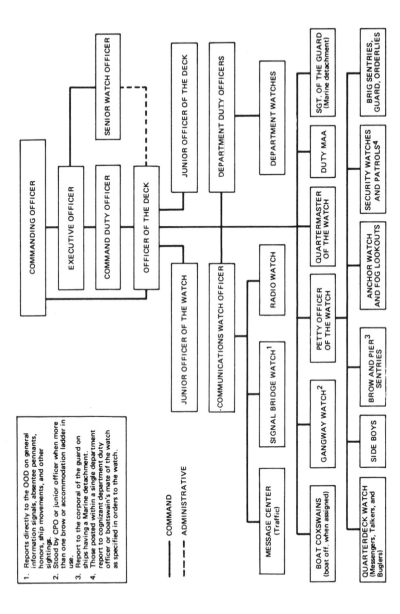

Figure 10-4. Watch organization in port.

1. Reports directly to the OOD on general information signals, absentee pennants, honors, ship movements, and other sightings.
2. Stood by CPO or junior officer when more than one brow or accommodation ladder in use.
3. Report to the corporal of the guard on ships having a Marine detachment.
4. Those posted within a single department report to cognizant department duty officer or boatswain's mate of the watch as specified in orders to the watch.

—— COMMAND
- - - ADMINISTRATIVE

for each of the bills in use. As its title states, it lists the watches, berthing assignments, and bill assignments for each officer and enlisted person. The working document for the division officer, it should receive his or her best efforts. It should be kept up-to-date, be neatly written, and be posted for ready reference by all personnel. A standard tabular form is used, which can be obtained from the Navy supply system. Division officers should adjust the watch, quarter, and station bill daily for personnel on leave, returning from leave, transferring in or out of the division, or sick or otherwise disabled for an extended period of time.

Ship's Regulations

Ship's regulations are an integral part of every ship's organization. Chapter 5 of *SORN* contains a set of typical regulations. Those in your ship may vary somewhat. It is important for a ship to have a good set of regulations giving guidance to all persons in matters that are not important enough to be included in *Navy Regulations.* They must be duly approved and posted.

Chief of the Boat/Command Chief Petty Officer

The idea of choosing and assigning a chief of the boat is not covered in *SORN*, although it is set forth in the submarine type commander's addenda. A chief of the boat has been used by submarine COs with good results for many years. Some small surface ships have also used it. The master chief petty officer of the Navy and the command chief petty officer are outgrowths of the position of chief of the boat.

The chief of the boat, or the command chief petty officer, is that person chosen by the CO as being the outstanding CPO assigned to that ship or submarine. In most instances this billet is filled by NAVMILPERSCOM. He has authority over all enlisted persons. In submarines he serves as chief master at arms in addition to his other duties. He is a vital link between the CO and enlisted personnel.

Organization Communications

No organization can function unless the will of the commander is known to those who carry it out. Also, information must come up the chain of command if the commander is to make sound decisions and communicate them back down the chain.

Methods of Communication. Every ship has several methods and systems of communication. The oldest and most reliable systems are writing and speaking. Normally these are used to indoctrinate the crew so that the policies of the CO are properly inculcated prior to battle, action, or emergency. They may be used in battle or emergency when other, more complicated methods break down. Many severely damaged ships have been steered by voice orders passed through a series of men posted along the deck, and many orders have been sent in written form to isolated areas.

In normal conditions, all ships are equipped with several additional systems that serve specialized functions, such as ship control. They depend upon electrical power and are degraded by the noise of battle. One is the intercommunications voice (MC) system linking major areas with multistation transmitter-receivers. This ensures receipt of messages as long as someone is present in the area and can approach the transmitter-receiver. Other MC systems, such as the IMC, are one-way systems that announce orders or information to various areas or to the entire ship. This system is also degraded by battle noise, needs electrical power, and has no way of ensuring the receipt of orders.

Many large ships have a ship's service telephone system linking stations throughout the ship. Theoretically this is an administrative system, but it can be used operationally when other systems are out.

In battle and in emergencies the most reliable system is the sound-powered telephone system. It does not need electrical power for its operation and can thus be used under all conditions. Its parts are more rugged and less liable to casualty. Headphone systems give it some protection against battle noise. Several individual circuits are installed depending upon the function to be served by the circuit. It is possible to cross-connect the circuits. This system is usually manned for battle, condition watches, and other evolutions where reliable communications are required. The great advantage of the system is that talkers provide instant monitoring and answering; the disadvantage is that the system is no better than its talkers. This requires continuous talker training.

Other communication systems are the general alarm, chemical alarm, collision alarm, and boat gongs. They are simple alarms whose sound, of distinctive character, can be initiated by special switches located on the quarterdeck and bridge and carried throughout the ship. The special alarms give instant notice of the threat they are designed to warn about. Boat gongs are used to announce boat departures and to warn of the approach of boats conveying distinguished officials.

II

STAFF ORGANIZATION AND FUNCTIONS

NO MILITARY OR NAVAL FORCE, IN WAR, CAN
ACCOMPLISH ANYTHING WORTHWHILE UNLESS THERE IS
BACK OF IT THE WORK OF AN EFFICIENT, LOYAL, AND
DEVOTED STAFF.

—*Lieutenant General Hunter Liggett*

AND SO, WHILE THE GREAT ONES DEPART TO
THEIR DINNER,
THE SECRETARIAT WORKS—AND GETS THINNER
AND THINNER.

—British military jingle

Staffs are absolutely essential for the smooth functioning of a military organization. No commander, however versatile and intelligent, can hope to gather and collate all of the intelligence available, make a reasoned and correct decision, organize his personnel and forces, and then issue detailed orders for the execution of his decision. The organization necessary to assist the commander in doing all these things is called a staff. Staffs vary from the five officers and dozen men working for a destroyer squadron commander to the vast assemblage of officers and enlisted persons assisting the chairman of the JCS.

General Staff Functions

A staff exists for one purpose: to assist the commander in carrying out the functions of command for which he is responsible. These include operational functions and supporting functions. Operational functions are the missions assigned to the command: decision-making, evaluating intelligence, formulating plans for executing missions, and providing the means by which command can be exercised. Supporting functions provide for the personnel's physical and mental welfare, for their morale and training, and for the supply and allocation of personnel, bases, and fighting equipment.

The magnitude of these functions will vary with the command's type and size. For instance, an administrative or type commander is concerned mainly with support to the fleet as a whole—personnel administration, basic type training, and initial conditioning of ships and aircraft. These support tasks then form the basis for operational functions. An operational or tactical commander is more directly concerned with purely operational functions: overall training for combat, and planning, supervising, and evaluating the execution of combat operations. Regardless of the size and type of an organization, however, basic functions are common to all commands.

If a staff is to furnish maximum assistance to the commander, it must be organized to function effectively. Efficient staff work, no less than effective management, depends upon sound organization. For this reason, much emphasis is placed on the formulation of a basic plan for dividing the work of the staff, for assigning personnel to positions on the staff, and for delegating authority and assigning duties within the staff.

Liaison with Other Commands. The following discussion of duties applies to those serving on all types of staffs.

Coordinated teamwork is the essence not only of successful military operations but of efficient staff functioning as well. The operations of a naval task force or battle group, often involving all the elements of the armed forces of the United States and of allied powers, require extensive liaison between members of the staff and commanders and staff members of other armed services. Liaison must be conducted in a courteous and cooperative manner, so as to reflect credit, not only on the Navy in general, but on your command in particular. In conducting such liaison, the commander must be kept fully informed. Tentative agreements reached on lower staff levels do not constitute decisions binding upon commanders. Tentative agreements must be presented to the commanders for approval or revision before becoming effective. The vast scope of naval and joint operations, particularly of amphibious warfare, and the complex interrelation of forces and types make this procedure essential.

Completed Staff Work. Occasionally a staff officer feels that, when a problem has been presented in general terms and a solution has been recommended to the chief, full duty has been performed. It is the duty of all staff officers to present to the chief in adequate detail the facts and figures on which he or she can base decisions and implement them. A recommended action should accompany this information, and it should be assembled in such a fashion that the chief may indicate approval or disapproval. This is completed staff work. Do not ask your boss what he or she wants or what is to be done. Put yourself in the commander's place, analyze what you think he or she needs, and then provide it. Make sure you have touched base with the other members of the staff who share responsibility in areas of the paper you are working on; then indicate this fact on your paper. If possible, avoid giving a rough draft to your chief. Deliver a letter or plan in final form so that he or she may sign it. You may have to type it over, but that is better than handing over a rough draft. As a final test, ask yourself if you would sign it. If not, you have not done "completed staff work."

In another area of staff work the word *no* has a positive function. It is your duty as a staff officer to make sure that both sides of every problem are presented and considered. If, in doing so, you feel that the commander's decision is wrong, you have an obligation to say so. As Major General Orland Ward, USA, said in 1934, "A yes man on a staff is a menace to a commander. One with the courage to express his convictions is an asset."

You will be chosen for duty on a staff because you have proved that you "know your business." Other considerations may play into the decision, such as that voiced by Napoleon when he said, "When I want good headwork done, I always choose a man, if otherwise suitable, with a long nose." Don't worry if your nose is short, for you will be chosen if you are worthy.

Naval Staff Organization

Organization. The basic organization of an operational navy staff is shown in figure 11-1. It adheres to the principles of unity of command and span of control. The functions of command should be assigned homogeneously to each of the five divisions.

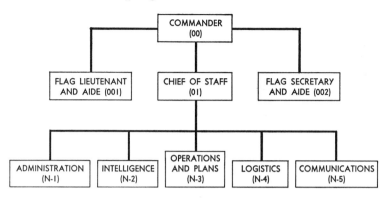

Figure 11-1. Organization of a typical naval operational staff.

Before considering in detail the assignment of functions and duties to staff divisions, certain characteristics of the organization plan should be stressed. The fact that the five divisions shown in figure 11-1 are on the same level has no significance as far as the rank of a division head is concerned. The chain of staff authority extends from the commander to the chief of staff and on down through each division, but it does not cross from one division to another. A division head may be designated by the chief of staff to coordinate staff work on some particular project.

It should be noted that the divisions are numbered N-1 through N-5. If a sixth division is required, it is numbered N-6. The first four divisions of this typical Navy staff resemble the Army's and Marine Corps' G-1, G-2, G-3, and G-4, S-1, S-2, S-3, and S-4, and the Air Force's A-1, A-2, A-3, and A-4 divisions. In those services, the four staff sections represent a division of the command functions or duties that a commander must perform, as follows: 1-personnel, 2-intelligence, 3-operations and plans, and 4-logistics. Structures for Army and Marine Corps staffs at the various echelons of command are generally fixed. An Air Force commander has more freedom in organizing his staff, because the Air Force, like the Navy, must mold its task organization for particular situations, and the staff must meet the requirements of the command.

In the Navy, every function of command, except decision-making, is assigned to a staff division. Decision-making, as mentioned previously, must be performed by the commander himself. The Navy does not have a special staff group (with a signal officer, engineer officer, etc.) as the command organizations of other services do. In the Navy, all officers—line, staff corps, or specialist—are fully integrated into the five divisions. Specialist officers may have direct access to the commander and to the chief of staff because of the nature of their particular duties, and the commander will often seek specific information from them directly. Nevertheless, they are under their respective heads for administrative purposes, and their estimates and plans are included in the division estimates and plans. The special staff officers in command organizations of services other than the Navy provide technical and special advice and assistance to the commander and the general staff (or coordinating or executive) divisions. They may also command subordinate units in the commander's organization.

The question often arises as to why communications (N-5) is given divisional status in the Navy. Rapid communications (electronic transmissions, flashing lights, and signal flags, rather than correspondence or hand-carried messages) play a vital role in every naval operation. Actually, they are the means by which command is exercised and should be considered a major function of command. A communications division does more than send and receive messages; it is responsible for other functions, which require direct access to the chief of staff and which affect all other divisions of the staff, including subordinate commanders. The head of the communications division must cooperate with other staff divisions in meeting their communications requirements and in coordinating staff planning for communications.

Naval Staff Functions

Duties of Staff Members. In this discussion, we will be referring to a combatant staff. Hence, all of the members are men. If the staff is a noncombatant one, any of the members can be women.

The chief of staff (or chief staff officer to a nonflag officer) is the senior officer of the staff. It is his responsibility to keep the admiral informed of the condition and situation of command, of subordinate commands, and of other commands in the theater of operations; and to advise the admiral on administrative matters, to supervise administrative work, and to coordinate staff activities.

The commander of the Sixth Fleet meets with his commanders and staff.

With regard to correspondence, the chief of staff signs routine papers, except for those concerning policy, action on legal papers, leave requests of flag officers, or approval of a previous recommendation or action of a flag officer. All such correspondence is signed by the admiral. The chief of staff signs papers concerning matters on which the policy of the admiral is known, action on requests for repairs and alterations, endorsements forwarding letters from higher authority quoted for compliance or guidance, and orders to all officers except flag officers.

The flag secretary is another personal aide who, on many staffs, acts as assistant chief of staff for administration. He is responsible for intrastaff administration and receives dispatches, maintains records, routes, and files, and assumes responsibility for the control and security of all official correspondence. He authenticates and distributes copies of plans, orders, and multiple-address correspondence; is responsible for the correct form of correspondence originated by the staff and for the expeditious handling of correspondence requiring action; and is top secret control officer. He arranges for the handling of U.S. and guard mail, administers the flag office, supervises the flag division of-

NAVAL OFFICER'S GUIDE

ficer's performance, and deals with matters pertaining to printing. He is also responsible for preparing the war diary, keeping a chronology of events during war and peacetime exercises, preparing fitness reports for the admiral, and assigning staff quarters.

The personal aide (the flag lieutenant) looks out for such matters as salutes, honors, presentation of awards, official calls, uniforms, entertainments, invitations, and liaison to promote cordial relations with local organizations. He is responsible for the admiral's calls and call book. He is the staff boarding officer. He maintains the boarding book, arranges transportation for the admiral, afloat and ashore, and keeps the chief of staff, staff duty officer, OOD of the flagship, and other interested persons advised as to the prospective movements of the admiral.

He tends the side upon the arrival and departure of the admiral, visiting flag and general officers and other important dignitaries. He also acts as flag signal officer. As such he is responsible to the staff communication officer for his communication duties. In most flagships he takes over and is responsible for all visual signaling to and from the flagship and for the performance of all signal personnel, whether assigned to the ship or to the staff.

The administration division (N-1) is under the assistant chief of staff for administration, who is often the flag secretary. In addition to the duties already enumerated for that officer, he is responsible for advising the admiral on the formulation of command administrative policies; for publishing command letters; for compiling a quarterly command administration organization book and staff roster and directory; for compiling all data for reports and other papers concerning enlisted personnel; and for procuring, assigning, paying, promoting, transferring, and replacing all officer and enlisted personnel.

In conjunction with the legal officer, he supervises rewards and punishments and oversees the individual training of enlisted personnel for advancement in rating. He prepares for, and reviews reports on, administrative inspections and writes the quarterly command summary.

The assistant chief of staff for intelligence heads the intelligence division (N-2). This division is responsible for the formulation and implementation of policies pertaining to combat intelligence, counterintelligence, propaganda, psychological warfare, and public information.

The intelligence officer also keeps the admiral and staff informed as to the capabilities of present and potential enemies by the collection, evaluation, interpretation, and dissemination of information regarding the enemy, hydrography, terrain, and weather. Through liaison with subordinate, parallel, and higher commands, and by use of all existing sources of intelligence, including aviation, satellite, and submarine visual and photographic reconnaissance, he strives to keep his intelligence of an actual or potential enemy current and accurate.

He supervises counterintelligence, propaganda, counterpropaganda, and psychological warfare. He prepares strategic estimates, intelligence studies of prospective operating areas, and the intelligence annex of all operation orders and plans. He keeps the intelligence journal and maintains situation maps during combat operations or training exercises. He supervises the photolab, photo interpretation, and cartographic work. He processes information obtained from prisoners of war and from the examination of captured documents. He supervises the training of intelligence personnel.

The assistant chief of staff for operations heads the operations division (N-3). This is the primary executive element of the staff, charged with those functions that relate to organization and command: training, planning, preparing, and issuing directives for combat operations and training exercises; executing such operations and exercises; and correlating reports pertaining to them. The operations officer has specific responsibility for making a continuous study of the existing situation and for preparing tentative plans for the admiral's consideration. He must also prepare operation plans and orders, including the annexes dealing with task organization, general concept, movement plan, the attack or order-of-combat plan, and protective measures for the force at the objective. He supervises and coordinates the preparation of other annexes.

The operations officer prepares the command employment schedule, issues the necessary movement orders, and keeps track of the location and movement of ships and units of the command. He advises the admiral about organization and command and about assigning ships, air groups, and other elements of the armed services to task groups for specific tasks. He is responsible for readiness inspections and for the review of inspection reports.

All matters relating to the training of individuals, ships, units, and special task organizations, including, in amphibious commands, all aspects of the ship-to-shore movement, come to the operations officer's attention.

The assistant chief of staff for logistics heads the logistics division (N-4), which is responsible for advising the admiral on all matters relating to logistics, maintenance, and material. Essential to strategy and the execution of operations, too often ignored in wars before World War I, logistics was finally recognized as important in World War II, from the local all the way to the worldwide arena. Since World War II logistics has been emphasized in all planning.

The assistant chief of staff for logistics prepares studies for proposed operations and the logistics annex for all operational orders and plans. He must maintain full liaison with subordinate, parallel, and senior commands with respect to material, repair, supply, and service of all forces assigned to the command. He conducts, supervises, and reports on engineering competitions and training and material inspections. In consultation with the operations officer, he recommends alterations to ships and craft and improved characteristics for new design.

The assistant chief of staff for communications heads the communications division (N-5), responsible for providing adequate rapid communications within the command and with other commands; for the custody and supervision of publications distributed through the registered publication system; and for communication security, communication discipline, communication/intelligence, electronic communication material requirements, and postal matters. The communications division may operate a staff message center or crypto-center, or it may take over the flagship centers.

Other officers, formerly members of the special staff, are now assigned to one of the five divisions. The legal officer, medical officer, and chaplain all are usually assigned to the administration division, although on some amphibious staffs, the medical officer is in the logistics division.

Small staffs combine duties and sections and may have relatively few officers and men. Nevertheless, the duties such staffs must perform are not as overwhelming as they may sound upon first reading a description of them. If tasks for a small staff arise at all, they do not usually do so simultaneously.

Staff Duty Officers. Certain line officers of the staff are designated by the chief of staff to take turns being staff duty officer on watch at sea and to perform a day's duty in port. Specific authority to exchange duty must be obtained from the chief of staff.

In port, the staff duty officer receives routine reports and acts on routine matters as necessary in the absence of staff officers. He regulates the use of staff boats and tends the side on all occasions of ceremony or when officers of command or flag rank are visiting. He sees all dispatches, initials them, and takes action if the proper officer is not aboard. In the absence of the flag secretary, he examines mail received and decides what action is to be taken. Upon the return of any officer for whom he has acted, the staff duty officer must inform that officer of his action.

The duties of the staff duty officer assume special importance when, in the absence of the admiral, chief of staff, or other staff officer, he is called upon to make decisions in an emergency or on matters that cannot be delayed. For this reason, it is imperative that officers on duty keep informed as to the status quo, the policies of the admiral, and the manner of taking action on various matters. In port, in an emergency, and in the absence of the admiral and chief of staff, he must be ready to refer the situation to the senior CO present in his unit.

When the ship is under way, the staff duty officer is on the bridge at all times during his watch. He represents the admiral in much the same way that the OOD represents the captain of a ship. He must inform himself of the formation and location of ships and units, of land and lights to be sighted, and of any other significant particular.

In an emergency, or in the absence of the admiral or chief of staff, he makes the required signals, reporting his action immediately to the admiral, chief of staff, and operations officer.

He makes reports to the admiral and chief of staff about the safe navigation of the formation, the flagship's position, and the hazards and aids to navigation. He keeps the staff log, which is submitted daily to the staff navigator.

The staff duty officer, when the ship is under way, must have in his grasp all necessary information with which to maneuver and fight the unit.

Relationships between Staff and Flagship Personnel

If you are serving in a flagship or on the staff of an embarked commander, you will be involved daily in relationships between the people of the staff and the flagship. These are discussed in detail in *SORN*, Arts. 370–75. You should refer to them for exact information. The following information will guide you in your day-to-day relationships.

Relationship between Flag and Flagship Officers.   Officers serving in a flagship must recognize and consider at all times the dual role played by a flagship. The CO is at all times responsible for the safety of his ship and for her individual performance, but he and his ship are answerable to the embarked commander. While under way the flagship maneuvers in obedience to signals from the officer in tactical command (OTC). When the embarked commander is OTC, he may orally direct the flagship to maneuver, in which case the flagship must notify other ships of her movements or of any independent maneuvers.

The embarked commander takes over responsibility for the operation of all communications of the flagship, absorbing into his organization the members of the flagship communication unit. This unit is then responsible to the flagship for all her communication needs. As a ship's officer you must remember these limitations and added responsibilities of your ship.

Staff Officers' Responsibilities.   Staff officers embarked in a ship must always be careful to respect the flagship's unity of command. Requests to the ship in the name of the admiral should always be made directly to the captain or executive officer and should be prefaced, "The admiral desires that you. . . ."

All officers and enlisted personnel who serve in a ship, with the exception of the flag officer or unit commander, are subject to the authority of the CO and to his discipline and punishment. The staff officer should remember that he has no authority of his own, and that all of his authority comes from the admiral. Not uncommonly, pleasant relationships between staff and flagship have been jeopardized by the thoughtless action of some junior staff officer or by the antagonistic attitude of a senior officer toward junior officers. The following notes may help you to avoid some such pitfalls.

Leave and liberty for men assigned to duty with the flag must conform as closely as possible with that of the flagship. The flag division officer must be zealous in regard to routine personnel reports, individual requests, liberty lists, disciplinary matters, uniform, and presence at quarters.

Marines are assigned to the flag muster with the flagship

Marine detachment and are administered and trained by the CO of the Marine detachment.

Flag watch, quarter, and station bills should be kept up-to-date. Flag CPOs and petty officers should be given time to perform their divisional duties.

Flag personnel, unless excused by proper authority, should observe calls to general drills promptly.

Staff compartments, lockers, bedding, and messing areas should be kept in a condition on a par with or better than that of similar ship facilities.

The flag lieutenant is in charge of staff boats, boat crews, drivers, automobiles, and members of the flag mess. The flagship is responsible for the maintenance and upkeep of all flag boats and automobiles and the observance of all safety precautions.

The captain is responsible for the station-keeping of the flagship. As staff duty officer, do not heckle the flagship unless you are directed to do so by the admiral or chief of staff.

When the admiral has retired, all reports are given to the staff duty officer, who decides which reports warrant the admiral's attention.

In an underway ship, the admiral's night order book is shown to the flagship CO for his information and initialing.

Always be considerate of the officers and enlisted personnel of the flagship.

Staff Organization and Functions

The young naval officer will rarely have an opportunity to serve on other than a naval staff. However, he or she may have occasion to deal with higher echelon staffs, and for this reason should be familiar with their nomenclature and purposes. In later years a more thorough knowledge of the organization and functions of joint, combined, and allied staffs will be necessary, especially with the passage of the Goldwater-Nichols Act. This legislation requires that virtually all aspirants to flag rank possess joint staff experience. Since most such staffs are shore-based, women officers will have a good opportunity to serve on them.

Joint Staff. A joint staff is one assigned to the commander of a joint command. A joint command is made up of forces from more than one U.S. service. The commander may belong to any U.S. service, and his staff generally includes officers from all services furnishing components of his command. A joint staff is usually organized along the lines of the naval staff, except that additional staff divisions are sometimes added and the plans division is sometimes separate. The letter *J* precedes the number designations. A joint staff is shown in figure 11-2.

Combined or Allied Staff. A combined staff is the staff assigned to a combined commander. It is also referred to as an allied staff. A combined commander may be an officer in the service of any country or group of allies. The NATO complex has many such staffs and commands. A typical combined staff organization is illustrated in figure 11-3.

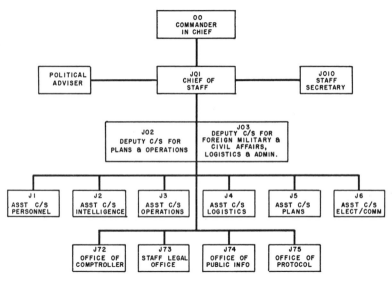

Figure 11-2. Typical joint staff organization.

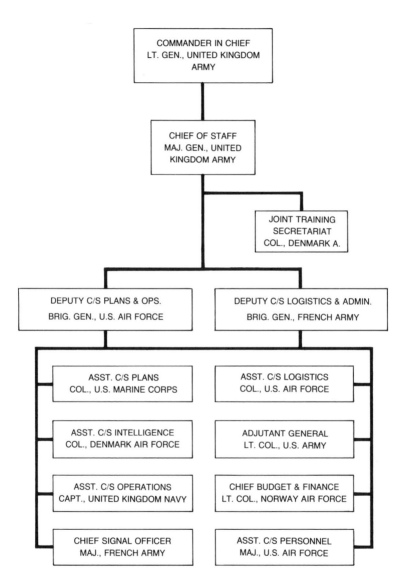

Figure 11-3. Typical combined (allied) staff organization.

12

THE OPERATING FORCES OF THE NAVY

NOT ONLY ON THE DEEP SEA, THE BROAD BAY, AND THE
RAPID RIVER, BUT ALSO UP THE NARROW MUDDY
BAYOU, AND WHEREVER THE GROUND WAS A LITTLE
DAMP, THEY HAVE BEEN AND MADE THEIR TRACKS.

—*Abraham Lincoln,* letter

THE NAVY EXISTS TO OPERATE FORCES OVER, UNDER
AND IN THE SEA. SOME ARE CHOSEN TO COMMAND
THESE FORCES; THEY ARE OUR CUTTING EDGE. SOME
REMAIN TO SUPPORT THAT EDGE; THEY ARE THE HILT
OF THAT INSTRUMENT. BOTH ENDS OF A SWORD ARE
NECESSARY IF IT IS TO DO ITS BUSINESS.

—*Secretary of the Navy John Connally*

The operating forces of the Navy comprise the several fleets, shore-based long-range air forces, strategic submarine forces, fleet marine forces (FMF) and other assigned marine forces, the Military Sea Transportation Service, and shore activities of the Navy assigned by the president or the secretary of the Navy.

Command of the operating forces is assigned to the CNO, subject to the authority vested in the president by the Constitution and the secretaries of defense and Navy by law. The CNO is responsible for executing the directives of the National Command Authorities (NCA), the chairman of the Joint Chiefs of Staff, and the Joint Chiefs as a collective body insofar as they affect the Navy. Nevertheless, for those forces assigned to unified and specified commands, command goes from the commander in chief through the chairman of the JCS, and to the unified and specified commanders.

Task Force/Battle Force Organization

Ships and units of the operating forces are organized under three different systems. First, the majority of forces are assigned to type commanders for administrative control and for operational control during primary and intermediate training phases. Second, these same forces are later assigned to numbered fleet commanders for advanced training and operations. Third, some elements of these forces are further assigned to task force or battle force organizations for specific operations and missions, including assignment to unified commands.

Type Organizations. The first system of organization an officer will come into contact with is the type organization. All ships are organized into broad categories under commanders whose titles are self-explanatory, such as surface, air, and sub-

The aircraft carrier, with her embarked air wing, is the heart of the battle group and the fleets.

Guided-missile cruisers are integral parts of battle groups and can also operate independently.

SSBNs make up the Navy's strategic submarine forces.

Marine Corps amphibious troops provide the offensive punch for the FMF.

marine. Each type command contains further administrative subdivisions. Normal administration is carried on by this organization, and a ship or unit is always under the administrative control of its type commander, even though it is also under the operational control of a numbered fleet, task force, or battle force commander. Normally a ship or unit remains under the operational control of its type commander during primary and intermediate training; upon completion of the training cycle it is shifted to the operational control of a numbered fleet commander.

Fleet Organization. There are four regularly constituted, numbered fleets, the Third and Seventh Fleets in the Pacific under the Commander in Chief, Pacific Fleet (CinCPACFLT), and the Second and Sixth Fleets in the Atlantic under the Commander in Chief, Atlantic Fleet (CinCLANTFLT). Under normal peacetime conditions, the Third Fleet exercises control over all forces on the Pacific Coast and in the Hawaiian area, and the Seventh Fleet exercises control over forces in the Far East and Indian Ocean. Similarly, the Second Fleet commands forces in the Atlantic and the Sixth Fleet exercises operational control over forces in the Mediterranean.

A small force of ships, varying in size with the regional situation, is based in the Persian Gulf at Bahrain. This force, the Middle East Force (MIDEASTFOR) is provided by the Atlantic and Pacific fleets and is under the operational command of the

U.S. Central Command. Since 1987, Commander Joint Task Force Middle East (CJTFME) has been the commander of this force, which operates in the Persian Gulf and the Gulf of Oman. Primary responsibility for operations elsewhere in the Indian Ocean rests with the Seventh Fleet.

Task Force and Battle Force Organizations.   The numbered fleet commanders are not given structured, tactical commands. In order to provide flexibility of command and ease of communication, the task force organization (more properly the task fleet organization) was formed during World War II. In order to meet the varied military requirements of vast areas, the fleets are now further divided into forces, groups, units, and elements. Each subdivision has a numbered designator and communication call signs. Depending upon the type and scope of the operation, the force will be assigned a task force or battle force designation under the operational control of the numbered fleet commander. By definition a battle force consists of assigned ships and at least one aircraft carrier. Normal operations are conducted by the task force organization. The task or battle force commander reassigns the forces assigned to him to appropriate subdivisions of the organization, which gives him a flexible, battle-ready organization. Both the task force and battle force organizations are adaptable to any magnitude of organization.

In a typical task-fleet numbering system, the commander of the Sixth Fleet, for example, would assign his major forces to numbered forces, such as striking forces to Task Force (TF) 61, the amphibious forces to TF 62, and the service forces to TF 63. Within each force he would assign logical subdivisions to task groups; for example, within Task Group (TG) 61 would be TG 61.1, Carrier Group, and TG 61.2, Heavy Support Group. Within each task group, further subdivision produces task units. Task Group 61.1, Carrier Group, would be subdivided into TU 61.1.1, Carrier Unit, and so forth.

Each task unit may be divided into task elements. In this case, Task Unit (TU) 61.1.2, Screen Unit, would become Task Element (TE) 61.1.21, Advanced Screen Element. Note that elements are formed by adding a second number to the unit number without adding a decimal.

The chain of command can be determined at a glance. Changes, additions, and deletions can be made easily by dispatch. Battle forces are designated as part of the numbered fleet, such as Battle Force, Seventh Fleet. It is further divided alphabetically to the group level and numbered in the same manner as the group using a TG 60.X or TG 70.X designator.

Allied Organizations. The United States is a member of the United Nations and is signatory to numerous pacts and agreements. Many of our agreements commit us to the use of force in the event of attack on us or our allies. Under some agreements we have committed ourselves to provide components of armed forces in advance of armed attack.

Frequently we exercise as part of an allied organization under NATO. A description of the NATO organization and chain of command is given in the chapter on overseas organizations. Tactical maneuvering under the NATO command system is accomplished by using the allied tactical publications (ATP) and communications systems. All officers must be familiar with these publications.

Employment

Employment Schedules. Earlier we reviewed the several organizational systems through which the CNO exercises command. Obviously it is not possible for the CNO to direct the movements of several hundred units on a daily basis. He therefore delegates authority to subordinate commanders to direct necessary movements. He issues an overall employment plan listing the major exercises, deployments, and other commitments expected. In implementing this schedule, he issues a fleet operating policy that gives general guidelines for subordinate commanders, and he determines an overhaul schedule.

With the foregoing information in hand, fleet commanders are able to draw up annual employment schedules listing major categories of assignments to ships of their fleets. Quarterly schedules are customarily issued incorporating the latest known changes and additional details. Type commanders are then able to make their own annual and quarterly employment schedules using those of their superior commanders as guides. The type commander's employment schedule is generally quite detailed, assigning authority to unit commanders and COs to make required movements.

In summary, each descending echelon implements the schedule of the senior echelons so that an overall training schedule is carried out for advanced training; units of the fleet will progress through their stages of training in order to be prepared at the proper time for the proper degree of advanced training. The detailed methods whereby this is accomplished will be discussed later.

Fleet Training Cycles. Ships, submarines, and air squadrons deploy to meet overseas commitments in regular cycles. Periods of deployment are long enough to take advantage of the unit's advanced state of training, but not so long as to put undue hardship on the unit's personnel. This is true for normal peacetime schedules. Unfortunately, crises often require additional forces overseas.

Deployments are scheduled for a maximum of six months, port to port. This may be extended by two to three weeks with the fleet commander's approval and, in the event of an emergency or contingency operation, may be extended one to two months. Any longer extension may interrupt the normal cycle completely. When possible, the cycle is resumed. In peacetime the cycle is based on the unit's overhaul schedule and its projected over a five-year employment schedule.

Normally, upon completion of overhaul, the unit commences refresher training, a period during which new personnel can be shaken down and integrated into the ship's company. This period lasts about six weeks and is followed by a brief maintenance period. The unit then commences a period of intermediate training under its type commander, followed by an advanced training period under a numbered fleet commander, lasting about six or seven months.

Next, the unit is given a brief period (about thirty days) of preparation for overseas movement (POM) and is deployed for six months. After deployment the unit is given a thirty-day leave and upkeep period. This change requires further intermediate and advanced training. During this time the unit also renders some services to other types. Current procedures require scheduling a minimum of twelve months' duty in the continental limits of the United States (CONUS), including maintenance and time in home port between overseas deployments. Next comes another POM period and a second deployment. Upon return, the unit will enter overhaul and then start the cycle all over again. Aviation units usually debark from their parent carriers and conduct training at nearby air bases whenever the carrier is in maintenance for extended periods.

A typical training cycle for a destroyer follows:

Months of Cycle	Employment
0–9	Shipyard overhaul (this may last as long as 18 months depending on the extent of the overhaul)
9–10	Refresher training
11	Post-shakedown availability
12–16	Type training
17	Advanced training
18–24	Transit; deployment; transit
25–26	Post-deployment leave and upkeep
27–33	Intermediate training; services
34–35	Advanced training
36	POM
37–42	Transit; deployment; transit
43–44	Post-deployment leave and upkeep
45–60	Services; type training; preparation for overhaul (a third deployment may be required)

Shipyard Overhauls. Shipyard overhauls are controlled by two factors. First is the ship's need for a regular overhaul. The interval between successive overhauls should be short enough to ensure maintenance of the ship and long enough to ensure that maximum use is made of her capability before expending shipyard funds. The second factor is the economical use of all shipyards and repair facilities. They should be neither overcrowded nor idle. These two factors are reconciled in an annual overhaul schedule published by the CNO. For each type, an overhaul period is fixed and a maximum time between overhauls determined. For example, a destroyer has, approximately, a nine- to eighteen-month overhaul with a five-year period between overhauls. An attempt is made to give smaller ships priority on yards near their home ports.

During a regular overhaul, maintenance work is done, major repairs are undertaken, and alterations and improvements are made. The amount of work accomplished depends on time and the money available for the ship. Planning for such an event starts long before entry into the shipyard and involves all officers.

The ship's routine is altered radically in the shipyard. Many officers and enlisted personnel are ordered to schools and training activities. Much of the ship is uninhabitable, and a move ashore to barracks, if they are available, is made.

After completion of overhaul, a period of about ten days, known as readiness-for-sea period, is scheduled for such tasks as reloading equipment and calibrating batteries and compasses.

Deployments. Battle is the reason ships exist. It would be ideal to have all naval units ready for war at all times. This is not feasible because of personnel and equipment shortages. Those units reduced in readiness are those in overhaul or about to go into overhaul. Other units, when deployed, are as ready as possible. Ships are expected to deploy ready and to stay ready throughout their period of deployment. As pointed out earlier, units deploy two or three times during a training cycle and stay deployed for six months, or longer if necessary.

Units deployed can expect to spend two or three weeks exercising as a fleet or as a lesser unit with port visits covering as many of the liberty ports as possible to avoid overcrowding. Transit to and from deployment is usually made as a battle group or amphibious task group, which provides exercise services and mutual support.

Some ships are given home ports overseas and follow modified schedules, which permit them to spend as much time as possible in their home ports. Fleet ballistic-missile submarines have two crews that rotate every three months. The ship deploys for about four two-month periods each year in a five-year cycle.

Successful completion of a deployment should be a source of great satisfaction to a ship and her personnel. All will have done their share to maintain the necessary security of the United States. In addition, they will have gained professional experience in naval tactics and operations and been educated through exposure to several foreign countries.

Type Competition. A competitive system of conducting and scoring certain exercises and inspections is traditional in our Navy, except during periods of crisis or war. The system stimulates individuals and ships, boosts morale with awards, and measures the readiness of ships and fleets. The current form of competition is organized on the basis of intratype competition, so that each ship competes only with other ships of her class. The CNO establishes basic rules for the competition, together with a standard scoring system, certain standard exercises for each type, and a system of awards.

All phases of the competition are scored with words, such as *outstanding, excellent,* etc. A corresponding numerical system is prescribed for convenience in calculating. A system is used to give each exercise and each department proper weight. Using this system, each ship of a type can be described simply by the use of a word and can be compared in detail with other ships using a score.

General standards and scoring rules, and methods of conducting, observing, and reporting exercises, are prescribed by the CNO. Each type commander then prescribes certain preparatory noncompetitive exercises followed by a series of competitive exercises to be completed by each ship each competitive year. The scheduling and conduct of these exercises is then carried out by the unit commanders.

At the end of the competitive year, awards are presented to those ships standing highest in the competition. Additional awards are authorized for certain outstanding departments, regardless of the overall standing of the ship concerned. Awards are made at a suitable ceremony and are displayed until the end of the next competitive year. Enlisted personnel earn prize money and all members of the unit winning the award earn the right to wear an "E" (for *excellent*) ribbon on their uniforms.

A young officer should keep informed about all aspects of the "Battle E" competition. A knowledge of methods of scoring is important. A ship is supposed to take advantage of benefits in the scoring system to the fullest extent possible. You should know in what part of a prescribed range your ship can shoot best if you are in gunnery, and what bearings give you best radar coverage if you are in operations. You need to know and use this knowledge in war; the competition is meant to prepare you for war.

13

THE ARMED FORCES
OF THE
UNITED STATES

THE DETERRENCE OF WAR IS THE PRIMARY OBJECTIVE
OF THE ARMED FORCES.

—*General Maxwell D. Taylor*, The Uncertain Trumpet

THE CONGRESS SHALL HAVE THE POWER TO RAISE AND
SUPPORT ARMIES . . . TO PROVIDE AND MAINTAIN A
NAVY; TO MAKE RULES FOR THE GOVERNMENT AND
REGULATION OF THE LAND AND NAVAL FORCES.

—*Constitution of the United States*

Organization for National Security

The Commander in Chief. The president of the United States is, by provision of our Constitution, commander in chief of the armed forces. The president is advised in security matters by several agencies that are part of the executive office of the president. These agencies include the National Security Council (NSC) and the Central Intelligence Agency (CIA).

The National Command Authorities (NCA). The NCA consists of the president and the secretary of defense, who have the sole authority for making certain types of defense-related decisions. The CINCs report to the NCA through the chairman of the JCS.

The National Security Council. Established by the National

Security Act and modified by the Goldwater-Nichols Defense Reorganization Act of 1986, the NSC has as statutory members the president, vice-president, secretary of state, and secretary of defense. The director of the CIA, chairman of the JCS, counselor to the president, White House chief of staff and deputy chief of staff, and the national security adviser also normally attend NSC meetings. The act provides that the secretaries and under secretaries of other executive departments and of the military departments may serve as members of the NSC, when appointed by the president with the advice and consent of the Senate. The NSC staff is headed by a civilian executive secretary appointed by the president. The staff of about one hundred persons includes officers and civilian officials from the Departments of State and Defense and the four military services. The secretariat conducts the routine business of the NSC.

The NSC's function is to advise the president on domestic, foreign, and military policies and problems relating to national security, so as to enable the military services and other departments and agencies of the government to cooperate more effectively in matters involving national security. The duties of the NSC are to assess and appraise the objectives, commitments, and risks of the United States in relation to the actual and potential military power of the nation; to consider policies of common interest to the departments and agencies of the government concerned with national security; and to make recommendations to the president on subjects that may affect the national policies of the government.

The Central Intelligence Agency.   The agency is administered by a director appointed by the president with the advice and consent of the Senate. The director may be either a military officer or a civilian. If an officer, he or she is completely separated from military service while serving as director.

The agency coordinates intelligence activities of the government. The CIA advises the NSC concerning the intelligence activities of the government that relate to national security, makes recommendations to the NSC for coordination of these intelligence activities, correlates and evaluates intelligence, and disseminates such intelligence within the government, using existing agencies where appropriate, and performs additional intelligence services that the NSC determines.

The Department of Defense

Mission. The Department of Defense (DOD) was created to provide for the security of the United States through the establishment of integrated policies and procedures for the departments, agencies, and government functions relating to the national security. The DOD coordinates and directs civilian control of three military departments (including naval aviation and the Marine Corps), with their assigned combat and service components.

The Secretary of Defense. The secretary of defense is the principal assistant to the president in all matters relating to the DOD. A civilian, he is appointed by the president with the advice and consent of the Senate. Under the president, and subject to the provisions of the National Security Act, the secretary exercises control over his department.

The Deputy Secretary of Defense. The deputy secretary of defense is responsible for the supervision and coordination of the activities of the DOD as directed by the secretary. He acts for and exercises the powers of the secretary in his absence or disability.

The Armed Forces Policy Council. This council is composed of the secretary of defense (chairman), the deputy secretary of defense, the service secretaries, and the service chiefs. It advises the secretary on matters of broad policy.

The Office of the Secretary of Defense. Various agencies, offices, and positions created under the National Security Act, together with certain other agencies that assist the secretary of defense, are referred to as the Office of the Secretary of Defense. They constitute the primary staff of the secretary. Its principal members are mentioned in the paragraphs that follow.

The deputy secretary of defense acts on all matters in the secretary's absence.

The under secretary of defense for acquisition is responsible for all matters involving acquisition.

The under secretary of defense for policy handles policy matters.

The assistant secretary of defense (legislative affairs) takes care of all legislative matters except for those pertaining to the appropriation committees of Congress.

The assistant secretary of defense (comptroller) is responsible for all budgeting matters and for liaison with the appropriation committees of Congress.

The assistant secretary of defense (for management and personnel) handles all manpower planning and administration.

The assistant secretary of defense (command, control, communications, and intelligence) is responsible for all matters involving those areas.

The assistant secretary of defense (health affairs) handles health planning and administration.

The assistant secretary of defense (public affairs) handles public affairs and media relations.

The assistant secretary of defense (program analysis and evaluation) is responsible for identifying issues and formulating programs.

The assistant secretary of defense (reserve affairs) handles all National Guard and reserve affairs.

The assistant secretary of defense (low-intensity conflict) is responsible for policy guidance and oversight of special operations and low-intensity conflict.

The general counsel handles all legal matters.

The executive assistant to the secretary of defense acts as his executive and office manager.

The special assistant to the secretary of defense handles affairs assigned to him.

The assistant to the secretary of defense (intelligence oversight) handles matters assigned to him.

Defense Agencies. The following DOD agencies operate under the control of the secretary of defense:

National Security Agency
Defense Legal Service Agency
United States Inspection Agency
Defense Communication Agency
Defense Contract Audit Agency
Defense Intelligence Agency
Defense Investigative Service
Defense Logistics Agency
Defense Mapping Agency
Defense Nuclear Agency
Defense Security Assistance Agency

Department of Defense

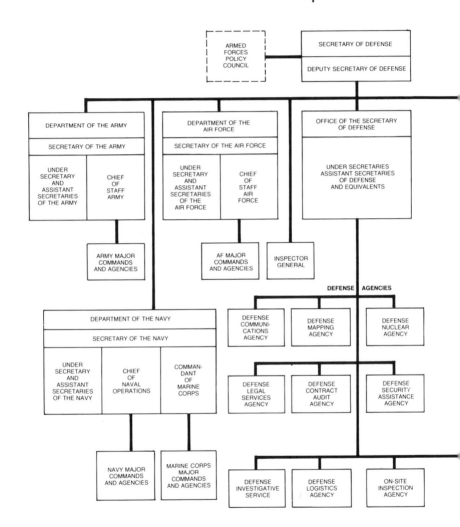

Figure 13-1. Organization of the DOD.

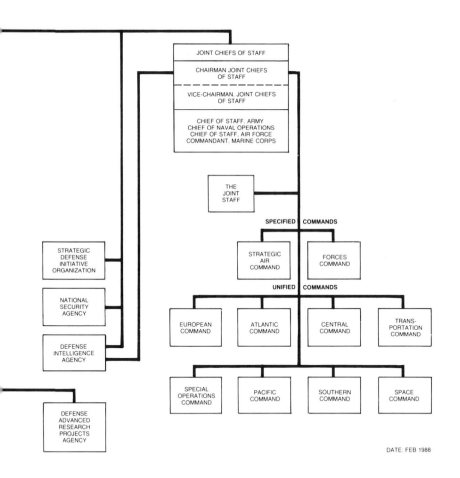

DATE: FEB 1988

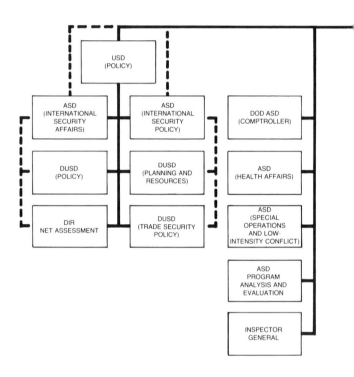

Reflects reporting structure during
period of USD (Policy) vacancy per
DEPSECDEF memo dated 29 Jan 88

Figure 13-2. Organization of the Office of the Secretary of Defense.

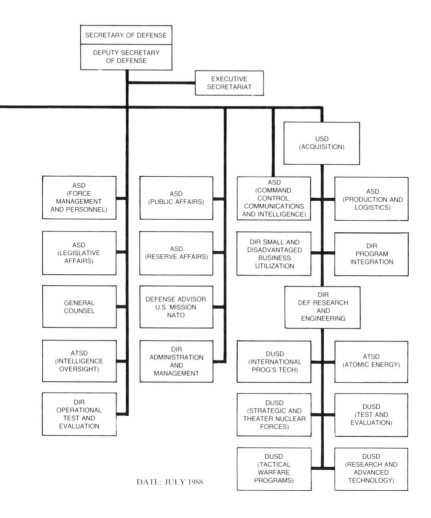

SECRETARY OF DEFENSE

DEPUTY SECRETARY OF DEFENSE

EXECUTIVE SECRETARIAT

USD (ACQUISITION)

ASD (FORCE MANAGEMENT AND PERSONNEL)

ASD (PUBLIC AFFAIRS)

ASD (COMMAND, CONTROL, COMMUNICATIONS AND INTELLIGENCE)

ASD (PRODUCTION AND LOGISTICS)

ASD (LEGISLATIVE AFFAIRS)

ASD (RESERVE AFFAIRS)

DIR SMALL AND DISADVANTAGED BUSINESS UTILIZATION

DIR PROGRAM INTEGRATION

GENERAL COUNSEL

DEFENSE ADVISOR U.S. MISSION NATO

DIR DEF RESEARCH AND ENGINEERING

ATSD (INTELLIGENCE OVERSIGHT)

DIR ADMINISTRATION AND MANAGEMENT

DUSD (INTERNATIONAL PROG'S TECH)

ATSD (ATOMIC ENERGY)

DIR OPERATIONAL TEST AND EVALUATION

DUSD (STRATEGIC AND THEATER NUCLEAR FORCES)

DUSD (TEST AND EVALUATION)

DATE: JULY 1988

DUSD (TACTICAL WARFARE PROGRAMS)

DUSD (RESEARCH AND ADVANCED TECHNOLOGY)

Defense Advanced Research Projects Agency
Strategic Defense Initiative Organization

The National Security Act. The National Security Act of 1947, amended in 1953, 1958, and 1962, is the basic military legislation of the United States.

The policy section of the act reads, "It is the intent of Congress to provide a comprehensive program for the future security of the United States; to provide for the establishment of integrated policies and procedures for the departments, agencies, and functions of the Government relating to national security." In so doing, the act

1. Provides for three military departments, separately administered, for the operation and administration of the Army, the Navy (including naval aviation), the Marine Corps, and the Air Force, with their assigned combatant and service components

2. Provides for coordination and direction of the three military departments and four services under the secretary of defense

3. Provides for strategic direction of the armed forces, for their operation under unified control, and for the integration of the four services into an efficient team of land, naval, and air forces.

Unification has been accomplished by giving the secretary of defense authority, direction, and virtual military control over the four services. He also has authority to eliminate duplication in procurement, supply, transportation, storage, health, and research.

The Joint Chiefs of Staff

History. The authority of the president as commander in chief of the Army and Navy was formerly exercised through the secretaries of war and Navy. During World War II, a need was felt for more personal control. The president wanted direct access to his military advisers and improved coordination between the Army and Navy. He ordered the organization of the JCS with Admiral William D. Leahy as chief of staff to the president. He became the senior member and presiding officer of the JCS. The first members were General George C. Marshall, Chief of Staff of the Army, and Admiral Ernest J. King, CNO. Lieutenant General H. H. Arnold, Chief of the Army Air Corps, was added as a third

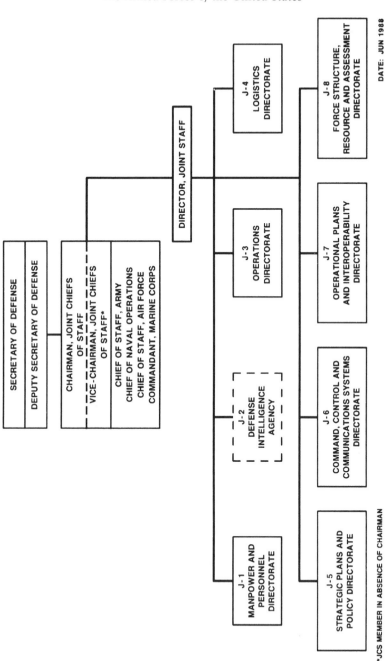

*JCS MEMBER IN ABSENCE OF CHAIRMAN

DATE: JUN 1988

Figure 13-3. Organization of the JCS, June 1988.

member. These four officers, later promoted to five-star rank, conducted the global warfare of World War II.

During the war, the JCS functioned as a part of the Combined Chiefs of Staff, an Anglo-American military agency whose members were the U.S. Joint Chiefs and two senior British Army general officers, one British admiral, and one British air vice-marshal.

At meetings, often held twice a day, the JCS discussed the grand strategy of the war and formulated directives. The chief of staff of the Army and the commander in chief of the U.S. Fleet acted as executive agents in carrying out their plans and directives. Meetings of the Combined Chiefs of Staff integrated the plans and operations of the U.S. Armed Forces into the broad scheme of strategy of the Allied powers.

With the coming of peace and the retirement of Fleet Admiral Leahy, reaching unanimous decisions on important issues became difficult. Accordingly, when the National Security Act came up for amendment in 1949, a chairman was authorized specifically to preside at the meetings of the JCS in order to expedite the business of that organization, but he was not to be considered a chief of staff to either the president or the secretary of defense or of the armed services, nor would he have a vote in deliberations.

Composition and Functions. The JCS consists of a chairman appointed from one of the services by the president, the chief of staff of the Army, the chief of staff of the Air Force, the CNO, and the commandant of the Marine Corps.

It should be noted that the JCS organization includes not only the chiefs themselves, but the joint staff, the secretariat, and various boards and organizations. The organization includes about four hundred officers.

The functions of the JCS are set forth in DOD Directives 5100.1 and 5158.1 of 31 December 1958 and in the National Security Act. These are

    1. To serve as advisers and as military staff in the chain of operational command with respect to unified and specified commands, to provide a channel of communications from the President and Secretary of Defense to unified and specified commands, and to coordinate all communications in matters of joint interest addressed to the commanders of the unified or specified commands by other authority.

    2. To prepare strategic plans and provide for the strategic direction of the armed forces, including the direction of op-

erations conducted by commanders of unified and specified commands and the discharge of any other function of command for such commands directed by the Secretary of Defense.

3. To prepare integrated logistic plans, which may include assignments to the armed forces of logistic responsibilities in accordance with such plans.

4. To prepare integrated plans for military mobilization.

5. To provide adequate, timely, and reliable joint intelligence for use within the Department of Defense.

6. To review major personnel, material, and logistic requirements of the armed forces in relation to strategic and logistic plans.

7. To review the plans and programs of commanders of unified and specified commands to determine their adequacy, feasibility, and suitability for the performance of assigned missions.

8. To provide military guidance for use by the military departments and the armed forces as needed in the preparation of their respective detailed plans.

9. To participate, as directed, in the preparation of combined plans for military action in conjunction with the armed forces of other nations.

10. To recommend to the Secretary of Defense the establishment and force structure of unified and specified commands in strategic areas.

11. To determine the headquarters support, such as facilities, personnel, and communications, required by commanders of unified and specified commands and to recommend the assignment to the military departments of the responsibilities for providing such support.

12. To establish doctrines for (a) unified operations and training and (b) coordination of the military education of members of the armed forces.

13. To recommend to the Secretary of Defense the assignment of primary responsibility for any function of the armed forces requiring such determination and the transfer, reassignment, abolition, or consolidation of such functions.

14. To prepare and submit to the Secretary of Defense for information and consideration in connection with the preparation of budgets, statements of military requirements based upon United States strategic considerations, current national security policy, and strategic war plans. These statements of requirements shall include tasks, priority of tasks,

force requirements, and general strategic guidance for the development of military installations and bases and for equipping and maintaining military forces.

15. To advise and assist the Secretary of Defense in research and engineering matters by preparing: (a) statements of broad strategic guidance to be used in the preparation of an integrated Department of Defense program, (b) statements of over-all military requirements; (c) statements of the relative military importance of development activities to meet the needs of the unified and specified commanders, and (d) recommendations for the assignment of specific new weapons to the armed forces.

16. To prepare and submit to the Secretary of Defense for information and consideration general strategic guidance for the development of industrial mobilization programs.

17. To prepare and submit to the Secretary of Defense military guidance for use in the development of military aid programs and other actions relating to foreign military forces, including recommendations for allied military force, material, and facilities requirements related to United States strategic objectives, current national security policy, strategic war plans, and the implementation of approved programs; and to make recommendations to the Secretary of Defense, as necessary, for keeping the Military Assistance Program in consonance with agreed strategic concepts.

18. To provide United States representation on the Military Staff Committee of the United Nations, in accordance with the provisions of the Charter of the United Nations, and representation on other properly authorized military staffs, boards, councils, and missions.

19. To perform such other duties as the President or the Secretary of Defense may prescribe.

The Goldwater-Nichols Defense Reorganization Act modified these guidelines. The chairman now has far wider power than before and, in most cases, is not required to canvas the Joint Chiefs concerning operational matters.

Operation. A problem for the JCS may be presented by the president or the secretary of defense; it may be brought up by one of the chiefs; it may be forced on them by the exigencies of war or national emergency; it may come to them through JCS representation on the Military Committee of NATO; or it may come up internally in the course of making or reviewing plans. However it originates, it is presented to the JCS on paper through the Joint Secretariat.

From the Joint Secretariat it is referred to the appropriate Joint Staff Directorate. The appropriate directorate studies the problem, coordinates it with other Joint Staff directorates, the services, and other affected agencies and government departments. Usually, agreement is reached between all concerned; however, a dissenting view is occasionally passed forward with the completed action. If necessary, a decision brief, attended by the Joint Chiefs, is used to resolve differences.

Two or three times a week in peacetime and several times a day in war or national emergency the chiefs meet in the JCS conference room in the Pentagon. Usually present are each chief and his principal assistant (known as his "OPSDEP"), the director of the Joint Staff, and the chairman. Other officers and civilian officials may be invited to attend; occasionally a JCS action officer is invited. The chiefs may discuss the subjects informally among themselves, or may allow presentations to be made.

The majority of JCS decisions are unanimous, although an occasional major decision is split.

Unified Commands

Structure. Unified commands were established during World War II. These commands came directly under the JCS, which appointed an officer of the dominant service as commander and assigned forces to that commander. One of the three services was assigned as "executive agent" to furnish support to the command. Since WW II, the command chain for unified commands has changed. A variation of the unified command is a specified command such as the Strategic Air Command, where the forces are all of the same service but under the direct command of the NCA through CJCS. All forces not assigned to a unified or specified command remain in their departments, as does the administration of the forces assigned to the unified and specified commands.

The unified and specified commands are:

U.S. European Command
U.S. Southern Command

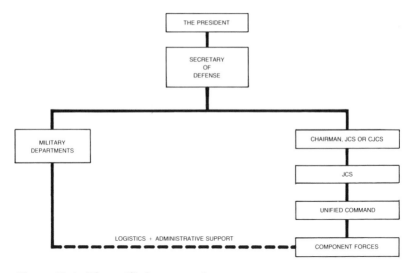

Figure 13-4. The unified command structure.

U.S. Atlantic Command
U.S. Pacific Command
U.S. Central Command
U.S. Special Operations Command
U.S. Transportation Command
U.S. Space Command
Strategic Air Command (specified)
Forces Command (specified)

The executive agency system has been abolished. Orders now go from the president to the secretary of defense and then to the commander of the unified or specified command, with the JCS acting as a corporate body.

The Department of the Army

Mission. The Department of the Army is charged with providing support for national and international policy and the security of the United States by planning, directing, and reviewing the military and civil operations of the Army establishment.

The U.S. Army includes land-combat and service forces, which include some aviation and water transport. Of the three

Army troops make a practice assault on a training range in Germany.

major services, the Army has primary interest in all operations on land.

Functions. The functions of the Department of the Army are set forth in the DOD Directive 5100.1 of 31 December 1958, as follows:

> The Army, within the Department of the Army, includes land combat and service forces and any organic aviation and water transport assigned. The Army is responsible for the preparation of land forces necessary for the effective prosecution of war and military operations short of war, except as otherwise assigned and, in accordance with integrated joint mobilization plans, for the expansion of the peacetime components of the Army to meet the needs of war.

> *The primary functions of the Army are:*

> To organize, train, and equip forces for the conduct of prompt and sustained combat operations on land—specifi-

cally, forces to defeat enemy land forces and to seize, occupy, and defend land areas.

To organize, train, equip, and provide forces for appropriate air and missile defense and space control operations, including the provision of forces as required for the strategic defense of the United States, in accordance with joint doctrines.

To organize, equip, and provide Army forces, in coordination with the other Military Services, for joint amphibious, airborne, and space operations and to provide for the training of such forces, in accordance with joint doctrines. Specifically, the Army shall:

1 Develop, in coordination with the other Military Services, doctrines, tactics, techniques, and equipment of interest to the Army for amphibious operations and not provided for elsewhere.

2 Develop, in coordination with the other Military Services, the doctrines, procedures, and equipment employed by Army and Marine Corps forces in airborne operations. The Army shall have primary responsibility for developing those airborne doctrines, procedures, and equipment that are of common interest to the Army and the Marine Corps.

3 Develop, in coordination with the other Military Services, doctrines, procedures, and equipment employed by Army forces in the conduct of space operations.

To organize, train, equip, and provide forces for the support and conduct of special operations.

To provide equipment, forces, procedures, and doctrine necessary for the effective prosecution of electronic warfare operations and, as directed, support of other forces.

To organize, train, equip, and provide forces for the support and conduct of psychological operations.

To provide forces for the occupation of territories abroad, including initial establishment of military government pending transfer of this responsibility to other authority.

To develop doctrines and procedures, in coordination with the other Military Services, for organizing, equipping, training, and employing forces operating on land, except that the development of doctrines and procedures for organizing, equipping, training, and employing Marine Corps units for amphibious operations shall be a function of the Marine Corps coordinating, as required, with the other Military Services.

To organize, train, equip, and provide forces, as directed, to operate land lines of communication.

To conduct the following activities:

1 Functions relating to the management and operation of the Panama Canal, as assigned by the Secretary or Deputy Secretary of Defense.

2 The authorized civil works program, including projects for improvement of navigation, flood control, beach erosion control, and other water resource developments in the United States, its territories, and its possessions.

3 Certain other civil activities prescribed by law.

A collateral function of the Army is to train forces to interdict enemy sea and air power and communications through operations on or from land.

Army responsibilities in support of space operations include the following:

1 Organizing, training, equipping, and providing Army forces to support space operations.

2 Developing, in coordination with the other Military Services, tactics, techniques, and equipment employed by Army forces for use in space operations.

3 Conducting individual and unit training of Army space operations forces.

4 Participating with other Services in joint space operations, training, and exercises as mutually agreed to by the Services concerned, or as directed by competent authority.

5 Providing forces for space support operations for the Department of Defense when directed.

Other responsibilities of the Army. With respect to close air support of ground forces, the Army has specific responsibility for the following:

1 Providing, in accordance with inter-Service agreements, communications, personnel, and equipment employed by Army forces.

2 Conducting individual and unit training of Army forces.

3 Developing equipment, tactics, and techniques employed by Army forces.

Organization.   Command flows through the secretary of the Army and military channels to Army units and installations throughout the world.

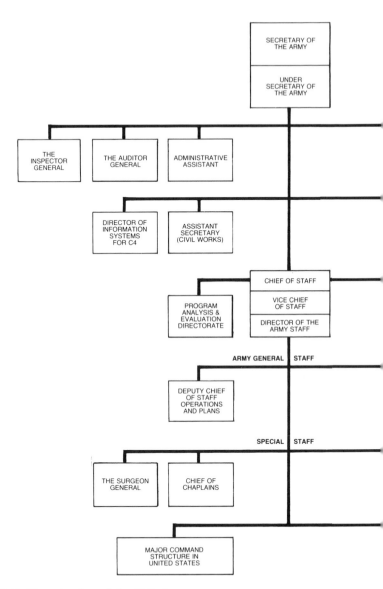

Figure 13-5. Organization of the U.S. Army.

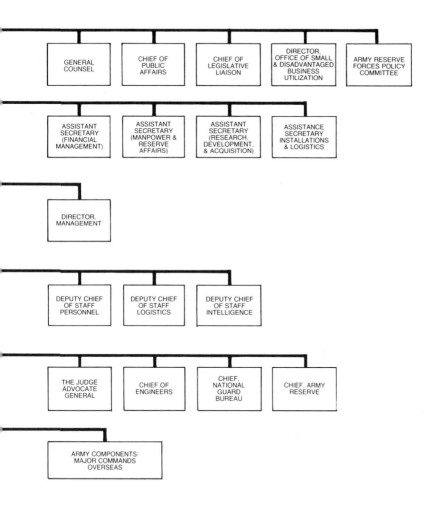

In the field the Army is divided into armies made up of corps and divisions, all of which contain a balance of combat arms and administrative and logistic services to make them effective and independent. The units of the Army, from the lowest echelon up, are reviewed in the following paragraphs.

A squad is the smallest unit, led by a noncommissioned officer. Its size varies.

A platoon is led by a lieutenant. It usually has three squads. Armored platoons have four tanks.

A company is commanded by a captain. It usually has three or four platoons. It is capable of receiving and controlling additional combat and support units. An artillery unit of equivalent size is called a battery. An armored or air cavalry unit is called a troop.

A battalion is commanded by a lieutenant colonel and is usually composed of five companies. It is self-sufficient and capable of independent operations. There are combat, combat support, and combat service support battalions. An armored cavalry (ground) or air cavalry unit of equivalent size is called a squadron.

A brigade is commanded by a colonel, who oversees the tactical operations of two to five attached combat battalions. Combat support and combat service support battalions are attached as needed for mission.

A regiment is commanded by a colonel and consists of headquarters, three armored cavalry squadrons, one combat aviation squadron, and a combat support squadron. It is a self-contained tactical and administrative unit.

Each division has a common division base, which includes such units as command and control, aviation, military police, signal, engineer, and the other units necessary to support it. There are five types of divisions, commanded by major generals: infantry, mechanized infantry, airborne, air assault, and armored. Each has about 12,000 to 18,000 personnel. Major units assigned vary according to the mission of the division.

A corps is commanded by a lieutenant general who controls two to five divisions.

An army contains two or more corps and supporting troops and is commanded by a general.

The U.S. Army has the following specialty branches, which provide individuals to the organizational units:

Infantry
Armor (includes cavalry)
Artillery
Corps of Engineers
Signal Corps
Adjutant General's Corps
Quartermaster Corps
Finance Corps
Ordnance Corps
Chemical Corps
Transportation Corps
Military Police Corps

Judge Advocate General's Corps
Chaplains
Medical Corps
Dental Corps
Veterinary Corps
Army Nurse Corps
Army Medical Services Corps
Aviation
Special Forces
Air Defense Artillery
Military Intelligence

The Secretary of the Army and His Assistants. The secretary of the Army heads the Department of the Army and is responsible for all affairs of the Army establishment. In addition, the secretary has certain quasi-civil functions, such as supervising the Alaska Communication Service, the Corps of Engineers' civil works programs, U.S. battle monuments, the civilian marksmanship program, and functions in connection with the District of Columbia.

Immediately under the secretary of the Army are the following assistants and major agencies:

Under secretary of the Army
Administrative assistant
Army Policy Council
Assistant secretary of the Army for civil works
Assistant secretary of the Army for financial management
Assistant secretary of the Army for manpower and reserve affairs
Assistant secretary of the Army for research, development, and acquisition
Assistant secretary of the Army for installations and logistics
General counsel
Chief of legislative liaison
Chief of public affairs
Director, Office of Small and Disadvantaged Business Utilization
Auditor General
Army Reserve Forces Policy Command

Inspector General

Director of Information Systems for Command, Control, Communications, and Computers

Army Staff. The Army Staff is the staff of the secretary of the Army. It includes the chief of staff and his immediate assistants, a general and a special staff, and a technical staff.

The duties of the Army Staff include preparing the plans for national security, both separately and in conjunction with the other military services; investigating and reporting questions affecting the efficiency of the Army and its state of preparation for military operations; executing approved plans and instructions; and acting for the secretary and chief of staff in informing all officers of plans and in coordinating the Army establishment.

The Chief of Staff. The chief of staff is the principal military adviser to the secretary of the Army and is charged by him with the planning, development, and execution of the Army program. The chief of staff supervises all members and organizations of the Army and performs the duties prescribed for him by the National Security Act and other laws. The chief of staff, by virtue of his position, takes rank above all officers on the active list of all the services, except the chairman of the JCS, the CNO, and the chief of staff of the Air Force, if their appointments antedate his.

The Office of the Chief of Staff. This office comprises the following:

Vice chief of staff
Director of the Army Staff
Deputy to the director of the Army Staff
Director of program analysis and evaluation
Director of management

The Army General Staff. This is made up as follows:

Deputy chief of staff for operations and plans
Deputy chief of staff for personnel
Deputy chief of staff for logistics
Deputy chief of staff for intelligence

The Army Special Staff. This is made up as follows:

Chief of engineers
Surgeon general
Chief of chaplains

Judge advocate general
Chief, National Guard Bureau
Chief, Army Reserve

Major Army Commands. The following are major Army commands:

Forces Command
Training and Doctrine Command
Army Material Command
Corps of Engineers
Military Traffic Management Command
Health Services Command
Intelligence and Security Command
Military District of Washington
Information Systems Command
Criminal Investigation Command
1st Special Operations Command

Army Commands Overseas. The Army has forces overseas in U.S. Army Europe and Seventh Army; in U.S. Forces, Korea, and Eighth Army, U.S. Army, Japan; in U.S. Army, Western Command, Hawaii; and in U.S. Army, South, Panama.

The Regular Army. The Regular Army is on full-time duty. Other components are ordinarily inactive in peacetime. All components may be called to active duty in war or national emergency. The duties of the Regular Army are to

Perform occupational duties
Garrison U.S. and overseas bases
Train the National Guard, Organized Reserve, and ROTC
Provide an organization for the administration and supply of the peacetime military establishment
Provide educated officers to become leaders, in the event of war, of the expanded U.S. Army
Advance and record the body of military knowledge so as to keep this country up-to-date and prepared
Constitute, with the National Guard and units of the Organized Reserve, a covering force in case of a major war
Cooperate with the Marine Corps, Navy, and Air Force in carrying out missions

Ready and Standby Reserve Corps. Army Reserve units train in local armories and are subject to orders to active duty in

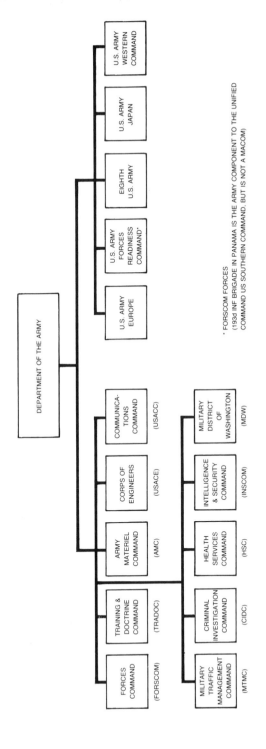

Figure 13-6. Chain of command for Army forces.

much the same way as the National Guard. Individual members are assigned to organizations in or near their home towns. The Organized Reserve is made up of members in organized units— as distinct from reservists in large pools—who will be assigned to Regular Army units in case of emergency. The Organized Reserve is not subject to state control.

Women in the Army.   Women have served in the U.S. Army for many years, first as civilian nurses, then as Army nurses, and finally as members of the Women's Army Corps and the women's medical specialist corps. They are now part of the Regular Army in accordance with a congressional act of 1948.

Education of Officer Candidates.   Three school systems train candidates for commissions in the Army: military academies, OCSs, and the Reserve Officer Training Corps (ROTC).

The United States Military Academy, at West Point, New York, was established in 1802 for the purpose of training young gentlemen as commissioned officers. The academy is commanded by a superintendent, an Army general. The four-year curriculum includes cultural subjects as well as military and other sciences. The cadet graduates with a B.S. degree, and, if physically fit, is usually commissioned as a second lieutenant.

OCS's are conducted for men and women at the U.S. Army Infantry Center, Fort Benning, Georgia. The course is usually six months. Most candidates come from the Regular Army, the Reserve, and the National Guard.

ROTC units are located at about 250 civilian universities and colleges. Candidates are commissioned into the Regular Army and U.S. Army Reserves from the four- and two-year courses.

National Guard

The National Guard is the civilian militia of the United States. In time of peace, the National Guard of any state can be called to active duty by the governor of that state to perform emergency duties. Units or individual members of the National Guard can be called to active duty by the federal government only during war or national emergency; in peacetime they may choose whether to perform active duty.

The Department of the Air Force

Mission.   The Department of the Air Force and the U.S. Air Force were established in 1947 by the National Security Act. The

Office of the Secretary of the Air Force

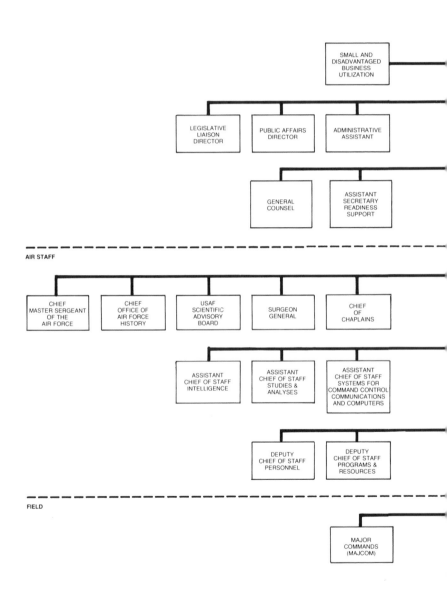

Figure 13-7. U.S. Air Force organization chart.

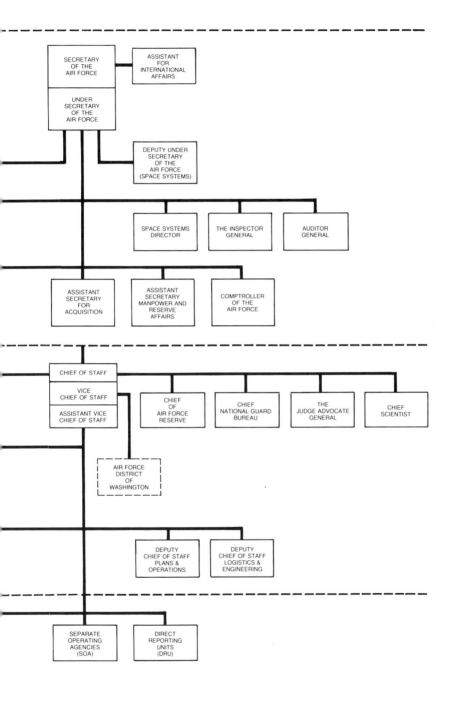

SECRETARY OF THE AIR FORCE

UNDER SECRETARY OF THE AIR FORCE

ASSISTANT FOR INTERNATIONAL AFFAIRS

DEPUTY UNDER SECRETARY OF THE AIR FORCE (SPACE SYSTEMS)

SPACE SYSTEMS DIRECTOR

THE INSPECTOR GENERAL

AUDITOR GENERAL

ASSISTANT SECRETARY FOR ACQUISITION

ASSISTANT SECRETARY MANPOWER AND RESERVE AFFAIRS

COMPTROLLER OF THE AIR FORCE

CHIEF OF STAFF

VICE CHIEF OF STAFF

ASSISTANT VICE CHIEF OF STAFF

CHIEF OF AIR FORCE RESERVE

CHIEF NATIONAL GUARD BUREAU

THE JUDGE ADVOCATE GENERAL

CHIEF SCIENTIST

AIR FORCE DISTRICT OF WASHINGTON

DEPUTY CHIEF OF STAFF PLANS & OPERATIONS

DEPUTY CHIEF OF STAFF LOGISTICS & ENGINEERING

SEPARATE OPERATING AGENCIES (SOA)

DIRECT REPORTING UNITS (DRU)

Air Force includes both air combat, missile, and service forces. It is organized, trained, and equipped for prompt and sustained offensive and defensive combat operations in the air. The mission of the Air Force is to preserve, with the cooperation of the other armed forces, the peace and security of the United States by providing air combat, air-service, aerospace, missile, and airlift forces.

Components.   The U.S. Air Force is composed of the Regular Air Force, the Air National Guard, and the Air Force Reserve. The U.S. Air Force provides for air and space security and defense of the United States. These component organizations are similar to those of the Army.

Functions.   The functions of the Air Force are set forth in DOD Directive 5100.1 of 3 April 1987 as follows:

Functions of the Department of the Air Force

(1) The Air Force, within the Department of the Air Force, includes aviation forces, both combat and service, not otherwise assigned. The Air Force is responsible for the preparation of the air forces necessary for the effective prosecution of war and military operations short of war, except as otherwise assigned and, in accordance with integrated joint mobilization plans, for the expansion of the peacetime components of the Air Force to meet the needs of war.

(2) The primary functions of the Air Force include:

(a) To organize, train, equip, and provide forces for the conduct of prompt and sustained combat operations in the air—specifically, forces to defend the United States against air attack in accordance with doctrines established by the Joint Chiefs of Staff, gain and maintain general air supremacy, defeat enemy air forces, conduct space operations, control vital air areas, and establish local air superiority except as otherwise assigned herein.

(b) To organize, train, equip, and provide forces for appropriate air and missile defense and space control operations, including the provision of forces as required for the strategic defense of the United States, in accordance with joint doctrines.

(c) To organize, train, equip, and provide forces for strategic air and missile warfare.

(d) To organize, equip, and provide forces for joint amphibious, space, and airborne operations, in coordination with the other Military Services, and to provide for their training in accordance with joint doctrines.

(e) To organize, train, equip, and provide forces for close air support and air logistic support to the Army and other forces, as directed, including airlift, air support, resupply of airborne operations, aerial photography, tactical air reconnaissance, and air interdiction of enemy land forces and communications.

(f) To organize, train, equip and provide forces for air transport for the Armed Forces, except as otherwise assigned.

(g) To develop, in coordination with the other Services, doctrines, procedures, and equipment for air defense from land areas, including the United States.

(h) To organize, train, equip, and provide forces to furnish aerial imagery for use by the Army and other agencies as directed, including aerial imagery for cartographic purposes.

(i) To develop, in coordination with the other Services, tactics, techniques, and equipment of interest to the Air Force for amphibious operations and not provided for elsewhere.

(j) To develop, in coordination with the other Services, doctrines, procedures, and equipment employed by Air Force forces in airborne operations.

(k) To provide launch and space support for the Department of Defense, except as otherwise assigned.

(l) To develop, in coordination with the other Services, doctrines, procedures, and equipment employed by Air Force forces in the conduct of space operations.

(m) To organize, train, equip, and provide land-based tanker forces for the in-flight refueling support of strategic operations and deployments of aircraft of the Armed Forces and Air Force tactical operations, except as otherwise assigned.

(n) To organize, train, equip, and provide forces, as directed to operate air lines of communications.

(o) To organize, train, equip, and provide forces for the support and conduct of special operations.

(p) To organize, train, equip, and provide forces for the support and conduct of psychological operations.

(q) To provide equipment, forces, procedures, and doctrine necessary for the effective prosecution of electronic warfare operations and, as directed, support of other forces.

(3) Collateral functions of the Air Force include the following:

(a) Surface sea surveillance and antisurface ship warfare through air operations.

(b) Antisubmarine warfare and antiair warfare operations to protect sea lines of communications.

(c) Aerial minelaying operations.

(d) Air-to-air refueling in support of naval campaigns.

(4) Air Force responsibilities in support of space operations include:

(a) Organizing, training, equipping, and providing forces to support space operations.

(b) Developing, in coordination with the other Military Services, tactics, techniques, and equipment employed by Air Force forces for use in space operations.

(c) Conducting individual and unit training of Air Force space operations forces.

(d) Participating with the other Services in joint space operations, training, and exercises as mutually agreed to by the Services concerned, or as directed by competent authority.

(5) Other responsibilities of the Air Force include:

(a) With respect to amphibious operations, the Air Force will develop, in coordination with the other Services, tactics, techniques, and equipment of interest to the Air Force and not provided for by the Navy and Marine Corps.

(b) With respect to airborne operations, the Air Force has specific responsibility to:

1 Provide Air Force forces for the air movement of troops, supplies, and equipment in joint airborne operations, including parachute and aircraft landings.

2 Develop tactics and techniques employed by Air Force forces in the air movement of troops, supplies, and equipment.

(c) With respect to close air support of ground forces, the Air Force has specific responsibility for developing, in coordination with the other Services, doctrines and procedures, except as provided for in Navy responsibilities for amphibious operations and in responsibilities for the Marine Corps.

The Secretary of the Air Force and His Assistants.   The secretary of the Air Force heads the Department of the Air Force and the Air Force establishment and is responsible for all matters pertaining to their operation. He has the following assistants:

Under secretary of the Air Force
Director, Small and Disadvantaged Business Utilization

Deputy under secretary of the Air Force for international affairs

Assistant secretary of the Air Force for financial management and Comptroller

Assistant secretary of the Air Force for acquisition

Assistant secretary of the Air Force for manpower, reserve affairs, installations, and environment

Assistant secretary of the Air Force for space

Administrative assistant

General counsel

Auditor general

Director, Office of Legislative Liaison

Director, Office of Public Affairs

Military assistant

Inspector General

Chief of Staff.   The chief of staff supervises the Air Force and exercises command over the major air commands. He is responsible for formulating policies and plans that will accomplish the Air Force mission and serves as principal military adviser and executive to the secretary of the Air Force.

Under the chief of staff, the following assistants and agencies perform staff functions:

Vice chief of staff

Assistant vice chief of staff

Scientific Advisory Board

Surgeon general

Chief of chaplains

Judge advocate general

Chief of Air Force Reserve

Chief, National Guard Bureau

Assistant chief of staff for intelligence

Assistant chief of staff for studies and analyses

Chief, Office of Air Force History

Assistant chief of staff, systems for command, control, communications, and computers

Chief master sergeant of the Air Force

Chief scientist

Director of administration

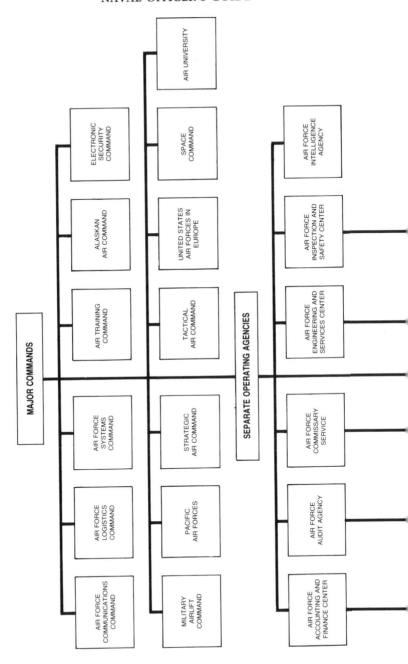

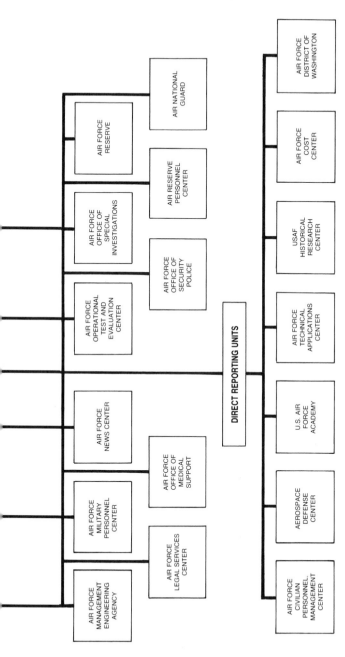

Figure 13-8. U.S. Air Force major commands.

The Air Staff is composed of the following:

Deputy chief of staff for personnel
Deputy chief of staff for programs and resources
Deputy chief of staff for research, development, and acquisition
Deputy chief of staff for plans and operations
Deputy chief of staff for logistics and engineering

Major Commands.   The Air Force has the following major commands:

Air Force Communications Command
Air Force Logistics Command
Air Force Systems Command
Air Training Command
Alaskan Air Command
Electronic Security Command
Military Airlift Command
Pacific Air Forces
Strategic Air Command
Tactical Air Command
U.S. Air Force in Europe Command
Air University

North American Aerospace Defense Command (NORAD).
This is a joint Canadian/U.S. organization that coordinates Air

An Air Force F-16C carrying two AIM9-L Sidewinder missiles, four Maverick missiles, two 390-gallon fuel tanks, and an ALQ/131 ECM pod.

Force, Navy, and Marine fighter units, as well as all air-warning services and Army antiaircraft, for the continental United States.

Education of Air Force Officer Candidates. Officer candidates are trained at the U.S. Air Force Academy, Air Force ROTC, and Officer Training School (OTS).

The U.S. Air Force Academy in Colorado Springs provides the main input of regular officers for the Air Force. The curriculum includes cultural, military, and science subjects, and leads to a B.S. degree and a commission in the Regular Air Force as a second lieutenant.

The Air Force ROTC is similar in nature to the Army ROTC program.

OTS is located at Lackland Air Force Base, San Antonio, Texas. It is coeducational. The curriculum allows each graduate to be commissioned as an active duty Air Force officer with a reserve commission as a second lieutenant.

14

THE DEPARTMENT OF THE NAVY

IT FOLLOWS THEN, AS CERTAIN AS NIGHT SUCCEEDS
DAY, THAT WITHOUT A DECISIVE NAVAL FORCE WE CAN
DO NOTHING DEFINITIVE, AND WITH IT EVERYTHING
HONORABLE AND GLORIOUS.

—*George Washington,* letter to the Marquis de Lafayette

EVERY DANGER OF A MILITARY CHARACTER TO WHICH
THE UNITED STATES IS EXPOSED CAN BE MET BEST
OUTSIDE HER OWN TERRITORY—AT SEA.

—*Rear Admiral Alfred Thayer Mahan*

Mission and Functions

The fundamental policy of the Department of the Navy is "to maintain the Navy and Marine Corps as a part of the Department of Defense in sufficient strength and readiness to fulfill its responsibilities as set forth in the *National Security Act of 1947* as amended and the *Functions of the Department of Defense* and its major components issued by the Secretary of Defense on 31 December, 1958" (*Navy Regulations* Art. 0102).

The section of the National Security Act of 1947 that applies to the Department of the Navy reads as follows:

> Sec. 206. (a) The term "Department of the Navy" as used in this Act shall be construed to mean the Department of the Navy at the seat of government; the headquarters, United States Marine Corps; the entire operating forces of the United States Navy, including naval aviation, and of the United States Marine Corps, including the reserve components of such forces; all field activities, headquarters, forces,

bases, installations, activities, and functions under the control or supervision of the Department of the Navy; and the United States Coast Guard when operating as a part of the Navy pursuant to law.

(b) In general the United States Navy, within the Department of the Navy, shall include naval combat and service forces and such aviation as may be organic therein. It shall be organized, trained, and equipped primarily for prompt and sustained combat incident to operations at sea. It shall be responsible for the preparation of naval forces necessary for the effective prosecution of war except as otherwise assigned, and, in accordance with integrated joint mobilization plans, for the expansion of the peacetime components of the Navy to meet the needs of war.

All naval aviation shall be integrated with the naval service as part thereof within the Department of the Navy. Naval aviation shall consist of combat and service and training forces, and shall include land-based naval aviation, air transport essential for naval operations, all air weapons and air techniques involved in the operations and activities of the United States Navy, and the entire remainder of the aeronautical organization of the United States Navy, together with the personnel necessary therefor.

The Navy shall be generally responsible for naval reconnaissance, antisubmarine warfare, and protection of shipping.

The Navy shall develop aircraft, weapons, tactics, technique, organization, and equipment of naval combat and service elements; matters of joint concern as to these functions shall be coordinated between the Army, the Air Force, and the Navy.

(c) The United States Marine Corps, within the Department of the Navy, shall include land combat and service forces and such aviation as may be organic therein. The Marine Corps shall be organized, trained, and equipped to provide Fleet Marine Forces of combined arms, together with supporting air components, for service with the fleet in the seizure or defense of advanced naval bases and for the conduct of such land operations as may be essential to the prosecution of a naval campaign. It shall be the duty of the Marine Corps to develop, in coordination with the Army and the Air Force, those phases of amphibious operations which pertain to the tactics, technique, and equipment employed by landing forces. In addition, the Marine Corps shall provide detachments and organizations for service on armed vessels of the Navy, shall provide security detachments for the protection of naval property at naval stations and bases, and shall perform such other duties as the President may direct: Provided, That such additional duties shall not detract from or interfere with the operations for which the Marine Corps is primarily organized. The Marine Corps shall be responsible, in accordance with integrated joint mobilization plans, for the expansion of peacetime components of the Marine Corps to meet the needs of war.

The mission of the Navy was further interpreted by the delineation of the functions of the United States Navy in Department of Defense Directive 5100.1 of December 31, 1958, which is given below.

FUNCTIONS OF THE DEPARTMENT OF THE NAVY

The Department of the Navy is responsible for the preparation of Navy and Marine Corps forces necessary for the effective prosecution of war except as otherwise assigned and, in accordance with integrated mobilization plans, for the expansion of the peacetime components of the Navy and Marine Corps to meet the needs of war.

Within the Department of the Navy, the Navy includes naval combat and service forces and such aviation as may be organic therein, and the Marine Corps includes not less than three combat divisions and three air wings and such other land combat, aviation, and other services as may be organic therein.

PRIMARY FUNCTIONS OF THE NAVY AND THE MARINE CORPS

a. To organize, train, and equip Navy and Marine Corps forces for the conduct of prompt and sustained combat operations at sea, including operations of sea-based aircraft and land-based naval air components—specifically, forces to seek out and destroy enemy naval forces and to suppress enemy sea commerce, to gain and maintain general naval supremacy to control vital sea areas and to protect vital sea lines of communication, to establish and maintain local superiority (including air) in an area of naval operations, to seize and defend advanced naval bases, and to conduct such land and air operations as may be essential to the prosecution of a naval campaign.

b. To maintain the Marine Corps, having the following specific functions:

(1) To provide Fleet Marine Forces of combined arms, together with supporting air components, for service with the Fleet in the seizure or defense of advanced naval bases and for the conduct of such land operations as may be essential to the prosecution of a naval campaign. These functions do not contemplate the creation of a second land Army.

(2) To provide detachments and organizations for service on armed vessels of the Navy, and security detachments for the protection of naval property at naval stations and bases.

(3) To develop, in coordination with the other Services, the doctrines, tactics, techniques, and equipment employed by landing forces in amphibious operations. The Marine Corps shall have primary interest in the development of those landing force doctrines, tactics, techniques, and equipment which are of common interest to the Army and the Marine Corps.

(4) To train and equip, as required, Marine Forces for airborne operations, in coordination with the other Services and in accordance with doctrines established by the Joint Chiefs of Staff.

(5) To develop, in coordination with the other Services, doctrines, procedures, and equipment of interest to the Marine Corps for airborne operations and not provided for in Section V, paragraph A 1 c (2).

c. To organize and equip, in coordination with the other Services, and to provide naval forces, including naval close air-support forces, for the conduct of joint amphibious operations, and to be responsible for the amphibious training of all forces assigned to joint amphibious operations in accordance with doctrines established by the Joint Chiefs of Staff.

d. To develop, in coordination with the other Services, the doctrines, procedures, and equipment of naval forces for amphibious operations, and the doctrines and procedures for joint amphibious operations.

e. To furnish adequate, timely, and reliable intelligence for the Navy and Marine Corps.

f. To organize, train, and equip naval forces for naval reconnaissance, antisubmarine warfare, and protection of shipping, and mine laying, including the air aspects thereof, and controlled mine field operations.

g. To provide air support essential for naval operations.

h. To provide sea-based air defense and the sea-based means for coordinating control for defense against air attack, coordinating with the other Services in matters of joint concern.

i. To provide naval (including naval air) forces as required for the defense of the United States against air attack, in accordance with doctrines established by the Joint Chiefs of Staff.

j. To furnish aerial photography as necessary for Navy and Marine Corps operations.

COLLATERAL FUNCTIONS OF THE NAVY AND THE MARINE CORPS

To train forces:

a. To interdict enemy land and air power and communications through operations at sea.

b. To conduct close air and naval support for land operations.

c. To furnish aerial photography for cartographic purposes.

d. To be prepared to participate in the over-all air effort as directed.

e. To establish military government, as directed, pending transfer of this responsibility to other authority.

Certain specific collateral functions of the Navy and Marine Corps are listed below:

1. To interdict enemy land and air power and communications through operations at sea.

2. To conduct close air support for land operations.

3. To furnish aerial photography for cartographic purposes.

4. To be prepared to participate in the overall effort as directed by the Joint Chiefs of Staff.

History

The government of the United States is founded upon a single document, the Constitution. The Constitution contains provisions for governing the armed forces that have not changed since the document was written.

The Congress, under the powers granted to it by the Constitution, has passed many laws forming and regulating the Navy. In turn, the secretary of the Navy has approved regulations and orders giving detail to these regulations.

In 1798 *Navy Regulations* provided for the establishment "at the seat of the government an executive known as the Department of the Navy, and a Secretary of the Navy, who shall be the head thereof."

A board of naval commissioners, with three members, was created by an act of 7 February 1815.

On 31 August 1842 the "bureau system" was established by Congress.

The congressional acts of 11 July 1890, 3 March 1891, and 20 June 1940 provided for an under secretary and an assistant secretary.

On 3 March 1915 the Office of the Chief of Naval Operations was provided for by an act of Congress.

On 12 July 1921 Congress created the Bureau of Aeronautics, and on 24 June 1926 Congress authorized the assistant secretary for air.

By 1942 *Navy Regulations* read as follows:

> The business of the Department of the Navy not specifically assigned by law shall be distributed in such manner as the Secretary of the Navy shall judge to be expedient and proper among the following bureaus:
> First, a Bureau of Yards and Docks.
> Second, a Bureau of Naval Personnel.
> Third, a Bureau of Ordnance.
> Fourth, a Bureau of Ships.
> Fifth, a Bureau of Supplies and Accounts.
> Sixth, a Bureau of Medicine and Surgery.
> Seventh, a Bureau of Aeronautics.

The National Security Act established the DOD in 1949 as an executive department of the government to include the military departments of the Army, Navy, and Air Force. The secretary of the Navy was demoted to subcabinet rank. The Reorganization Act of 1958 established the number of assistant secretaries at three. The titles of these positions have changed over the years. In 1966 the Naval Material Command was organized and in subsequent years various bureaus have been retitled as commands.

Congress and the Department of the Navy

Of the three branches of government, the legislative branch has the sole power to appropriate funds. From this and from the constitutional responsibility to "raise armies and navies" Congress derives the power to determine the nature of the Navy and Marine Corps and the amount of money used to purchase and operate ships, weapons, and personnel. Both the Senate and the House have committees on armed forces. These committees hold annual hearings for the purpose of authorizing ships and weapons. The appropriations committees of both houses then appropriate money for their construction and additional funds for supplies, pay, and other support.

The Navy Department has a chief of legislative liaison, several legislative officers, and an office in the House and the Senate to provide rapid liaison with the committees and members.

The comptroller of the Navy, under the supervision of the assistant secretary of the Navy for financial management, directs the preparation of the Navy budget and supplementary appropriation requests, which are forwarded to the comptroller of DOD. The budget is based on requirements carefully screened by the JCS.

Proposals for legislation affecting the Navy may be originated by members of Congress, by the Navy Department, or by other offices of DOD. No matter where they originate, they are referred to appropriate committees of the Congress for hearing and further processing.

Most of the laws affecting the Navy are contained in a grouping called US Code 10, which can be found in the library of every Navy Department office.

The Naval Establishment

The Organization of the Department of the Navy. The basic organization of the Department of the Navy was set forth in the section of the National Security Act of 1947 quoted earlier in this chapter. Figure 14-1 gives additional detail.

The name Department of the Navy is synonymous with the term naval establishment. The three principal parts of the Department of the Navy are:

1. The operating forces of the Navy, which comprise the fleets and their assigned forces, the fleet Marine forces (FMFs) and other assigned Marine Corps forces, the Military Sea Transportation Service, and those shore activities assigned to the operating forces of the Navy by the president or the secretary of the Navy.

2. The Navy Department, which is the central executive authority of the Department of the Navy, located at the seat of the government. It comprises the Office of the Secretary of the Navy, the Office of the Chief of Naval Operations, and the headquarters organizations of the Marine Corps, the Naval Material Command, the NMPS, the Bureau of Medicine and Surgery, the Office of the Comptroller of the Navy, the Office of the Judge Advocate General, the Office of Naval Research, the offices of the staff assistants to the secretary, and the Coast Guard, when operating as a service of the Navy.

3. The shore establishment, which comprises all activities of the Department of the Navy not assigned to the operating forces and not a part of the Navy Department. This includes those operating forces of the Marine Corps not assigned to the operating forces of the Navy or to a unified or specified command.

Policy of the Department of the Navy. It is the policy of the Department of the Navy, as part of DOD, to maintain the Navy and Marine Corps as an efficient, mobile, integrated force of multiple capabilities, sufficiently strong and ready at all times to fulfill their responsibilities, in conjunction with the other armed forces, to support and defend the Constitution against all enemies; to ensure, by timely and effective military action, the security of the United States, its possessions, and areas vital to its interest; to uphold and advance the national policies and interests of the United States; and to safeguard the internal security of the United States. This policy imposes upon the executive administration of the Department of the Navy four principal tasks:

1. To interpret, apply, and uphold the national policies and interests within the Department of the Navy. This task may be described as the "policy control" of the Department of the Navy.

2. To command the operating forces and, with respect to those Navy and Marine Corps forces assigned to unified and specified combatant commands, to exercise command in a manner

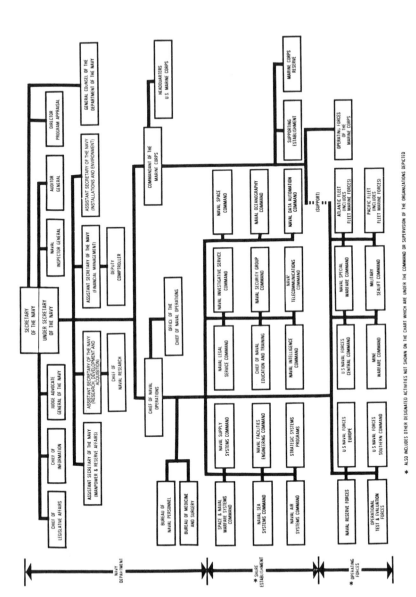

Figure 14-1. Organization of the Department of the Navy.

consistent with the full operational command vested in their unified and specified combatant commanders; to maintain the operating forces in a state of readiness to conduct war; and to promulgate to the Department of the Navy directives embracing matters of operations, security, intelligence, discipline, naval communications, and similar matters of naval administration. This task may be described as the "naval command" of the Department of the Navy.

3. To coordinate and direct the effort of the Navy Department and the shore establishment, in order to assure the development, procurement, production, and distribution of material, facilities, and personnel to the operating forces. This task may be described as the "logistics administration and control" of the Department of the Navy.

4. To develop and maintain efficiency and economy in the operation of the Department of the Navy with particular regard to matters of organization, staffing, administrative procedures, the utilization of personnel, materials, facilities, and the budgeting and expenditure of funds. This task may be described as the "business administration" of the Department of the Navy.

The Executive Organization.   The executive administration of the Department of the Navy is carried out by:

1. The secretary of the Navy, who is responsible under the direction of the secretary of defense for the operation of the Department of the Navy as well as its efficiency, including the policy, administration, and control of all matters within the Department of the Navy

2. The civilian executive assistants to the secretary of the Navy, who are the under secretary of the Navy and the assistant secretaries of the Navy

3. The naval professional assistants to the secretary, who are

   (a) the principal naval professional assistant and the naval command assistant (the CNO)

   (b) the Marine Corps command assistant (the commandant of the Marine Corps)

   (c) the commandant of the Coast Guard, when the Coast Guard is operating as part of the Navy.

The four principal tasks of the executive administration of the Department of the Navy are assigned to the secretary, his civilian executive assistants, and his naval professional assistants, as set forth in the following paragraphs:

1. The secretary of the Navy is responsible for the policy, administration, and control of the Department of the Navy, and for its operating efficiency.

2. The civilian executive assistants, all of whom function under the direction of the under secretary, are responsible to the secretary of the Navy for the supervision of those particular duties the secretary assigns.

3. The CNO is the senior military officer of the Department of the Navy and is responsible to the secretary of the Navy for the command, use, and administration of the operating forces of the Navy. With respect to those Navy and Marine Corps forces assigned to unified and specified combatant commands, this responsibility shall be discharged in a manner consistent with the full operational command vested in their unified and specified combatant commanders. The CNO is the principal naval adviser to the president and to the secretary of the Navy on the conduct of war and the principal naval adviser and naval executive to the secretary on the conduct of the activities of the Department of the Navy. He is the Navy member of the JCS and is responsible for keeping the secretary fully informed on matters considered or acted upon by the JCS.

The commandant of the Marine Corps is the senior officer of the Corps. He commands the Marine Corps and is directly responsible to the secretary of the Navy for its administration, discipline, internal organization, unit training, requirements, efficiency, and readiness, and for the total performance of the Marine Corps. The commandant is not a part of the permanent command structure of the CNO. However, there must be close cooperation between the CNO, as the senior military officer of the Department of the Navy, and the commandant of the Marine Corps. The commandant has an additional direct responsibility to the CNO for the readiness and performance of those elements of the operating forces of the Marine Corps assigned to the operating forces of the Navy. Such Marine Corps forces are under the command of the CNO.

From the secretary stems policy control; from the CNO, naval command and consumer logistics; and from the civilian executive assistants, business administration and producer logistics.

The Secretary of the Navy. The secretary superintends construction, manning, armament, equipment, and maintenance of all vessels and aircraft and performs other duties assigned by the secretary of defense. He has direct cognizance of officer and enlisted personnel and of public and legislative relations.

The Staff Assistants to the Secretary of the Navy. These are the assistant for administration, the general counsel, the chief of information, the chief of legislative affairs, the director of the Office of Program Appraisal, the auditor general, the inspector general, and the heads of any other boards and offices established. The duties of the individual assistants are assigned by the secretary.

The Executive Office of the Secretary. The various boards, directors, and chiefs reporting to and performing staff functions for the secretary and his civilian executive assistants are referred to as the Executive Office of the Secretary (EXOS).

The Office of the Judge Advocate General. This office has cognizance of all major phases of military, administrative, and legislative law pertaining to the operation of the naval establishment. It reviews the records of court-martial proceedings and other courts and boards. Matters of international law are also reviewed.

The Office of the Comptroller. This office, under the assistant secretary for financial management, is responsible for budgeting, accounting, progress and statistical reporting, and internal audit for all organizations of the Navy Department and for liaison with the comptrollers of DOD and the other services.

The Office of the General Counsel. This office is responsible for providing, throughout the Department of the Navy, legal services and advice in the field of business and commercial law.

The Office of Information. This office handles all phases of the public information and public relations program of the Navy.

The Office of Legislative Affairs. This office assists the senior officials of the Navy in their relations with Congress and handles liaison with individual members of Congress and with all committees except the appropriations committees.

The Office of Program Appraisal. This is a personal staff office of the secretary that provides appraisals of Navy and defense plans, studies, and proposals.

The Office of Naval Research.　This office, under the assistant secretary for research, engineering, and systems, initiates and coordinates naval research.

The Administrative Office.　This office is responsible for the general administration and business management of the department and administers certain management programs and appropriations applying to the naval establishment.

Navy Department Boards.　The National Naval Reserve Policy Board, the Decorations and Medals Board, and the Correction of Naval Records Board have been established to represent the secretary in the matters to which their titles refer.

Navy Council of Personnel Boards.　Certain naval personnel boards and councils have been established either by law or by administrative action to assist the secretary in promoting the welfare of Navy personnel. The duties of most of the boards are indicated in their titles. Details of their charters can be obtained from the management engineer of the Navy Department.

Joint Boards and Committees.　Joint boards are established either by law or by order of the president or the secretary of defense. A number of these are mentioned in the discussion of the functions of the JCS.

The Office of the Chief of Naval Operations

The responsibilities of the CNO and his subordinates are set forth in detail in OPNAVINST 5430. The following is a condensed version. The various offices under the CNO are collectively referred to as the Office of the Chief of Naval Operations (OPNAV). They assist the CNO in executing command and in providing consumer logistics. See figure 14-2.

The Chief of Naval Operations (OP-00).　The CNO is the senior military officer in the Department of the Navy. He has authority over all other officers of the naval service, except an officer of the naval service serving as chairman of the JCS. He is the principal naval adviser to the president and to the secretary of the Navy on the conduct of war, and the principal naval adviser and naval executive to the secretary on the conduct of the activities of the Department of the Navy. He is the Navy member of the JCS, and is responsible, with the commandant of the Marine Corps, for keeping the secretary fully informed on matters considered or acted upon by the JCS. He commands the operating forces of the Navy and such shore activities as are assigned by the Secretary of the Navy.

The Vice Chief of Naval Operations (OP-09). The VCNO has authority and duties delegated by the CNO. Orders issued by the VCNO in performing such duties have the same effect as if issued by the CNO.

The VCNO's principal job is to act as executive for the CNO. In addition the VCNO coordinates the performance of the various boards, staff assistants, deputy chiefs of staff, and directors of major staff offices.

The CNO/VCNO Staff Assistants. These assistants advise the secretary of the Navy, CNO, and VCNO on matters within their area of responsibility. They are the master chief petty officer of the Navy, the assistant for special projects, the special counsel to the CNO, the executive director of the CNO executive board, and the assistant for public affairs.

The Deputy Chief of Naval Operations (Manpower, Personnel, and Training) (OP-01)/Chief of Naval Personnel. This DCNO appraises and implements the programs of the CNO relating to manpower, personnel, and training resources and also sets professional standards and supervises human resource management and religious ministry.

ACNO (Undersea Warfare) (OP-02). Implements the programs of the CNO regarding shipboard and related support requirements, as well as submarines and deep submergence systems. This ACNO is the principal adviser on submarine and deep submergence systems.

ACNO (Surface Warfare) (OP-03). Implements the programs of the CNO with respect to shipboard requirements and the major characteristics of surface ships (except for carriers and submarine support ships). Implements surface warfare programs, including those in the Naval Reserve, and supervises surface ship training (but not that of carriers and submarine support ships).

DCNO (Logistics) (OP-04). Plans and provides for the logistic support of the operating forces, except for those areas assigned elsewhere, and serves as the principal adviser to the CNO on the conduct of logistics and physical security.

ACNO (Air Warfare) (OP-05). Implements the programs of the CNO with respect to naval aviation, determines shipboard

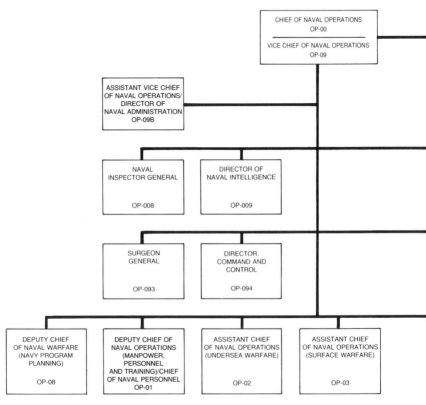

Figure 14-2. Organization of the Office of the CNO.

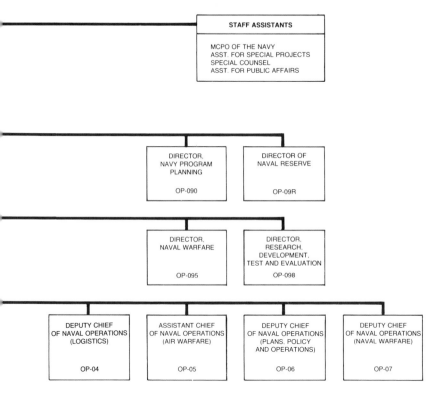

and related support requirements for aircraft carriers and specified aviation ships, and acts as the CNO's principal adviser on aviation matters.

DCNO (Plans, Policy, and Operations) (OP-06). Develops and disseminates plans and policies. Serves as the principal adviser to the CNO on JCS matters and as the principal adviser to the CNO and secretary of the Navy on strategic planning, nuclear weapons systems, national security affairs, international political-military affairs, technology transfer, foreign military assistance, and naval operational information.

DCNO (Naval Warfare) (OP-07). Provides centralized coordination of Force Warfare System's architecture and engineering, provides planning and requirements for fleet tactical readiness, force modernization, and force levels.

DCNO (Navy Program Planning) (OP-08). Exercises supervision over Navy program planning and study effort and serves as principal OPNAV staff executive for other than JCS matters.

Assistant VCNO/Director of Naval Administration (OP-09B). Serves as executive to the VCNO and sees to organizational matters regarding OPNAV and the commands assigned to the CNO. Also administers the Office of the Oceanographer of the Navy and the Naval Observatory.

Directors and Bureau Chiefs. The duties of directors and bureau chiefs belong to the positions set out in the following paragraphs:

The naval inspector general (OP-008) investigates all matters of importance to the Department of the Navy.

The director of naval intelligence (OP-009) is responsible for intelligence, cryptology, counterintelligence, and investigative and security matters.

The director of Navy program planning (OP-090) supervises and coordinates the Navy program planning and study effort.

The director of the Naval Reserve (OP-09R) administers the policy of the Naval Reserve.

The surgeon general (OP-093) formulates and directs all health-care programs.

The director, command and control (OP-094), establishes policy and integrates requirements for Navy command and control.

The director, naval warfare (OP-095), plans and establishes requirements for fleet readiness, modernization, and force levels.

The director, research, development, test and evaluation (OP-

098), carries out the responsibilities of the CNO and assists the assistant secretary of the Navy (R & D) in research, development, test, and evaluation.

Systems Commands

The Naval Sea Systems Command. This command is responsible for the design and integration of all displacement ships, ground-effect machines, and hydrofoil craft. It includes construction, overhaul, modernization and conversion, and covers combat systems, propulsion, navigation, habitability, ship-mounted sonar, search radar, the naval tactical data system, degaussing, minesweeping, and salvage equipment.

The Naval Air Systems Command. This command is responsible for aircraft, air-launched weapons systems, airborne electronics, air-launched underwater sound systems, airborne pyrotechnics, astronautics, catapults and arresting gear, airborne minesweeping equipment, aircraft drone and target systems, and photographic and meteorological equipment.

Space and Naval Warfare Systems Command. This command is responsible for shore electronics, the sound surveillance system, material support of certain Air Systems Command electronics equipment, certain space programs, shore-based strategic data systems, data link systems external to ships and aircraft, radio equipment, and electronic test equipment.

The Naval Facilities Engineering Command. This command is responsible for the design and construction of public works and public utilities of the shore establishment.

The Naval Supply Systems Command. This command is responsible for the procurement, custody, cataloging, inventory control, shipment, warehousing, issue, sale of and accounting for all supplies including food, fuel, clothing and general stores, retail store stock, and other property and services.

The Supply Systems Command prepares and serves food in all general messes except at naval hospitals and administers a centralized storage-operating organization for the control of all storage facilities.

Direction of Staff Offices. Under the VCNO, the staff offices of Naval Intelligence, Naval Reserve, Space, Command and Control Director of Naval Medicine/Surgeon General, Oceanography, Director of Religion Ministries/Chief of Chaplains, and Research and Development Requirements, Test and Evaluation support the CNO.

Other Commands and Bureaus

The Naval Military Personnel Command. The NMPC is responsible for the procurement, education, training, discipline, promotion, welfare, morale, and distribution of officers and enlisted personnel. The command has responsibility for all records of medals and awards, for places of confinement, and for prisoners. It supervises welfare and recreation activities, except those under the Marine Corps, and it controls all libraries.

The Bureau of Medicine and Surgery (BUMED). BUMED, headed by the surgeon general, is responsible for the health of Navy and Marine Corps personnel. It trains and educates the officers and enlisted personnel of the bureau and maintains all health records.

The Military Sealift Command. This command provides ocean lift to meet Navy responsibilities.

The Navy Intelligence Command. This command collects, processes, and disseminates intelligence materials.

The Naval Security Group Command. This command conducts the Navy's counterintelligence programs.

The Naval Investigation Service Command. This command conducts investigations of naval matters.

Naval Telecommunications Command. This command carries out the Navy's communications responsibilities.

Board of Inspection and Survey. This command conducts inspections of naval vessels, aircraft, and commands.

Naval Legal Service Command. This command conducts the Navy's legal affairs.

Naval Space Command. This command carries out the Navy's space program.

Naval Education and Training Command. This command conducts the Navy's education and training activities.

The Civil Engineer Corps (CEC). This corps mushroomed during World War II. The increasing complexity of warfare has made the logistics problem urgent. In World War II and subsequent wars the CEC was required to build hospitals, dry docks, housing, and other facilities rapidly, both here and overseas.

Naval Construction Battalions. Naval construction battalions, popularly known as SeaBees, were established during World War II to meet the need for uniformed men to perform construction work in combat areas. It became apparent early in the war at places like Wake and Guam that civilian workers could not do the job under combat conditions. As initially established, a battalion was composed of four companies of construction workers and a headquarters company of yeomen, cooks, etc., for a total of 34 officers and 1,083 men. SeaBees took part in every major amphibious landing in the Pacific. They unloaded supplies, rehabilitated airfields, and constructed buildings and roads. Later they built dry docks, fleet operating bases, and major bases.

Because their outstanding contribution had clearly established the need for such a force, the SeaBees were made a permanent part of the Navy in 1946, but were reduced to a peacetime level of less than 5,000. Just before the Korean crisis in June 1950, there were 3,300 SeaBees on active duty. They participated in the Korean conflict, including the Inchon and Wonsan landings, as well as in the Vietnamese War. They will continue to be a vital part of our Navy.

The U.S. Marine Corps

Origin. The Continental Marines, based on an organization of the Royal Navy, was established by resolution of the Continental Congress on 10 November 1775. The Marine Corps was established by act of Congress on 11 July 1798.

Tradition. As they enlist, marines learn that Marine Corps traditions are as much a part of their equipment as their pack and rifle. These traditions are many: devotion to duty and to discipline, loyalty to country and to Corps, self-sacrifice, versatility and dependability. Tradition is reinforced by distinctive uniforms and insignia, faultlessly kept, excellent equipment, and a continuously fostered readiness to fight in peace or in war.

The Commandant of the Marine Corps. The commandant is responsible directly to the secretary of the Navy for procurement, discharge, education, training, discipline, and distribution of officers and enlisted men of the Corps, including the Marine Corps Reserve and its equipment, supply, administration, and general efficiency. The commandant is one of the naval professional assistants to the secretary of the Navy and a principal adviser to both the secretary and the CNO.

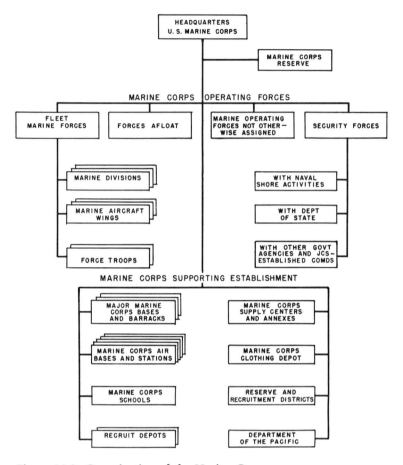

Figure 14-3. Organization of the Marine Corps.

The staff of the commandant is composed of the positions described in the following paragraphs.

The assistant commandant and chief of staff is responsible for execution of the policy of the commandant and for coordinating the work of the staff. There is a special projects directorate under him.

The deputy chief of staff for plans, programs, and operations is responsible for the formulation of plans and programs and for the operations of those forces under the commandant.

The deputy chief of staff for manpower and reserve affairs is responsible for all manpower and personnel management, procurement, and service.

The deputy chief of staff for aviation is responsible for aviation plans and policies.

The assistant chief of staff for reserve affairs administers all Marine Corps Reserve matters.

Other officers at Marine Headquarters are the inspector general, the judge advocate, the public affairs officer, the deputy chief of staff (DCS) for installations and logistics, the DCS for requirements and programs, the DCS for command, control, communications, computers, intelligence and interoperability (C4I2), the legislative assistant, the medical and dental officers, and the chaplain. Two other organizations have a special relationship to the Headquarters Marine Corps: the Marine Corps Research, Development and Acquisition Command (MCRDAC), and the Marine Corps Combat Development Command (MCCDC).

The Shore Establishment. This includes two recruit depots (Parris Island, NC, and San Diego, CA) where recruits receive their basic training. The major continental bases for the East Coast are at Camp Lejeune and the Marine Corps Air Stations at Cherry Point, NC; New River, NC; and Beaufort, SC; for the West Coast they are at Camp Pendleton and the Marine Corps Air Stations at El Toro, CA, Tustin, CA, and Yuma, AZ.

The Marine Corps Schools. These are located at Quantico, VA. The basic school trains and indoctrinates new officers taken into the service as second lieutenants from the Naval Academy, from among civilian university graduates, or from the ranks. The eight-month course emphasizes individual and crew-served weapons, small-unit tactics and leadership, and basic administration and military law. Upon graduation, the young officer is ordered to duty in the FMF or in a marine detachment aboard ship. Another source of marine officers is the Naval Aviation Cadet Program.

After becoming a captain (five to eleven years), an officer becomes eligible for the Amphibious Warfare School, which trains the officer for action and command on the battalion and regimental levels. As a major (twelve to sixteen years), the officer is eligible for the senior course at the Command and Staff College, which trains officers in staff and command duties at the division and corps level. Naval officers and personnel from the other services attend these schools on a quota basis.

Marine Corps Reserve. Allowing for functional differences, the Marine Corps Reserve organization parallels that of the Naval Reserve and is, in fact, governed by the same basic legislation. Most of the organized ground units of the Marine Corps Reserve are composed of infantry battalions, although an adequate number of specialist units, such as artillery, tracked vehicle, engineer, and communication organizations, are likewise operating. More than thirty squadrons are included in the air reserve.

Operating Forces. The operating forces of the Marine Corps are a balanced blend of air and ground arms, and are primarily trained, organized, and equipped for offensive amphibious employment. The marines are divided into two Fleet Marine Forces (FMFs): FMFLant and FMFPac. FMFLant consists of II Marine Expeditionary Force (II MEF), and FMFPac consists of I and II MEF. Each MEF is composed of a Marine division, a Marine aircraft wing and a Force Service Support Group (II MEF also includes an extra Marine Expeditionary Brigade located in Hawaii). The primary mission of the Fleet Marine Forces is to seize objectives held by enemy forces. They may also be used for defense of forward bases. The forces are trained for immediate deployment by ship or air anywhere in the world.

Marine Air-Ground Task Forces (MAGTFs) are combined arms teams of air and ground forces controlled by a single commander. There are three basic kinds of MAGTFs, depending on size. However, regardless of size, each MAGTF consists of a Command Element (CE), a Ground Combat Element (GCE), an Aviation Combat Element (ACE), and a Combat Service Support Element (CSSE).

The largest type of MAGTF is the Marine Expeditionary Force (MEF), described above. A typical MEF will have 48,000 marines and 2,600 Navy personnel and requires 50–51 amphibious ships for transport. The MEF's ACE will have a full range of fighter and strike aircraft, as well as helicopters.

The next-largest MAGTF is the Marine Expeditionary Brigade, or MEB. A MEB will typically have 14,800–16,500 marines and 550–875 Navy personnel. A MEB may be embarked on 20–22 amphibious ships or may be designed to mate with prepositioned equipment and supplies. Three MEBs (1st, 6th, and 7th) are specifically designed for this purpose. For example, the Second Maritime Prepositioning Squadron ships located at Diego Garcia in the Indian Ocean are earmarked for the 7th MEB, which is based in California and would be flown to meet contingency requirements in the Middle East. The MEB's ACE has a full range of combat aircraft and helicopters (approximately half as many as the MEF).

The smallest MAGTF is called the Marine Expeditionary Unit–Special Operations Capable, or MEU–SOC. A MEU–SOC typically has 2,050 marines and 100 Navy personnel and is embarked aboard three to five amphibious ships. The MEU–SOC will have helicopters and will often include a small number of AV-8 Harrier aircraft as well.

The commanding generals of the FMFs, wearing the three stars of a lieutenant general, have the status of type commanders in the two fleets.

Marine Security Forces. Marines man marine security detachments at many naval bases all over the world and provide special guard detachments at American embassies.

The Naval Shore Establishment

The naval shore establishment comprises the field activities of the bureaus and offices of the Navy Department and includes all shore activities not assigned to the operating forces. Its function is to supply, maintain, and support the operating forces. Administration of the shore establishment and of the shore activities assigned to the operating forces is defined in detail in General Order 19.

Naval Districts. All naval districts except the Naval District of Washington have been abolished and their functions turned over to appropriate naval station commanders. In time of war naval districts will be reestablished. Therefore, the following description of the duties of a naval district commandant has been included.

Each naval district is commanded by a commandant, a flag officer of the line eligible to command at sea, who directly represents the secretary of the Navy and the CNO for all matters pertaining to discipline, area standardization, coordination, defense, and security. The commandant is the direct representative of the bureaus and offices of the Navy Department for matters specifically assigned to them, and for public relations.

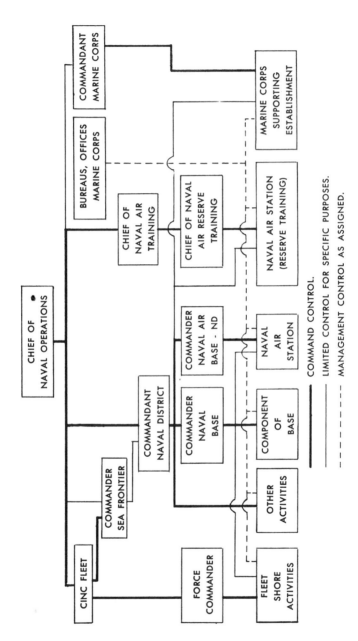

Figure 14-4. Naval command relations ashore.

The organization of a naval district establishes, between the commandant and the COs of the groups and units included in the district, relations similar to those between the commander in chief of a fleet and the various units of his command.

District craft, including vessels, aircraft, and small boats, are administered by the commandant. Craft assigned to specific units are under the immediate jurisdiction of the COs of the naval bases, shipyards, or stations to which the craft are assigned.

Certain activities within the geographical limits of a naval district may, for good reasons, not be under the command of the commandant or may be under his control only in a limited sense. Examples of these are fleet bases such as Guantánamo, Cuba, the amphibious bases at Little Creek, VA, and Coronado, CA, and air stations under the Naval Air Training and Experimental Commands.

Within the geographical confines of the Fifth Naval District, the naval district of Washington, DC has the same relationship to shore activities and to the Navy Department as set forth for numbered districts.

Among the many functions exercised by the commandant are logistical and operational support of the operating forces, the defense of the district and control of local disasters or emergencies, public relations, maintenance of industrial mobilization plans for the district, and control of Naval Reserve matters (except for matters relating to the Naval Air Reserve).

Naval Bases. A naval base is an area where shore activities are concentrated. The activities furnish direct logistic support to ships of the operating forces, with a naval base commander in military command of the group. A typical naval base includes a shipyard (commanded by an officer professionally and technically qualified in industrial matters), a naval station, a supply center or depot, a fuel depot, an ammunition and net depot, and a degaussing station.

It should be noted that the naval district commandant—who is an area commander—is in the military chain of command of the naval base; through the naval base commander he discharges his duties relating to logistic support of ships of the operating forces and carries out any other appropriate responsibilities.

The COs of the several component activities under the military command of a naval base commander receive most of their direction on matters involving administrative and technical guidance directly from the responsible bureaus and offices of the Navy Department.

Naval Air Bases. Naval air base commands comprise those activities of the shore establishment pertaining to aviation logistic support of the operating forces.

The commander of a naval air base in a naval district is under the command of the district commandant, as is the commander of a naval base. Activities of a naval air base command are directed by the naval air base commander, who also coordinates them with other activities of the command. Administrative and technical guidance of such activities, unless otherwise delegated, comes from the responsible bureau or office of the Navy Department.

Air activities within naval districts that are not assigned to the commander of naval air bases include the Naval Air Training Command and the Experimental Command, which are under their respective functional chiefs except in case of emergency.

The Commanders, Marine Corps Air Bases Eastern Area and Western Area. These officers, under the command of the commandant of the Marine Corps, coordinate their work with and are guided by the district commandants.

The Pacific Missile Range and the Naval Air Rocket Test Station. These, like other activities of the shore establishment not connected with a naval base, a naval air bases command, or a functional command, are under the command of the district commandant.

The Operating Forces

The operating forces are the several fleets, the FMF, and those shore activities and other forces assigned to the operating forces by the president or the secretary of the Navy (see chapter 12).

The Regular Navy

The U.S. Navy consists of the Regular Navy and the Naval Reserve. Together, these two components, the military and civilian elements of the Navy, have long provided for our country's first line of defense and for the security of the vital sea-lanes.

The Regular Navy and the Naval Reserve are dependent on one another; they must work closely and harmoniously, not only with each other, but with all elements of their sister services, if the armed forces of the United States are to achieve the teamwork of which they are capable. The Naval Reserve is discussed in the next chapter.

Consisting of many officers and enlisted personnel who have elected to make a career out of the naval service, the Regular Navy is our permanent professional naval force.

Officers of the Regular Navy are divided, as they are in the Naval Reserve, among the line and seven staff corps. Line officers exercise the military command of the Navy. The senior line officer present anywhere at any time is accountable for the exercise of his or her authority and cannot delegate this responsibility. Only line officers can command at sea. In general, only line officers can command ashore, except that members of certain corps, such as the medical, supply, and civil engineer corps, command shore activities under the technical control of their respective bureaus.

Among officers of the line are certain officer specialists who have been designated to perform engineering duty only, such as naval constructors and naval engineers, and others who perform limited duties in specialized fields, such as hydrography, communications, and law. These officers may not command at sea, but some of them will command at specialized shore stations.

Line officers, then, are the officers who command, administer, train, and fight the ships and larger units of the fleet. Their specialty is command in war.

Medical Corps.   The officers of the medical corps are composed exclusively of doctors of medicine. Under the Bureau of Medicine and Surgery, they are charged with the administration of members of the nurse corps and the Medical Service Corps (MSC).

Dental Corps.   The officers of the dental corps are composed exclusively of doctors of dentistry. Their opportunities for specialization are similar to those offered to medical officers. Although a separate corps, the dental corps comes under the administrative control of the Bureau of Medicine and Surgery. At naval hospitals, the dental department and dental officers are under the command of the CO of the hospital.

Medical Service Corps.   The officers of the MSC are men and women who, in civilian life, have acquired specialized competence in the fields of optometry, pharmacy, or such related medical sciences as bacteriology, biochemistry, psychology, sanitation engineering, and medical statistics. The MSC is under the Bureau of Medicine and Surgery. At naval hospitals the MSC is under the command of the CO of the hospital.

Supply Corps. Commissioned and warrant officers of the supply corps administer supplies for the Navy and receive and disburse naval funds for supply, pay, subsistence, and transportation. The supply corps is the business branch of the Navy. Its officers pay all the Navy's public bills and make payroll disbursements, both afloat and ashore.

Chaplain Corps. Officers of the chaplain corps are ordained ministers of various denominations and faiths. They serve under a chief of chaplains, but report to a commanding officer of the line. The officers of the chaplain corps conduct religious services aboard ships, at Navy and Marine Corps shore stations, and with the marines in the field. Although their duties are primarily religious, they have close daily contact with the young people of the commands in which they serve and are therefore able to promote their moral and spiritual welfare. Chaplains are authorized to conduct services of all denominations.

The U.S. Coast Guard

The functions of the Coast Guard, in general terms, are to enforce maritime law, save and protect life and property, provide navigational aids to maritime commerce and to transoceanic air commerce, promote the efficiency and safety of the American merchant marine, and remain in a state of readiness for military duty.

History. Created by act of Congress on 4 August 1790 at the request of the first secretary of the treasury, Alexander Hamilton, the Coast Guard has been variously known as the Revenue Marine, Revenue Service, and Revenue Cutter Service. As early as 1799, Congress provided for cooperation between the cutters and the Navy whenever the president directed. An act of Congress in 1915 consolidated the Revenue Cutter Service and the Life-Saving Service into the Coast Guard, which was to operate under the secretary of the treasury in peacetime and under the secretary of the Navy in wartime, or whenever the president directed.

In addition to its peacetime service to the country, the Coast Guard has given effective service in wartime. It participated with the Navy in the quasi-war with France in 1798, in the War of

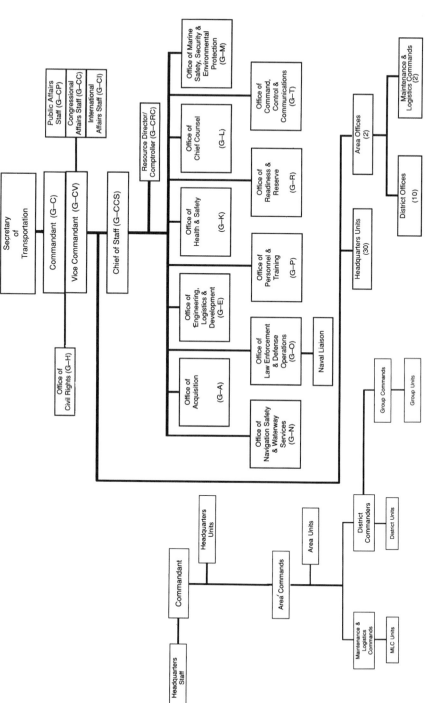

Figure 14-5. Organization of the U.S. Coast Guard.

1812, in the Seminole War, and in the Mexican War, and is said to have fired the first maritime shot in the Civil War (the revenue cutter *Harriet Lane* fired across the bow of the steamer *Nashville* while Fort Sumter was being bombarded).

In World War I, the Coast Guard not only hunted submarines but also performed convoy duty, principally between Gibraltar and the British Isles. Peace after World War I brought the Coast Guard its greatest expansion and a most difficult duty, the enforcement of Prohibition. With the repeal of the Eighteenth Amendment, the Coast Guard was drastically cut. In 1939 the Lighthouse Service of the Department of Commerce was transferred to the Department of the Treasury and the Coast Guard. In 1940 the Coast Guard established the Atlantic Weather Observation Service, patroling weather stations for protection of transatlantic air commerce. The Coast Guard Auxiliary (then called the Reserve) was established in 1939 and the Reserve in 1941. By November 1941 the Coast Guard was operating as part of the Navy. In World War II, in addition to guarding the continental coastline, the Coast Guard manned 351 vessels of the Navy. The Coast Guard now operates as part of the Department of Transportation.

Headquarters. The commandant of the Coast Guard directs the administrative affairs of the Coast Guard and maintains his office in the Coast Guard headquarters in Washington, D.C. The commandant is assisted by an organization as shown in figure 14-5.

Law Enforcement. The Coast Guard is charged with the enforcement, or with assisting in the enforcement, of all applicable federal laws upon the high seas and waters subject to the jurisdiction of the United States.

Through its captains of the ports, it enforces rules and regulations governing the anchorage and movement of vessels in territorial waters.

Saving Life and Property and Protecting Marine Commerce. To conduct search and rescue and to assist vessels and aircraft in distress, the service maintains an established organization of inshore and offshore rescue surface vessels, aircraft, lifeboat stations, and radio stations, together with rescue-coordination stations in each Coast Guard district.

Safety and Efficiency of Merchant Marine. The Coast Guard functions that relate to the merchant marine include the following: investigating marine disasters and collecting statistics relating to them; approving materials, equipment, and appliances; issuing certificates of inspection and permits approving vessels for operations that may be hazardous to life and property; regulating the transportation of explosives and other dangerous articles on vessels; administering load-line requirements; controlling logbooks; numbering undocumented vessels; licensing officers, pilots, and seamen; enforcing requirements for manning, for citizenship, and for the mustering and drilling of crews; suspending and revoking licenses and certificates; licensing motorboat operators; guarding the shipment, discharge, and welfare of merchant seamen; and promulgating and enforcing rules for lights, signals, speed, steering, sailing, passing, anchorage, movement, and towlines for vessels.

Navigation Aids. The Coast Guard establishes and maintains aids to maritime navigation.

Aviation. The Coast Guard maintains aviation stations along the coasts and on the Great Lakes. These stations engage in search-and-rescue work and in aerial reconnaissance and cooperate with other federal agencies in such matters as law enforcement and mapping.

Coast Guard Academy. The Coast Guard Academy is maintained at New London, Connecticut, for the professional instruction of cadets, who become eligible to receive commissions upon graduation from a four-year course.

Coast Guard Reserve and Auxiliary. The Coast Guard Auxiliary (then called the Reserve), established on 23 June 1939, and the Coast Guard Reserve, established on 19 February 1941, are administered by the commandant pursuant to act of Congress.

Publications. The Coast Guard publishes various pamphlets as well as light lists and Loran and radio-beacon system charts, which give information on aids to navigation.

Coast Guard Districts. For purposes of administration, the United States and its territories and possessions are divided into twelve Coast Guard districts, each under a district commander.

Women in the Navy

Nurse Corps. The Navy Nurse Corps was established by an act of Congress in 1908 to serve as a nursing unit in the medical department. In 1942 Congress enacted legislation giving members of the Corps rank relative to that of commissioned officers of the Navy. By an act of Congress in April 1947, the Nurse Corps was authorized and established as a staff corps of the Navy. Nurses appointed to the Navy hold regular commissions.

Female Yeomen and the Women's Reserve.   During 1917, as the United States was reaching a final decision to enter World War I, the Civil Service Commission could not meet the growing need of naval shore stations for clerical assistance. The act of 29 August 1916, which established the Naval Reserve Force, did not use the term *male,* so women were declared eligible for enrollment.

Immediately after the United States entered the war, the enrollment of women was undertaken on a large scale to release men for combat duty. As a result, 11,275 female yeomen were in service at the Armistice. They served not only as clerics but also as translators, draftsmen, fingerprint experts, and recruiters. They were stationed in Guam, the Canal Zone, Hawaii, France, and the United States. All were released from duty by July 1919.

The Women's Reserve of the Naval Reserve was authorized by Congress on 30 July 1942 in order to permit women volunteers to serve at shore stations within the continental United States and thereby release men for overseas duty. The Women's Reserve was an integral part of the naval service and in no sense a separate corps.

Women in the Regular Navy.   The Women's Armed Services Integration Act of 1948 provided that all laws or parts of laws regarding commissioned and warrant officers of the Regular Navy would apply equally to women officers. Enlisted women have the same opportunities as women officers. All benefits are the same except that husbands of women are not considered as dependents unless they are actually dependent.

Women attend all schools and are brought into the Navy via all sources. They serve in all billets for which they are qualified except in combatant ships and aircraft.

Women Marines.   In August 1918 Secretary of the Navy Daniels granted authority for women to enroll in the Marine Corps Reserve for clerical duty. The records show that 305 women were enlisted; the highest rank any of them attained was sergeant. The women wore a uniform similar to the men's and were subject to the same rules and regulations. After World War I they were discharged. At the beginning of World War II the Marine Corps

Women in the Navy are part of the regular and reserve components. They serve in noncombatant ships and aircraft and in all other billets.

Women's Reserve was activated, with an authorized strength of 1,000 officers and 18,000 enlisted women.

Women marines in the Regular Marine Corps were authorized by the Women's Armed Services Integration Act of 1948. They are integrated into the regular establishment. Enlisted women are given training at Parris Island. Women officer candidates are trained at the Women Officer's Training Class at Quantico. Their training closely parallels that of male marines.

Women in the Coast Guard. The women's reserve of the Coast Guard Reserve, formerly called SPARS (from the Coast Guard motto, *semper paratus*, meaning "always ready"), was established by the same amendment to the Naval Reserve Act that authorized the WAVES in July 1942. SPARS served with distinction during World War II.

The place of women in the Regular Coast Guard was assured by the same legislation that integrated women into the other services in 1973.

15
THE NAVAL RESERVE

THE REGULAR NAVY SHOULD ALWAYS BE READY TO
FIGHT, BUT IT CANNOT DO SO FOR A PROLONGED
PERIOD WITHOUT A TRAINED AND READY RESERVE.

—*Secretary of the Navy Thomas Gates*

WE DON'T HAVE TWO NAVIES, THERE'S JUST ONE NAVY.
MAKING THE BEST USE OF BOTH ACTIVE AND RESERVE
ELEMENTS IS ESSENTIAL IF WE ARE GOING TO MAINTAIN
OUR MARITIME SUPREMACY IN THE 1990s.

—*Admiral Frank B. Kelso II,*
Chief of Naval Operations

The Naval Reserve is of such continuing importance to the Navy that this complete chapter is devoted to educating regular officers about the Reserve and informing those reserve officers either entering or about to enter the Naval Reserve.

History of the Naval Reserve

The U.S. Naval Reserve was officially formed on 3 March 1915, although the use of naval reserve forces can be traced to colonial days and the Revolutionary War. Predecessors of the citizen-sailors of the 1980s include the members of naval militias in Massachusetts (1888) and then New York, Pennsylvania, and Rhode Island (1889). In 1891 the Office of Naval Militia was established in the Navy Department. Six years later sixteen states had naval militias whose personnel served with the Regular Navy during the Spanish-American War.

The Division of Naval Affairs replaced the Office of Naval

Militia in the Navy Department in 1914. By November 1918, at the end of World War I, approximately 20,000 reserve officers and 280,000 reserve enlisted members served alongside 230,000 active-duty Regular Navy personnel at sea and ashore.

In the period between World Wars I and II, there were no Ready Reserve units as we know them today and no reserve officers on extended active duty. Reserve officers were trained during voluntary two-week active-duty tours on combatant ships or at shore stations. Just prior to World War II, a few junior officers were brought directly from NROTC graduation to extended active duty with fleet units, so that in the opening days of the war a few members of the Reserve were on duty in ships and at shore stations. After Pearl Harbor, reservists helped man and command the ships, submarines, and aircraft that made up the largest navy ever built. At the end of World War II, the Navy was manned by a majority of reservists, many of whom remained either on extended active duty as reservists or as members of the Regular Navy. During the Korean War many reservists returned to active duty, again swelling the ranks of those manning the ships and aircraft that fought the war. During the conflict in Vietnam, the political administration decided not to call the reservists, with the exception of selected air and Seabee units, but to use the draft to obtain extra manpower. Some individual reservists returned to active duty on a voluntary basis. The decision not to call the reservists has been the subject of much debate.

Today's attitude toward the Naval Reserve was formed when the conflict in Vietnam wound down. Defense Department planners realized that the next war would be unlike any past wars and that, in the future, regular forces and their reserves would have to be equally ready to fight on short notice. The years to follow would also see increasing financial austerity, which would require maximum efficiency in the use of funds. Consequently, in 1970 the Secretary of Defense established a policy known as the Total-Force concept. Under this new policy, the services would make maximum use of their reserve forces: two reserve units (such as ships or air wings) would be maintained with the same annual budgetary expenditure as a similar Regular unit. Over the years the Total-Force policy has produced a strong Naval Reserve, manned by well-trained personnel and equipped with modern ships, aircraft, and weapons.

Mission of the Naval Reserve

The mission of the Naval Reserve, like that of other reserve components of the U.S. armed forces, is to provide trained units and qualified individuals for active duty in time of war or national emergency and at any other time the national security requires them.

The units are to have the necessary training, manning level, and equipment to be capable of joining regular units on short notice. Some reserve units have missions not usually needed in peacetime, such as censorship or control of merchant shipping.

Individual reservists not part of trained units must maintain a level of individual training that will enable them to join regular units.

Call to Active Duty

Peacetime. In normal times the majority of the Naval Reserve has an inactive status. Those officers who enter the Reserve from NROTC contract programs, OCS, and certain other procurement programs serve varying numbers of years of service under obligation before entering the Regular Navy or being released to inactive duty for completion of their remaining years of service in the Reserve. A few officers are voluntarily recalled for specific assignments of varying duration. Many officers (and enlisted personnel) perform annual fourteen-day tours of active duty in ships or squadrons for training purposes. Some reserve officers, selected for the Training and Administration of Reserves (TAR) program, are ordered to TAR and other related billets and perform extended active-duty tours.

Full Mobilization. In time of national emergency, declared by the president or declared and authorized by law, the secretary of the Navy, without the consent of the reservists concerned, may order any unit and any ready reservist not assigned to a unit to active duty for a period not to exceed twenty-four months.

In time of war or national emergency, when authorized by the Congress, the secretary of the Navy may, without the consent of the reservists concerned, order to active duty any unit or ready reservist or any other member of the Naval Reserve for the duration of the war or for six months thereafter.

Selective Mobilization. Selective mobilization is the expansion of the active Navy by the call-up of Naval Reserve units or individual ready reservists to satisfy an emergency requirement. It is used not only to deal with domestic emergencies such as civil disturbances but also to protect life or federal property and to prevent the disruption of federal actions.

Partial (External) Mobilization. Partial mobilization means the expansion of the active-duty Navy by call-up of Naval Reserve units and/or individual ready reservists. Partial and selective mobilization require the same authority as full mobilization.

Involuntary Recall. Since 1976, the president has had the authority under 10 USC 6737 to recall reservists for up to six months (90 days with the option to extend the recall an additional 90 days) for "any operational mission" that he may determine to be necessary. This authority, used for the first time in support of Operation Desert Shield, permits the president to recall involuntarily up to 200,000 selected reservists for operational requirements.

Members of the Selected Reserve who receive pay for drill and annual active-duty training accept the condition of immediate recall following a mobilization alert as part of their assignment to a billet. Once recall procedures have been initiated, ready reservists must execute mobilization orders; only legal exemptions or requests based upon extreme personal or community hardship will be considered valid reasons for failure to meet one's obligations. Figure 15-1 illustrates the foregoing options.

Composition of the Naval Reserve

Categories of Reservists. Reserve personnel are divided into several categories as follows:

1. The Ready Reserve consists of the Selected Reserve and the Individual Ready Reserve, liable for active duty as indicated in the previous section.

2. The Selected Reserve consists of that portion of the Ready Reserve made up of organized units required to participate in active-duty training and annual training in a pay status. Also included are persons performing initial active duty for training.

3. The Standby Reserve consists of those members of the Naval Reserve (other than those in the Ready Reserve or Retired Reserve) who are liable for active duty as indicated in the section

FORCE EXPANSION OPTIONS

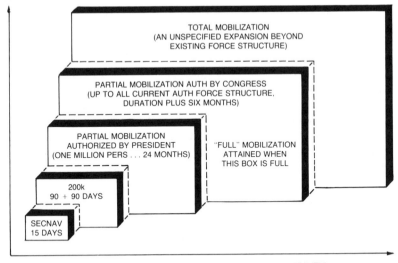

Figure 15-1. Force expansion options.

of this chapter on recall. The Active Standby Reserve is composed of those reservists who are completing their statutory military service obligation, are retained in active service by law, are screened from the Ready Reserve for their talent or experience, or are temporarily assigned to undertake some hardship. The Inactive Standby Reserve is composed of those individuals who are not required by law or regulation to remain members of the active-status program but who desire to retain their reserve affiliation in a nonparticipating status and who have skills that may be of future use to the Navy.

4. The Retired Reserve consists of those persons who have completed their service and been placed on the retired list. See chapter 21 for details and conditions under which reserve retirees may be recalled, paid retiree pay, and entitled to benefits.

Examples of Reservists. Lieutenant Able Officer is a ready reservist (USNR) and thus is in an active status. He is assigned to a pay billet with a Naval Reserve unit that meets the second weekend each month at the Pentagon. In January he performed two weeks' active-duty training with the Navy Command Center, for which he received full pay and allowances. His CO made sure he executed a Ready Reserve agreement (RRA) for an indefinite period when he joined and has counseled him regarding appropriate Navy officer billet classification codes. The NMPC has just notified Able Officer that he was selected for promotion to lieutenant commander by a Naval Reserve selection board.

Lieutenant Commander Win Scott is a standby reservist-active (USNR-S1) and thus is in an active status. In March he accepted a temporary appointment to a key position in his federal agency and was therefore screened from the Ready Reserves. He expects to return to his civilian position and resume drilling with his unit next year. For the present he may not receive pay or allowances. If the upcoming selection board finds him otherwise qualified, he may be promoted like Lieutenant Able Officer. He is liable for recall to active duty without his consent in time of war or national emergency, or when otherwise authorized by law, upon approval by the director of the selective service system.

Data Processing Technician 2 (DP2) Joe Bit is a standby reservist-inactive (USNR-S2), and thus is in an inactive status. His civilian employer has scheduled him for nine months of intensive technical and managerial training, so he had to allow his enlistment contract and RRA to expire for the duration. He passed the recent examination for DP1 but may not be advanced unless he returns to active status prior to the "limiting date" for this exam cycle. An officer in the S2 category cannot be considered for promotion by a selection board until one year after returning to active status. Similarly, even if selected by a board, the officer cannot be promoted unless he or she is appointed before being transferred to S2 status.

Commander Robin Law and Chief Petty Officer Long Career are retired reservists (USNR-Retired) and are thus in an inactive status. Commander Law is fifty-eight years old and does not yet receive pay or allowances of any kind. Chief Career is sixty-one and has received retirement pay since reaching his sixtieth birthday. Neither will receive retirement point credits for any additional service except extended active duty. Both remain liable for involuntary active duty in time of war or national emergency, or when otherwise authorized by law.

Manpower and Units

Size of the Reserve Force

For fiscal year 1988 Congress authorized 152,789 personnel for the Selected Reserve and 19,788 on full-time active duty as support personnel. This constitutes about 20 percent of the total Navy. There are also 7,300 people in the NROTC, 72,000 on active duty, and 87,000 in the Individual Ready Reserve for a total in the Ready Reserve of about 250,000.

Individual Ready Reserve. The Individual Ready Reserve contains approximately 87,439 persons who are ready to meet the Navy's mobilization requirements. They do not receive the amount of regular training that members of the Selected Reserve do. When ordered to active duty they are used to fill the complements (wartime allowances) of ships, squadrons, and stations.

Reserve Units. Most ready reservists are assigned to commissioned or augmentation reserve units, which are categorized in the following sections.

Commissioned Units. These are the units with equipment such as ships, aircraft squadrons, or construction battalions, tasked to deliver complete operational entities to the operating forces. In 1990 they comprised:

52 ships
    30 ASW frigates
    16 minesweepers
     3 tank landing ships
     3 salvage ships
 4 special boat units
28 mobile inshore undersea-warfare units
17 mobile construction battalions
13 cargo-handling battalions
41 fixed-wing squadrons
    4 fighter squadrons
    2 carrier airborne-early-warning squadrons
    3 strike fighter squadrons
    1 light attack squadron
    2 medium attack squadrons
    2 tactical electronic warfare squadrons
    2 fighter composite squadrons
   13 maritime patrol squadrons

helicopter squadrons
    2 carrier-based ASW
    1 combat support
    2 mine countermeasures
    2 combat support, special
    3 LAMPS

Reinforcing Units. These units augment active Navy commissioned units and operating staffs (and some Marine Corps combat commands) with trained personnel to provide the capability for combat forces to operate at the highest level of readiness for an indefinite period of time.

Sustaining Units. These units augment fleet and force support activities with the trained personnel necessary to provide a surge capability and to sustain the high level of activity required to support the deployed forces.

There are approximately 3,000 reinforcing and sustaining units that support or reinforce thirty-six diverse programs such as the submarine force and the selective service.

Reserve Shore Facilities. The Naval Reserve has over 250 Naval Reserve centers, combined Naval and Marine Corps Reserve centers, Naval Air Reserve facilities, and other stations lo-

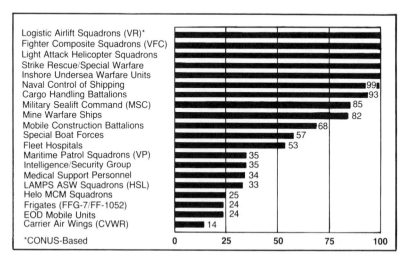

Figure 15-2. Major Naval Reserve mission areas—percentage of Navy's total capability (FY 89).

cated throughout the United States. Some have armories and elaborate training facilities, others are limited to more modest facilities, but all provide a home and a center for reservists and their activities.

Modernization of Naval Reserve Units. The defense policy shifts of 1970 began the modernization phase of the Naval Reserve. It was gradually outfitted with first-line ships, aircraft, and equipment.

In the area of ships, aircraft, and equipment, eight *Knox*-class (FF-1052) frigates have already been transferred to the Naval Reserve force, and sixteen new *Oliver Hazard Perry*–class (FFG-7) guided-missile frigates are being transferred. All have the latest equipment available.

The air arm of the Reserve is being modernized with E-2C, A-7E, F-14, and F/A-18 aircraft. Squadrons equipped with these aircraft will receive the same shore support and training as fleet units. Thus, reserve air units will be fleet compatible, which will ensure immediate augmentation upon mobilization.

The Naval Reserve mans modern, capable, first-class ships.

The same F/A-18 aircraft are flown by reserve squadrons and fleet squadrons. The reserve squadrons are trained and ready to join fleet units on very short notice.

Organization

Responsibility for the organization, administration, training, and equipping of the Naval Reserve, and for mobilization planning to reinforce and augment the active forces, rests with the CNO. The Naval Reserve command structure is headed by a rear admiral, the chief of Naval Reserve and as such the director of Naval Reserve and commander of Naval Reserve Forces.

Responsibilities of the DIRNAVRES. The DIRNAVRES, under the CNO, controls the policy direction, administration, and management of the Naval Reserve. He establishes plans, programs, priorities, organizations, procedures, and standards and monitors the state of mobilization readiness of Naval Reserve units and personnel. He also provides budgetary support for all Naval Reserve activities and programs.

Responsibilities of the COMNAVRESFOR. The COMNAVRESFOR commands the Naval Reserve from his headquarters in New Orleans. Obviously command of two such widely separated staffs requires a maximum of travel, communication, and expertise. The command organization for the COMNAV-

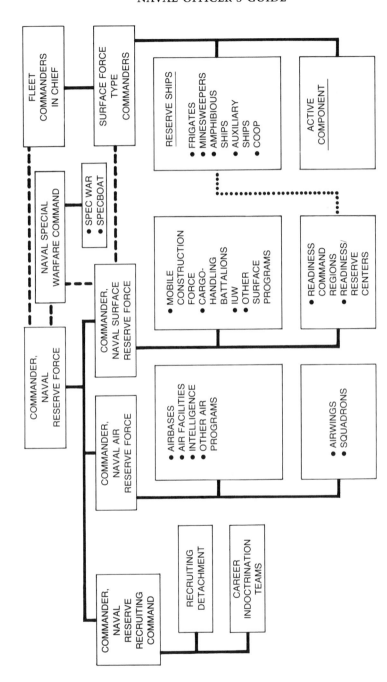

Figure 15-3. Organization of the Naval Reserve.

RESFOR is outlined in figure 15-3 and consists of five major subordinate commands.

1. The Naval Reserve surface unit and readiness command. Figure 15-4 shows the location of the sixteen subordinate Naval Reserve readiness command regions. Figure 15-5 shows the locations of Naval Reserve force ships and assets. Naval Reserve force ships and staffs are assigned to the active fleet commanders for operations and administration.

2. The Naval Air Reserve shore facilities. Figure 15-6 shows the sites of naval air stations, naval air facilities, Naval Air Reserve units, and Naval Air Reserve centers. These commands include all Naval Air Reserve shore facilities, except for Reserve air units.

3. The Naval Air Reserve force squadrons. Figure 15-7 indicates the types of squadrons in this command and their locations. Command of these units is exercised through subordinate reserve air wing commanders.

4. Naval Reserve mobile construction battalions. Figure 15-8 shows the location of reserve mobile construction battalions. The command is exercised through a brigade commander.

5. Naval Reserve intelligence units. Individual Reserve intelligence units are commanded by the director of the Naval Intelligence Program.

Support and Training

The Naval Reserve is supported by a unique combination of active-duty military and civilian personnel. The military group, known as full-time support (FTS) personnel, includes Regular Navy personnel who have one or more assignments in support of the Naval Reserve, a limited number of reserve officers who are voluntarily recalled to active duty for a specific assignment, and approximately 19,800 reservists in a special Navy active-duty career program called Training and Administration of Reserves (TAR).

Training. Training to achieve mobilization readiness is the primary peacetime task of the Naval Reserve. Training objectives are established, based on the specific unit mission, and set forth annually in each unit's long-range training plan. This plan establishes the minimum number of drills and active-duty training

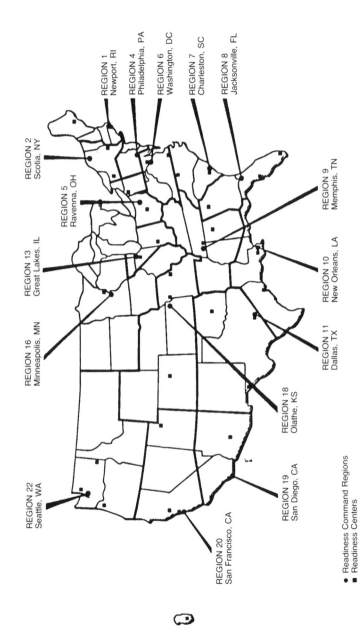

Figure 15-4. Naval Reserve Readiness Command regions.

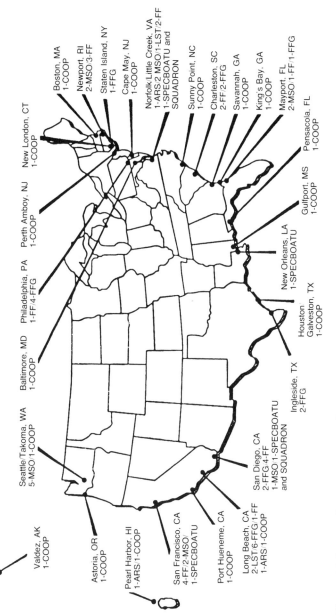

Figure 15-5. **Naval Reserve Force ships and assets as of 1988.**

Boston, MA
1-COOP

Newport, RI
2-MSO/3-FF

Staten Island, NY
1-FFG

Cape May, NJ
1-COOP

Norfolk/Little Creek. VA
1-ARS 2 MSO/1-LST/2-FF
1-SPECBOATU and
SQUADRON

Sunny Point, NC
1-COOP

Charleston, SC
2-FF/2-FFG

Savannah, GA
1-COOP

King's Bay, GA
1-COOP

Mayport, FL
2-MSO-1-FF-1-FFG

Pensacola, FL
1-COOP

New London, CT
1-COOP

Perth Amboy, NJ
1-COOP

Philadelphia, PA
1-FF/4-FFG

Baltimore, MD
1-COOP

Gulfport, MS
1-COOP

New Orleans, LA
1-SPECBOATU

Houston
Galveston, TX
1-COOP

Ingleside, TX
2-FFG

Seattle/Takoma, WA
5-MSO/1-COOP

San Diego, CA
2-FFG 4-FF
1-MSO/1-SPECBOATU
and SQUADRON

Port Hueneme, CA
1-COOP

Long Beach, CA
2-LST/6-FFG/1-FF
1-ARS 1-COOP

San Francisco, CA
4-FF 2-MSO/
1-SPECBOATU

Pearl Harbor, HI
1-ARS 1-COOP

Astoria, OR
1-COOP

Valdez, AK
1-COOP

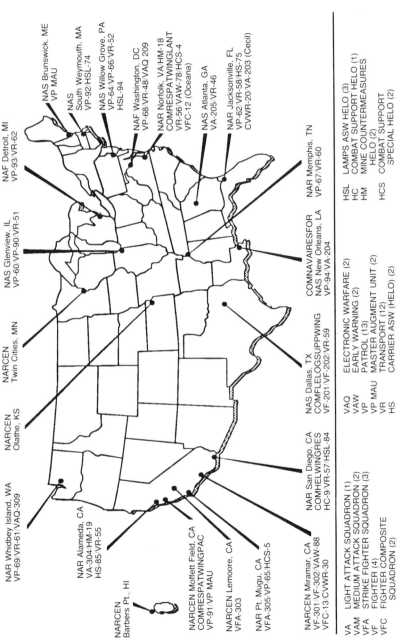

NAS Brunswick. ME
VP MAU

NAS
South Weymouth. MA
VP-92/HSL-74

NAS Willow Grove. PA
VP-64/VP-66/VR-52
HSL-94

NAF Washington. DC
VP-68/VR-48/VAQ 209

NAR Norfolk. VA/HM-18
COMRESPATWINGLANT
VR-56/VAW-78/HCS-4
VFC-12 (Oceana)

NAS Atlanta. GA
VA-205/VR-46

NAR Jacksonville. FL
VP-62/VR-58/HS-75
CVWR-20/VA-203 (Cecil)

NAF Detroit. MI
VP-93/VR-62

NAR Memphis. TN
VP-67/VR-60

HSL   LAMPS ASW HELO (3)
HC   COMBAT SUPPORT HELO (1)
HM   MINE COUNTERMEASURES
       HELO (2)
HCS   COMBAT SUPPORT
       SPECIAL HELO (2)

NAS Glenview. IL
VP-60/VP-90/VR-51

NARCEN
Twin Cities. MN

COMNAVAIRESFOR
NAS New Orleans. LA
VP-94/VA-204

NARCEN
Olathe, KS

NAS Dallas. TX
COMFLELOGSUPPWING
VF-201/VF-202/VR-59

VAQ   ELECTRONIC WARFARE (2)
VAW   EARLY WARNING (2)
VP   PATROL (13)
VP MAU MASTER AUGMENT UNIT (2)
VR   TRANSPORT (12)
HS   CARRIER ASW (HELO) (2)

NAR Whidbey Island, WA
VP-69/VR-61/VAQ-309

NAR San Diego, CA
COMHELWINGRES
HC-9/VR-57/HSL-84

VA   LIGHT ATTACK SQUADRON (1)
VAM   MEDIUM ATTACK SQUADRON (2)
VFA   STRIKE FIGHTER SQUADRON (3)
VF   FIGHTER (4)
VFC   FIGHTER COMPOSITE
       SQUADRON (2)

NAR Alameda. CA
VA-304/HM-19
HS-85/VR-55

NARCEN
Barbers Pt.. HI

NARCEN Moffett Field. CA
COMRESPATWINGPAC
VP-91/VP MAU

NARCEN Lemoore. CA
VFA-303

NAR Pt. Mugu. CA
VFA-305/VP-65/HCS-5

NARCEN Miramar. CA
VF-301/VF-302/VAW-88
VFC-13 CVWR-30

Figure 15-6. Naval Air Reserve sites and squadrons.

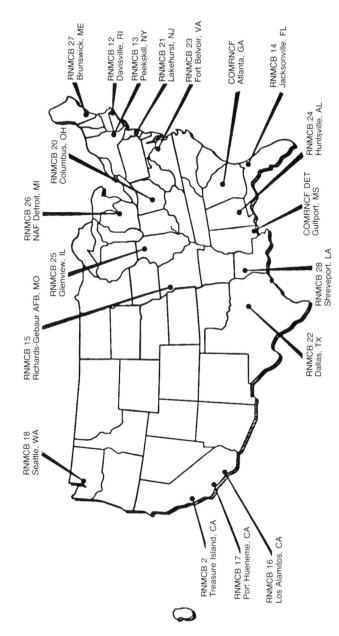

RNMCB 27
Brunswick, ME

RNMCB 12
Davisville, RI

RNMCB 13
Peekskill, NY

RNMCB 21
Lakehurst, NJ

RNMCB 23
Fort Belvoir, VA

COMRNCF
Atlanta, GA

RNMCB 14
Jacksonville, FL

RNMCB 24
Huntsville, AL

RNMCB 20
Columbus, OH

RNMCB 26
NAF Detroit, MI

COMRNCF DET
Gulfport, MS

RNMCB 25
Glenview, IL

RNMCB 28
Shreveport, LA

RNMCB 15
Richards-Gebaur AFB, MO

RNMCB 22
Dallas, TX

RNMCB 18
Seattle, WA

RNMCB 2
Treasure Island, CA

RNMCB 17
Por: Hueneme, CA

RNMCB 16
Los Alamitos, CA

Figure 15-7. Naval Air Reserve Force squadrons.

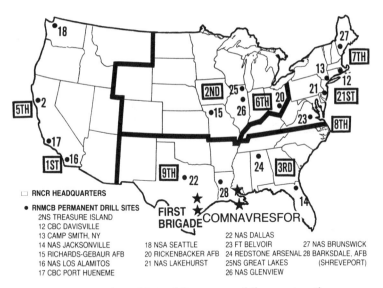

Figure 15-8. Location of Naval Reserve mobile construction battalions.

days needed to meet established unit-readiness criteria, individual qualification standards, and mobilization billet requirements. Emphasis is placed on individual training, unit training, and functional team training. Proven training techniques are set forth by a unit's active counterpart or the activity to which a unit will report upon mobilization. Unit-training syllabi, developed to implement the long-range training plan, help the individual maintain professional qualifications and skills and enable the unit to achieve established readiness criteria.

Training normally takes place during one weekend each month. Two drills which last at least four hours each are scheduled, one for Saturday and one for Sunday. Satisfactory participation is achieved through attendance at 90 percent of the scheduled regular drills and completion of two weeks' annual active-duty training. Additional drill programs, which range from twelve to seventy-two drills depending upon the criteria established for individual and unit-readiness and mobilization requirements, are conducted for a significant portion of the commissioned units of the Naval Reserve. Naval Reserve training programs recognize that over 85 percent of the enlisted members and virtually all of the officers in the Naval Reserve have had the initial and on-the-job training associated with two or more years of active duty.

Active duty for training and weekend-away training at mobilization sites give reserve units the opportunity to become familiar with the latest fleet equipment and with the work they would actually perform in the event of mobilization. One of the great benefits of this type of training is that the individual reservists is qualified and ready to perform with little or no time lost after mobilization.

Reservists use the correspondence-course facilities of the Navy to supplement their regularly scheduled training program.

The Naval Reserve training and mobilization capabilities are benefitting from modernized hardware in the commissioned units. There is increased involvement in Regular Navy–sponsored training programs and fleet training schools. Shipboard simulators (SBSs) have been installed at centralized drill locations. More emphasis is being put on the use of the weapon systems training devices and operational flight trainers. Improved classroom training aids and curricula are meeting the PQS used in the active fleet. Participation in fleet and command staff exercises also provides excellent training for reservists.

The Navy will continue to integrate reserve force units into fleet exercises, providing "hands on" training in the use of new equipment for those manning reserve force units. Improved training will be achieved through an increase in weekend-away training, simulator training, and funds to pay for attendance at formal schools.

An important feature of much Naval Reserve training is the direct support provided to active-duty units of the Navy. The phrase "mutual support" has been adopted to describe those Naval Reserve training evolutions that involve direct support and assistance to active-duty units in the performance of their daily mission.

Fortunately, training results can be measured. The effectiveness of training is reflected in PQS and advancement exams. Training visits and inspections focus on the unit training program; individual members may be interviewed and detailed training records reviewed. In a broader sense, training results will show up as additional Navy officer billet codes (NOBC) for unit officers and new Navy enlisted classification (NEC) codes for enlisted members. For both specific programs and the Naval Reserve as a whole, the standard Navy force-status reporting system is one indicator of training quality and may highlight areas where additional effort is required.

Participation Requirements. Current U.S. law requires registration of males for the selective service but does not specify a military obligation. By voluntary membership in an armed force, each person under the age of twenty-six incurs a six-year obligation to serve in the active and reserve components of that force.

Management and Administration

Overall Management. As pointed out earlier, the overall management of the Naval Reserve is under the control of DIRNAVRES/COMNAVRESFOR, who issues directives as necessary to implement his responsibilities. The *NMPC Manual* contains some basic regulations that set policy for the reserve program. Most of these repeat pertinent parts of U.S. Code 10, the basic law governing the armed forces. The *NMPC Manual* sets forth categories of reserve units and personnel, qualifications for drill pay, and mobilization definitions, and describes the TAR program. The manual also includes information on physical qualifications, retirement instructions, and the methods of shifting personnel from one category to another. However, the manual's regulations are sparse and have been expanded upon by parallel DIRNAVRES/COMNAVRESFOR instructions. Many essential functions of the reserve program are not covered at all in the *NMPC Manual* and are addressed solely by DIRNAVRES/CNAVRES directives.

Administration of Reservists on Active Duty. Reservists on active duty are administered in most areas in a manner similar to that used for regular members of the Navy. Orders, fitness reports, pay, and entitlements are similar. All reservists on active duty are subject to the UCMJ and are disciplined accordingly.

Reservists on active duty are selected and promoted along with their reserve contemporaries and are retired or ordered to inactive duty according to the provisions of the *NMPC Manual.*

Inactive Reservists Attached to Reserve Units. Reservists attached to reserve units are administered by the commanding officer of their unit in accordance with DIRNAVRES directives and the *NMPC Manual.* Selection, pay, retirement, and drilling are governed by the *NMPC Manual* and the NMPC Instruction 5400 series.

Inactive Reservists Not Attached to Units.   Reservists not attached to units are administered directly by the DIRNAVRES. The same criteria and directives are used for them and other reservists.

Training/Pay Categories.   NMPC Manual Art. 1880100 outlines the various drill categories, classified A through N. The definition of these categories is complicated; anyone interested should consult the manual.

Transfers between Reserve Programs.   NMPC Manual Art. 1880180 covers transfers to and from the Ready Reserve and between other programs.

Retirement.   Retirement of reservists, including the benefits to which they are entitled, is covered in chapter 21. More detailed information is contained in *NMPC Manual* Art. 3860100.

Annual Report on Retirement.   An annual report on retirement and qualified service for retirement is furnished to all officers of the Ready Reserve who are not on extended active duty and to all officers of the Active Standby Reserve by the Naval Reserve Personnel Center. If the report does not coincide with your personal records, consult *NMPC Manual* Art. 502040 for actions to be taken.

Career Patterns and Promotion or Advancement.   Reserve officers and enlisted personnel compete for pay billets and for promotion or advancement. Upon completion of twenty satisfactory years of participation, they may become eligible for retirement at age sixty with pay and benefits.

Officers who serve in Selected Reserve units will normally have an opportunity to perform in many familiar billets: personnel, administration, security, facilities, operations, training, public affairs, executive, and CO. In certain units they may be project directors, analysts, instructors, researchers, or staff officers. Units are organized to accomplish a function or task, thus providing a range of experience for members over a period of several years. Junior members may be able to fill several billets successively in the same unit, depending upon requirements and their qualifications. Senior members, on the other hand, often transfer to other units after one or two tours (two to four years) in order that they may continue to progress in their careers.

Promotion and advancement opportunities are determined each year by the Navy contingent upon mobilization requirements, authorized strength, and the numbers of qualified competitors for each vacancy. Enlisted personnel through pay grade E-6 compete in Navy-wide advancement examinations.

Selection Boards.   The procedures used by selection boards, which are approximately the same for all boards, are described in chapter 17.

Naval reservists are selected for promotion to the ranks of O-3 and above and advancement to E-7 and above by boards convened for that purpose. Each member is responsible for ensuring that his official record maintained by the NMPC contains complete and accurate information. From time to time Naval Reserve readiness commanders convene boards for the selection of officers and enlisted personnel for certain duties, including the vital role of unit commands. Each reservist must take positive measures to verify field records maintained by the Naval Reserve Readiness Command and the NMPC.

If reserve officers on active duty are being considered, board membership includes an appropriate number of reserve officers. Members from groups of officers restricted in the performance of duty, including reserve officers of these categories, are included in the line board when it considers officers of each group.

Separate selection boards are appointed to consider reserve officers not on active duty, reserve officers on temporary active duty, and TAR officers. They are composed of five or more members, all senior to the officers under consideration. At least half must be reserve officers.

Failure of Selection.   Rules governing Naval Reserve officers who have failed selection to the same grade twice are the same as for Regular Navy officers. Naval Reserve officers serving on active duty who have failed selection to the same grade twice and who are within two years of retirement eligibility will usually be continued on active duty until eligible for retirement. Those below the rank of lieutenant commander and not within two years of retirement will be released from active duty.

Honorably discharged officers, except those in the TAR community who receive severance pay, remain eligible for an appointment in the Naval Reserve so that they may continue serving in an inactive status and earn years of service toward retirement.

Fitness Reports and Enlisted Evaluations.   Naval reservists are evaluated on the same basis as active-duty naval personnel. The forms used are identical, and policies are stated in the same directive used by the active component. Any differences in the evaluation procedure derive from reserve component cycles, which use the fiscal year as a reference for unit training and many administrative functions.

Retention.   The purpose of the Navy retention program is to maintain the strength of active and reserve components at required levels by a volunteer force of qualified personnel. Naval Reserve units use the *Navy Retention Manual* (NAVPERS 15878), employ the same management techniques as their active counterparts, and rely upon affirmative leadership by exemplary senior officer and enlisted personnel to implement a successful program.

Conditions for Naval Reserve participation vary widely throughout the United States, making generalizations about retention somewhat limited in scope. A common factor in achieving high retention rates, however, is unit performance of tasks that are directly related to the Navy mission and that receive support from the active component. Unit readiness and retention are vitally linked, and both demand an imaginative and vigorous training effort.

Officer Qualification Questionnaires (OQQs) and Annual Qualification Questionnaires (AQQs).   Two questionnaires used in managing officer personnel are the OQQ (CNAVRES Form 1301/4) and the AQQ (NMPC Form 1210/2). Responsibility for compiling and organizing the needed information rests with individual officers; the material collected is subject to verification by seniors in the chain of command. The forms provide information that affects decisions about unit billet assignment, selections for active duty for training, qualification for NOBC codes, and promotion. They must be maintained to reflect current mobilization qualifications and are updated at least once a year.

Officers who require additional information or assistance in reserve training matters should contact the appropriate Naval Reserve coordinator or the nearest Naval Reserve center CO.

The tradition of citizen-sailors contributing to their country's defense began during America's fight for independence and has been maintained for two centuries. During the past three and a half decades of fiscal constraint, Congress and the chief executive have recognized the value of the Naval Reserve. The vitality and importance of the Navy's reserve component depends on the informed involvement and active participation by all uniformed personnel, active and reserve. The Total-Force concept can be realized only by teamwork and positive leadership.

16

OVERSEAS ORGANIZATIONS

WE ARE A STRONG NATION. BUT WE CANNOT LIVE TO
OURSELVES AND REMAIN STRONG.
—*General George C. Marshall*

THE RESPONSIBILITY OF THE GREAT STATES IS TO SERVE
AND NOT TO DOMINATE THE WORLD.
—*President Harry S. Truman*

Each naval officer should have an understanding of the alliances and organizations of which the United States is a member. Further, each should know the essentials of any organization or alliance that affects the national security of the United States.

The United Nations

Origin. The charter of the United Nations developed from proposals made at the Dumbarton Oaks Conference in 1944 by delegates from the United States, Great Britain, the USSR, and China.

In April 1945, 1,400 representatives from fifty nations met in San Francisco for a conference on international organization. The Dumbarton Oaks proposals were put before the conference, and the charter was signed after amendments were made. The required number of states ratified the charter on 24 October 1945.

Aims. The United Nations is an association of nations pledged to maintain international peace and security and to establish the political, economic, and social conditions necessary to that aim. The primary purpose of the UN, then, is to keep the peace. The secondary goal is to develop friendly relations among nations "based upon respect for the principle of equal rights and self-determination of peoples." The UN seeks also to achieve international cooperation in solving economic, cultural, and humanitarian problems. It strives to promote recognition of human rights and of fundamental freedoms for all without distinction as to race, sex, language, or religion. Finally, the UN acts as a center where nations may meet to discuss their problems and try to find solutions to them.

Organization

The UN has six basic divisions called "principal organs": the General Assembly, the Security Council, the Economic and Social Council, the Trusteeship Council, the International Court of Justice, and the Secretariat.

General Assembly. The General Assembly is the only organ of the UN that includes all members. Each member nation may have five representatives but only one vote. The General Assembly meets regularly once a year, and special sessions are called. The chief task of the assembly is to consider and make recommendations on the ways nations can cooperate to keep the peace. Voting on important questions is by a two-thirds majority; on other questions it is by a simple majority.

Security Council. The Security Council has the primary responsibility of keeping the peace. It investigates any situation that might lead to friction. It calls upon countries concerned to settle their differences. It may also recommend that members break off relations with recalcitrants. The Security Council has the power to use armed forces contributed by member nations, as it did in the Korean and Persian Gulf wars.

The Security Council consists of eleven members, five of which are permanent: China, France, the USSR, the United Kingdom, and the United States. The other six are elected to a two-year term by the General Assembly.

Economic and Social Council. This council works to further the economic and social purposes of the UN. It arranges for studies and makes reports and recommendations. The council is made up of eighteen members elected by the General Assembly.

Trusteeship Council. Territories not yet ready for self-government are placed under the international trusteeship system by the powers administering them. The Trusteeship Council assists the Security Council in governing these territories.

International Court of Justice. This court, the principal judicial body set up by the UN charter, judges cases brought before it by UN members. All members of the UN automatically belong to the court, which has fifteen judges, no two of whom may be from the same country.

Secretariat. The Secretariat is run by the secretary general, who is the chief administrative officer of the UN. He or she is appointed by the General Assembly on the recommendation of the Security Council. The secretary general appoints the staff, which does the clerical and administrative work of the UN.

Specialized Agencies. The UN has various specialized intergovernmental agencies such as the World Health Organization, the International Refugee Organization, and the International Monetary Fund.

Changing Character of the UN

When the UN was first formed, there were two distinct blocks, one headed by the United States and the other by the USSR. During the debate over the Korean crisis, the Soviet representative walked out of the Security Council room and was therefore unable to veto the motion to intervene with a UN force. Since the Korean War the USSR has been careful not to miss the opportunity to cast a veto. In the 1990–91 Persian Gulf crisis, the UN played a key role, passing several resolutions involving the Iraq invasion of Kuwait. The United States and other allies freed Kuwait under the UN aegis. The Soviet Union participated in the debate, but did not furnish any forces.

The UN has changed character in recent years with the admission of numerous Third World countries. Over the years, the UN has shifted its attention from rebuilding the countries victimized by World War II to improving the living standards of the world's poor.

The UN serves as a forum for debate, which will keep it in existence for some time. Naval officers should understand the scope of the UN's powers and should keep abreast of its debates and actions. An officer is appointed under the CNO as the U.S. Navy's representative to the UN, and many officers are assigned duties with UN peacekeeping and police forces.

North Atlantic Treaty Organization

In sea service in the Atlantic and Mediterranean and overseas assignments in Europe, you will operate with a NATO organization or under a NATO command. You will need to know as much as possible about NATO. The *NATO Handbook* (published annually by the NATO Information Service, Brussels, Belgium) will give you full information.

The Formation of NATO. When World War II came to an end, Western democracies hoped they were entering a period of security. They demobilized the majority of their armed forces and, for the maintenance of peace and the settlement of international disputes, invested their faith in the current spirit of understanding among the great powers.

Such hopes were rapidly doomed to disappointment by the policy of the Soviet Union. Having taken over the Baltic countries and parts of Finland, Czechoslovakia, and Germany, the USSR set about extending its rule still further. The solidarity of the Communist bloc was cemented by the creation of a network of alliances made up of twenty-three bilateral treaties.

The maintenance of peace in the face of this increasingly threatening situation was supposedly the function of the UN. By 1949, however, no less than thirty Soviet vetos had convinced free peoples that the UN could not preserve world order.

Faced with the failure of the UN, the Western countries united for their common defense. On 17 March 1948 the Brussels Treaty was signed by the United Kingdom, France, Belgium, Luxembourg, and the Netherlands. The participation of the United States was recognized as necessary to strengthen the treaty. The United States was reluctant to enter into alliance, but on 11 June 1948 the Vandenberg Resolution, which authorized the government to associate itself with a mutual defense agreement, was adopted. Discussions took place between the Brussels Treaty signatories, the United States, Canada, Italy, Iceland, Denmark, Norway, and Portugal, and on 4 April 1949 the representatives of the twelve countries signed the North Atlantic Treaty in Washington, D.C.

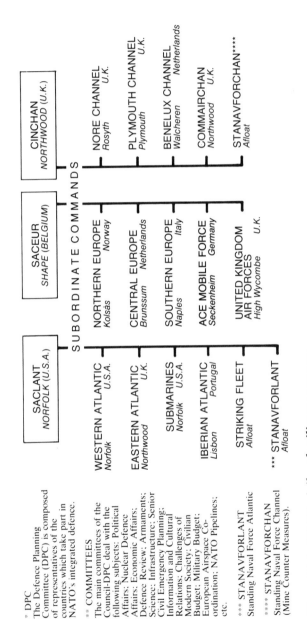

Figure 16-1. NATO civil and military structure.

* DPC
The Defence Planning Committee (DPC) is composed of representatives of the countries which take part in NATO's integrated defence.

** COMMITTEES
The main committees of the Council-DPC deal with the following subjects: Political Affairs; Nuclear Defence Affairs; Economic Affairs; Defence Review; Armaments; Science; Infrastructure; Senior Civil Emergency Planning; Information and Cultural Relations; Challenges of Modern Society; Civilian Budget; Military Budget; European Airspace Co-ordination; NATO Pipelines; etc.

*** STANAVFORLANT
Standing Naval Force Atlantic

**** STANAVFORCHAN
Standing Naval Force Channel (Mine Counter Measures).

SACLANT
NORFOLK (U.S.A.)

SACEUR
SHAPE (BELGIUM)

CINCHAN
NORTHWOOD (U.K.)

SUBORDINATE COMMANDS

WESTERN ATLANTIC   U.S.A.
Norfolk

EASTERN ATLANTIC   U.K.
Northwood

SUBMARINES   U.S.A.
Norfolk

IBERIAN ATLANTIC   Portugal
Lisbon

STRIKING FLEET
Afloat

*** STANAVFORLANT
Afloat

NORTHERN EUROPE   Norway
Kolsås

CENTRAL EUROPE   Netherlands
Brunssum

SOUTHERN EUROPE   Italy
Naples

ACE MOBILE FORCE   Germany
Seckenheim

UNITED KINGDOM   U.K.
AIR FORCES
High Wycombe

NORE CHANNEL   U.K.
Rosyth

PLYMOUTH CHANNEL   U.K.
Plymouth

BENELUX CHANNEL   Netherlands
Walcheren

COMMAIRCHAN   U.K.
Northwood

STANAVFORCHAN****
Afloat

Greece, Turkey, and the Federal Republic of Germany have subsequently joined the alliance.

The Treaty.   The text of the treaty is short and clear. It conforms with both the letter and the spirit of the UN charter. Briefly, it sets forth the following as desirable goals:

1. Peaceful settlement of disputes and abstinence from force or the threat of force
2. Economic collaboration between the signatories
3. Strengthening the means of resisting aggression by individual effort and mutual assistance
4. Consultation in the event that any signatory is threatened

The North Atlantic Council.   The council is the highest authority of NATO. It is composed of representatives from the member countries. All decisions are taken unanimously.

The president, who must be the foreign minister of a state, is chosen on a rotating basis, and the chairman is the secretary general of NATO. The council may meet at the level either of ministers or of permanent representatives.

Defense Planning Committee (DPC).   The DPC, composed of representatives of the member countries taking part in NATO's defense system, discusses military policy.

Military Committee.   The Military Committee is the senior military authority of NATO. It is composed of the chiefs of staff of member countries, except for Iceland, which is represented by a civilian. It meets regularly and makes recommendations and supplies guidance on military operations to subordinate authorities.

In 1966 France withdrew from the Military Committee of NATO and required that all Allied military forces and activities be removed from her land. The council decided to establish an integrated military staff responsible to the Military Committee. Supreme Headquarters Allied Powers Europe (SHAPE) was transferred to Casteau, Belgium, and the political headquarters to Brussels.

Commands.   The strategic area covered by NATO is divided into three commands and a regional planning group. The three major commands are the European Command, the Atlantic Command, and the Channel Command. Each command has subordinate commands. See figure 16-1.

Ships of the Standing Naval Force, Atlantic, operate in the Norwegian fjords during a NATO exercise.

The forces of member countries include those assigned in peacetime to NATO commands and those remaining under national command. The NATO commanders develop defense plans and determine requirements for forces, deployments, and exercises.

Other Treaty Organizations and Agreements

There are other treaty organizations and agreements that naval officers should be familiar with. Your ship or staff will have to include these organizations in your plans, using their strength for the benefit of our country and avoiding entanglements where necessary.

Organization of American States (OAS). On 30 April 1948 the twenty-one republics of the Western Hemisphere signed the charter forming the OAS. The charter describes the organization as a regional planning agency of the UN, but it is actually independent.

The collective security systems of the Inter-American Treaty of Reciprocal Assistance—known as the Rio Treaty, which became part of the OAS—represented the American states' general

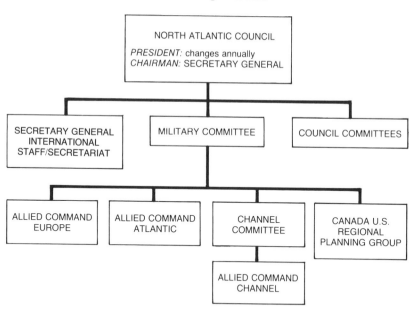

Figure 16-2. Major NATO commanders.

acceptance of the principle underlying the Monroe Doctrine: an attack upon an American state by a non-American state would be an attack upon all. The OAS is represented in Washington by the Inter-American Defense Board.

South Korean Mutual Defense Treaty. This treaty, signed in 1953, allows the United States to station troops in South Korea.

Japanese Mutual Defense Treaty. Under this bilateral treaty, signed in 1951, U.S. forces in Japan and the Japanese self-defense forces have agreed to cooperate.

Philippine Mutual Defense Treaty. This mutual-defense treaty, signed in 1951, covers the stationing of U.S. forces in the Philippines and the cooperation of defense forces in the event of emergency.

Anzus Treaty. This treaty, signed in 1951 by Australia, New Zealand, and the United States, provides for cooperation among the armed forces of the signatories.

Executive Agreements. The United States has entered into executive agreements which, although they do not have the force of treaties, cover defense arrangements with Denmark, Iceland, Spain, Canada, Liberia, Turkey, Pakistan, and the Philippines.

Congressional Resolutions. Congress has the power to pass resolutions in response to international crises. Some are in effect now, and all can be renewed if necessary. Those in effect are

1. A Middle East resolution (1956) proclaiming U.S. policy to help defend the Middle East countries against aggression from any country controlled by international communism.

2. A Cuban resolution (1962) to defend Latin American countries against Cuba and to oppose the deployment of Soviet forces to Cuba.

3. A Berlin resolution (1962) reaffirming U.S. determination to use force to defend West Berlin and its accesses.

U.S. Organizations for Foreign Policy Overseas

The Foreign Service of the United States

The Foreign Service, a branch of the Department of State, is a career corps of men and women who are specially selected and trained to carry out the foreign policy of our nation in day-to-day relations with other countries. Their specialty is diplomacy, the art of conducting negotiations between nations. Some seven thousand people serve abroad in more than one hundred countries. It is important that naval officers understand the structure of the Foreign Service, for there are ample opportunities during a naval career to interact with its members.

The Mission of the Foreign Service. The mission of the Foreign Service is to protect and promote the welfare and interests of the United States and of the American people, to establish relations between peoples as well as between their governments, to help friendly or developing nations achieve their goals, and to represent our government before the many permanent international organizations.

Embassies. Our country has an embassy in the capital of each major country with whom we have diplomatic relations and of many small ones. Embassies are headed by ambassadors who, in addition to acting as personal representatives of the president to the heads of host governments, are in charge of the team of agencies and attachés operating from the embassy. The ambassador also has authority over the various consuls in major ports and cities of that country. The official place of business of an ambassador is known as a chancery or chancellery.

Missions. Some countries are not of sufficient size to warrant an ambassador. The diplomatic agents sent to such countries are called ministers, their posts missions.

Consular Posts. Consulates general and consulates are established in the important cities of a foreign country. Consuls are not authorized to represent the president in negotiations. They perform such services as issuing visas and passports, protecting American citizens and property, assisting American business people, and serving American shipping and seamen.

Foreign Service Personnel. Foreign Service officers are members of the Foreign Service officer corps, the career professionals who perform the principal work of the service. They may be assigned to any kind of diplomatic or consular duty in any country where the United States maintains diplomatic or consular posts.

Foreign Service reserve officers are specialists in some skill; they are appointed by the secretary of state or by the president to be diplomatic and consular officers.

Consular Agents. Appointed by the secretary of state, consular agents are usually businessmen or women, of either American or foreign nationality, whose duties relate mostly to shipping and certification of invoices.

Titles. The Foreign Service officer holds a class and a title determined by his or her assignment. The officer's title establishes status at his or her post, whereas the officer's class establishes relative seniority for internal purposes.

The principal officer at a diplomatic post is the chief of mission. His or her principal assistant is the deputy chief of mission.

Titles and Address

Diplomatic	How To Address	Consular	How To Address
Ambassador	Mr. Ambassador	Consul general	Mr. Parker
Minister	Mr. Minister	Consul	″
Counselor	Mr. Harbisen	Vice consul	″
First secretary	″		
Second secretary	″		
Third secretary	″		
Attaché	″		

Titles and Positions at an Embassy

CLASS	TITLE	POSITION
Career minister	Ambassador or minister	Chief of mission
Foreign service officer, class 1 to 3	Minister counselor or counselor of embassy for political affairs	Deputy chief of mission and chief of the political section (supervises political reporting)
Foreign service officer, class 1 to 4	Economic counselor, first or second secretary	Economic officer (responsible for reporting on economic affairs)

Titles and Positions at a Consular Post

CLASS	TITLE	POSITION
Foreign service officer, class 1 to 3	Consul general	Principal officer at a consulate general
Foreign service officer, class 3 to 5	Consul	Principal officer at a consulate
Foreign service officer, class 6 to 8	Vice consul	Visa officer

Note: If an ambassador or minister is a woman, she should be addressed as Madam Ambassador or Minister; in all other cases, Mr. becomes Mrs. or Ms.

The chargé d'affaires *ad interim* is temporarily in charge of a diplomatic post in the absence of the chief of mission.

An attaché performs a specialized function. There are, among others, labor, agricultural, and commercial attachés, Army, Navy, and Air Force attachés. The senior military attaché is normally designated the defense attaché.

In many of our diplomatic missions, officers of the rank of counselor and below hold diplomatic and consular titles concurrently.

The Public Affairs Officer. The public affairs officer, although an employee of the U.S. Information Agency (USIA), is an integral member of the staff of an American embassy. He or she heads the information section of the embassy and is in charge of the country's USIA program.

The public affairs officer supervises the operation of USIA cultural centers in the country. These centers show films, distribute pamphlets, maintain libraries, and in general make the culture of the United States available to the host country.

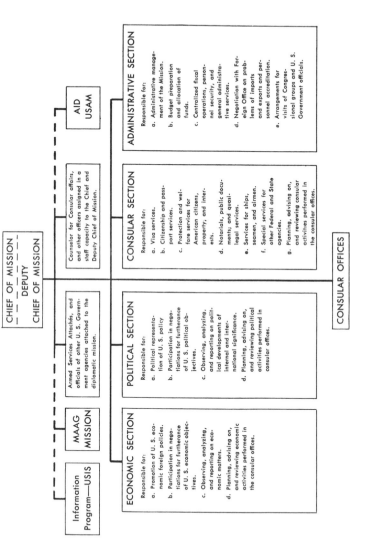

Figure 16.3 Basic organization of a typical U.S. diplomatic mission.

Agency for International Development

The Agency for International Development (AID), a semiautonomous unit within the Department of State, is responsible for coordinating all mutual-defense and assistance programs. The field offices are called AID missions and, like all other overseas operations, are under the control of the ambassador. AID is usually managed by a director and a central staff. Many of the AID staff are lent by separate federal agencies; others are on contract from universities and businesses.

Development Assistance. In most countries aided by the United States today, the development of human resources remains the priority need. Technical assistance is the heart of the development program. Development lending provides needed capital for investment and imports.

In Latin America U.S. contributions to the Alliance for Progress are administered by AID's bureau for Latin America, the head of which is also the coordinator of the Alliance for Progress.

Strategic Assistance. Both military and economic aid are used in strategic-assistance programs to strengthen free-world defenses and preserve the security and stability of friendly countries.

The largest element in strategic assistance is the military assistance program, which provides military equipment, training, and related services to help other countries protect themselves against internal subversion or external aggression.

Other AID Programs. AID helps promote the growth of private enterprise in Third World countries through its regular development programs and through special programs to encourage U.S. overseas investment. AID also administers much of the Food and Peace program, which donates surplus U.S. food stocks.

The Country Team

Every American governmental employee, whether he or she be the chief of another mission or a minor technician or clerk, takes his or her direction from the ambassador as captain of the team, and is responsible, through the chief of mission to the ambassador, for all his or her actions. While the chiefs of other missions are responsible directly to their Washington agencies, they are also responsible to the ambassador, who in turn is responsible to all branches of government through the Department of State for the operation of the country team in his charge.

17

CAREER PLANNING

LET RULE ENTRUSTED BE
TO HIM WHO TREATS HIS RANK
AS IF IT WERE HIS SOUL.

—*Lao Tze*, The Way of Life

THERE WILL BE NO MONEY IN IT; BUT THERE WILL
ALWAYS BE HONOR AND QUIETNESS OF MIND AND
WORTHY OCCUPATION—WHICH ARE FAR BETTER
GUARANTEES OF HAPPINESS.

—*Rear Admiral Alfred Thayer Mahan*, The Navy as a Career

From the day of reporting to first ship or station to the day of assuming highest command, an officer is continuously in training. At sea the officer is trained to assume the duties of the next senior billet in the ship's organization; ashore the officer is educated in the broader aspects of command responsibilities. In both areas training enables the officer to advance his or her career. This progression is carried out by a group of detail officers in the NMPC and in various staff corps headquarters. They are the best group of officers available, chosen on the basis of their top performance and carefully supervised, but you should still monitor them.

Detailing

There are two groups of officers in the officer distribution section of the NMPC collectively known as detailers. The first group, the rank detailers, has an officer, with assistants, for each rank. These officers keep a permanent file on the officers under their care and look out for the career and interests of all officers of that rank. The second group, consisting of placement officers, looks after the interests of the ships and stations in which they place officers.

When an officer in a billet is due for rotation, the placement officer controlling that billet informs or posts that billet with the detailer for that rank, who then assigns the best qualified officer available at that time. The detailer takes into account the personal preferences and career pattern of the officer concerned. The detailer and the placement officer confer on the needs of the service and the details of the orders to be written. The result is a set of orders.

The system does the utmost to reconcile the needs of the service with the aspirations, needs, and personal preferences of the individual officer. Nevertheless, the changing needs of the service, changes in detailing rules, differences of opinion about what is best for you, and your changing needs mean that you should always play a key role in planning your career.

Admiral Nimitz summed it up well while talking with a group of young destroyer captains when they called on him at his World War II headquarters on Guam. Being asked for advice on career planning, he said, "First, determine what career you want to follow, and plan it all the way to the top. Then ask for the best and toughest job available that suits your career path. If you present your case well to your detailer, you should get your requested job, then just continue on up the ladder as far as you can. If you don't get it, plead your case firmly and honestly. If you are turned down a second time, keep quiet, go to your assigned duty, and carry it out better than it was ever done before. If you do so, the chances are that the detailer will ask you what job you want the next time around. After all, he has to fill difficult and prestigious jobs with good men. If you have proved that you are a good man, he will need you. Remember, you are always allowed one objection. If you don't succeed, never say another word about it."* Admiral Nimitz's philosophy resulted in a long and rewarding career for him. You can do well, too.

Restricted line officers have detailers who handle all ranks, since the numbers they deal with are much smaller. Staff corps detailing is done by separate detailing systems in corps headquarters.

Preference Cards. Take pains to fill out your officer's pref-

*From the authors' personal notes.

erence and personal information card (NAVMILPERS 1301/1). If data changes radically, submit a change immediately. The detailer is only as good as the information he has.

Professional Development Paths

Career Patterns. Career patterns or paths, known as professional development paths, usually fall into well-defined sequences of duties. They are followed as closely as possible by the detailers, but the needs of the service and other contingencies frequently require deviations. The patterns used are shown graphically in the *Unrestricted Line Officer Career Planning Guidebook*, OPNAV P-13-1-86. This publication also contains much information on paths for restricted line and staff corps officers.

In the sections following, information on career professional development paths, taken from OPNAV P-13-1-86 and modified somewhat, is presented for each category of officer. Commentary for each group is included.

Surface Warfare Officer (SWO) (11XX). Figure 17-1 shows a typical professional development path for SWOs. They fill billets that will give them qualifications or that require an achieved expertise in surface warfare. Officers will generally follow the path shown, but no two officers will follow exactly the same sequence. Officers entering this field attend SWO School in Newport or Coronado. Additional functional training for the specific billet in which the CO intends to place the officer will be given en route.

Nuclear Surface Warfare Officer (NSWO) (11XX). Figure 17-2 shows a typical professional development path for NSWOs who begin their careers with nuclear-power training and then attend SWOS functional training. Thereafter these officers complete all other requirements and qualifications for SWOs. In addition, they must complete qualification as an engineering officer on a nuclear-powered ship in their first tour. This qualification is required for later command of a nuclear-powered ship. The NSWO usually has a split first tour, which enables him to complete engineering qualification in one half and normal surface warfare qualification in the other half. NSWOs may spend more time at sea than their SWO counterparts because of the shortage of NSWOs. This shortage will disappear in coming years.

Aviation Warfare Officer (13XX). Figure 17-3 shows a typ-

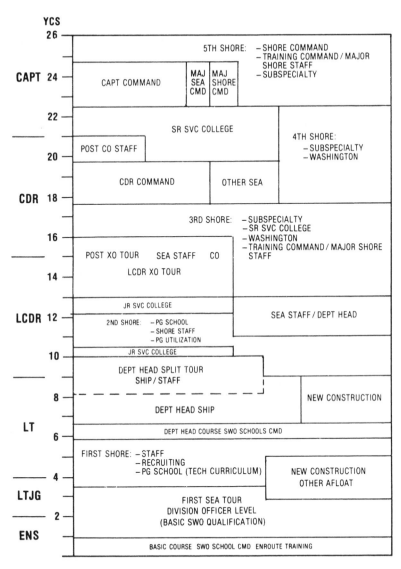

Figure 17-1. Surface warfare officer—professional development path.

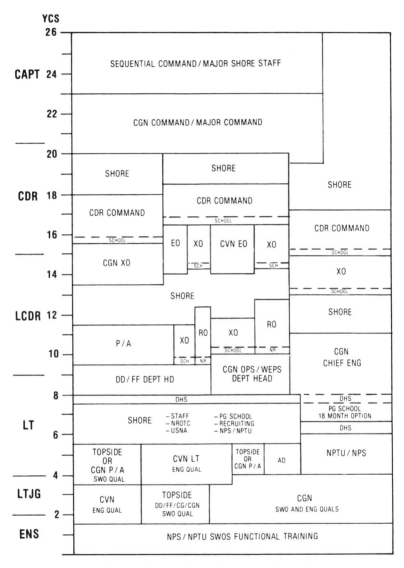

Figure 17-2. Nuclear surface warfare officer—professional development path.

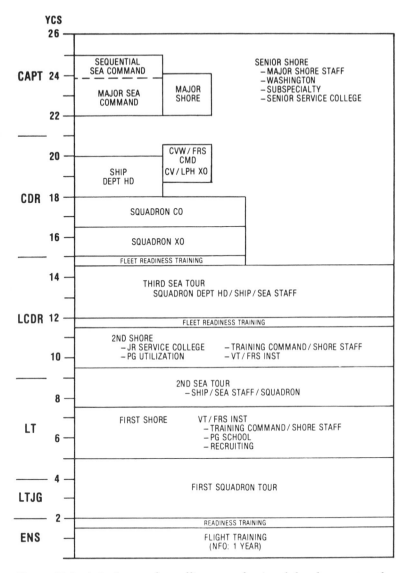

Figure 17-3. Aviation warfare officer—professional development path.

ical professional development path for aviation warfare officers. All officers with a 13XX designator belong to this community. This includes pilots, NFOs, and aviation generalist officers. All pilots and NFOs begin training at Pensacola. Pilots take general aviation pilot training for twelve to eighteen months and then continue with training in specific aircraft types in fleet readiness squadrons. Type assignment is competitive, but it is also influenced by the needs of the Navy. NFOs train in a shorter period of about one year, since no pilot time is needed. NFOs then go to fleet-readiness squadrons. After reporting to the fleet, both pilots and NFOs generally follow the patterns shown in figure 17-3.

Submarine Warfare Officer (112X).   Figure 17-4 shows a typical professional development path for a submarine warfare officer. After initial training, the program is much less flexible than those for other officer communities because of a shortage of officers. Sea tours are often extended and shore tours are shortened or skipped.

After about eight years of service, a critical decision must be made as to whether to remain a 112X officer and strive for eventual SSN (nuclear-powered attack submarine) or SSBN (nuclear-powered fleet ballistic missile) command or to ask for an ASR (a submarine rescue ship) command, or a change to an engineering duty (144X).

General Submarine Officer (112X).   Figure 17-5 shows a typical path for a general submarine officer. These assignments provide the GSO with the broad experience necessary for sea command and senior management, both inside and outside the submarine community. GSOs do not command nuclear submarines.

General Unrestricted Line Officer (110X).   Except for those with warfare specialties described in preceding paragraphs, these officers serve in a variety of shore billets. Career progression is described in figure 17-6.

Weapons Systems Acquisition Management.   The WSAM program provides an opportunity for unrestricted and restricted line and staff corps officers to fill vital weapons systems acquisition billets. Professional development paths exist for officers from various sources. For additional information, consult the *Unrestricted Line Officer Career Planning Guidebook*.

Special Warfare Officer (118X and 113X).   Figure 17-7 shows

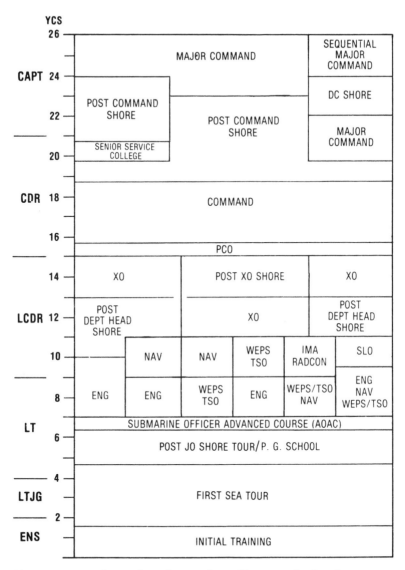

Figure 17-4. Nuclear submarine warfare officer—professional development path.

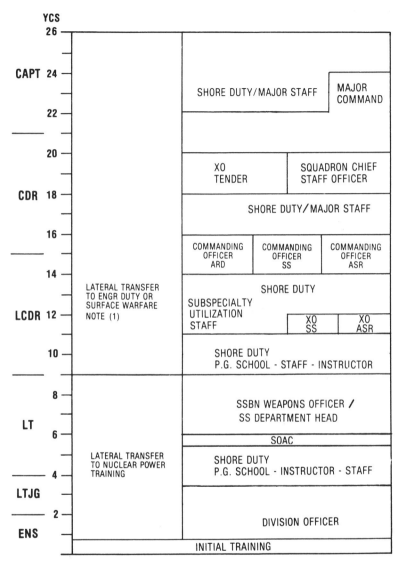

Figure 17-5. General submarine officer—professional development path.

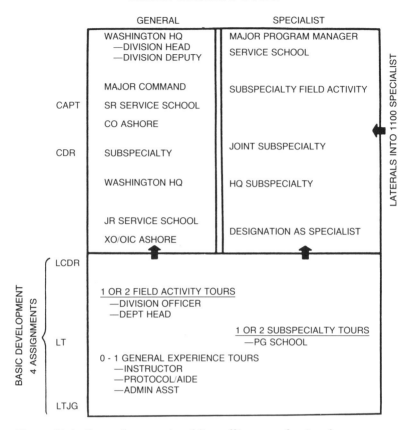

Figure 17-6. General unrestricted line officer—professional development path.

the professional development path for special warfare officers who serve in the areas of unconventional warfare, counterinsurgency, coastal and riverine interdictions, and tactical intelligence collection. Such officers must pass a rigid physical examination, volunteer for hazardous duty, and receive basic underwater demolition training (SEAL/BUDS). Initial assignment is to an underwater demolition team (UDT) or SEAL team, with a split tour allowing service in both. Upon qualification, the designator is changed from 118X to 113X. Subsequent tour patterns are shown in figure 17-7.

Special Operations Officer (114X). Figure 17-8 shows the professional development path for special operations officers. This

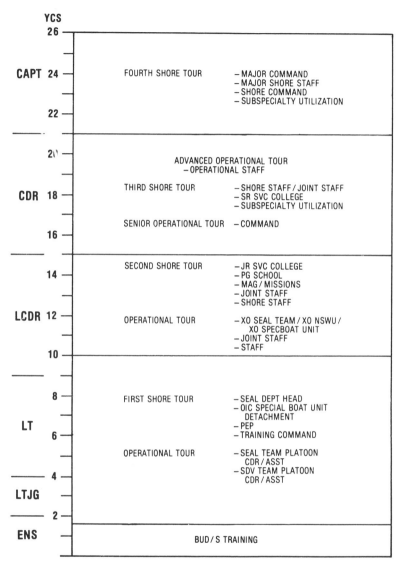

Figure 17-7. Special warfare officer—professional development path.

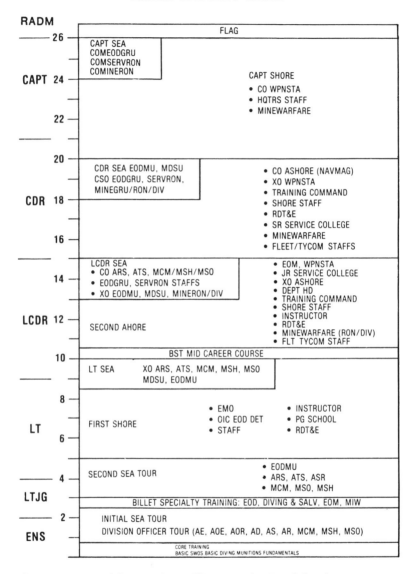

Figure 17-8. Special operations officer—professional development path.

community was created in 1978 to function in the areas of explosive ordnance disposal (EOD), operational diving and salvage, and expendable ordnance management (EOM). These officers serve aboard fleet ocean tugs (ATFs), salvage ships (ARSs), and ASRs, at harbor clearance units (HCUs), on major staffs, and at ordnance shore stations.

Officers may specialize in one area but must be familiar with all three. Newly acquired officers are designated 119X and receive initial training to qualify them for their first assignment. Thereafter additional training is given for qualification in the other two areas. After specialty training and warfare qualification, the designator is changed to 114X.

Engineering Duty (ED) Officer (144X/146X). ED officers follow professional development paths as shown in figure 17-9. These officers are technical specialists who serve in research and development, acquisition, construction, and maintenance of ships, combat systems, ordnance systems, and electronic systems.

The ED career path is divided into two phases. ED officers serve an initial sea tour, earn a postgraduate degree (if they do not already have one), and complete an ED qualification program. Thereafter, they may specialize in one of four areas: ships and ship system engineering, electrical system engineering, combat system engineering, and ordnance system engineering. After qualification, rotation is as shown in figure 17-9.

Aeronautical Engineering Duty Officer (151X). An aeronautical engineering duty officer is a technically educated and operationally experienced naval officer who provides professional management and technical direction in the design, development, acquisition, production, and logistic support of naval aircraft, air weapons, air weapons systems, and related support equipment. These officers relinquish line functions and serve in management billets. Each officer progresses through a succession of jobs of increasing responsibility, as indicated in figure 17-10. Most 151X officers are designated as naval aviators.

Aeronautical Maintenance Duty Officer (AMDO) (152X). AMDOs must complete the aviation maintenance officer and joint aviation supply maintenance material school. Like aeronautical engineering duty officers, they gain experience with each assignment and are rotated as shown in figure 17-11.

Cryptology Officer (161X). These officers provide support to the fleet and defense organization in cryptology and allied skills.

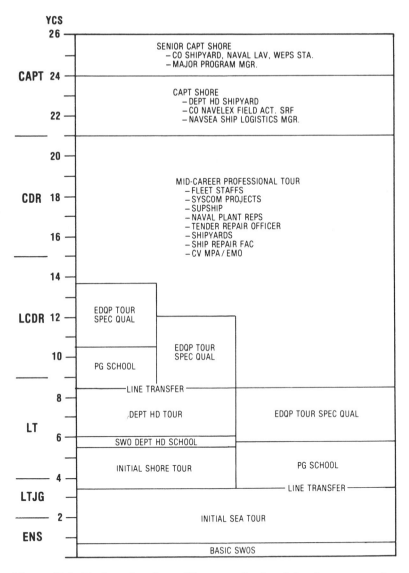

Figure 17-9. Engineering duty officer—professional development path.

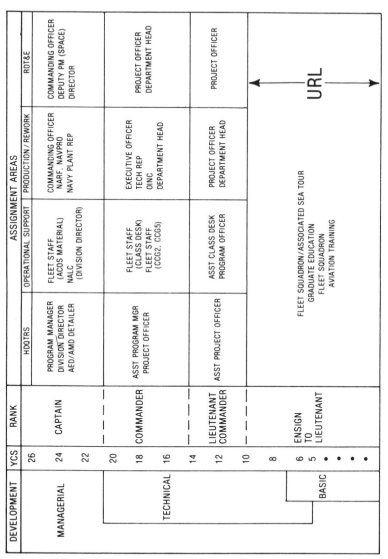

Figure 17-10. Aeronautical engineering duty officer—professional development path.

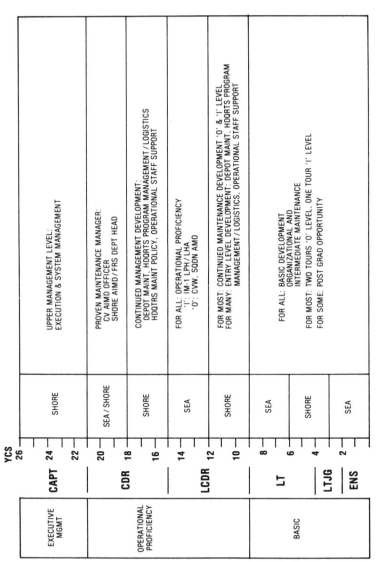

Figure 17-11. Aeronautical maintenance duty officer—professional development path.

They are members of the Naval Security Group (NAVSECGRU). The fields of service are signals intelligence (SIGINT), signals security (SIGSEC), and electronic warfare.

The professional development path begins with initial training and experience in a large NAVSECGRU station and thereafter follows the sequence shown in figure 17-12.

Special Duty Officer (Intelligence) (163X). Intelligence officers are trained in their specialty before serving in their first billets. This training is conducted at the Armed Forces Air Intelligence Center. First tours are air oriented, and subsequent tours branch out into other areas. The professional development path is shown in figure 17-13.

Special Duty Public Affairs Officer (165X). These officers specialize in the Navy's public affairs program. The group is relatively small; rotation provides continuous coverage of billets, which results in officers of different ranks succeeding each other in the same billet. A standard professional development path is difficult to predict. The ideal is shown in figure 17-14.

Oceanographic Officer (18XX). The oceanographic community comprises officers qualified by education and experience to serve in meteorology and mapping, physical oceanography, charting, and geodesy. The community evaluates and predicts environmental effects on weapon systems performance and fleet operations. There is a heavy emphasis on scientific education. Lateral transfers in all ranks are possible. Figure 17-15 gives an idealized professional development path; the requirements of the service usually govern rotation.

Supply Corps Officer (31XX). Officers of the supply corps first attend the six-month course at the Navy Supply School in Athens, Georgia. Their first tour is at sea, with those receiving highest school marks going to coveted independent billets on small ships. Supply officers handle supplies, disbursing, ship's stores, and food service. On small ships all are handled by the one officer. On large ships a supply corps officer may be assigned to one area only. The supply corps professional development path is usually followed as shown in figure 17-16. Assignment is much more regular than in other communities.

Civil Engineer Corps (51XX). Officers of this corps maintain the shore establishment. Therefore, they must attain both engineering and management skills. There are four basic types of duty available: public works, contract administration, construction

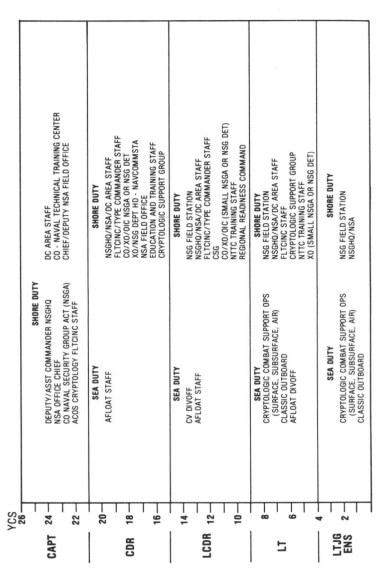

Figure 17-12. Cryptology officer—professional development path.

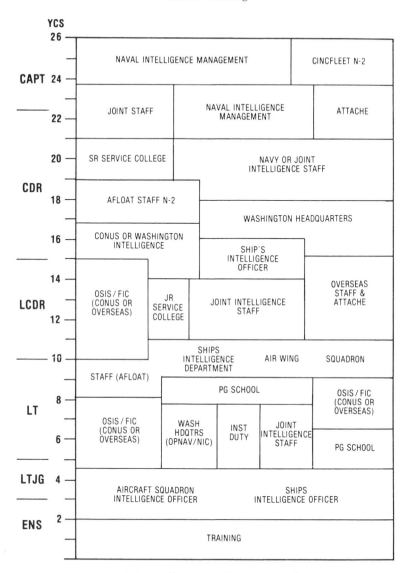

Figure 17-13. Special duty officer, intelligence—professional development path.

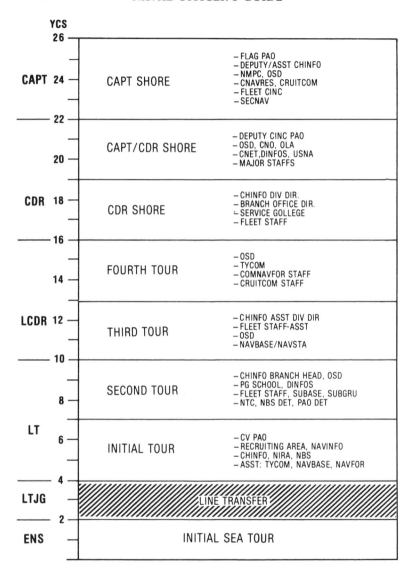

Figure 17-14. Special duty public affairs officer—professional development path.

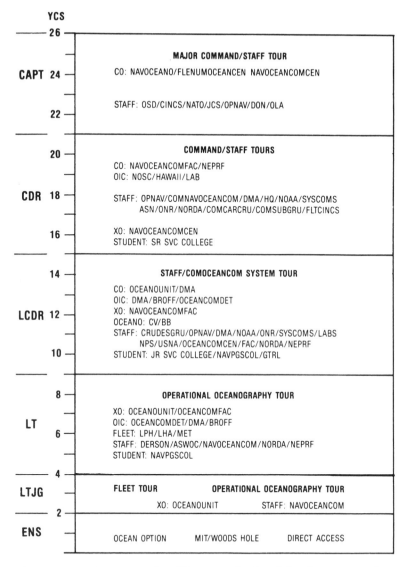

Figure 17-15. Oceanography officer—professional development path.

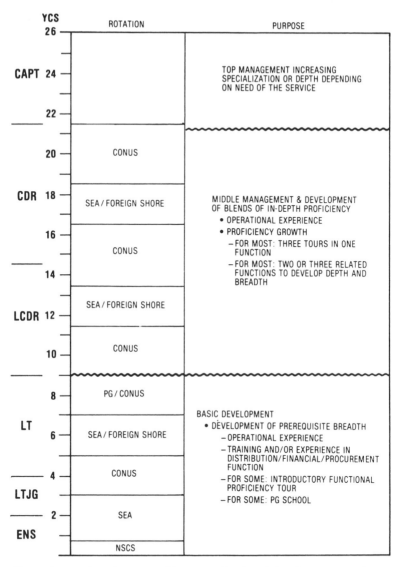

Figure 17-16. Supply corps officer—professional development path (generalized).

battalion operations, and staff assignments. Although there is no typical career pattern, figure 17-17 shows the more common professional development paths.

Medical Corps (21XX). Officers of the medical corps are quite varied in rank upon commissioning, total naval service, and professional qualifications. They may be commissioned as ensigns while still in medical school, and as lieutenant commanders by direct procurement. They may, in the first case, have many years of service by the time they reach lieutenant commander; or, in the second case, have none. They may be general practitioners, surgeons, and specialists of every kind. They may be without certification, or they may be board certified. With this variety in the community it is difficult to predict professional development paths for individual officers. Each medical officer pursues his or her individual path, experience and qualifications mounting with each year of service. The chief of the bureau details each officer to provide the necessary specialists at each hospital and clinic and the necessary coverage for each ship and staff. Medical officers attain administrative experience as they progress and are detailed where possible as heads of hospital departments. In these billets they are able to qualify as future COs of hospitals and eventually for flag rank.

Dental Corps (22XX). Officers of the dental corps are more uniform in experience than those of the medical corps. Their rank at entrance is usually the same and their qualifications are not as varied. They serve on staffs and in hospitals, dental clinics, and ships. There are specialists in the dental corps, but the majority of dental officers are generalists.

Dental officers follow fairly uniform professional development paths. Most serve one tour at sea in their first two tours and some return for second sea tours. Most of their service is ashore, with occasional tours overseas. They attain administrative experience by serving as heads of departments in dental clinics and eventually qualify for one of twenty command billets and two flag billets.

Medical Service Corps (23XXO). The MSC is made up of officers who have a great variety of medical specialties, ranging from administration and food service to bacteriology, pharmacology, and therapy. Officers of this corps do not rotate much and do not have professional development paths. They may command major medical units.

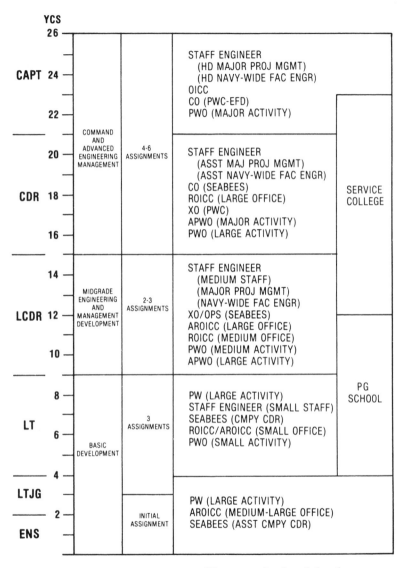

Figure 17-17. Civil engineer corps officer—professional development path.

Nurse Corps (29XX). The nurse corps is composed of men and women who are graduates of accredited nursing schools. They may be commissioned ensign or lieutenant junior grade, depending upon experience. Rotation is between shore and overseas commands. As nurses acquire more experience they assume a growing number of responsibilities. Some become specialists in diet or in operating rooms and stay in their specialties. No professional development path can be predicted.

Legal Officer (25XXO). Members of the judge advocate corps are commissioned as lieutenants junior grade and after indoctrination serve in large ships or at shore stations for their initial tours. Each legal officer serves at least one tour at sea. Thereafter legal officers progress through a series of billets of increasing responsibility. Most legal billets require duty in some aspect of court-martial procedure or legal review. Others require knowledge of contract law and business law. Many senior billets require the exercise of the entire gamut of legal expertise. Legal officers move to billets of increasing responsibility roughly in accordance with increasing rank and do not have formal professional development paths.

Chaplains (41XX). Members of the chaplains corps must be ordained in their denominations and, if acceptable, are commissioned as ensigns or lieutenants junior grade. After indoctrination they are ordered to a sea billet as soon as possible. Thereafter they serve at a variety of shore and overseas stations, rotating from sea to shore in a normal pattern. Some stations have more than one chaplain. Each chaplain has to be prepared to conduct services in all creeds.

An attempt is made by the chief of chaplains to detail chaplains so that major faiths are represented at each station where more than one chaplain is stationed. Chaplains do not command, but senior chaplains at large stations have heavy administrative requirements and eventually may be selected for flag rank.

Limited Duty Officer (6XXX). LDOs fill the need for technical management skills at mid-grade. Such officers are usually CPOs and warrant officers who have been commissioned. They are assigned so that they may use their qualifications in their occupational fields. They rotate between sea and shore stations and do not have professional development paths.

Warrant Officers. Warrant officers are procured from a wide variety of ratings and serve in billets where they can use their expertise. They do not have professional development paths; they rotate from sea to shore as the needs of the service dictate.

Woman Officer (110X). Women are restricted by law from serving in combat ships or in combat aircraft in combat areas. They may, however, qualify as naval aviators and serve aboard certain types of naval vessels designated as noncombat ships.

Women who choose to qualify as warfare specialists follow the appropriate professional development path for that specialty, serving their sea tours in noncombat ships such as tenders, tugs, and ARSs. They may qualify in all types of aircraft, but in case of war are restricted to flying noncombat aircraft in noncombat areas. Women warfare specialists follow the career patterns outlined in figures 17-18 and 17-19.

Women who do not choose to qualify as warfare specialists follow the professional development path shown in figure 17-18. They do not rotate from sea to shore, but serve outside the United States in lieu of sea duty. Commissioned women who are not warfare specialists serve in communications, port service, special services, mess management, public affairs, personnel administration, intelligence, and a variety of other billets. They may become subspecialists; they may command shore stations and other commands.

Training and Administration of Reserve Officers (XXX7). TARs are from all communities. Each community has a professional development path. Space does not permit illustration of more than the general unrestricted line path (figure 17-20). Other paths are shown and described in detail in the *Unrestricted Line Officer's Career Planning Guidebook.*

Fitness Reports

The fitness report is the key to your career, for it governs your selection for important billets, for command, for schooling, and finally, for promotion.

Changes in Fitness Report Forms. For many years, the fitness report form has had two distinct sections, one for arithmetical marks in personal qualities and another for a written summary of the officer's performance. Over the years numerical marks have been changed into percentages and boxes to be checked, and comparative systems and classes of recommendations for promotions have been added.

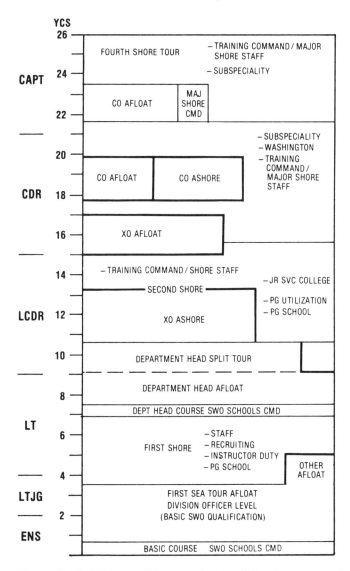

Figure 17-18. Woman officer—professional development path.

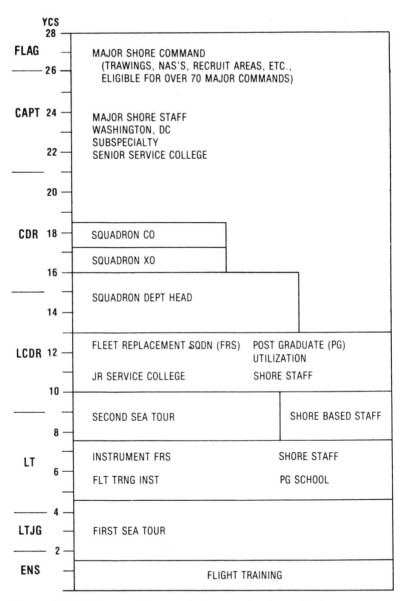

Figure 17-19. Woman officer, aviation—professional development path.

Rank	YCS	Assignments
CAPT	28	
	26	
	24	MAJOR STAFF
	22	REDCOM COMMAND
		NAVAL RESERVE CENTER (CO)
		COMNAVRESFOR STAFF (DCOS)
	20	NAVAL RESERVE CENTER (CO)
	18	RESERVE READINESS COMMAND (CSO)
		SENIOR SERVICE COLLEGE
		XO, NAVAL AIR STATION
CDR	16	MAJOR STAFF
		READINESS COMMAND DEPARTMENT DIRECTOR
		TRAINING/ADMINISTRATIVE COMMAND
LCDR	14	MAJOR STAFF
	12	TRAINING/ADMINISTRATIVE COMMAND
		COMNAVRESFOR STAFF
	10	JUNIOR SERVICE COLLEGE, PG SCHOOL
		NAVAL RESERVE CENTER (CO/XO)
		RESERVE READINESS COMMAND STAFF (TRAINING)
LT	8	NAVAL RESERVE CENTER (ADMIN, TRAINING, XO)
	6	NAVAL RESERVE AIR ACTIVITY (ADMIN, PERSONNEL, TRAINING)
		NAVAL RESERVE RECRUITING
		OFFICER IN CHARGE, PSD
		RESERVE READINESS COMMAND STAFF (ADMIN/PERSONNEL, TRAINING) (SPLIT TOUR WITH REDCOM)
		PG SCHOOL
LTJG	4	INITIAL ACTIVE DUTY TOUR
ENS	2	NAVAL RESERVE AIR ACTIVITY
		NAVAL RESERVE CENTER
		RESERVE READINESS COMMAND STAFF

Figure 17-20. TAR unrestricted line officer—career development path.

These changes were made to help reporting officers make accurate and meaningful reports. After each form was introduced, reporters found that accurate and honest marking began to hurt the persons so marked because other less conscientious markers used higher marks to protect their officers. Selection boards had to resort to reading between the lines of the written summaries in order to make selections. Complaints by the selection boards soon reached the ears of the chief of naval personnel, who then tightened the marking requirements of the forms with various devices. Perhaps the Navy has reached the ultimate in fairness with the present forms, which rate officers of the rank of lieutenant commander and above relative to the other members of their group.

There are some points about fitness report writing that officers making out reports should keep in mind. Regardless of the form, reports should be consistent. Numerical marks should match written comments. Performance should be marked consistently in succeeding reports. If there are changes, justification or explanation should be given.

Examining Your Fitness Report. As pointed out previously, you can review your file in Washington and examine your own fitness report file with some idea of what the marks mean. Chapter 2 of the *Unrestricted Line Officer Career Guidebook* gives an excellent summary of what you should look for in such a review.

Remember that your detailer is the best source of information you will have in career planning; he or she is also an expert on fitness report interpretation, having read hundreds of reports a day. He or she has access to all the recorders on recent selection boards (most of them are detailers) and to the letters to the presidents of each board. Detailers will have statistics of past board results and know of expected future changes.

Influencing Your Fitness Reports. An officer can influence the scoring of a fitness report only by performing excellently. No marking officer will improve your marks because of personal plea. However, it is your right and duty to point out certain matters regarding your performance of duty. If you have completed a correspondence course or acquired a watch qualification, these accomplishments will eventually find their way into your official records; to speed up the process, send a simple memorandum to the officer making out the rough of your fitness report and request that any new qualifications be mentioned in your next fitness report. Some reporting seniors ask that you submit memoranda listing your activities and accomplishments during the period of the report. Don't be modest whether or not you are lucky enough to have such a senior.

Selection Boards

Selection boards are convened to decide such issues as promotion, transfer from reserve to regular status, transfer from unrestricted line to restricted line and staff corps, attendance at postgraduate school, attendance at service colleges, ship command, air squadron and group command, and subspecialty designation.

Procedures of Selection Boards. Each selection board receives a precept addressed to its president, informing the board of its purpose and the results it is expected to produce. Promotion boards for higher ranks receive a special letter of instruction from the secretary of the Navy. Other boards may or may not receive special letters of instruction, but all receive adequate briefings on the subject matter before the board.

Selection boards meet in specially isolated areas in Arlington Annex. Board rooms are provided together with a special theater, where summaries of fitness reports can be viewed on multiple screens by all members of the board. A special electrical voting system is provided.

Although the actual proceedings of any one board are considered confidential, the general process can be described. Each board determines how it will proceed. Most have each record examined in complete detail by two members of the board and then the whole board is briefed by them during the viewing process. A system of voting is agreed upon, with the first votes usually grouping officers into those sure to be selected, those sure to fail, and those in contention. Additional screenings, votings, and briefings are conducted until a final group is reached of small enough size to permit final discussion and voting. A selection board whose purpose is other than promotion operates in much the same way.

The procedure is extremely fair, and the board members are invariably hardworking and conscientious. An unfair selection process cannot be attributed to the board but rather to those reporting seniors who failed to write accurate fitness reports.

Shore Billets, Unrestricted Line

If not an educational billet, the first shore tour is relatively unimportant to a career. If you can combine both career enhancement and desirable location, you are fortunate. Most pilots are assigned to a shore-flying billet in a training role.

The second shore tour is important, but still not vital. Recruiting billets and Naval Academy billets are career enhancing. The best billet is to be chosen for a service college with a subsequent tour on a staff or in Washington. Because service on a joint staff or in some other joint billet is virtually a prerequisite for flag rank, these billets are the most career enhancing.

The third shore tour is as important to your career as sea duty. Assuming you have done well at sea, your performance ashore will then make or break your next selection. You will want to seek a service college and then a billet in the Washington complex. Being on a major staff is a good billet as well. Assignment to a subspecialty billet is next on the list of career-enhancing assignments; assignment to the Naval Academy as a head of department follows.

For the fourth shore tour, command at a shore station is excellent. An equally good assignment is to a key billet in the Washington complex or to a senior billet on a fleet staff. Assignment to a subspecialty billet is next. Assignment to almost any other billet is a signal to start thinking of retirement.

Educational Programs

The education of naval officers can be divided into three major periods.

The Basic Period. This comprises the first three years of an officer's career. Most officers go to sea, to aviation training, to submarine schools, or to staff corps school. SWOs normally will attend SWOS and receive surface nuclear-power training. Officers going to submarines may first go to nuclear-power school or missile school and submarine basic school. This period, despite variations, is mainly one of professional training, education, and development. The primary requirement of this period is to qualify in a warfare specialty. Officers generally remain at sea until they qualify.

The Command and Technical Education Period. The education of this period is received between an officer's fourth and tenth years, although not always. Officers attend postgraduate institutions, junior service colleges, and technical schools. By this time no two officers will follow the same career path. You need to be aware of the possibilities open and should communicate freely with your detailer. You should indicate by official application which postgraduate school or which service college you desire. However, assignment is by selection, and the exact courses are not always available. As discussed in chapter 1, if you are not selected for schooling, do not be discouraged. Begin your self-education by correspondence course and by reading. The demonstrated effort, if reflected in your fitness report, may help you get selected the following year.

The Command and Staff Period. This may be anywhere from the eleventh to the thirtieth year. The officer, with the preparatory period of education and training over, is ready for a third tour of shore duty. While attendance at advanced schools is not a prerequisite for promotion, completion of these schools makes assignment to important billets much easier. Assignment and selection personnel recognize further schooling as an achievement that prepares the individual for increasing responsibilities.

Specialization

Specialization Programs. An officer may wish to specialize permanently by entering a staff corps or becoming a restricted line officer. Programs in the following areas are available to both men and women:

Engineering duty	Special duty
Aeronautical engineering duty	cryptology
aeronautical engineering	intelligence
aviation maintenance	public affairs
	oceanography
	Supply corps
	CEC

Career patterns for these categories are given in the *Unrestricted Line Officer Career Guidebook* (restricted line officers are covered in this book).

The methods of application, the criteria, and the times of

application submission are covered generally in the *Naval Military Personnel Manual* and in the NAVMILPERS 1120 series.

Operational Technical Management System (OTMS). In the late 1960s the post–World War II practice of requiring breadth of experience in the assignment of officers to shore duty was increasingly difficult to administer. No single officer could hope to master each kind of job to which he was assigned on successive shore tours if all were radically different. Both the job and the officer suffered.

OTMS was developed in 1972 to correct this situation. It is set forth in OPNAVINST 1000.16E and described in the *Unrestricted Line Officer's Career Planning Guidebook*. The program is now popularly described as the subspecialist system.

Under OTMS, the first aim of the unrestricted line officer is to develop an operational specialty, which leads to command at sea or in the air. Each officer should then subspecialize in either the technical or management area, through education and/or experience. Specialization should lead to designation as a proven subspecialist by board action. Thereafter, instructions to selection boards will assure that officers compete with each other on the basis of their specialty and their proven subspecialty. An officer may obtain more than one subspecialty.

Weapon Systems Acquisition Management (WSAM). Officers with subspecialties in management, engineering, and applied science are prime candidates for WSAM selection, which is by board action. Officers become candidates through education and assignment to qualifying billets.

Major Procurement Program Management. Operationally successful officers who have been in a WSAM billet are considered for assignment to key positions as directors of major weapons systems and weapons acquisition and production programs.

Functional Schools

Functional schools provide training in the various technical functions performed by Navy personnel. The courses offered by these schools are short (one to sixteen weeks) and are usually conducted by forces afloat or by the training commands. As courses change frequently, you should check into them before applying.

Attendance at functional schools is usually on a temporary-additional-duty basis. Occasionally officers attend functional schools en route to their station, particularly if they are to be assigned to a particular billet. The quota and travel are then arranged by the detailer in consultation with the CO.

Tactical Action Officer's School.   This school trains officers assigned to combat systems departments of ships and staffs with tactical data systems.

Optical and Gunnery Officer's School.   This school trains officers and men in the upkeep and operation of the fire-control installations to which they are currently assigned.

Fleet Sonar and Electronics School.   These schools train officers and men in the techniques of operating sonar and electronic equipment and the tactical employment of it.

Naval Amphibious Training Commands.   Schools at these commands conduct a variety of courses for personnel in the land, sea, and air elements of all four services. The basics of the conduct of amphibious joint operations are taught.

Fleet Air Defense Training Centers.   These centers train officers and personnel in the techniques of air defense. There are many other functional schools and courses on the subject listed in training command pamphlets.

Leadership Management Education Training.   This school was covered in more detail earlier. Eventually all personnel in the Navy will attend LMET school en route to new stations at one of fourteen locations. Basic leadership and management are taught.

Correspondence Courses

Correspondence courses cover a wide variety of naval activities. Some courses are designed to prepare the student for attendance as a resident student. Other courses are complete in themselves and give the officer expert guidance in a subject.

The Naval War College.   This college, located in Newport, Rhode Island, conducts courses in strategy and policy, defense, economics, and decision making (management), and employment of naval forces.

There are additional elective programs in international relations and international law. Three core subjects and one elective must be completed to earn the correspondence course diploma.

The off-campus graduate study program offers three seminars

in strategy and policy and two seminars in defense economics in the Washington, D.C., area. These seminars are taught by highly qualified instructors and are supplemented by lectures given by Naval War College resident faculty members.

Self-administered graduate seminar study programs are offered for strategy and policy in the Jacksonville, Florida, area and defense economics and decision making in the Norfolk, Virginia, area. These seminars are led by moderators from within each group and augmented by the Naval War College resident faculty.

These seminars provide active-duty naval officers an excellent opportunity to continue their professional military education on an off-duty basis. Off-campus and self-administered seminar course completions may be substituted for core areas of the correspondence course diploma. Further information concerning Naval War College continuing education may be obtained by contacting the director of the continuing education program.

The Naval School, Naval Intelligence. This school conducts a correspondence course in naval intelligence that parallels and prepares officers for the resident course.

The Naval Correspondence Course Center. At the Naval Supply Depot in Scotia, New York, this center conducts a variety of courses for both regular and reserve officers.

The U.S. Armed Forces Institute. This school provides armed forces personnel with educational opportunities in subjects normally taught in civilian institutions.

Postgraduate Schools

After three to five years, usually spent at sea in ships, submarines, and aircraft of the fleet, officers become eligible for their first permanent shore duty. Because of the shortage of nuclear-qualified officers, they may be at sea for several more years before coming ashore. When shore duty does begin, officers have an opportunity to advance their formal education, work on their subspecialty base, and gain general knowledge.

Programs. Several avenues are available for obtaining a master's degree. The first is the Postgraduate Education Program, which starts with a year at the Naval Postgraduate School in Monterey, California, and continues at various civilian universities. It is fully funded. A second alternative is the Advanced Education Program, which allows an officer up to two years of full-time study to complete a master's degree. Tuition expenses must be paid by the individual. A third alternative is the Scholarship Program, where the officer applies for a grant, fellowship, or scholarship to pay tuition expenses for up to two years of study. Pay and allowances are continued during the period. The final alternative is off-duty study.

You may also conduct off-duty study at your own expense or use the Veteran's Educational Assistance Program, G.I. Bill, or the Tuition Assistance Program.

Selection for the Postgraduate Education Program is made by an annual board. You are considered at regular intervals and may receive additional consideration if you request it.

Selection for the Advanced Education Program is based upon your application and record and by a board that meets annually.

Selection for the Scholarship Program is made by a continuing board. You must obtain your own scholarship, grant, or fellowship before applying for the program.

Naval Postgraduate School. A total of thirty-four curricula, taught at Monterey, receive full credit from the Western Association of Schools and Colleges and from the Engineer's Council for Professional Development. The following general programs are taught:

Administrative science
Aeronautical engineering
Antisubmarine warfare
Electronics and communications
Environmental science
Naval engineering
Naval intelligence
Operations research/systems analysis
Weapons system engineering

Other Technical Schools. In addition, officers are ordered to a number of specialized schools, some of which are discussed below. Refer to your type commander for information on other schools.

Damage control schools and other schools at the Naval Technical Training Center, Treasure Island, California, and the Damage Control Training Center, Philadelphia, Pennsylvania, offer an eight-week course as well as shorter courses to officers and CPOs. The eight-week course trains damage control assistants for their duties aboard ship; four weeks are devoted to theory and the rest to fire fighting, chemical warfare, radiological safety, and allied subjects.

The School of Naval Justice in Newport, Rhode Island, trains naval officers in the administration of military law and naval discipline in accordance with the UCMJ. Senior yeomen are given courses to prepare them for their administrative jobs as court reporters.

Marine Corps Schools. The Marine Corps conducts two schools at Quantico, Virginia, to which naval officers of appropriate rank are assigned.

Amphibious Warfare School, Junior Course. This course places emphasis on the coordinated employment of naval, air, and ground elements of the armed forces in amphibious operations. Naval lieutenants and lieutenant commanders are eligible. The course is nine months long.

Communications School. This course offers formal instruction and exercises on communications in amphibious operations. Subjects include technical and operational communications. Navy lieutenants are eligible. The course lasts nine months. Graduates are usually assigned to communications duties with amphibious forces.

Service Colleges

Service colleges further an officer's professional development and prepare the student for entry into important policy-making billets in large staffs and in the Washington complex. Service colleges are divided into two groups, intermediate and senior. Selection is made by a board, which chooses officers with superior records. Some officers may attend both an intermediate and a senior service college. An obligation of two years' service is incurred by attendance.

In August 1984 a new system of selection policy was established. It is discussed in the *Unrestricted Line Officer's Career Planning Guidebook.*

The Intermediate Colleges. These are usually attended in an officer's sixth to eighth year. They are designed to prepare officers for command and staff duties in all echelons of their parent services and in joint and allied commands.

The Army Command and General Staff College in Fort Leavenworth, Kansas, has a forty-week course for officers of all services, but predominantly Army. The purpose of this college is to prepare officers for duty as commanders and general staff officers at division, corps, and Army levels, and at a comparable level in the communications zone, and for duty in the specific general staff section in which they specialize.

Instruction is given to all students in the School of the Commander and of the General Staff, after which the students are assigned to specialize in one of the schools of personnel, intelligence, operations and training, or logistics.

The College of Naval Command and Staff in Newport, Rhode Island, is predominantly for naval officers but is attended by officers of other services as well. This forty-four-week course provides a basic education in the science of war, with special emphasis on the operational functions of command and the organizational procedures of an operational staff. The course includes the study of problems in strategy and tactics, chart and game board maneuvers, capabilities of ships and aircraft and their weapons, international law and international relations, logistics, communications, intelligence, and nuclear physics.

The Marine Corps Command and Staff College in Quantico, Virginia, is predominantly for Marine officers, but is attended by a few officers of other services. The forty-three-week course teaches staff functions and procedures for middle ranks and command functions for all ranks.

The Air Command and Staff College in Montgomery, Alabama, is predominantly for Air Force officers, but attended by some officers of other services. Naval officers ordered as students are usually naval aviators. The forty-three-week course prepares officers for command of air groups and wings and for appropriate staff duties. Subjects covered are logistics, personnel, operations, intelligence, and organization.

The Armed Forces Staff College in Norfolk, Virginia, is part of the JCS National Defense University. Each of the four services has a balanced representation in both the faculty and the student body, and the commandant and his deputy are always from a different service. The twenty-two-week course is designed to train students in joint operations and for staff duty on joint and naval staffs. The methods of instruction include conferences, lectures, practical staff problems, exercises conducted by the students, and familiarization visits to Army, Navy, and Air Force installations in the Norfolk area. Normally officers do not attend both the intermediate college of their service and the Armed Forces Staff College.

The course at the Armed Forces Staff College covers the organization, characteristics, and employment of Army, Navy, Marine Corps, and Air Force and their relation to each other in joint operations; joint staff procedures; and new weapons and scientific developments that affect joint operations. Each student is required to submit a thesis on a subject of importance to national defense.

Senior Service Colleges.   These schools are attended for ten months by carefully chosen officers in the rank of commander and captain. Selection is made by a board. The colleges prepare officers for senior command and staff billets and for staff positions in the Washington complex and in multinational organizations such as NATO.

The National War College in Fort McNair, Washington, D.C., is part of the National Defense University. The school is attended by officers of all services and civilian students from the State Department and other agencies.

The course prepares students for high command and joint staff duties in the highest echelons of the armed forces, for joint high-

The Naval Postgraduate School is located at Monterey, California.

The Armed Forces Staff College, an intermediate service college and part of the National Defense University, is in Norfolk, Virginia.

level policy, and for strategic planning. A flag or general officer of one of the services serves as commandant, with deputy commandants from the other two departments and the Department of State. Officers with wide-ranging professional experience and knowledge comprise the military staff. Outstanding professors, scientists, and authors from civilian life are on the civilian faculty.

The course includes the study of the interests and international objectives of the United States and other powers; the United Nations; regional pacts, and bilateral and multilateral agreements as means of avoiding war and furthering peace and national security; the military force necessary to implement national policy in peace and in war; the strategy and integration of military policy and foreign policy; the impact of science and modern technology upon the armed forces; and war planning and employment of forces on a joint expeditionary force and at higher levels.

Instruction is by lecture and seminar. Students are assigned to committees to evaluate and study problems given to them, and each student is required to submit a thesis on a subject chosen from a wide range of topics.

The Industrial College of the Armed Forces, located adjacent to the National War College, is also part of the National Defense University. The course is for officers from all four military services and for selected civilian officials from the Defense Department and other government agencies.

The course prepares students for important assignments in command, staff, and planning in the Department of Defense and other agencies and for industrial-mobilization planning. The course provides a thorough study of the relation of joint logistic planning to joint strategic planning, to national policy planning, and to governmental organization. In their lecture and seminar courses students consider the economic factors pertinent to war and analyze how our economic potential affects political, military, and psychological factors in our national strategy. They study the organization and administration of the Department of Defense and other government agencies.

The Army War College conducts a course predominantly for Army officers, but it is attended by officers of all services. The course covers the duties of commanders and staffs of higher Army echelons.

The Naval War College, located in Newport, Rhode Island, is predominantly for naval officers, but is attended by officers of all services. The course, initiated in 1886 with the lectures of Alfred T. Mahan, helps senior officers further their understanding of naval strategy and its employment in future warfare. Besides logistics and the solution of major naval and military problems, this course teaches the principles that govern the administration and operation of forces and fleets. The course prepares officers for the exercise of command in flag rank, in single and multiple commands in lower ranks, and for duty as senior staff officers.

The Air War College, in Montgomery, Alabama, is predominantly for Air Force officers, but it is attended by officers of all services. The course focuses on the broad aspects of air power in order to prepare graduates for key staff and command assignments with large Air Force units. The curriculum, in its academic phase, teaches an objective method of approaching and solving military problems; in its evaluation phase, analyzes the effectiveness of World War II organization, plans, operations, training and logistics; and in its projection phase, studies the problems involved

The National War College, senior college of the National Defense University, is located in Washington, D.C.

The Naval War College is located in Newport, Rhode Island.

in maintaining the present and future security of the United States. The problems arising from specific objectives are considered; each seminar group presents a solution, both oral and written.

Foreign Service Colleges. Foreign service colleges teach courses on both senior and intermediate levels. The objective of the courses is to expose U.S. naval officers to foreign doctrine and methods of operation and planning. Officers attending these colleges should have the potential for a tour of duty in a foreign country or on a NATO staff. They must be fluent enough in the language of the host country to undertake the course. Preparatory language training is available.

Promotion

The end product of career planning is, of course, measured by promotion. In the Navy all promotion, except to lieutenant junior grade, is done by the selection process. We have already described the workings of the selection board.

The times at which officers are promoted are governed by the size and composition of the Navy. Congress fixes the size of the Navy by the annual authorization and appropriation processes. The number of officers in each rank is fixed by legislation. The NMPC then monitors the number of officers in each rank, determines when vacancies will occur, schedules selection board meetings, and issues promotions as vacancies arise.

Promotion Flow. The timing of the flow of promotion can be predicted fairly accurately. At present it is, in accumulative years:

To lieutenant (jg)	2 years
To lieutenant	4 years
To lieutenant commander	9–11 years
To commander	15–19 years
To captain	21–23 years
To flag rank	about 26 years

Promotion flow changes as the size of the Navy changes.

Frocking. The practice of frocking, or granting the privileges and authority of rank except for pay, is about twenty years old. An officer is frocked if he or she is on a promotion list and receives permission to wear the uniform of the higher rank and to exercise the authority of that rank. The officer is entitled to higher pay only upon full promotion.

The officer frocked must be serving in a billet calling for the increased rank. This rule is strictly enforced. An officer frocked has the full authority of increased rank, even over those who may have been senior to him or her. However, the officer frocked retains the same relative precedence on the lineal promotion list.

18

THE NAVAL OFFICER ASHORE

YOU CANNOT STAY AT SEA FOREVER; WHEN YOU GO
ASHORE DETERMINE TO DO YOUR BEST. THOSE YOU
LEFT BEHIND AT SEA WILL BE DEPENDING ON YOU.

—Admiral Chester Nimitz

THE BUSINESS OF THOSE NAVAL PERSONS ASHORE IS TO
BUILD SHIPS AND AIRCRAFT AND TO REPAIR AND
SUPPLY THEM. IF IT IS DONE WELL, THE NAVY WILL
FIGHT WELL.

—Secretary of the Navy William B. Franke

Shore duty to a seagoing naval officer is just an awkward interlude between sea assignments. To others shore duty is a relatively restful period between sea assignments during which an officer can sample some of the Navy's other important and interesting sides. An officer may attend a school, specialize in the development of new equipment, or simply have the time to become more closely acquainted with family and community.

Definitions Used in Assignment Ashore

Shore Duty.   Shore duty means all duty on shore within the United States, at desirable locations overseas, and in vessels and craft assigned to the Naval Reserve for training purposes.

Foreign shore duty is duty ashore at all stations overseas. For rotational purposes it is divided into two classes:

1. Desirable locations classed the same as shore duty in the United States.

2. Other locations designated as "foreign shore duty" and sometimes combined with sea duty in one cruise (tour of sea duty) for rotational purposes. Since localities and total personnel requirements vary for this type of duty, a list of stations or assignments would be unreliable. Rotation to and from shore duty is examined in the light of conditions at each station and the balanced career assignment for the officer involved.

Sea Duty. Sea duty entails service in seagoing ships of the fleet and aircraft. Some other services have been officially designated as sea duty, including duty at certain overseas stations not considered as desirable for shore duty as those in the United States. Sea duty commences on the date of reporting on board ship and continues until the date of detachment. For officers ordered to seagoing ships of the active fleet and to foreign shore duty, sea duty for rotational purposes commences with the date of reporting on board or sailing from a port after detachment. Service in all ships commissioned in the Navy is considered sea duty for record purposes. So are periods of a month or more of temporary duty on board a vessel in commission during a normal tour of shore duty.

Rotation between Sea and Shore Duty. Normal sea duty for line officers is two years for commanders and above and three to five years for officers below the grade of commander, except for warrant officers. Sea duty for warrant officers is determined by the number of sea and shore billets within a given category.

Normal tours of shore duty are three to four years for captains and above, two and a half to four years for commanders, and two to four years for officers below the grade of commander, depending on the needs of the service and funds available for transportation.

For officers of the staff corps, a regular alternation between sea and shore cannot always be made. A normal sequence generally will be shore—sea—shore—foreign shore. This may be modified by the needs of the service and in order to make the type of service performed by officers of the same grade as uniform or equal as possible.

The rotation of limited-duty officers between sea, shore, and foreign shore duty is planned to approximate the rotation of unrestricted line officers.

Shore Duty

Stations Available. Duty stations ashore, both at home and abroad, are many and varied. Each year the commander of the NMPC publishes the *Annual Officer Billet Summary* (NAVMIL-PERS 15994), which lists all the billets available for junior officers and includes information on geographic location, required designator, rank, subspecialty, and primary duties.

A typical naval base has a station, ammunition depot, supply center, and shipyard. An air station may be part of the same complex or may be nearby.

The Naval Academy, the Naval Postgraduate School, the Naval War College, and other school complexes provide large numbers of shore billets. Recruiting centers, NROTC units, and Naval Reserve training centers provide billets in widely scattered areas.

The largest number of shore billets is located in the Washington complex of the Pentagon, Arlington Annex, and peripheral buildings. The billets in commands and agencies in Washington are assigned largely to the ranks of commander or above.

Overseas there is a wide geographical range of billets for most ranks.

Organization. Naval stations are organized in much the same way as a ship, but there are some physical differences. Sound management and the need for security require that the headquarters, instead of having a ship's high concentration of activity, be dispersed over a wide area. In some bases, shipyards and other units may be entirely outside of the basic compound. Housing may be quite distant from working areas.

Regardless of differences between a ship and a naval station, both need a strong organization and adequate regulations, understood and carried out by all.

Housing. Most officers and personnel, both bachelor and married, live off base. Single officers who choose to live on base live in bachelor officers quarters (BOQ) and single enlisted persons in barracks.

The BOQ is often integrated with the officer's club, but may be found in a separate building. The rooms are completely furnished. The more senior bachelors have correspondingly better quarters.

A station may have both a "closed" officer's mess—where

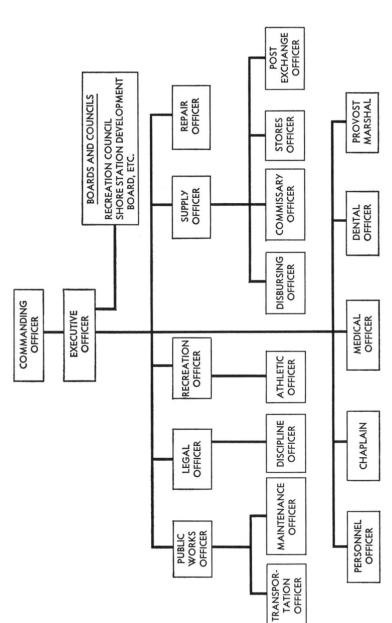

Figure 18-1. Organization of a small naval station.

only residents and their personal guests dine—and an "open" mess as part of the officer's club, where authorized members use all of the facilities. Closed messes are being reduced in numbers.

Married officers may live in government quarters on stations, which are comfortable residences furnished and maintained by public works. Others may live in so-called emergency housing developments, such as Wherry Housing units. Still others may have to seek their own quarters off base. Many officers buy a house in a large area such as Washington, Norfolk, or San Diego, which they rent when they are away and to which they may return later.

Medical Care. Medical facilities at a naval station may range from a small dispensary to the outpatient section of a large hospital. Dental care is provided at most bases for officers but not for dependents. Care for your dependents will vary widely. If a large dispensary or a hospital is available, care will be good. If facilities are inadequate, the Civilian Health and Medical Program of the Uniformed Services (CHAMPUS) may be used.

The following persons are covered by the Uniformed Services Health Benefits Program (USHBP):

1. Spouse
2. Unremarried widow or widower
3. Children, including adopted, illegitimate, and stepchildren under twenty-one, or in certain cases when older and enrolled in a course of instruction
4. Dependent parent or parent-in-law

Identification required for medical care is DD Form 1173 (uniformed services identification and privilege card). Application for this card should be made on DD Form 1172, which you may get from the ship's office or personnel office. Other identification may be used in an emergency. Children under ten do not require a card. Claims for payment for care are relatively simple if the directions are followed. The proper form for care in hospitals is DA Form 1863-1. Other care is reimbursed following the submission of CHAMPUS Form 500.

All officers and their dependents are eligible for care in uniformed service facilities if they are available and have the necessary space and assigned personnel. Spouses and children of officers not residing with their sponsors have the choice of using civilian medical facilities. Spouses and children residing with their sponsors will be given civilian medical care only if there is no armed service facility in the vicinity (set at a limit of forty miles) or if required care cannot be given in the armed service facility. A statement of nonavailability must be obtained from the armed services medical facility unable to provide the service.

The provisions of CHAMPUS are detailed and changeable; you should inquire frequently into current regulations in the area where your dependents live.

To expedite care of your dependents, enroll them in the Defense Enrollment Eligibility Reporting System (DEERS). DEERS also helps management by providing data on the population eligible to receive medical care.

The Commissary. The privilege of making purchases in the commissary of any armed service is restricted to regular (active and retired) armed services personnel, to reserve personnel on active or training duty, to certain governmental civilians in special situations, and to their dependents. A valid identification card must be presented.

Stocks and services vary depending upon the size of the facility. The use of a commissary is a privilege and not a right; the purchases must be for the use of the purchaser and his or her family.

Exchanges. Exchanges are maintained at almost all naval facilities. The amount and kind of stock vary with the size of the facility, which is designed to provide at reasonable prices the items a family needs for everyday use. Luxury items are not stocked, although many larger items can be ordered. Some exchanges have barber shops, beauty shops, garden annexes, and shoemakers. Uniform items are stocked in almost all stores.

Anyone eligible (eligibility is the same as for the commissary) may use the facility of any armed service. Profits of the exchanges go to the recreation system.

Welfare. The American Red Cross and the Navy Relief usually have representatives at large stations. Your chaplain will arrange services for you if needed. Most stations can also provide you with legal assistance.

Recreation. Most posts provide excellent recreational opportunities. Sports facilities and hobby shops are open to all. Every station has a library.

Participation in Community Life. Naval officers stationed

ashore have always been noted for participation in the life of their community. Any community profits from the leadership and help of Navy families.

Active participation in partisan politics is prohibited. However, the naval officer, as a citizen, has the right and obligation to vote, and must understand the political and foreign relations problems of the United States. There is no better arena for the study of politics than the small community.

Foreign Shore and Sea Duty

There are many bases overseas—Pearl Harbor, Guam, Subic Bay, Yokosuka, Alaska, Guantánamo. There are shore opportunities in London, Tokyo, Naples, and many other smaller locations. Naval missions and military assistance advisory groups serve in many countries.

The Seventh Fleet cruises Far Eastern waters and visits ports from Japan and Korea to Australia. The Atlantic Fleet visits many Atlantic ports, and the Sixth Fleet visits many Mediterranean ports regularly. Many ships and staffs have home ports overseas, giving families an opportunity to travel and learn the customs of a host country thoroughly.

Overseas Travel. Each family member over a certain age will require a passport to foreign countries. The NMPC or your sponsoring office will help you. Passport agencies of the Department of State are located in major cities, and the post offices of large cities also assist in issuing passports. When you visit, have the following documents with you:

Original orders
Birth certificates for all members of the family
Evidence of naturalization, if required
Old passports, if any
ID cards
Three passport-sized photos for each member (in your picture you should be in uniform)

Ask your sponsoring office to obtain visas on all passports for any countries you will stop in en route or where you will be on duty.

Physical Examinations and Immunizations. All members of your family must have physical examinations before going overseas. Get the required immunizations as early as possible. Have them recorded on an international certificate, and also carry in your wallet a Navy immunization card.

Medical and dental services are often inadequate overseas. Have your family and yourself in the best possible physical condition before departure.

Accompanied Baggage. Ascertain what restrictions are in force regarding baggage weight and numbers. Use sturdy baggage, well marked, with copies of your orders placed inside each piece.

Government Air and Sea Transportation. The Navy uses aircraft of the Military Airlift Command (MAC), although you may travel commercially and occasionally by MAC charter.

MAC military transport flights are usually made in combination passenger-freight aircraft, and the accommodations can vary from good to sparse. Box lunches are usually provided if needed. Baggage limitations are severe.

Mail. Learn in advance your new mailing address and send change-of-address forms to all your correspondents and periodicals. When possible, have magazines, parcels, and dutiable articles sent via your nearest fleet post office or Army post office. This will enable you to obtain low domestic prices for your magazines and to receive parcel post without the trouble of going through customs.

Customs. Since you will be traveling under orders with a special passport, you will probably have little difficulty with local customs or immigration. Your embassy or mission will assign a representative to greet you and to help you get settled.

Shore Leave. In foreign countries outstanding conduct ashore is even more important than at home. The reputation of the Navy and the country is at stake, and thoughtless or irresponsible conduct by either officers or enlisted personnel is offensive to the local people and damaging to good relations with their government. Take proper action to correct any Navy person's breach of good manners.

Meet the people of the country, not only in hotel lobbies and in bars, but in markets, in parks, and on streets. Practice the language if you have any facility for it. If stationed overseas for any length of time, learn the native language.

Senior officers are expected to visit the American consulate. Others will find it educational to do so.

Schools. Inquire into available facilities. If your child is young, you may want to seek out a school that teaches half in English and half in the language of the country to give your child the opportunity to learn a second language at an early age.

Sanitation.   Sanitation may not be up to the standards you are used to. Find out from the old hands and the medical officer what treatment water and food need.

Customs and Traditions.   Customs and traditions vary widely throughout the world. Climate, religion, heritage, and standard of living all forge a people's way of life. To understand the people of a country, you must know about their history and economic background. Greater understanding of a culture will help you appreciate the hospitality and courtesy that are deeply rooted in the traditions of a people.

The position of women in most countries is quite different from that in our country. In some localities women are kept in complete seclusion and may not even be seen by men other than husbands and close relatives. In others women have a completely subordinate position to men, by both custom and law. Some cultures grant women a superior position; they must be treated with great deference. The institution of marriage varies widely; polygamy and child marriage are the norm in some countries. In some places marriage is a formality and keeping mistresses is an acceptable practice.

In older societies there is strong social stratification, with classes clearly defined and with little mixing between them. Discrimination, based on color or race, is intense in many countries.

You will find that the manners of the people of the country you are assigned to are quite different from the manners you are used to. Study them carefully and then adopt those you feel are compatible with your American background. Kissing a woman's hand is automatic in most European countries. Americans usually adopt a modified version of the act. Most Europeans are very effusive in greeting others. Be prepared to shake hands frequently.

Most people offer tea or coffee to arriving guests. Do the same. Expect to spend several minutes in polite conversation before getting down to business. Dinners start quite late in most foreign countries and finish late. The best defense against the onslaught of sleepiness at these affairs is a siesta.

Religion.   You will encounter many religions. No subject can get you in as much trouble as religion if you are not well informed about it. Learn the fundamentals and taboos of the religions you will encounter. By all means never ridicule or make light of any belief. If doing so does not compromise your own beliefs, observe the peculiar customs that go with a religion. Never serve or drink alcoholic beverages in a Muslim country. In some countries you uncover when entering a place of worship; in others you cover. Never talk loudly near a place of worship. When you want to take pictures, ask if it is permitted before breaking out your camera.

Language. If you go to a diplomatic post or to a military assistance group, you will probably be given language instruction before you depart; your spouse may be allowed to participate. Keep up the initial instruction after you arrive in the country and encourage your family to participate.

Protocol. If you go to duty in an embassy, you will find that your State Department colleagues place great importance on protocol. The pamphlet "Social Protocol and Usage," published by the Navy Department and made available to you, will answer any questions you may have.

Entertainment. Entertain modestly and within your means. Try to repay all of your social obligations, if with no more than an occasional small reception. Warmth of hospitality will do more to cement your relationships with your foreign friends than ostentation. You will find that your natural American friendliness will be appreciated by the peoples of all countries and will serve to make your foreign tour memorable.

19

COMMAND

I CONSIDER IT A GREAT ADVANTAGE TO OBTAIN
COMMAND YOUNG, HAVING OBSERVED AS A GENERAL
THING THAT PERSONS WHO COME INTO AUTHORITY
LATE IN LIFE SHRINK FROM RESPONSIBILITY, AND OFTEN
BREAK DOWN UNDER ITS WEIGHT.

—*Admiral David G. Farragut,* journal entry

YOU SHOULD ENTER THE NAVY FOR ONE PURPOSE, TO
COMMAND SHIPS, SUBMARINES, AND AIRCRAFT.
ONCE YOU GET SUCH A COMMAND ENJOY EVERY
MINUTE OF IT.

—*Fleet Admiral Chester Nimitz*

Command is, and should be, the aspiration of every naval officer. This entire book is, in a sense, advice to officers on preparing themselves for command, for preparation must start from the first day of an officer's career.

Obviously the full range of advice and counsel on command cannot be presented to you in this chapter. You should refer for more complete advice to the book *Command at Sea,* which covers the subject thoroughly.

Preparation for Command

Administrative Preparation

Preparing for command either at sea or ashore is a matter first of learning all you can about the succeeding echelons of responsibility to which you are exposed in various billets. Secondly, it involves learning all you can by observing the performance of others in billets to which you are not assigned. Finally, as you progress up the ladder of responsibility, you should fill in gaps of information and knowledge by reading and asking questions.

You must do your utmost to climb each rung of the ladder you have chosen as your career path. Missing one does not mean eventual failure. Rather it means you will have to find some way to demonstrate that you are qualified in that missed assignment. Many officers have become COs of destroyers without having been executive officers in destroyers; they qualified by serving as executive officers in other types of ships or by serving as heads of departments. Such qualification does not come automatically. You may have to ask to understudy the executive officer, or you may have to ask the exec to indicate on the rough copy of your fitness report that you are qualified.

Examine the duties of officers senior to you, particularly of the executive officer and CO, and observe their daily routine and methods of carrying out responsibility. You will soon find out that you need to do a little studying. This means reviewing *Navy Regulations, SORN*, the *Manual of the Judge Advocate General*, Navy Department directives, and subsidiary publications and directives that control the daily routine of a ship and her crew. It is not enough to wait until each variety of problem arrives at your personal doorstep; reach out to find how problems are resolved before they become your responsibility.

Shiphandling

Every CO should know how to handle a ship well. This skill does not come easily. First, it means thorough preparation. Study *Naval Shiphandling* until you are familiar with the parts that can control the movement of a ship (screws, rudder, lines) and with the uncontrollable forces you will encounter (wind, tide, currents). This knowledge must become ingrained. Then find every opportunity to use it. Don't just stand around at your special sea detail station. Mentally record every boat coxswain's landing you observe. Prior to the last frantic hour before entering port, go up to the bridge and try to find out where the ship will berth. Study the approach charts. Plan in your mind how you would make the approach and landing or anchorage. Then when you are stationed at special sea detail, make the approach and landing in your mind and compare it with the one actually made. If your CO is a good one, you will get your turn to observe from the bridge and even-

NAVAL OFFICER'S GUIDE

Shiphandling in formation is one of the important qualifications of a future CO.

tually to conn the ship. If you are the executive officer, ask the CO to let you handle the ship until you have convinced both him and yourself that you can competently do it.

Do the same for replenishment operations. If you are not on watch or otherwise engaged, try to find a quiet place abaft or above the bridge where you can observe. You will learn, and eventually the CO should note your interest and offer to help you. In other words, seek shiphandling knowledge and opportunities, don't just wait for them to come to you.

When in port look up the schedule of emergency shiphandling school. Try to find a time when you can be spared and ask to be sent. You can also ask questions of officers who are serving in other types of ships. Again, take the initiative.

Watchstanding

Some officers look upon watchstanding as a necessary chore to be gotten over with as soon as possible. It may be, but you will be happier if, early on, you determine that, as far as you are concerned, it is a privilege. Think of it as a chance to be in command for four short hours. While an OOD, you will be as close to command as you will get until you are actually ordered to command. Take advantage of every minute of it. Go to your watch station early. Do a thorough job of familiarizing yourself with the situation and review in your mind what might happen during the watch. If you stand a good watch, your seniors will soon know, and your eventual qualification for command will follow.

Schools

There is no single school that will graduate you as a full-fledged CO. School for prospective COs will help you review and undertake final preparation, but circumstances may preclude your attendance. Schooling should start as early as you can be assigned.

Emergency shiphandling school has already been mentioned. To this should be added other schooling, which can be fit in during yard and upkeep periods or between duty stations. These include, but are not limited to, fire-fighting school, sonar school, damage-control school, nuclear effects school, and other technical schools teaching propulsion and weapons.

Early in your career you must make a key decision: whether to apply for nuclear power school. Remember that in years to come the majority of large ships will be nuclear powered. If you look forward to commanding one of them, you must pay the price now by going through the selection and schooling process. It is a small price to pay for the privilege.

Qualifications

Some qualifications are partially under your control. Obviously you should qualify as OOD in port and under way as soon as possible. Seek the opportunity to qualify as CIC watch officer, communication watch officer, and engineering officer of the watch. Do not use the excuse that you were not assigned to all departments. Go to them and learn. Spend your off time in the engineering spaces, even if you are not assigned to engineering, until you have completed the required notebook for the type. Ask to be assigned to a watch, and eventually ask to be examined so that you can demonstrate your qualifications. During overhaul periods, examine the insides of disassembled machinery. Apply the same initiatives to other departments. The ship's senior officers will be sympathetic (it is their duty to be so) and most will assist you in your attempts.

If you go directly to aviation without a sea assignment, when you next go to sea with a squadron, volunteer to stand JOOW watches. Study and work at learning about your ship. The ship's

CO will be sympathetic and will either qualify you as OOD or will ask your squadron commander to note in your fitness report that you made the effort to qualify. This may sound useless, but it also may be the deciding factor in declaring you qualified to command a carrier in later years.

Command Ashore

For the unrestricted line officer, qualification for command ashore usually follows automatically after a successful command at sea. There are relatively few commands ashore, and the probability of such assignment before the third or fourth shore tour is low. Some commands require special qualifications, which either have been accumulated in previous shore tours or schools or will be taken care of en route.

The acquired education of restricted line officers and staff corps officers is usually sufficient to qualify them for command ashore. Engineering duty officers are expected to serve in a succession of qualifying billets before being declared qualified to command a naval shipyard. Medical and supply officers similarly serve in head-of-department and executive officer billets or the equivalent before qualifying as COs of hospitals and supply depots.

Summary of Command Preparation

The preparation for command is command itself. This means considering your division as a command and carrying out your responsibilities in the same complete and dedicated manner you would expect to display later as the CO of a surface ship or submarine. It means commanding your aircraft just as if it were a carrier. Do an excellent job of command with each echelon of responsibility and you will be ready for an independent command when called.

Assumption of Command

If selected and ordered to command, you will take over in one of two ways: by relieving the CO of an active ship or air squadron or by assuming command of a newly commissioned vessel.

Relieving Command. Assuming command usually means relieving a regularly ordered CO who is completing his tour. You may also relieve an executive officer who has been ordered to relieve his former CO. In any event, your part in the process will be the same.

You will be ordered to such preparatory schooling as the type commander and the commander of the NMPC mutually arrange. Turnover time will vary from about four days to thirty days (the latter for nuclear-powered ships). When your schedule is firm, notify the officer you are to relieve and establish a turnover schedule. You will have to be flexible, since the ship's schedule is relatively fixed.

The CO being relieved has the responsibility of arranging the relief ceremony and of inviting the guests. He should ask you for a list of the persons you want invited and should then make out and mail all of the invitations.

During your turnover period you will want to follow the guidance given in *Navy Regulations* Art. 0707 and the appropriate type commander's instructions. *Navy Regulations* require that both officers inspect the command, exercise the crew at general quarters and general drills, discuss defects, and transfer all unexecuted orders, official correspondence, and information concerning the command and its personnel. Specifically, an audit must be made of the Navy post office, if there is one, and magazine and other keys must be turned over. An inventory and audit of registered publications must be made, and the CO being relieved must complete and sign fitness reports, logs, books, and journals.

Ideally the turnover period should permit the CO to determine the ship's combat readiness. A ship whose crew performs well at general quarters and drills related to combat, that has the required number of specially qualified personnel such as air-controllers and boiler tenders, and that has no equipment, material, or supply deficiencies, can be assumed to be combat ready. Determining combat readiness is vital in wartime and should be given first priority. In peacetime other qualifications should be given higher priority, and the determination of combat readiness can be shortened. Precautions should be taken to assure that the ship can navigate safely and that she will not burn, explode, or sink. If only a limited period for turnover is available, priority should be given to determining whether the ship has the charts, personnel,

Members of VAW-121 receive an ADMAT inspection from COMFAIRNorfolk and their commanding officer.

and equipment to navigate safely, whether the fire and collision bills are adequate and qualified fire-fighting and damage-control personnel are on board and properly assigned, and whether dangerous materials such as ammunition, fuel oil, nuclear fuel, high-pressure steam, and nuclear munitions are stored, accounted for, and used safely. These danger areas must be brought under control immediately. Other areas can wait.

Review carefully with the previous CO the handling characteristics of the ship. Ask how she accelerates and handles in various seas. You will have to take this information on faith until you have had a chance to handle the ship yourself. If you have not had duty in a similar type of ship, review appropriate sections of *Naval Shiphandling*. With information from this book you should be able to handle your ship adequately even before you have gained familiarity with her.

Other areas to look into are registered publications, postal matters, and supplies in small ships without supply officers.

Review the last administrative inspection checklist, the last material, supply, and medical inspection checklists, the last operational-readiness-inspection checklists, naval technical proficiency inspection results, and in the case of nuclear-powered ships, recent reactor safeguards results.

Give careful attention to the letter report of change of command. Substantial deficiencies affecting the operational readiness and safety of the ship should be listed. Any machinery that is inoperative, any armament that is not fully ready, any lack of spare parts, munitions, and supplies, and any abnormal personnel shortages should be noted.

Navy Regulations Art. 0707 says that at the time of turning over command, all hands are to be mustered, and the officer to be relieved is to read orders of detachment and turn over command to his or her successor, who in turn is to read his or her orders and assume command. The remainder of the change-of-command ceremony is described in chapt'

Assuming Command of a Newly Commissioned Ship. Placing a new ship in commission is a challenging task. You will not have the relative luxury of taking over a functioning, organized command. You will have the assistance of your type commander, but most of the task will be yours.

The duties of a prospective commanding officer (PCO) are clearly defined by *Navy Regulations* and type commander's policies. Until the ship is commissioned, the PCO has no independent authority over her. The PCO reports to the type commander and sets the standards for constructing the ship and training the crew. This means studying the ship's plans and inspecting and monitoring construction. You must do so with limited personnel; crew members report to the ship in distinct groups, and you will never think you have enough.

On conventional surface ships, the crew is generally split into a nucleus and a balance detail. The nucleus detail consists of experienced personnel who help assemble the precommissioning outfit and witness tests of machinery and equipment. They are assisted by the fleet introduction team (FIT) assigned to the building yard. This team of experienced operators can provide a wealth of knowledge in areas of quality control, crew organization, and equipment operation. The balance detail generally reports to the ship immediately before commissioning and after extensive en route training.

In the case of nuclear-powered ships, the PCO is designated CO of naval personnel assigned to the precommissioning unit. The first group of personnel reports three months prior to initial reactor plant testing in order to participate in the new-construction reactor plant test program. Unlike the crews of conventional ships, nuclear ship crews are responsible for conducting new-construction tests on the propulsion plant.

Launching is entirely the province of the builder, and any participation by the PCO and the precommissioning unit is strictly by invitation. The builder customarily allows the PCO and a number of the precommissioning detail to ride the ship down the ways. You will have to decide whether you want to ride the ship or be present with the sponsor at the bow when she christens the ship. The sponsor is chosen by the secretary of the Navy. You will be maintaining your relationship with the sponsor for many years.

Fitting out means placing on board a ship or craft the material specified in the allowance lists. During both the construction process and fitting out, you will be responsible for making periodic progress reports, which are described in OPNAVINST 9030.2.

Two final operational ship checks and crew-training evolutions take place prior to going to sea. Dock trials demonstrate that all equipment will operate satisfactorily and that all fitting-out material is aboard. Fast cruise (meaning fast in a dock) is the final check of the crew's ability to operate safely under simulated at-sea conditions.

There are two sets of sea trials for any new-construction ship. Those conducted by or for the builder are called builder's trials. Those conducted for the government are called acceptance trials. The *NAVSEA Technical Manual* contains a complete description of these trials.

Delivery and commissioning can occur simultaneously or separately, depending on where fitting out is to take place. Delivery is purely a contractual matter and can be deferred until the final requirements laid down by the government have been met.

After commissioning, the ship will undergo a shakedown and guarantee period, a post-shakedown availability, and final acceptance trials. It is then ready for refresher training.

Organization and Administration

Setting Command Policy. Whether you relieve command or commission a new ship, one of your first tasks should be to set command policy.

Each CO, during the years of preparation for command, will have studied leadership texts, observed many seniors, and spent much time thinking about how command should be exercised. His or her officers and personnel will be waiting to find out what the policies are and how they will be communicated.

The new CO may choose to reveal his or her philosophy of command through time and events. Many successful COs have followed this path. However, most find it better to establish a quick rapport with their officers and personnel by addressing them as soon as possible. The address need not be formal or all-inclusive, but it should be carefully prepared and should include the most important of the many facets of command.

Your policies and philosophy are your own, but you will find guidance available if you need it. Most successful COs agree that one of your primary goals should be to know your ship. Then you should expect your officers and personnel to know her.

You must be loyal to your subordinates and at the same time let them know that you expect their loyalty. Vow to keep your crew informed. They will respond if they know what you want. Let them know that you want a clean, combat-ready ship. Make sure that they are mentally and physically ready by allowing them adequate rest and recreation.

There will be more to your philosophy of command than the above points, but you should consider them the bare bones of your approach to command.

Organization. SORN describes the basic principles of ship organization, most of which are mandatory. SORN gives excellent guidance for solving your organizational problems. The type commanders publish annexes that set the organization for your type. If your ship is already in commission, the organization will need little change. If you are commissioning a new ship, you will find that SORN and the type commander's annex are all you will need to establish a sound organization.

Personnel. SORN sets forth the duties of the officers and personnel of your ship. You may, of course, alter or combine the duties of the officers assigned to you. Frequent correspondence and liaison with the placement officer (detailer) for your type in the NMPC will help you anticipate detachments, arrivals, qualifications, and other officer problems. You can also get together with the personnel assignment staff of your type commander for problems with enlisted personnel. Make sure that all ship's rosters and personnel documents are up-to-date so that those designated to help you will have the data they need.

Be aware of the educational and training requirements of your officers and enlisted personnel. This means administering a sound PQS so that each of your personnel is in training for the next job and rate. An overall training program is executed by a training officer. Input is provided by a training board. The training program analyzes the career needs of officers and helps them prepare for postgraduate school or war college and attain higher qualifications.

Discipline starts with fair but firm administration of military justice. Make sure that mast is conducted properly and that all of your officers and men understand the restrictions on the assignment of extra duty.

The officers and personnel of your ship are her most important asset. Your entire career should be spent gaining the wisdom and information you will need for their efficient administration. If you succeed in this task, you will run a successful ship.

Maintenance. Navy Regulations Art. 0768 states that the CO will have inspections and tests conducted to ensure the proper maintenance and operation of any ship, aircraft, vehicle, or equipment assigned to his or her command.

In carrying out this responsibility, the most efficient method you can use is to establish a "zero defects policy." To institute such a policy you may want to challenge a group of personnel to prevent defects; they will want to excel individually and at the same time function as part of a team with the same goals. What begins as a program will, if it is successful, become a way of life.

You must still have the few defects that do occur corrected. Today's Navy consists of complex and highly capable ships. A single casualty or material failure to the ship, quickly corrected, will seldom detract from the ship's readiness for war. If it is not corrected, a single defect can precipitate an avalanche of problems.

A large majority of maintenance errors can be prevented by conscientious planning. Officers and senior petty officers should teach good engineering practice, which means instilling in personnel a respect for and an understanding of the equipment being operated; this applies not only to the broad aspects of shipboard plant operation but to everyday operations and maintenance routines. Problems such as abnormal temperatures, unusual noises, and minor leaks should be corrected before they cause major damage.

The Navy's 3-M system was created to solve problems related to the growing complexity of shipboard maintenance, the increased tempo of operations, and the steady decline in available resources. Three-M has two subsystems, the planned maintenance subsystem (PMS) and the maintenance data collection system (MDCS). When properly used by carefully indoctrinated officers and petty officers, these systems can provide the basis for an efficient maintenance system.

Over the past several years, type commanders have made progress in automating the current ship's maintenance project (CSMP) and making its maintenance document meaningful. The document provides the information necessary to evaluate and quantify the back log and scope of work for the ship's force, tender, or yard; it also gives information about planning, scheduling, and funding these activities.

One of the characteristics of a good CO is the ability to inspect. A good inspector knows what to look for, a skill learned from years of experience, usually on the receiving end of inspections.

Availability is the period of time assigned a ship for repair activity ashore or afloat. The key to its success is early planning and complete preparation, which start with educating all workcenter supervisors in the proper preparation of work requests for repairs. Problems must be identified accurately, equipment must be listed completely, shipboard contacts for the repair activity must be identified, and the submission of work requests must be monitored closely as they pass up the chain of command to ascertain action of higher authority.

Normal dry-docking is scheduled during the regular overhaul period. Dry-docking may also be done between regular overhauls (interim dry-docking) for routine maintenance or for repairs. Dry-docking is usually carried out in a Navy yard, a Navy repair facility, or a commercial yard. Prior to docking, a conference is held by the CO and the docking officer or commercial dockmaster to arrange docking schedules and other housekeeping details for the visit. At this conference, information on last docking and ship's plans must be ready.

Navy Regulations Art. 0752-4 says that when a ship operating under her own power is being dry-docked, the CO is fully responsible until the extremity of the ship first entering the dock crosses the sill and the ship is pointed fair. The docking officer then assumes responsibility and retains it until the dock is pumped dry. In undocking, the docking officer assumes responsibility when flooding commences and returns it to the CO when the last extremity of the ship crosses the sill and the ship is pointed fair. In dock, the CO is responsible for ensuring closure of all valves and openings in the ship's bottom on which no work is being done by the repair facility. The CO of the repair facility is responsible, at the end of working hours, for closing all valves and openings in the ship's bottom being worked on by the repair facility.

The success of a regular overhaul depends on the preparations made by the CO before overhaul. During the overhaul, heavy demands are placed on the crew for auxiliary plant operation, preventive maintenance, ship's force overhaul work, and surveillance of shipyard work and training. Early preparation will minimize these demands.

Logistics. Afloat, logistics has become the business of determining what individual ships need to carry out their projected tasks and then supplying the necessary items and services before ships leave port and on a continuing basis by underway replenishment at sea. In a ship this function is the responsibility of the CO and the supply officer.

In a large ship the supply officer should be well qualified. In a small ship, a recently commissioned supply officer may need help. He or she has one of the most difficult jobs the Navy can assign a young officer. The supply officer is responsible for procuring, receiving, storing, issuing, shipping, transferring, selling, accounting for, and maintaining all stores and equipment of the command.

The Coordinated Shipboard Allowance Lists (COSAL) show the repair parts, special tools, and other materials required on board the ship to support installed equipment. The COSAL, an effective management tool, is adjusted periodically as usage information is obtained. Make sure your supply officer is keeping this data accurately.

Controlled equipage such as power tools is a growing problem, since higher costs have made replacement costly. Minimize the number of items requiring custody cards if you can, but remember to maintain accountability, which will reduce the chances of pilferage.

Educate those who originate requisitions so that they do not assign them higher priorities than necessary. Like any such system, over-assignment will kill the system.

The financial account for spare parts and supplies is the operating target (OPTAR). In a small ship your unit commander maintains the account and you do the spending. In a large ship you maintain your own. Watch the accounts carefully to avoid embarrassment and possible disciplinary action in case of overspending. Even though your unit commander maintains the account, you have the ultimate responsibility for it.

The CO can monitor a ship's supply readiness in several ways. The most obvious is to learn the important details of the supply system and to ask the supply officer all the right questions. You can monitor the supply edit audit SIM system report. This monitoring system uses a copy of each requisition to provide a measure of consumption rate versus obligation rate. Supply inspections are an excellent assessment of the supply system condition. Unfortunately they are normally conducted at only eighteen- to twenty-month intervals; a lot can go wrong between inspections. If supply inspections are not so scheduled, it is prudent to request one six months prior to a deployment.

Each type commander administers an improvement system that lists approved alterations, alterations equivalent to a repair, and field changes. Your program will be based on the Navy's FMP, an integrated program combining technical and military alterations. Under the FMP, items in scheduled ship overhauls are listed.

Good food is important to the morale of your crew. You may assign a separate food service officer if you have enough officers, but most supply officers are assigned to carry out this function. In most small ships the wardroom mess subsists from the general mess. All messes should be closely supervised. Random sampling of meals should be required of the CO, executive officer, and OOD, but this is not effective unless follow-up sampling is done to see if any discovered deficiencies have been corrected.

Each ship should leave her base, tender, or last port as fully supplied and provisioned as possible. Normal fleet operations will provide for replenishment at sea when necessary. You should know how to communicate your needs as required by *Operational Reports* (NWP 7) and *Replenishment at Sea* (NWP 14). You must attain skill in bringing your ship alongside for replenishment and in receiving and striking down supplies and provisions both from ships and helicopters.

Safety. Prior to World War II, safety was a relatively simple matter; today it is much more complex. In 1940 safety was divided into three major categories. First, the ship had to sail safely, which meant groundings and collisions had to be prevented by good navigation and shiphandling. Second, fireroom casualties had to be avoided, which meant observing safety precautions closely. Third, ammunition had to be received, stored, moved, and fired safely. These latter tasks generated elaborate, almost sacrosanct safety precautions that were observed to the letter. The safety program, although it was effective, was not even dignified by a name. Today nuclear power, nuclear weapons, high-pressure steam plants, exotic missile propellants, more powerful conventional explosives, aviation fuels, automatic gun-loading systems, complex logistic replenishment machinery, the threat of biological and chemical warfare, and the possibility of nuclear-fallout contamination require a formal and far-reaching safety program.

SORN gives the CO ultimate responsibility for all safety matters and outlines safety programs. You are required to assign a safety officer to be your principal adviser on safety matters.

With respect to safety at sea, the ship is administered departmentally, but her safe operation is accomplished by watches. *SORN* requires that the CO establish watches and that the engineering officer of the watch and an OOD be placed on continuous watch under way. Within the bounds of these fundamental requirements you must train and assign competent and well-qualified watch officers. Upon your own skill and training ability depends the safety of your ship.

Navigational readiness is another area vital to safety. Make sure all your officers know your policy with regard to shifting the conn.

Training

The first step in your training program is to assign a training officer as required by *SORN*. Large ships can afford a fairly senior officer, but small ships must depend heavily on the executive officer. No matter whom you appoint, you and your executive officer must give him or her full backing. Next, you will need to appoint a planning board for training. Its composition is dictated by *SORN*. With these two steps taken, the next is to develop the training program itself. *SORN* Art. 0810 provides a detailed training program that you should follow with appropriate changes and modifications to suit your ship. It is important to the success of your program that you keep good records showing the status of all subprograms.

Refresher training is an intensive, concentrated period of training designed to take a ship that is materially ready, fully manned, and fully supplied, and at the end of a period of about two months turn her into a ship capable of performing any individual ship function required of her type.

This period is preceded by an assessment and administrative inspection by the training command staff to determine if the ship is reasonably ready for refresher training. The training period begins with a series of lessons, drills, and battle problems of increasing complexity and difficulty. These events culminate in an advanced battle problem designed to test every facet of the ship's machinery, equipment, and armament, and all of the officers and enlisted personnel, first as individuals and then as members of various teams and parties.

Inspections. Inspections are a means of ascertaining the battle readiness, administrative efficiency, preservation, and cleanliness of a ship or squadron. The oldest and most basic inspection is the weekly CO's inspection. Historically it has been held on Saturday. It is preceded by an inspection of the lower decks on Friday. No other inspections are permitted on the weekend. Most type commanders expect these inspections to be held each week. If you cannot be present, let your executive officer conduct the inspection.

Large ships are separated into zones. You may want to inspect only one or more zones each week and let other officers cover the remaining zones. By alternating zones, you can cover the entire ship over a reasonable period of time.

Over the years other inspections have been imposed by higher authority. The most important is the operational readiness inspection, which is designed to test the ability of the ship to operate in wartime conditions and in battle. It is conducted over a period

Captain's inspection in a small ship. Regular inspections allow the CO to keep track of the condition of ship and crew.

of twenty-four hours by a chief inspector (normally your unit commander) assisted by a large party. Most of the inspection is conducted under way with the ship either in condition watches or at general quarters. Realistic battle problems and drills are held, including live firing if it is feasible.

The next most important is the administrative inspection, usually held twice a year, once as a surprise inspection. Given in port in a twenty-four-hour period, it starts with a formal personnel inspection and then proceeds to examine all facets of administration including logs, journals, records, and procedures. Other lesser inspections, such as supply and medical, may be given at the same time or separately.

Perhaps the most demanding inspection is that given by the Propulsion Examination Board (PEB). OPNAVINST 3540.4 (series) covers conventionally powered ships and OPNAVINST 3540.3c (series) covers nuclear-powered ships. Inspections are made by permanently established boards and are very rigorous. PEBs examine personnel to determine their training and qualifications, witness and evaluate the conduct of propulsion plant drills and evolutions, inspect the material condition of the propulsion plant, and review the administration and records of the entire engineering plant.

The conventional ship is given a light-off examination (LOE) and an operational propulsion plant examination (OPPE). The nuclear-powered ship is given a precritical reactor safeguards examination, a post-overhaul reactor safeguards examination (PORSE), an operational reactor safeguards examination (ORSE), and a radiological control practice evaluation (RCPE). Failure to pass any of these inspections can result in weeks of hard work for you and your crew. Prepare well and pass them the first time.

Certain other inspections are prescribed for nuclear-capable ships, submarines, and aircraft. Since the inspections are classified, not much detail can be presented here. The inspections are designed to ascertain that each ship or aircraft is technically equipped and that each crew is proficiently trained in the handling, stowage, and use of nuclear weapons before the ship or aircraft is allowed to acquire the weapons. Periodic reinspections assure maintenance of qualifications.

Each CO should master the details of handling nuclear weapons personally. The inspections are very stringent and go into every detail of handling, training, and record keeping. Many failures on these inspections occur as the result of a single administrative error in personnel records, maintenance logs, or equipment histories. Such meticulousness is justified by the enormous consequences of failure, which might lead to a nuclear disaster.

Inspections are also made by the Board of Inspection and Survey during the period prior to regular overhauls.

Operations

With your ship organized, a sound training program established, and refresher training behind you, your ship is now ready to join the fleet.

Reports. You must make prompt reports on the daily operations of your ship. The movement report (MOVREP) is the most important one you will make. NWP 7 contains all the information you will need to compile the MOVREP. Be meticulous in making this report. Failure to do so, coupled with damage to your ship, could be disastrous both to your ship and career. When you are operating as part of a fleet unit, the unit commander is supposed to render the report. Review chapters 9, 10, and 11 of NWP 7 to make sure the unit commander reports the correct information about your ship.

A submarine notice (SUBNOTE) is a movement report peculiar to submarines. It should include all the information required for a movement report. Further details are contained in chapter 12 of NWP 7.

NWP 7 Art. 1003 reminds you that MOVREP information is used by postal authorities to verify the forwarding information they have on file, but MOVREPs do not relieve you of the responsibility of submitting separate mail-routing instructions to the appropriate fleet commanders in accordance with either the CINCLANTFLT 5110.1 series or the COMNAVLOGPACINST 5112.1 series.

The purpose of a casualty report (CASREP) is to provide seniors and others with early information concerning personnel, equipment, machinery, and hull damage that impairs the readiness of your ship. If you submit a CASREP, you must also submit a report under the combat-readiness reporting system. You must submit follow-up reports when the casualty is reduced or corrected (CASCOR).

Section 405 of NWP 7 covers reports of accidental death or injuries to Navy personnel on or off duty.

Section 410 of NWP 7 covers the requirement for combat-readiness reports. OPNAVINST C3501.66 and fleet and type instructions cover details of readiness categories.

Logistic requirement reports (LOGREQs) are discussed in NWP 7. Under the LOGREQ system, each ship or unit must submit a logistics requirements report forty-eight hours in advance of arrival at a British, Canadian, or U.S. port.

Independent Operations. Navy Regulations covers the responsibilities of a CO operating singly. He or she must conform to the applicable regulations for the senior officer present. These are in *Navy Regulations* Chap. 9; if you are to operate independently you should study them carefully.

Two seemingly simple actions will keep you out of most trouble. First, understand your orders, and second, make all required reports promptly and accurately.

Independent operations of submarines are conducted frequently and provide exceptional training opportunities. For the fast attack submarine, independent operations provide training opportunities much like wartime operations. For both SSBNs and SSNs, deployed operations are truly independent and the CO has much latitude.

Heavy weather, the ever-present hazard to ships, may require that you act independently. Prepare your ship for any kind of weather by reviewing your heavy-weather plan and making sure all hands know how to implement it. Your studies of heavy weather should cover weather patterns both worldwide and in your particular area. A good text to refer to is *Weather for the Mariner*. Piloting instructions include useful weather information for your area.

Search and rescue (SAR) may also call for independent operations. You may come across a vessel in distress or you may hear a report from one on the international distress frequency. Higher authority may also divert you to an SAR mission. *Navy Regulations* Art. 0925 spells out your responsibilities, and *SORN* contains sample bills for implementing them.

Combat

The ultimate purpose of your ship is to engage in combat in defense of our country. All of the preparations we have been talking about, and which you have been carrying out, are undertaken to ready your ship for combat.

Kinds of Warfare. Obviously the warfare you must prepare for is unlikely to be like that of the past, but you must still be ready for conventional war. The most intense warfare would be the annihilation of total nuclear exchange. The most likely warfare lies somewhere between conventional and total nuclear war.

Strategic planners foresee various kinds of war. These include strategic nuclear exchange, or a total use of nuclear weapons by both sides; partial strategic nuclear exchange, or a mutual limitation following an initial exchange; tactical nuclear exchange ashore, or a limited exchange of tactical nuclear weapons ashore; tactical nuclear exchange at sea; conventional war at sea; conventional war, with no nuclear use; and incidents short of war, such as confrontation, harassment, and blockade.

Each kind of war requires your thought and preparation. In the event of war, you will have to decide for the first time how to cope with a mutilated topside; a lack of repair facilities, replacement equipment, and ammunition; morale problems among a crew wondering what has happened to their homeland and what will happen to them; and many other unique and catastrophic problems.

There are several publications you may refer to for information, among which are *Shipboard Damage Control* (NWIP 50-3), *Nuclear Fallout Forecasting and Warning Organization* (ATP 25), and *Armed Forces Doctrine for Chemical and Biological Defense* (NWP 36).

Combat Housekeeping. You will have to make sure that all of your weapons systems and detection equipment are in peak condition. You will be dependent upon radar, electronic countermeasures, and even lookouts for information that will help you to survive.

The cleanliness of your ship will become more rather than less important—it will minimize infection in case of explosion or damage. Security, particularly when you are in port, will have to be increased.

Combat Philosophy. You will have to formulate a combat philosophy that can be transmitted to your officers and men. They will fight better if they are well informed and well led.

Review the combat qualities our Navy has traditionally commended. They include, but are not limited to, tenacity, courage, aggressiveness, ingenuity, and the ability of young officers and enlisted men to display initiative when their seniors are incapacitated. You, as CO, may supplement the qualities honored by the Navy, but you must never adopt a policy that discourages them.

Ready your ship and crew; be prepared for any eventuality; and then hope that the strength of our country and of our Navy will make the use of power unnecessary.

20

RETIREMENT

MY SWORD I GIVE TO HIM THAT SHALL SUCCEED ME IN
MY PILGRIMAGE, AND MY COURAGE AND SKILL TO HIM
THAT CAN GET IT. MY MARKS AND SCARS I CARRY WITH
ME, TO BE A WITNESS FOR ME, THAT I HAVE FOUGHT
HIS BATTLES WHO WILL NOW BE MY REWARDER.

—*John Bunyan,* Pilgrim's Progress

SO, SAFE ON SHORE THE PENSIONED SAILOR LIES,
AND ALL THE MALICE OF THE STORM DEFIES . . .

—*William Somerville,* The Author, an Old Man, to His Arm-chair

It is never too early to plan for retirement. Many of the qualifications you have attained and the education you have achieved
can be used to build a second career after retirement. With these
achievements and the decision-making abilities you have developed, your services will be marketable after retirement.

In any event, you need to prepare for retirement several years
before the actual event. This chapter is designed to help you in
this effort.

Retirement Procedures

General. Officers of the Regular Navy and the Naval Reserve
earn the right to retire under a variety of conditions. Regular
officers who retire usually receive reduced pay as compensation.
Retirement for Naval Reserve officers may be honorary or may
be accompanied by retired pay. The difference in retirement benefits has to do with the different sorts of service performed: regular
officers devote their life's work to the defense of their country,
whereas reserve officers offer their services primarily in a national

emergency or war. Officers of the Naval Reserve are entitled to retirement compensation similar to that received by regular officers if physical disabilities are received in the line of duty.

The retirement system for regular Navy officers is advantageous both to them and to the government. It is part of an officer's compensation for the rigors of naval life. The system also permits the government to release officers from active duty for medical reasons, because they have reached the statutory age for retirement, or in a few cases for lack of proficiency. The retirement system is a strong inducement for young people considering the Regular Navy as a career.

Most active-duty officers do not know enough about retirement benefits or the retirement process. For a basic discussion of the subject, see the *Navy Guide for Retired Personnel and Their Families* (NAVMILPERS 15891F), and for more information see the *Retired Military Almanac*, published annually by the Uniformed Services Publishing Company, and *Retiring from Military Service*, published by the Naval Institute Press.

Regular Navy

Voluntary Retirement. When an officer of the Regular Navy (or Naval Reserve) has completed more than twenty years of active service, ten years of which must have been active commissioned service, he or she may, upon request, be transferred to the retired list according to the discretion of the president (twenty-year retirements have been suspended from time to time).

When an officer of the Navy has completed at least thirty years of active service, he or she may, upon application and according to the discretion of the secretary of the Navy, be retired from active service and placed on the retired list with 75 percent of his or her active-duty pay. When an officer has completed at least forty years of active service, he or she will, upon application, be retired from active service with 75 percent of active-duty pay.

A request for retirement is submitted via the chain of command, through the commander of the NMPC, to the secretary of the Navy. The request should read as follows: "Having completed thirty [40, 20] years' service, I request a transfer to the retired list of officers of the Navy effective [date]." It is not necessary to state a reason or to refer to pertinent law. Orders for release from active

NAVAL OFFICER'S GUIDE

VOLUNTARY RETIREMENT PROGRAM
FOR COMMISSIONED AND WARRANT OFFICERS, USN

LAW— TITLE 10	TYPE OF RETIRE- MENT	APPLICABLE TO	CREDITABLE SERVICE	PAY	RANK ON RETIRED LIST
Sec. 6321	40 years service	Permanent officers	Full-time active duty in Regular or Reserve components of Armed Forces	¾ of applicable basic pay of rank in which retired	Rank held at time of retirement (unless entitled to higher rank under other law)
Sec. 6322	30 years service	Permanent officers	Same as above	Same as above	Same as above
Sec. 6326	30 years service	Temporary officers and warrant officers with permanent enlisted status	Same as above, less time lost for AWOL, SKMC or NPDI	Same as above	Rank held at time of retirement (unless entitled to higher rank under other law)
Sec. 6323	20 years service	Permanent officers and officers whose permanent status is enlisted	Active duty in Navy, Army, Marine Corps, Air Force, Coast Guard or Reserve components thereof, including active duty for training, at least 10 years of which shall have been commissioned	2½% × applicable basic pay of rank in which retired multiplied by the sum of the following: (a) total years of service creditable for basic pay purposes as of 31 May 1958; (b) total years of active service, including active duty for training, performed subsequent to 31 May 1958; (c) if not included in (a) above, total years of constructive service credited for basic pay purposes by the Act of 30 April 1956 (applicable only to MC and DC officers); and one day's credit (with maximum of 60 days credit for any one year) for each retirement point earned as a member of a Reserver component subsequent to 31 May 1958 through attendance at drills, periods of equivalent instruction or appropriate duty performed as authorized by competent authority, completion of correspondence courses, plus 15 points per year gratuitous credit for Reserve membership	Rank held at time of retirement (unless entitled to higher rank under other law)
Sec. 1293	20 years service	Warrant officers	Full-time active duty in Armed Forces or Reserve components		Warrant officer grade in which serving at time of retirement, unless entitled to higher rank or pay under other law, at member's election

Figure 20-1. Voluntary retirement program, USN.

VOLUNTARY RETIREMENT PROGRAM
FOR COMMISSIONED AND WARRANT OFFICERS—USNR

LAW—TITLE 10	APPLICABLE TO	CREDITABLE SERVICE	PAY	RANK ON RETIRED LIST
Sec. 6323 as amended	Commissioned officers 20 years service	Active duty in the Navy, Army, Marine Corps, Air Force, Coast Guard or Reserve components thereof, including active duty for training, *at least 10 years of which shall have been commissioned*	2½% ×applicable basic pay of rank in which retired multiplied by number of years service creditable in computation of basic pay	Rank held at time of retirement, unless entitled to higher rank under other law
Sec. 6327	Commissioned officers and Warrant officers 20 years service	Ful-time active service in the Navy, Army, Marine Corps, Air Force, Coast Guard or, Reserve components thereof. (Member must have been in Reserves on 1 January 1953)	50% ×applicable basic pay of rank in which retired	Highest rank in which service was satisfactory
Sec. 1293	Warrant officers 20 years service	Full-time active duty in Armed Forces or Reserve components	2½% ×applicable basic pay of rank in which retired multiplied by number of years service creditable in computation of basic pay	Warrant officer grade in which serving at time of retirement, unless entitled to higher rank or pay under other law, at member's election
Sec. 1331	Commissioned officers and Warrant officers 20 years satisfactory Federal service *and* age 60	All service in the Armed Forces prior to 1 July 1949; subsequent to 1 July 1949 any year in which a minimum of 50 retirement points is earned	Total number of retirement points divided by 360 and multiplied by 2½% of basic pay of rank in which retired	Highest rank satisfactorily held during entire period of service

Figure 20-2. Voluntary retirement program, USNR.

duty will provide for detachment in the month preceding the effective date of transfer to the retired list.

All retirements become effective on the first of the month following the month in which the request is approved, except in certain cases. Detachment depends on the availability of a relief.

No person may accrue more than sixty days' leave. Upon retirement unused leave up to sixty days is compensated by payment at current rate of pay.

After your request has been approved, if you are on sea duty or overseas, you may first be ordered to the nearest naval separation activity in the continental United States, where you will receive further orders releasing you from active duty. Officers of the rank of captain and above are ordered to report to the commandant of the nearest naval station or naval district (during wartime).

It is mandatory if you are contemplating voluntary retirement or are subject to involuntary or statutory retirement that you obtain a preliminary physical examination three or four months prior to the prospective date of retirement. Any minor problems can be corrected before retirement and will not complicate or delay release. If you are found to have a disability, you may, of course, be subject to physical retirement; in this case, adequate information must be received by COMNAVPERSCOM in time to stop final action on the retirement papers then being processed.

After a request for retirement has been approved and the retirement has become effective, there is no process of law whereby the retired status may be changed, unless a physical disability of over 30 percent is received while serving as a retired officer on active duty.

If you are not physically qualified for release, it does not necessarily follow that you will be ordered to appear before a physical-evaluation board. An operation or treatment may correct the problem.

Involuntary Separations and Retirement. In the discussion of retirement and separation from the service in this section, two definitions are of importance. Retired pay is the amount of pay received by an officer when he or she goes on the retired list. This amount will be increased by cost-of-living changes. Severance pay is a lump-sum payment made to an officer discharged from the naval service, based upon two months' active-duty pay for each year of commissioned service, not to exceed two years' pay.

Commissions of all officers are revocable for three years after the initial appointment.

The *NAVMILPERS Manual* references the various sections of U.S. Code 10 that cover involuntary retirement for all categories of officers. Officers not of the unrestricted line should consult these references. In general, the following provisions of the Defense Officer Personnel Management Act (DOPMA) of 1981 apply:

1. Lieutenants and Lieutenant Commanders—officers failing twice in selection to the next higher grade will be honorably discharged. If they are within 2 years of completing 20 years in service on the day of discharge they may be retained until qualified for retirement.

2. Commanders—officers failing twice in selection after completing 28 years in service are retired.

3. Commanders—officers failing twice in selection after completing twenty-eight years of commissioned service are retired.

4. Captains—officers not restricted in the performance of duty, having completed thirty years of service and failed twice in selection, and all other captains not on the promotion list upon completion of thirty years are retired. Captains of the restricted line and staff corps, if not on the promotion list and if not selected for continuation on the active list, are retired on the first of July after completing thirty-one years of commissioned service.

5. Limited-duty officers—officers who fail twice in selection have the option of being discharged with severance pay or being retired as provided above, or of reverting to warrant status to complete thirty years of service. All limited-duty officers will be retired after thirty years of service.

6. Transferees—those regular officers of the grade of lieutenant commander and above, who transferred to the Regular Navy and who have failed twice in selection, are involuntarily retired when the next junior Regular Navy officer who has not lost numbers or precedence completes the necessary active service for retirement. Such officers will receive a minimum of 50 percent of active-duty pay as retired pay, even though they have completed less than twenty years of active commissioned service.

7. Unsatisfactory officers—if the records of an eligible officer with less than twenty years' service indicate unsatisfactory performance of duty in his or her present grade and suggest that he or she would not satisfactorily perform the duties of the next higher grade, the officer will be discharged from the Navy on the thirtieth of June of that fiscal year with severance pay.

Selection for Retention in the Grade of Rear Admiral. Line rear admirals not designated for engineering, aeronautical engineering, or special duty must undergo selection in the fiscal year in which they complete five years of service in that grade or thirty-five years of total commissioned service, whichever may be later, to determine whether or not they are to continue on the active list. If they fail in selection, they are retired. At least 50 percent and not more than 75 percent of those eligible for such selection must be continued on active duty.

Selection of rear admirals for retention on the active list is also provided for engineering duty, aeronautical engineering duty, and special duty categories and for the staff corps. In these cases, rear admirals become eligible for selection in the fiscal year in which they complete seven years of service in that grade or thirty-five years of total commissioned service, whichever is later, and

434

NAVAL OFFICER'S GUIDE

in each fiscal year thereafter as long as they remain on the active list.

Physical Retirement.   The purpose of physical retirement is to remove those not able to perform their duties and at the same time to safeguard the rights of the individual.

The physical retirement provisions of the Career Compensation Act are too long to explain in detail here. Some of its provisions are described in the following paragraphs.

Members of the uniformed services unfit to perform duties of their office because of physical disability may be retired or separated from the service. If the percentage of disability is less than 30 percent and the member has completed less than twenty years of active service, the individual may be discharged with severance pay.

There is a temporary-disability retired list to which individuals are transferred unless they are already retired because of permanent disability. Retired pay on this list may be determined either from a percentage of basic pay, equal to 2.5 percent times the number of years of service, or from the percentage of disability with which the individual was placed on the list; the retired pay in no case will be less than 50 percent or more than 75 percent. Individuals placed on this list are given periodic physical examinations at intervals of not less than eighteen months. After five years, or earlier if examination shows the individual to be permanently disabled, he or she may be permanently retired. If the disability is less than 30 percent on any examination and less than twenty years' service has been completed, he or she may be separated with severance pay. If found fit, he or she is returned to duty. Consult the *NAVMILPERS Manual* for other provisions.

When an officer has been hospitalized for three months, a medical board will recommend that the officer appear before a physical evaluation board, return to duty or limited duty, or undergo further treatment and subsequent reexamination. In most cases, appearing before a physical evaluation board requires only part of a day. After that, the officer awaits further orders. Each case is reviewed by the Physical Review Council. Final determination on the case is made by the secretary of the Navy.

Statutory Retirement.   The statutory retirement age for regular officers is sixty-two. An officer is transferred to the retired list on the first day of the month following that in which he or she attains statutory age.

Retired Pay. As a general rule, an officer is retired in the rank in which he or she is serving prior to the time of retirement, unless some provision of law confers higher rank.

Retired pay is difficult to compute, and it is hard as well to predict future changes in retired pay. When you retire, your pay will be 2.5 times the number of years of service times your base pay upon retirement, up to a maximum of 75 percent. Thereafter you will be entitled to periodic raises tied to the Consumer Price Index (CPI). Prior to 1981 two raises per year were granted. In 1981 only one was given. CPI-based increases are determined by congressional action and may vary from year to year.

Naval Reserve

The Retired Reserve is composed of members of the Naval Reserve who have been transferred to it without pay. The Naval Reserve retired list is composed of members of the Naval Reserve transferred to it with pay. Officers in the Retired Reserve may eventually qualify for the Naval Reserve retired list.

Voluntary Retirement to Retired Reserve. An officer may be transferred to the Retired Reserve when he or she has completed twenty years of honorable service in any component of the armed forces or has been found physically disqualified for active duty as a result of a service-connected disability. See figure 20-2.

An officer of the Naval Reserve may be transferred to the Retired Reserve after he or she has completed ten years of active service, has been found physically disqualified for active duty (not a result of misconduct), is thirty-seven years old and has completed eight years of qualifying service subsequent to 1 July 1949, has completed honorable service on active duty in time of war or national emergency for at least six months, or has consistently supported the armed forces in an outstanding manner as determined by the secretary of the Navy.

Involuntary Retirement to the Retired Reserve. Except under special circumstances, an officer in an active or inactive status in the Naval Reserve in a grade of ensign or above will be retired at age sixty-two.

Naval Reserve Retired List. Any warrant or commissioned officer of the Naval Reserve who has completed twenty years of active service, at least ten years of which were commissioned service, may be transferred to the Naval Reserve retired list. Each officer retired under this section of U.S. Code 10 will be retired in the highest grade, temporary or permanent, in which he or she served satisfactorily. Retired pay will be computed at 2.5 percent of the basic pay multiplied by the sum of:

1. Total years of service creditable for basic pay purposes as of 31 May 1958
2. Total years of active service, including active duty for training, performed subsequent to 31 May 1958
3. If not included in the above, total years of constructive service credited for basic pay purposes in U.S. Code 10
4. One day's credit (with a maximum of sixty days' credit for any one anniversary year) for each retirement point earned as a member of a reserve component performing authorized reserve activity subsequent to 31 May 1958, and fifteen points per year gratuitous credit for reserve membership

Retired pay may not be more than 75 percent of basic pay.

Review Boards

The Naval Retiring Review Board and the Physical Review Council fully protect the interests of all officers when physical retirement proceedings are involved. These bodies review the actions of medical boards of hospitals and physical evaluation boards when the officer has been separated from the service without pay, providing the officer concerned formally applies for such review within fifteen years from the date of separation.

Retired Pay Accounts

The pay accounts of all officers retired are carried in the U.S. Finance Center in Cleveland, Ohio. Pay accounts are not transferred to the center until notification is received by certified copies of the final retirement letter.

Income tax is withheld except for those completely exempt from paying it. All allotments are automatically continued for insurance; others are stopped. To have state income taxes withheld from retirement pay, an officer must make a written request to the Navy Finance Center, Cleveland.

Commencing 1 January 1982, retirement pay years for members serving less than six months of a year are rounded to the nearest lower year. Members serving more than six months of a year have that year rounded to the nearest month.

Retired Officer Rights, Benefits, and Restrictions

Publications of Interest to Retired Officers. The Retired Officer's Association publishes a bimonthly magazine giving information of vital interest to the officers of all services. Every officer should join this association, which is in the forefront of the fight to preserve the rights and privileges of all retired officers.

Navy Times has up-to-date information on all developments in the Navy affecting retired officers and publishes an occasional retirement supplement. The NMPC (NMPC 643) also publishes "Shift Colors," a quarterly newsletter of information of interest to retirees from the Navy.

The NMPC publishes the *Navy Guide for Retired Personnel and Their Families* (NAVMILPERS 15891F). This publication, which will be sent to you prior to your retirement, contains all the information you will need to make the transition to retired status.

Employment Activities after Retirement. If you are physically able, you should seek employment after retirement, preferably a position covered by Social Security. Certain laws limit your freedom to accept employment. They can be found in the *Reference Guide to Employment Activities of Retired Naval Personnel* (NAVSO P-1778) and DOD Dir. 7700.15. If you have any doubt as to your eligibility for a particular job, write to the Office of the Judge Advocate General, Washington, D.C., 20370.

When you retire, you will be required to submit a statement of employment (DD Form 1357) within thirty days after retirement. Officers O-4 and above must file DD Form 1787 if they are employed by a prime defense contractor.

A retired regular officer is restricted for a period of three years after his retirement from selling any supplies or war materials to any agency of the government.

A retired officer, regular or reserve, may not represent anyone other than the United States in connection with a matter in which the United States is a party or has an interest and in which he or she participated personally for the government.

A retired officer, regular or reserve, may not, for one year after retirement, represent anyone other than the United States in connection with a matter in which the United States is a party or has an interest, and which was within the boundary of his or her official responsibility during the year after retirement.

A retired officer considering employment with a foreign government or by a firm employed by a foreign government should consult the judge advocate general prior to accepting employment.

Dual Compensation. All retired officers are eligible for employment in a civilian position with the federal government. Certain conditions must be met if employment is sought within 180 days.

Retired regular officers may receive the full salary of the civilian office, plus retired military pay at an annual rate approximately equal to the first $7,698 of pay (the amount changes annually based on Cost of Living Adjustment [COLA] increases) plus one-half of the remainder. Regular officers retired for combat disability are not so restricted, nor are reserve officers.

Survivors Benefit Plan. Public Law 92-425, enacted on 21 September 1972, established a new SBP within the uniformed-services retirement plan. The full facts regarding the plan are contained in the *Navy Guide for Retired Personnel and Their Families*, but the following summary will be adequate for preliminary planning. The Congress has indicated that it intends to make changes in this plan. Those nearing retirement should consult their personnel office for late changes.

The purpose of the SBP is to establish a program to complement the benefits of Social Security. The plan gives all career members who reach retirement eligibility, including reservists who qualify for retired pay at age sixty, an opportunity to leave a portion of their retired pay to their survivors at a reasonable cost.

Members who have a spouse and/or dependent children on the date of retirement automatically receive maximum survivor benefits. A member can elect not to participate in SBP or to participate in other plans by submitting a request to the CO of the Retired Pay Department, Anthony J. Celebrezze Federal Building, Cleveland, Ohio, 44199, via his or her own CO within thirty days of the retirement date.

If automatic full coverage is not desired, other options are available to provide for reduced coverage, or for reduced or no coverage for certain dependents.

Basic coverage is for the surviving spouse. Additional coverage may be obtained for dependent children. Because of recent changes in SBP rates and coverage, an officer who is planning for retirement should obtain detailed information from the nearest personnel office.

The total annuity may flow from one or more sources at various times, i.e., part from the VA dependency and indemnity compensation and part from Social Security benefits. These benefits replace equal amounts of the SBP annuity when and if the annuitant is eligible for them.

Social Security.   Social Security is a government-sponsored old-age and survivors' insurance program that provides protection to nine out of ten employed citizens of this country and their families. Social Security can provide you with a monthly income in addition to retirement pay and VA compensation. It is tax partially free. You receive it upon reaching age sixty-two (or as late as sixty-five if you so opt). If you die, your spouse and your children, if they are under eighteen, receive a payment; if your children become disabled while under eighteen, they continue to receive a payment past that age. Orphaned children and dependent parents also receive payments.

All officers on active duty pay into the Social Security program. You should keep track of your Social Security contributions for each year. As you approach sixty-two, visit or write your nearest Social Security office for consultation. They will help you calculate your Social Security payments after you decide whether you want to accept them at age sixty-two or later. If you accept them at age sixty-two, you will receive less per month than if you delay acceptance until age sixty-five; the total amount received in either case should be equal in the long run.

Social Security deductions are not taken from your retired pay. If you work after retirement you will have to contribute to Social Security from your pay. After you begin receiving Social Security payments, you are limited in the amount of money you may earn. This amount varies annually. At age 70 there is no limit.

Other Social Security Benefits.   If you are permanently disabled, you may be eligible at an earlier age for the same benefits you would otherwise receive at sixty-five.

When you die, your spouse or the person paying your burial expenses will be entitled to a lump-sum payment, in addition to a monthly annuity equal to three times the amount of the monthly old-age benefit—but not more than $255—which you would be entitled to receive at sixty-five.

Medical and Dental Care. A retired regular officer, or a retired reserve officer entitled to retired pay, and his or her dependents may be hospitalized on a space-available basis in naval and other uniformed-service and public-health-service hospitals for most ailments. Those with excepted ailments who still desire government hospitalization must apply to veterans' hospitals.

Those eligible for hospitalization are also eligible for out-patient care. Dental care is available only on an availability basis.

When medical care is not available at uniformed-service facilities, retired persons and their dependents may use CHAMPUS until they are sixty-five years old; after that Medicare may be used. For additional information on CHAMPUS, see *The CHAMPUS Handbook*, published by the CHAMPUS Public Affairs Branch.

A retired officer who is old and infirm may be admitted to the U.S. Naval Home in Gulfport, Mississippi, for domiciliary care.

Veterans' Benefits. All retirees are entitled to veterans' benefits even though they are receiving retired pay. Some benefits accrue to survivors of retired officers. Hospitalization in veterans' hospitals is available on a priority basis only to veterans with a service-connected disability.

If you can establish the existence of a service-connected disability to the satisfaction of the VA, you may, in addition to disability compensation, be eligible for other benefits such as tax exemption, priority hospitalization in VA hospitals, increased death benefits, and residence in VA homes.

Veterans of World War II and the Korean War are eligible for loan guarantees to buy, build, or improve a home, to buy a farm or farm supplies and equipment, and to buy or undertake a business.

The Korean GI Bill offers limited educational benefits. Money is paid directly to the individual. Some of these benefits extend to Vietnam veterans. An officer retired for disability may also apply to the VA for vocational rehabilitation.

Employment. You are entitled to use the specialized counseling and placement services provided by federal and state law. You may register with the appropriate state or local employment office.

Nondisabled veterans are entitled to a five-point preference in addition to their earned ratings in civil service examinations; disabled veterans are entitled to a ten-point preference.

Travel, Shipment, and Storage of Household Goods. A regular naval officer or a reserve officer retiring with pay with eight or more years of active service is entitled to receive allowances for travel from the last duty station to a new home. Travel must be completed within one year. Temporary storage is available.

Use of Titles. Retired persons are permitted to use their military titles in connection with commercial enterprises, but they must not discredit the service in so doing.

Commissary, Exchanges, and Officers' Messes. Officers retired with pay may be accorded the privileges of armed forces commissary stores, exchanges, and Navy clothing and small stores. Privileges at officers' messes are subject to possible limitation of facilities.

Uniform. On appropriate occasions, retired personnel are entitled to wear their uniforms. They are prohibited from wearing their uniform in connection with any civilian enterprise. Retired personnel in a foreign country may not be in uniform except when attending ceremonies or social functions where the uniform is required on the invitation, or when regulations or customs of the country permit.

APPENDIX A

MPCCs Manual for Officer Accession Programs

Each newly commissioned line officer should be aware of the professional knowledge the Navy expects of him or her. The following minimum professional core competencies (MPCC) have been approved for all officer accession groups. Naval Academy midshipmen are given about four times as much professional education as NROTC regular midshipmen and about eight times as much as contract NROTC midshipmen and OCS students. These objectives must be met by all Naval Academy midshipmen prior to graduation. NROTC and OCS graduates are expected to achieve these objectives as soon as possible after commissioning.

Preface

All Navy officer accession programs are designed to produce junior officers with a basic knowledge of the naval profession and to provide moral, mental, and physical development. The goal is to instill in each graduate the highest ideals of duty, honor, and loyalty in order to provide officers who have potential for future development of mind and character to assume the highest responsibilities of citizenship, military command, and government service.

This manual provides the professional competencies for developing course objectives for all officer accession programs. These competencies are in response to the policy statements of the chief of naval operations, which established a common category of professional and training requirements for all officer accession programs. The competencies listed in this manual are based upon fleet requirements. It should be noted that the competencies are the minimum which should be attained for the accession program.

The composite of all classroom and practical instruction provides the basis for the development of a sense of dedication and commitment to the naval service and establishes personal standards of excellence which will remain with the graduate throughout his or her professional career. Program emphasis is directed toward providing a foundation for future training, education, and professional growth.

Definition of Measurement Terms

I. Know—recall facts, bring to mind the appropriate material, recognize knowledge.

   Examples: *Know* the objectives of damage control aboard ship.

   Know the safety precautions used to provide the fullest measure of safe small-boat operations.

II. Comprehend—interpret principles and concepts and relate them to new situations.

   Examples: *Comprehend* the development of Soviet seapower and the threat it represents.

   Comprehend the concept of internal forces (e.g., stress, strain, shear).

III. Apply—utilize knowledge and comprehension of specific facts in new relationships with other facts, theories, and principles.

   Examples: *Apply* the active and passive sonar equations and radar equation in determining system performance.

   Apply piloting, celestial, and electronic navigation techniques in preparing a day's work in navigation.

IV. Demonstrate—show evidence of ability in performing a task.

   Examples: *Demonstrate* fundamental swimming skills and ability to cope with water emergencies.

   Demonstrate the correct procedure used in plotting LORAN fixes.

Executive Summary

The organization of this MPCC manual differs from the previous manual in that it is not organized to parallel the normal sequence of Naval Academy or NROTC professional naval science courses. This compilation is organized to expand on major domains of accumulated knowledge that a naval officer should have acquired by the time he or she is commissioned. Each section adds another item to the aspiring officer's "uniform" of competency to enter his or her chosen profession.

Not all of the major competency statements apply to all naval officer accession programs. For example, Marine Corps officer accessions are exempt from much of the entire section relating to shipkeeping, seamanship, and navigation. In addition, some accession programs are exempted from specific subordinate competency elements or related series of elements. In these cases, a statement of exemption is contained in parenthesis following the competency statement. This exemption applies, as well, to subordinate elements of the statement, if any.

An inclusive summary of each major competency area follows:

I. Academic Preparation—This statement outlines the requirement for an accredited baccalaureate degree which incorporates certain specified courses. The choice of academic major is free except where otherwise governed by institutional requirements. Navy specified courses include the following:

A. Required for all U.S. Navy officer accession programs except as modified in subparagraphs B and C below:

(1) Two semesters or equivalent of English grammar and composition.

(2) One semester course or equivalent of mathematics at or above the level of college algebra.

(3) One semester or equivalent of fundamentals of computers.

B. Required for NROTC (Navy Option) College Program in addition to A (1) and (3):

(1) Two semesters or equivalent of college level mathematics through college algebra or advanced trigonometry.

(2) Two semesters or equivalent of physical science courses.

C. Required for all USNA and NROTC (Navy Option) Scholarship midshipmen in addition to A (1) and (3):

(1) Two semesters or equivalent taken in naval or military history, political-military affairs, national security policy, or related areas.

(2) Two semesters or equivalent of calculus.

(3) Two semesters or equivalent of calculus-based physics.

In addition, it is recommended that new accessions from all sources gain appreciation for foreign cultures through study of languages, other cultures, geography, international economics, or foreign political systems. NROTC Scholarship midshipmen, including Marine Options, are required to take one course in a modern Indo-European language. If such course represents a significant overload, it may be waived.

II. Leadership and Management—This competency area covers the specific basic levels of knowledge of moral and ethical behavior, organizational design, goal setting, decision making, and objective attainment needed by a college graduate to function as a leader and manager of an organizational component, whether in the military or in the civilian sector. Theories of leadership, motivation, and group dynamics are prominently included.

III. Orientation and Naval Science—This section covers a broad spectrum of competencies required of a newly commissioned naval officer including: customs and traditions, organization of the armed forces and the Navy Department, missions of ships and aircraft, capabilities of weapon systems, warfare doctrines, communications, division officer administration, UCMJ and legal aspects, and many other subjects. This grouping of competency statements encompasses the majority of the naval science *training* required for new naval officers. Additional competency requirements regarding theory and operation of engineering and weapons systems and the ship-related nautical science areas of shiphandling, seamanship, damage control, and navigation, are covered in later sections.

IV. Sea power and Maritime Strategy—This section addresses the newly commissioned officer's requirement for understanding of the role of naval forces in national policy formulation and strategies. Specific competency statements address historical evolution of seapower, U.S. Navy and Marine Corps history, naval missions in the nuclear age, the rise and implications of Soviet seapower, and the impact of third-world development and terrorism. The current U.S. maritime strategy is included. Additionally, evolution of land warfare and more specific coverage of amphibious warfare development is included for Marine Option NROTC accessions.

V. Technical Foundations—Competencies in this section require that the newly commissioned officer be able to comprehend quantitative mathematical and scientific problem-solving techniques in relation to basic applications of Navy materiel systems. The major change in this area from the previous MPCC is a shift in focus from "know" level fact accumulation regarding weapons and engineering systems to comprehension and application of the physical principles and scientific theories underlying the systems. Competency statements by implication require solution of basic problems related to the principles and theories covered. Coverage includes: thermodynamic laws, propulsion systems, electrical power generation/distribution, electromagnetic wave theory and application, sound in water, ship design/stability, and fluid/aerodynamics.

VI. Shipkeeping, Navigation, and Seamanship—The competency statements of this section address the traditional nautical science base required of all seagoing officers. Specific areas include: seamanship, small boats, damage control, shiphandling, relative motion, formations, rules of the road, laws of the sea, and navigation. Also included are requisite levels of qualification in small-boat sailing.

VII. Personal and Personnel Excellence and Fitness and Navy/ Marine Corps Fitness and Wellness Programs—This section contains competency requirements for demonstration of physical fitness and swimming readiness on the part of newly commissioned officers. It also covers the junior officer leadership role in current Navy and Marine Corps fitness and wellness programs such as smoking elimination, weight control, control of hypertension, stress reduction, suicide prevention, drug and alcohol abuse, and drug-detection programs.

Appendix A. NROTC Marine Option Midshipmen Professional Lab—This appendix covers lab topics and requirements particular to the Marine Option program.

Appendix B. Aviation Officer Candidate School Competency Requirements—This appendix covers technical foundations of aerodynamics, aviation engineering, and air navigation for prospective aviation officers.

I. Academic Preparation

The newly commissioned officer must have completed the requirements of an accredited baccalaureate degree program which includes completion of the required courses below. These requirements, along with the competencies listed in Parts II through VII, form the foundation of knowledge needed to assume the technical, managerial, and leadership duties associated with an officer's commission.

A. Demonstrate a proficiency of the English language through usage, both spoken and written.

1. Satisfactorily complete a minimum of two semesters, or equivalent, of English, grammar, and composition, as part of the bachelor's degree program. (Required of all U.S. Navy officer accession programs).

B. Know the major developments in United States and world history with comprehension of the evolution of the political, military, and diplomatic history of the United States within the background of the modern world from 1785.

1. Satisfactorily complete two semesters, or equivalent, of courses in the area of modern United States or European political/military history, national security policy, modern western diplomatic history or equivalent, as part of the degree program. (Required for all USNA midshipmen and all NROTC Navy option scholarship midshipmen, and recommended for all other officer accession programs).

C. Apply sound working knowledge and ability to solve quantitative problems in a logical manner employing advanced mathematics and physical science theories.

1. Complete a minimum of two semesters, or equivalent, of mathematics through college algebra or advanced trigonometry. (Required of all U.S. Navy officer accession programs except as noted in 2. and 3. below).

2. Navy option NROTC College Program midshipmen shall, in addition to the mathematics courses above, be

required to complete two semesters, or equivalent, of physical science courses.

3. Navy option NROTC Scholarship midshipmen and all USNA midshipmen shall be required to complete, in lieu of the courses above, a minimum of two semesters, or equivalent, of calculus and two semesters, or equivalent, of calculus-based physics. (Recommended for all officer accession programs).

D. Know modern basic computer systems including hardware, software, and languages.

1. Satisfactorily complete one semester course or equivalent in basic computer science and programming. (Required of all U.S. Navy officer accession programs).

E. Be familiar with and appreciate other world cultures through study of language, geography, or political science.

1. All NROTC Scholarship midshipmen shall be required to take one course in a modern Indo-European language unless such course represents a significant academic overload. (Includes Marine Option).

II. Leadership and Management

The newly commissioned officer must understand and be able to apply leadership principles necessary to accomplish the Navy's mission through people.

A. Comprehend the inter-relationship between authority, responsibility, and accountability within a task-oriented organization.

B. Apply leadership and management skills to establish priorities among competing demands.

1. Demonstrate ability to establish meaningful goals and objectives.

2. Apply techniques of prioritization and time management to resources and personnel.

C. Apply leadership skills to achieve mission objectives through groups.

1. Comprehend the difference between informal and formal groups.

2. Comprehend the contribution that formal group organizations and standard procedures make to mission accomplishment.

3. Apply leadership and management skills to design work groups based on task requirements, group capability, and available resources.

4. Apply techniques and skills to measure organizational effectiveness by establishing qualitative and quantitative performance standards.

D. Comprehend the importance of planning and follow-up to mission accomplishment.

1. Comprehend the importance of planning and forecasting.

2. Comprehend the relationship between goal setting and feedback and apply this understanding to establishment of control systems.

3. Know the important reasons for development of and constant re-evaluation of alternatives in decision making.

4. Comprehend major reasons why change is resisted in organizations.

5. Comprehend specific techniques that may be used to bring about changes in organizations.

E. Demonstrate in junior-officer leadership situations an understanding of the influence of the following on a leader's ability to achieve organizational goals:

1. use of authority

2. degree of delegation and decentralization

3. the officer-enlisted professional relationship

4. chain of command

5. morale and esprit de corps

F. Comprehend the moral and ethical responsibilities of the military leader.

1. Comprehend the leader's moral and ethical responsibilities to the organization and society.

2. Comprehend the relationship of integrity, moral courage, and ethical behavior to authority, responsibility, and accountability.

3. Comprehend the standards of conduct for government officials.

4. Comprehend the provisions and reasons for official policies regarding fraternization.

G. Know the types of, and importance of, communication within the military.

1. Comprehend the communication process.

2. Comprehend the major causes of communication breakdowns.

3. Demonstrate characteristics of effective oral and written communication.

H. Demonstrate an understanding of basic counseling skills.

1. Comprehend the importance of feedback to mission effectiveness.

2. Comprehend various motivational techniques which may be useful in leadership situations encountered by the junior officer.

3. Apply counseling skills to performance evaluation debriefings, discipline infractions, career guidance, and personal problems.

I. Comprehend the following personal qualities and be able to relate them to a leader's effectiveness:

1. loyalty

2. honor

3. integrity

4. courage (moral and physical)

J. Comprehend the major principle of the Code of Conduct and be able to apply it to a leader's role in a prisoner-of-war situation.

III. Naval Orientation and Naval Science

The newly commissioned officer must have extensive knowledge of the special requirements, tasks, and unique characteristics of the naval services which make leadership and management in them different from that required in other formal organizations.

A. Know the missions and basic organization of the major components of the U.S. armed forces, including:

1. Know the current organization of the Department of the Navy and the relationship of this organization to the National Security Council, the Department of Defense, Joint Chiefs of Staff, and the unified and specified commands.

2. Comprehend the missions of the U.S. Navy and Marine Corps.

3. Know the major missions of the U.S. Army, U.S. Air Force, and U.S. Coast Guard.

4. Know the operational and administrative chains of command within the Department of the Navy.

5. Know each warfare specialty, restricted line specialty, and staff-corps community and how each contributes to the missions of the U.S. Navy.

B. Know the customs and traditions of the Navy and Marine Corps and relate them to current usage.

    1. Know the definition of custom and its origin

    2. Know the definition of tradition and its origin

    3. Know the legal effect of custom in the naval services

    4. Demonstrate the following:

        a. Wear the uniform in accordance with appropriate regulations.

        b. Correctly demonstrate military courtesy, etiquette, and greetings.

        c. Demonstrate proper shipboard protocol with respect to quarter-deck procedures, wardroom etiquette, boarding and disembarking, honors to passing ships, and boat etiquette.

        d. Conduct military ceremonial functions including parade formation, platoon drill, and officer's sword in accordance with the appropriate manual.

        e. Exercise a military unit in basic evolutions.

        f. Present a military unit for inspection.

    5. Know the Navy and Marine Corps rank and rate/grade structures and insignia and relate them to their equivalents in the Army and Air Force.

    6. Know relevant Navy and Marine Corps unrestricted and restricted line career paths and opportunities including the requirement for joint duty.

    7. Comprehend the role of commissioned officers as members the U.S. armed forces and know the obligations and responsibilities assumed by taking the oath of office and accepting a commission including the constitutional requirement for civilian control.

C. Comprehend the UCMJ, practice of military law, and applications of regulations as they may involve a junior officer in the performance of duties. (NROTC USMC option exempt from this section except C3 and C4).

    1. Comprehend the purpose, scope, and constitutional basis of *Navy Regulations* and the Uniform Code of Military Justice and relate these regulations to personal conduct in the military service.

2. Comprehend junior officer responsibilities relative to the military justice system including familiarization with:
   a. essential publications relating to military justice
   b. search and seizure
   c. apprehension and restraint
   d. nonjudicial punishment
   e. investigations
   f. courts-martial
   g. administrative discharges

3. Know secretary of the Navy published standards of conduct required of all naval personnel.

4. Be familiar with the International Law of Armed Conflict including rules of engagement, conduct of hostilities, rights of individuals, obligations of engaged parties, and the Code of Conduct for members of the U.S. Armed Forces.

D. Know shipboard command relationships and organization for both operational and administrative environments.

1. Know the shipboard administrative organization including the primary duties of commanding officer, executive officer, department heads, and division officers.

2. Know the organization of the shipboard battle, special operation, and peacetime routine watch teams, in port, at anchor, and underway, and the responsibilities, accountability, and duties of each watchstander.

3. Know the requirements for, and be able to demonstrate a proper watch relief and the requirements, procedures, and format for keeping the ship's deck log underway, in port, and at anchor.

E. Know basic administrative responsibilities of a junior officer including correspondence procedures, maintenance management, personnel management, security, and safety procedures and programs. (NROTC USMC option exempt from this section except E1, E8, and E11).

1. Know current Navy and Marine Corps policies and programs to assure equal opportunity for minorities and women.

2. Know financial, medical, and recreational benefits available to military personnel.

3. Know the basic elements of personal finances, including pay, taxes, death benefits, insurance, savings, investments, and wills.

4. Know the principles and administration of the PQS system.

5. Know the responsibilities of departments for specific bills, watch organization, administration and operational routine, and significant reporting requirements to the commanding officer.

6. Know the personnel administrative actions in dealing with actions with regard to officer and enlisted service records, performance evaluations, and advancement recommendations.

   a. Know the role of the enlisted performance evaluation with regard to advancement and detailing.

   b. Comprehend the role of officer fitness reports with regard to promotion and officer detailing.

   c. Know the general requirements for enlisted advancement including time in rate, required courses, practical factors, and examinations.

   d. Know the purpose and basic operation of an officer promotion selection board.

   e. Know the purpose for and typical contents of a division officer's notebook.

   f. Know the principal programs for achieving an officer's commission including those available to enlisted personnel.

   g. Know of the requirement for submission of the Officer Duty Preference Form, and comprehend its use in the officer assignment process.

7. Know the purpose of the Navy Maintenance Material Management (3-M) System and its PMS and MDCS subsystems including the duties of division officer and work center supervisor.

8. Know the requirements and procedures for proper handling and disclosure of classified material, consequences for inadvertent disclosure, and consequences for violation of the espionage laws, including:

   a. maintaining security over classified material including security for avoiding technology transfer.

   b. disclosure (clearance *and* need to know).

   c. the basic security classifications and the handling requirements for each.

9. Know the correct format, usage, and the general rules

pertaining to the different types of naval correspondence, and apply basic rules to draft correspondence.

10. Be familiar with the Navy Directives System.

11. Perform the proper handling and firing of U.S. service small arms using current safety procedures.

F. Know the characteristics and capabilities of the major weapons systems and platforms of the U.S. naval forces.

1. Know the designations, characteristics, capabilities, and missions of major ships, aircraft, and weapon systems of the U.S. Navy and the Marine Corps.

2. Comprehend the mission of the U.S. Merchant Marine relative to national security including its integration with the combat fleet.

3. Comprehend the broad tactical implications of the multi-threat environment.

4. Comprehend the role of active and passive electronic warfare and their employment in the fleet.

5. Comprehend the significance of intelligence in the application of naval warfare.

G. Know the major air, surface, and sub-surface assets which potential adversaries can employ to prevent accomplishment of the sea control and power projection missions of the United States naval services.

H. Comprehend the concept of command and control in the armed forces, know the Navy's command and control system and the essential elements necessary for command and control of naval forces. (NROTC USMC option exempt from this section except H1 and H2).

1. Comprehend the concept of command and control as the exercise of authority and direction by a properly designated commander over assigned forces in the accomplishment of a mission.

2. Know the chain of operational command from the national command authorities to the platform commander.

3. Know and be able to discuss the composite warfare commander (CWC) concept, the organization of a typical ship CIC, and understand their interrelationship in formation maneuvering and in accomplishing the ship's warfare mission.

4. Comprehend how each of the following doctrines con-

tribute to the basic sea control and power projection missions of the naval service:

a. anti-air warfare
b. anti-submarine warfare
c. submarine warfare
d. surface warfare
e. mine warfare
f. strike warfare
g. amphibious warfare
h. electronic warfare
i. mobile logistics support
j. special warfare

5. Know and be able to discuss the basic information found in Naval Tactical Publications (NTP), Naval Warfare Publications (NWP), and Allied Tactical Publications (ATP) systems.

6. Know the functions of tactical data systems and basic NTDS symbology.

7. Know the seven stages of a typical engagement sequence from indicators and warnings (I&W) to battle damage assessment (BDA).

I. Comprehend the requirement for rapid and secure communications for naval forces, and know the characteristics, advantages, and disadvantages of various systems. (NROTC USMC option exempt from this section except I1 and I3).

1. Know the purpose and scope of Defense/Naval Communications Systems including electronic systems such as fleet broadcast, ship-shore-ship, and tactical broadcasts.

a. Know the frequency spectrum selection for Navy communications and the reasons for frequency selection for various missions.

b. Demonstrate by drafting a naval message the use of proper procedures and correct format.

c. Demonstrate proper radio-telephone terminology procedure by simulating a radio-telephone communication.

2. Know various methods of visual communications including flags and pennants, flashing light, semaphore, and demonstrate procedures for their proper use as outlined below:

a. Know the use of ATP-1 Volume II and the International Code of Signals (HO-102).

b. Demonstrate a knowledge of international signal flags and allied tactical flag hoist procedures through simulated messages.

3. Be familiar with procedures for effecting communications security including the common causes of security compromise and safeguards to prevent unauthorized disclosure.

4. Know various systems for internal shipboard communications, and demonstrate proper sound-powered phone procedures.

J. Comprehend the requirement for operations security for military forces including the following elements:

1. Comprehend the OPSEC process.

a. Understand the need for OPSEC including recognition of the OPSEC threat.

b. Understand the concept of Essential Elements of Friendly Information (EEFI).

c. Know the protective measures used in OPSEC including the basic design of a system to reduce vulnerabilities and how to utilize counter OPSEC methods.

2. Comprehend the concepts of OPSEC and military deception as a means to preserve secrecy and the element of surprise.

VI. Role of Sea Power in National Policies and Strategies

Through a study of history, the newly commissioned officer must comprehend the part naval forces play in the current national policies and diplomatic and military strategies of the United States.

A. Know the significant events of U.S. naval history.

1. Know the significant milestones in the history of the evolution of the U.S. Navy and Marine Corps including the prominent leaders and their contributions.

2. Know the role U.S. naval forces played in the national strategies and policies of the United States in peacetime expansion and war until 1939.

B. Comprehend the historical evolution of sea power and its effects on world history.

1. Comprehend the importance of power projection by sea-borne forces and be able to cite historical examples.

2. Comprehend the rise of English sea power, in particular:

a. its role in confirming the independence and inviolability of an island nation.

b. its role in exploration and the growth of a mercantile empire.

c. its strategic importance in the wars with France to 1815.

3. Know the significant historical developments in the technical evolution of naval weapons systems and platforms from the era of sail to nuclear power.

4. Comprehend the contributions of 19th/early 20th century naval strategists including Mahan and Corbett, and relate their concepts to current situations.

5. Know the major historical facts in relation to sea power in the global wars 1914–1918 and 1939–1945 including the developments in submarine, amphibious, and air warfare at sea.

C. Know the fundamental national interests of the U.S. and the Soviet Union and the strategies of each for employment of military forces in furthering these interests.

1. Know the significant historical events of the Cold War period including:

a. the strategic direction of U.S. military forces in the postwar world of the atomic bomb.

b. the Korean War.

c. the Cuban missile crisis.

2. Comprehend the concepts of limited and total war.

3. Know the background facts of the rise of Soviet sea power, and comprehend the threat it represents to U.S. national interests. Know how Soviet naval forces fit into the national strategy of the Soviet Union.

4. Comprehend the national interests, policies, and overall military strategy of the U.S. and how these policies and strategies are formulated in the U.S. political system.

5. Comprehend the role of the military forces of the United States within the constitutional framework and the effect of the National Security Act of 1947.

6. Know the current U.S. maritime strategy for employment of naval forces.

D. Know the effect the evolution of third-world countries and the development of international terrorist movements have had on the interests, policies, and strategies of the U.S. and the Soviet Union.

1. Comprehend the Soviet use of wars of liberation to expand the Soviet sphere of influence since 1945.

2. Comprehend the policies and related military actions of the U.S. in developing countries since 1945, and know examples of successes and failures of these policies and actions.

3. Know instances where third-world involvements and commitments have become strategic liabilities or failures for the Soviet Union.

4. Comprehend the effect of uncontrolled terrorist movements relative to the super-power relations.

E. Comprehend the evolution of the means and methods of warfare, particularly land warfare, including the following topical areas: (NROTC USMC option only).

1. Know the preeminent leaders and military organizations of history and the reasons for their success.

2. Know the interrelationship between technological progress and military change in rendering obsolete previous successful strategies, policies, doctrines, and tactics.

3. Comprehend the evolution of the influence of economic, psychological, moral, political, and technological factors on strategic thought.

F. Comprehend the evolution of amphibious warfare. Include the following topical areas: (NROTC USMC option only).

1. Know the significant events of history relating to amphibious operations. Comprehend their impact on the evolution of amphibious warfare doctrine.

2. Comprehend the problems and advantages relative to employment of amphibious forces in the modern era including the impact of nuclear warfare on amphibious tactics and doctrine.

3. Know the major doctrinal principles associated with planning for amphibious operations

V. Technical Foundations

The newly commissioned officer must be able to apply quantitative mathematical and scientific problem-solving techniques in basic situations of Navy materiel systems. (NROTC USMC option and AOCS exempted).

A. Comprehend the basic physical principles of open and closed thermodynamic systems.

1. Comprehend the various forms of energy including potential, kinetic, thermal, and mechanical, and the process of energy conversion.

2. Comprehend the "laws of thermodynamics" and types of thermodynamic cycles.

3. Comprehend the concepts of "work" and "efficiency," and be able to apply these concepts to determine levels of output and efficiency in theoretical situations.

B. Apply understanding of the "laws of thermodynamics" and concepts of work, power, and efficiency to various shipboard propulsion systems.

1. Comprehend the basic operation, key components, and safety considerations within major propulsion systems, and contrast the advantages, disadvantages, and capabilities of the systems. Include the following:

   a. conventional steam propulsion plants.

      i. Apply the laws of thermodynamics to determine the changes in state/energy which water undergoes in the basic steam cycle, and comprehend the purpose of the various components and their effect on these energy and state changes.

      ii. Apply understanding of the energy transformations occurring within a turbine, know the components which perform the transformations, and be able to classify a turbine by staging, direction of flow, division of flow, impulse, or reaction.

      iii. Comprehend the purpose of routine feed water chemistry control aboard ship.

   b. nuclear steam propulsion plants.

      i. Comprehend the basic fission process.

      ii. Comprehend what is meant by the term SCRAM.

      iii. Comprehend the definition of the terms critical/subcritical/supercritical relative to nuclear reactors.

c. internal combustion engines (gasoline and diesel) and plants.

d. gas turbine (single and split shaft) and associated propulsion systems.

e. jet engines and associated propulsion systems.

f. Know the features of various fuel oil systems and how they provide fuel to the thermodynamic cycle in each of the applicable systems above.

C. Comprehend the basic operation, principal components, and safety considerations related to key shipboard auxiliary systems, and apply understanding of thermodynamics, output, and efficiency to situations involving such systems.

1. Comprehend the theory of operation, basic layout, and energy transformations which occur in distilling plants.

2. Comprehend the thermodynamic aspects of the refrigeration cycle.

D. Comprehend the theory of operation and key components of shipboard main propulsion power transmission from power source to propellers.

1. Comprehend the effects of each of the following in regard to propulsion:

a. controllable/reversible pitch propellers

b. cavitation

2. Apply comprehension of propeller design parameters to determine efficiency at different speeds.

E. Comprehend and be able to apply basic physical principles of electrical theory to shipboard power generation and distribution systems.

1. Apply basic electrical theory including Ohm's law and its derivations; compare AC and DC electrical power and their uses and transmission.

2. Apply generator theory to determine frequency and voltage in an AC generator, and comprehend fundamentals of generator construction and control mechanisms, including prime movers and power ratings.

3. Comprehend and be able to apply electric motor theory including construction, power rating, usages, and control mechanisms.

4. Comprehend the functions of the following elements in regard to electrical distribution applications:

a. buses

   b. circuit breakers
   c. controllers
   d. switches
   e. fuses
   f. transformers
   g. relays
   h. basic control circuits
5. Comprehend the components and principles of operation of a three-phase AC power distribution system, and know how to recognize a wye or delta connection on a schematic.
6. Comprehend the following with respect to shipboard electric power distribution systems:
   a. parameters which must be matched in paralleling generators
   b. measures to counter a ship's magnetic field
   c. identification of vital and nonvital systems
   d. functions of the main switchboard
   e. difference between ships service and emergency power distribution systems
   f. casualty power system
F. Comprehend the basic application of electronics systems, communications theory, and electromagnetic wave theory to maritime and naval applications in radars, communications, and radio navigation systems.
1. Comprehend the theory of operation and key components used with naval electronics and communications systems including:
   a. amplifiers
   b. antennas
   c. power amplifiers
   d. oscillators
   e. filters
2. Know the fundamental means of imparting information to radio waves, and comprehend the uses, advantages, and disadvantages of various means.
3. Comprehend the use of computers and digital electronics in naval and maritime communications and signal processing systems.
4. Be able to apply wave theory including relationship between frequency and wave length.

5. Comprehend refraction, polarization, and propagation as related to electromagnetic waves.

6. Know the definition and comprehend the effects of ground plane, free space, re-radiation, sky waves, space waves, ground waves, and tropospheric waves.

7. Know the frequency spectrum of electromagnetic waves, and comprehend the uses, advantages and disadvantages of various frequency ranges for communications, sensing, and radio navigation.

8. Know the characteristics of ELF, VLF, LF, HF, VHF, and UHF communications.

9. Be able to apply radar theory, and comprehend basic operation, major components, parameters, and radar-range equation.

10. Comprehend radio theory, basic operation, major components, and parameters.

11. Know electro-optic theory, basic device operation, major components, and parameters.

12. Know basic electromagnetic interference factors in ship and weapon design.

G. Comprehend the physical properties associated with sound travel in water and the application of these properties to sensing and detection systems.

1. Comprehend sound propagation including Snell's law, effects of temperature, pressure and salinity, sound velocity profiles, sound ray traces, sound channels, and convergence zones.

2. Comprehend sound propagation loss including spreading and absorption.

3. Comprehend concepts of self and ambient noises.

4. Apply the active and passive sonar equations.

5. Comprehend basic transducer and hydrophone theory.

6. Comprehend the differences between active and passive sonar systems; contrast advantages and disadvantages of each.

7. Know types of sonar systems in use in the fleet.

H. Comprehend the factors and criteria of ship design for seaworthiness, structural integrity, and operational employment.

1. Comprehend the trade-offs in the design priorities used in construction of various warship types.

2. Comprehend the factors involved in machinery plant layout and design.

3. Know basic ship hull and structural component nomenclature.

4. Comprehend effects of stress, strain, and shear forces on hull design, and know considerations involved in selection of materials for ship construction and basics of structural design.

5. Comprehend how ship stability and stability redundancy is designed into a ship before construction including allowance for future modifications.

6. Comprehend the factors involved in ship stability, and be able to apply them in determination of stability conditions.

    a. Comprehend hydrostatics, buoyancy, and Archimedes' principle.

    b. Comprehend static equilibrium and the relationship of center of gravity and buoyancy to righting arms and stability.

        1. Comprehend positive, neutral, and negative stability conditions.

        2. Comprehend the effect of movements of centers of buoyancy and gravity on stability.

        3. Comprehend the use of stability curves, know how they are derived, and be able to apply information derived from them in stability calculations.

        4. Comprehend the effect of loose water on stability characteristics.

I. Comprehend basic principles of fluid dynamics, and be able to apply them in shipboard situations.

1. Comprehend Bernoulli's principle, kinetic versus potential energy in terms of fluid flow, and the concept of pressure "head."

2. Comprehend Pascal's principle and basic hydraulics.

3. Comprehend fluid systems and be able to apply characteristic curves to basic pump operation.

4. Know the definition of boundary layers.

5. Comprehend the concepts of lift and drag, atmospheric properties and effect, subsonic and supersonic flow characteristics, and high-speed aerodynamics.

6. Comprehend aerodynamic and hydrodynamic controls of aircraft and submarines.

J. Comprehend and be able to apply the basic geometry of the fire-control problem and applicable principles of internal and external ballistics, propulsion, launching, and guidance.

1. Comprehend the basic concepts of relative motion, bearing rate and speed across and in the line of sight.

2. Know the nomenclature of the fire-control problem.

3. Comprehend the factors affecting solution of the fire-control problem.

K. Comprehend the fundamental chemical and physical principles of conventional and nuclear warheads, including fuzzing, and the principal effects of detonation of such warheads.

L. Comprehend basic principles of command and control and system dynamics.

1. Comprehend principles of computer operation, major components, and parameters.

2. Comprehend countermeasure principles including basic principles of electronic warfare.

VI. Shipkeeping, Navigation, and Seamanship

The newly commissioned officer must have knowledge of requirements unique to organizational leadership, management, and task accomplishment in a maritime environment. AOCS and NROTC USMC option exempt entire section except A2 (NROTC USMC option exempt A2c), B1, B2c(1), E6, G1, G2, G5.

A. Know terms and nomenclature of shipboard deck seamanship equipment and fittings and the fundamentals of their usage.

1. Know the use and safety precautions associated with the following groupings of shipboard equipment:

a. ground tackle, anchoring, towing, and mooring equipment and fixtures,

b. boat lifting and handling equipment,

c. weight handling equipment, and

d. fiber lines and wire ropes.

2. Know operational procedures, responsibilities, and safety precautions relative to small-boat operations.

a. Know the chain of command aboard a small boat and the duties of assigned boat crew personnel.

  b. Know practice and tradition of boat etiquette.

  c. Know boat handling procedures and theory.

B. Know the basics of shipboard safety and comprehend the reasons for extraordinary attention to safety and preparedness.

  1. Know Navy safety programs and precautions including ordnance, electrical, workplace, and environmental programs.

  2. Know the requirements for forehandedness in shipboard damage-control training and preparedness.

   a. Know the typical shipboard damage-control organization and responsibilities of key personnel assigned.

   b. Know how shipboard watertight integrity is obtained through installed shipboard features to increase material conditions of readiness.

   c. Know the procedures, objectives, and priorities in combating progressive deterioration from fire and underwater hull damage.

    (1) Know classes of fire and agents, equipments, and procedures used to extinguish them.

    (2) Know the use of equipment, materials, and procedures for countering progressive flooding and structural deterioration.

  3. Know standard procedures to be implemented prior to, during, and after NBC attack.

  4. Demonstrate donning and proper operation of oxygen-breathing apparatus (OBA) and standard Navy gas mask.

C. Comprehend the theory and practice of navigation at sea.

  1. Comprehend the theory and practice of marine navigation by celestial methods.

   a. Comprehend the motions of celestial bodies relative to nautical astronomy, and relate these motions to coordinate systems.

   b. Comprehend the fundamentals for the solution of spherical triangles by mathematical means, and

    (1) Apply nautical astronomy coordinate systems to establish unique celestial/navigational spherical triangles.

    (2) Apply computational and tabular means to solve navigational spherical triangles.

   c. Comprehend the longitude/time relationship, and

time conversion, zone time determination, and motions of the sun as the basis of time.

d. Apply correct procedures to determine the times of daily phenomena such as sunrise, sunset, moonrise, etc.

e. Apply the altitude intercept method to establish a celestial LOP and to position fixing by

(1) simultaneous observation of several celestial bodies

(2) running fixes

f. Apply correct procedures in determining latitude by means of Meridian Transit and Polaris observations.

g. Apply celestial triangle solutions to determine compass error.

h. Apply sextant altitude corrections to observed altitudes obtained with a marine sextant.

i. Perform celestial observations using the marine sextant and azimuth circle.

2. Apply electronic navigation system information to supplement other navigation methods.

a. Know advantages, disadvantages, system geometry, and features of principal radio navigation systems.

b. Know the basic principles and advantages of inertial navigation, navigation satellite, doppler, and bottom contour navigation methodologies.

c. Apply correct procedures to plot lines of position from radio navigation system information.

3. Apply the fundamentals of the practice of marine navigation while in pilot waters.

a. Comprehend the uses of various chart projections and know chart symbology, particularly those symbols pertaining to hazards and dangers.

b. Know how to select the proper chart and how to determine chart accuracy and reliability.

c. Apply correct plotting procedures when navigating in pilot waters.

(1) Apply the six rules of deduced reckoning in keeping a plot of ship movements.

(2) Comprehend the definitions of the terms: track, speed of advance, speed over ground, PIM, and course made good.

(3) Plot and interpret turn and danger bearings.

(4) Plot and interpret simultaneous and running fixes.

d. Apply ship's tactical data in precision piloting including precision anchoring.

e. Know the advantages, disadvantages, and applications of gyro and magnetic compasses.

(1) Apply terrestrial navigation methods to determine compass error.

(2) Apply magnetic variation and deviation or gyro error to convert from compass to true course or bearing and vice versa.

f. Know the capabilities and limitations of various instruments used in piloting to determine direction, speed, distance, and depth of water.

g. Know the essential publications and records used in navigation and comprehend their value in all applications.

h. Know the characteristics and application of various aids to navigation in piloting, and comprehend their importance in safe navigation, including:

(1) buoyage systems—U.S. lateral system

(2) lights

(3) sound signals

i. Apply correct procedures in planning and plotting approaches to harbors and anchorages, and know port anchorage control procedures.

j. Comprehend celestial and weather effects on tidal action; know tide classifications and reference planes.

(1) Apply correct procedures to determine daily tide and tidal current tables at given locations.

(2) Apply correct procedure to determine the tide height or tidal current velocity and direction at a given time at a particular location; conversely, determine the time when the height of tide or tidal current will be at a certain value

k. Apply correct procedures to work common current sailing problems.

D. Know environmental weather factors affecting naval operations.

1. Know the principles of basic weather phenomena including fronts, subtropical and tropical storms.

2. Know the relationship between wind and current in wind-driven current systems.

3. Know the sources of environmental predictions including pilot charts and weather broadcasts.

4. Know the earth's major wind and current systems.

5. Know how wind velocity relates to storm warnings and comprehend the effect of wind velocity on sea state.

6. Know the characteristics of the approach of tropical storms and hurricane/typhoon evasion techniques.

E. Comprehend controllable and noncontrollable forces as factors in shiphandling.

1. Comprehend the effects of controllable forces in shiphandling, such as engines, rudders, propellers, lines, anchors, and tugs.

2. Comprehend the effects of noncontrollable forces in shiphandling, such as wind, current, depth of water, etc.

3. Know the terms associated with tactical data and comprehend how tactical data tables may be employed in planning shiphandling evolutions.

4. Demonstrate procedures and standard terminology in giving engine, rudder, and line-handling commands.

5. Demonstrate the techniques for using binoculars, stadimeter, radar, and bearing circles when involved in shiphandling situations.

6. Demonstrate the operation of sail craft to attain qualification as skipper "B" or offshore crewman using current CNET/USNA standards.

F. Comprehend relative motion and demonstrate capability to solve problems associated with relative motion.

1. Comprehend the theory of relative motion as graphically displayed by the geographic and relative plot.

2. Comprehend the significance of bearing drift, and apply bearing drift to determine relative motion. Comprehend the following related terms: relative bearing and target angle.

3. Know the terminology used to describe the speed triangle and relative plot associated with maneuvering board.

4. Apply the principles associated with relative motion, and use the maneuvering board to accurately and rapidly:

a. Determine the CPA and time of CPA of an approaching vessel;

b. Determine the course and speed of a maneuvering ship; and

c. Determine courses and/or speeds for proceeding to a new station or to intercept another vessel.

5. Know the principal rules for maneuvering in formation and the use of ATP-1 (B) Volume I.

G. Know governmental and international laws and systems of regulations which govern conduct of vessels in national waters and on the high seas.

1. Know major aspects of the U.S. position on International Law of the Sea regarding territorial seas, contiguous zones, high seas, and rights of innocent passage.

2. Comprehend the difference between customary and conventional international law and how the customary international law is affected by treaties, conventions, and practices of nations.

3. Know the U.S. Inland Rules of the Road and the International Regulations for Preventing Collisions at Sea to include:

a. The purpose and scope of the rules including application.

b. Terms and definitions used in the rules.

c. Steering rules for vessels in sight of each other, including sound signals.

d. Lights and day shapes for frequently encountered vessel classes.

e. Use of radar and conduct of vessels in reduced visibility, including sound signals.

f. Definition of situations falling under "special circumstances."

4. Know the purpose and maneuvering rules associated with traffic separation schemes established by International Maritime Consultive Organization (IMCO) agreement.

5. Know the purpose and general details of U.S./Soviet Navy agreements to prevent mutual interference during the conduct of naval exercises at sea.

H. Comprehend the lessons that may be learned from the study and analysis of actual groundings, collisions, storm damage, and shipboard accidents, and know the publications where such information can be found.

VII. Personal and Personnel Excellence and Fitness and Navy–Marine Corps Fitness and Wellness Programs

The newly commissioned officer must demonstrate a high level of personal physical fitness and be able to apply leadership skills in implementing Navy or Marine Corps personal excellence and wellness programs.

A. Demonstrate personal physical fitness by excelling in Navy or Marine Corps physical fitness testing requirements.

B. Demonstrate fundamental swimming skills and ability to cope with water emergencies.

C. Comprehend current Navy or Marine Corps regulations, policies, and programs relative to the following wellness issues:

1. Substance and alcohol abuse including urinalysis testing programs, treatment, and consequences.

2. Physical fitness, nutrition, and weight control.

3. Smoking cessation.

4. High blood pressure detection and control and stress reduction.

5. Suicide prevention.

6. AIDS awareness and testing programs.

7. Safe driving

D. Demonstrate current methods and techniques of first aid, self-aid, and CPR.

Appendix A—U.S. Marine Corps Programs

To familiarize the NROTC Marine Corps option student and USNA midshipmen desiring USMC commissions with the missions and structure of the Marine Corps and to prepare the student for the Marine option 1/C cruise.

A. Be familiar with the organization structure of the USMC as outlined in the current edition of the *Marine Officer's Guide*.

B. Be familiar with the missions, status, and development of the Marine Corps as a separate service as outlined in the current edition of the *Marine Officer's Guide.*

C. Be familiar with the essential subjects contained in the U.S. Marine Corps Essential Subjects Book (MCIO 1552.14A).

D. Preparation for Officer Candidate School:

1. Know, and be able to command a detail in, the basic movements of close-order drill, including the manual of arms with the M-16.

2. Be familiar with the assembly, disassembly, care, cleaning, and functioning of the M-16.

3. Be familiar with basic fire team offensive tactics.

4. Be familiar with basic map reading and the use of the compass.

5. Be familiar with Marine Corps history, interior guard and basic general military subjects.

6. Be in an appropriate level of physical conditioning that emphasizes total body fitness.

E. Successfully complete Marine Option 1/C cruise (Officer Candidate School/Bulldog).

F. Understand the requirements for, and be able to perform at the requisite level of, physical conditioning necessary for Marine officers.

G. Conduct adventure training, emphasizing skills to enhance individual confidence and survivability on the battlefield. This training should be ground combat oriented.

Appendix B—Aviation Officer Candidate School

To provide aviation officer candidates with basic skills and knowledge needed for primary flight training and basic naval flight officer training.

A. *Aerodynamics.*

Demonstrate knowledge of basic aerodynamics fundamentals for actual naval flight officer or pilot flight training.

1. Know basic airplane nomenclature and terminology.

a. Know the five major components of an airplane.

2. Know the basic laws of physics, basic physical relationships, and the basic mathematical systems as they relate to aerodynamics.

a. Know the definitions of mass, weight, volume, force, work, energy, power, density, and moment.

b. Know Newton's three laws of motion.

c. Comprehend equilibrium, in terms of Newton's first and second laws of motion, and relate this to an airplane in flight.

3. Know the basic atmospheric properties and their relationships.

a. Know the definitions of static pressure, density, temperature, humidity, and viscosity.

b. Know the General Gas Law and apply it to establish the relationships between pressure, temperature, and density.

c. Know the standard atmosphere and describe its properties in terms of pressure, temperature, and density.

4. Know the basic aerodynamic properties and their application to airflow dynamics.

a. Comprehend velocity as it applies to airflow and know the four properties of airflow.

b. Know the definitions of steady airflow, streamline, and streamtube.

c. Comprehend the continuity equation and its relationship to a streamtube.

d. Comprehend Bernoulli's equation and its relationship to kinetic, potential, and total energy.

e. Comprehend the changes in total pressure, static pressure, and dynamic pressure within a streamtube, as stated in Bernoulli's equation, and know the factors affecting total pressure.

f. Comprehend Bernoulli's equation as it relates to the measurement of dynamic pressure.

g. Know the purpose of the pitot-static system and identify the pressures sensed by it.

h. Comprehend true airspeed and indicated airspeed and the relationship between the two. Given a constant indicated airspeed, recall the effects on true airspeed with variations in altitude.

i. Comprehend ground speed and relate the effect of wind to groundspeed and distance traveled.

j. Know the definition of Mach number and relate true airspeed to the local speed of sound with variations in altitude.

k. Know the definition of the boundary layer and the factors affecting its formation.

l. Know the definitions of turbulent and laminar flow in the boundary layer.

5. Know the basic airfoil nomenclature, the properties of

airflow about an airfoil, and the principal aerodynamic forces and their properties.

a. Know the definitions of the terms center of gravity, flight path, and relative wind.

b. Know the definitions of angle of attack, angle of incidence, and climb angle.

c. Know the chord, chordline, leading and trailing edges, mean camber line, and thickness of an airfoil.

d. Know the effects on dynamic and static pressure as air flows about a cambered and symmetrical airfoil, and identify the pressure distribution common to those airfoils.

e. Comprehend how the lifting force is generated around an airfoil and how this force varies with changes in angle of attack.

f. Know the definition of the center of pressure, and recall the effects of variations in angle of attack on its location in both cambered and symmetrical airfoils.

g. Know the definition of the aerodynamic center, and recall the effects of changing angle of attack on its location.

h. Know the importance of the aerodynamic center, and identify the forces acting about the aerodynamic center.

i. Know the definition of the aerodynamic force, pitching moment, lift, and drag.

j. Know the equations for aerodynamic force and lift, and identify the factors affecting the coefficient of force and the coefficient of lift.

k. Know graphically coefficient of lift and angle of attack.

l. Know the definition of wingspan, average chord, wing area, and aspect ratio.

m. Know airflow circulation, and recall its effects on the lift generated by a finite wing.

n. Know the differences in the coefficient of lift generated by cambered and symmetrical airfoils.

o. Know the equation for minimum straight level airspeed.

p. Comprehend, given a requirement to maintain a constant altitude, the relationship between angle of attack and velocity.

q. Know parasite drag, and recall the three major types of parasite drag and methods of reducing them.

r. Know the equation for parasite drag, and graphically depict parasite drag as it varies with velocity.

s. Define induced drag, and recall the cause of induced drag and the methods of reducing it.

t. Know the equation for induced drag, and graphically depict induced drag as it varies with velocity.

u. Know the variables affecting the total drag coefficient and graphically depict the coefficient of total drag versus angle of attack.

v. Contrast coefficient of drag and coefficient of lift graphically. Know the importance of (L/D) maximum.

w. Know the definition of total drag, state the equation for total drag, and graphically depict total drag, induced drag, and parasite drag.

6. Know the techniques, results, and effects of flight at high angles of attack.

a. Know the definition of a stall, its causes and what must be done to recover from a stall. Know the equation for stall speed and its variables.

b. Know the method of inducing a wing root stall and common methods of stall warnings.

c. Know the definition of a spin, the motions of a spin, and their causes.

d. Demonstrate graphically the effects the motions of a spin have on C_L and C_D for the upgoing and downgoing wing.

e. Know the two steps necessary for spin recovery.

f. Know the three basic types of spins and their characteristics.

g. Know, given an angle of bank, the effects on aircraft lift and the techniques for maintaining a level turn.

h. Know the load factor and the effects of angle of bank and load factor on stalling velocity.

i. Know the definition of turn radius and turn rate and the four primary limitations on turn performance.

j. Know the primary purpose of all high lift devices.

k. Know the effects of camber changes on coefficient of lift, the stalling angle of attack, the stalling speed, and the pitching moment about the center of gravity.

l. Know the various types of leading and trailing edge camber change devices, and contrast their coefficient of lift.

m. Know the effect of changes in wing area on stall speed.

n. Know the effects of boundary layer control on C_L maximum, stalling angle of attack, and stalling speed.

o. Know the three primary means of boundary layer control, identify various boundary layer control devices, and contrast their maximum coefficient of lift values.

7. Know the factors affecting takeoff and landing and their effect on takeoff and landing distance.

a. Know the forces acting on an aircraft during takeoff and landing.

b. Know ground effect and its effects on lift, drag, and thrust required.

c. Know the takeoff and landing distance equations and recall the effects on takeoff and landing distances due to variations in weight, pressure, altitude, temperature, and wind.

8. Comprehend the basis for the development of thrust/thrust horsepower curves and their application to airplane performance.

a. Know the thrust required and thrust available and their units of measure.

b. Know, graphically, thrust required versus thrust available curves for a turboprop-driven and a jet-driven airplane.

c. Know thrust horsepower in terms of thrust available and thrust required.

d. Know, graphically, the thrust horsepower required and thrust horsepower available curves for a turboprop-driven and a jet-driven airplane.

e. Know the importance of (L/D) maximum and its location on the thrust and thrust horsepower curve.

f. Know the definition of excess thrust and excess thrust horsepower.

g. Know, graphically, the regions of normal and reverse command, relate them to (L/D) max angle of attack and velocity, and label maximum and minimum velocities.

h. Apply the regions of normal and reverse command

to different phases of flight, and know the requirements for thrust in those phases of flight.

i. Know, graphically, the changes in thrust required and thrust horsepower required due to changes in airplane gross weight and altitude.

9. Know the basis for the development of thrust/thrust horsepower curves and their application to airplane performance.

a. Know the definitions of maximum angle of climb, maximum rate of climb, maximum range, maximum endurance, maximum glide range, and maximum glide endurance.

b. Know the relationship of fuel flow to thrust and thrust horsepower.

c. Know the angle of attack and velocity at which jet- and turboprop-driven airplanes achieve maximum range and endurance, and the effects on these parameters of changes in weight, altitude, and wind.

d. Know the angle of attack and velocity at which jet and turboprop airplanes achieve maximum angle of climb and maximum rate of climb, and the effects on these parameters due to changes in weight, wind, and altitude.

e. Know the angle of attack and velocity at which jet and turboprop airplanes achieve maximum glide range and maximum glide endurance, and relate the effects on these parameters due to changes in weight, altitude, wind, and angle of attack.

10. Know the factors affecting an airplane's structural strength and maneuvering limitations.

a. Know the definition of static failure and fatigue failure.

b. Know the definitions of limit load, ultimate load, maneuvering speed, accelerated stall line, and redline airspeed.

c. Know the airplane operating strength diagram and label the major axis, limit and ultimate load, the maneuver speed, stall speed, redline speed, and accelerated stall lines.

d. Know the four phenomena that occur beyond redline airspeed.

e. Know the definition of critical Mach number.

f. Know the effects on the operating strength diagram due to variations in gross weight, altitude, and configuration or due to flight in turbulent conditions or with asymmetrical loads.

11. Know the basic design characteristics and their effect on airplane stability.

a. Know the definition of static and dynamic stability and the three types of each.

b. Know the three motions of an airplane and the axis about which they occur.

c. Know the forces acting about an airplane's aerodynamic center, and relate these forces to the forces acting about an airplane's center of gravity.

d. Know the definition of trim angle of attack.

e. Know the relationship between airplane stability and the location of the aerodynamic center relative to the center of gravity.

f. Know the effects of the fuselage, wing, vertical and horizontal stabilizers, wing sweep, and thrust axis location on longitudinal static stability.

g. Know the definition of sideslip angle.

h. Know the effects of the fuselage, wing, vertical and horizontal stabilizers, wing sweep, and thrust axis location on directional static stability.

i. Know the definition of anhedral and dihedral.

j. Know the effect of the wing, wing sweepback, and the vertical stabilizer on lateral static stability.

k. Know the effect of the wing position on lateral static stability and the reasons for these effects.

l. Know phugoid oscillation, short period oscillation, spiral divergence/convergence, proverse roll, and dutch roll.

m. Know adverse yaw and the use of spoiler versus ailerons to reduce adverse yaw.

n. Know the function of trim tabs, and relate their use in correcting inflight imbalances.

o. Know the relationship between an airplane's stability and its maneuverability.

p. Know the various control surfaces on an airplane and their functions.

B. *Engineering*

Demonstrate, in accordance with NAVAVSCOLSCOMINST 1610.7H, knowledge of the fundamentals of power plants and associated accessory systems.

  1. Know the basic physical principles that relate to gas turbine engines.
     a. Know the definition of potential energy.
     b. Know the definition of kinetic energy.
     c. Know how pressure and velocity are related.
     d. Know Bernoulli's Theorem.
     e. Know how subsonic air reacts in a nozzle or diffuser.
     f. Know how supersonic air reacts in a nozzle or diffuser.
  2. Know the principles of operation for a gas turbine engine.
     a. Know what the five components of a gas turbine do.
     b. Know Newton's Second and Third Laws of Motion.
     c. Know how pressure, temperature, and velocity change throughout a gas turbine engine.
     d. Know the Brayton Cycle.
     e. Know gross thrust and net thrust.
     f. Know how pressure, temperature, altitude, humidity, and RPM affect the thrust produced by a gas turbine engine.
     g. Know how airspeed and the ram effect change the amount of thrust produced by a gas turbine engine.
     h. Know the various instruments found in the cockpit that are used to measure thrust.
  3. Know the functions of gas turbine engine components.
     a. Know the five sections of all gas turbine engines.
     b. Know the function of the inlet in the operation of the gas turbine engine.
     c. Know the difference between subsonic and supersonic inlets.
     d. Know the function of the gas turbine compressor.
     e. Know the three types of compressors.
     f. Know the function of the burner section.
     g. Know the three types of combustion chambers used in gas turbines.
     h. Know the function of the turbine section.
     i. Know the three types of turbines used in gas turbines.
     j. Know how heat and potential energy are converted into mechanical energy in the turbine section.

k. Know the function of the exhaust duct.

l. Know the two types of exhaust nozzles.

m. Know the function of the afterburner.

n. Know the components of the afterburner.

o. Know the operation of the afterburner.

4. Know the reasons for compressor stalls and how to avoid or reduce them.

a. Know the characteristics of a compressor stall.

b. Know what causes the compressor to stall.

c. Know the angle of attack of air on the compressor blades and the two factors that determine it.

d. Know how airflow distortions can cause compressor stalls.

e. Know the three possible mechanical problems that can lead to compressor stall.

f. Know how to avoid compressor stalls.

g. Know the steps to be taken if compressor stall occurs.

5. Know the construction and operating characteristics of a turbojet engine.

a. Know the definition of a gas generator.

b. Know the construction of a turbojet engine.

c. Know how the turbojet produces thrust.

d. Know the advantages and disadvantages of using a turbojet engine.

6. Know the construction and operating characteristics of a turbofan engine.

a. Know the construction of a turbofan engine.

b. Know how thrust is produced by a turbofan.

c. Know the advantages and disadvantages of the turbofan over the turbojet.

7. Know the construction and operating characteristics of a turboprop engine.

a. Know the construction of a turboprop engine.

b. Know how a turboprop produces thrust.

c. Know the advantages and disadvantages of the turboprop.

8. Know the construction and operating characteristics of a turboshaft engine.

a. Know the construction of a turboshaft engine.

b. Know how the turboshaft produces thrust.

9. Know the basics of hydraulic theory.

a. Know the definition of Pascal's Law.

b. Know force and pressure and how they relate to hydraulic theory.

c. Know how area affects the force produced in a hydraulic system and how it affects linear movement.

10. Know the basic operation of an aircraft hydraulic system.

a. Know why hydraulic systems are required on aircraft.

b. Know the function of basic hydraulic components used on aircraft.

c. Know the operation of a basic aircraft hydraulic system.

11. Know the basic operation of an aircraft electrical system.

a. Know the function of basic electrical components used on aircraft.

b. Know the operations of a basic aircraft electrical system.

12. Know the basic operation of an aircraft fuel system.

a. Know the function of basic fuel system components on aircraft.

b. Know the flow of fuel through a basic aircraft fuel system.

13. Know the basic operation of an aircraft lubrication system.

a. Know the functions of basic lubrication system components used on aircraft.

b. Know the operation of a basic aircraft lubrication system.

14. Know the basic operation of aircraft accessory, starter, and ignition systems.

a. Know the types of accessories used on aircraft and how they are driven.

b. Know the starting sequence for a gas turbine.

c. Know the four types of abnormal starts.

d. Know the three types of starters.

e. Know the two types of ignitors.

f. Know a basic aircraft ignition system.

C. *Navigation*

Demonstrate, in accordance with NAVAVSCOLSCOMINST 1610.7H, knowledge of the fundamentals of air navigation and dead-reckoning navigation skills necessary to enter pilot or naval flight officer training.

1. Know basic concepts, principles, and terminology used in air navigation.

    a. Know the definitions of the four types of navigation.

    b. Know the five flight instruments essential to dead-reckoning navigation.

    c. Demonstrate the accurate use of the elementary tools of air navigation in a classroom environment.

2. Know the characteristics of chart projections and plotting techniques.

    a. Apply the concepts of position, direction, distance, and time to air navigation.

    b. Know the specific characteristics of Mercator and Lambert Conformal projections.

    c. Demonstrate the navigation plotter and dividers by plotting courses and measuring directions to a tolerance of ± 2 degrees and distance to within ± 2 nautical miles.

    d. Demonstrate the use of the navigation plotter and chart, locating geographic points and plotting the positions to within ± 1 nautical mile using degrees and minutes of latitude and longitude.

3. Demonstrate the application of the computer side of the CR-3 Computer in air navigation.

    a. Apply the components, scales, and indexes of the CR-3 Computer.

    b. Demonstrate use of the navigation computer by solving rate, time, and distance problems to within ± 3 knots, ± 1 minute and ± 3 in the third significant figure.

4. Know and correlate the principles of the pressure and altitude structure.

    a. Know indicated altitude, calibrated altitude, true altitude, and absolute altitude.

    b. Know the effects that changes in density have on true altitude.

    c. Determine pressure altitude, given a calibrated altitude and the altimeter setting.

    d. Determine true altitude using the CR-3 Computer.

    e. Know indicated airspeed, calibrated airspeed, true airspeed, and groundspeed.

    f. Determine true airspeed using the CR-3 Computer.

5. Demonstrate the application of the wind side of the CR-3 Computer in air navigation.

a. Apply the effect of wind on the path of an aircraft over the ground.

b. Demonstrate use of the navigation computer by solving for unknown values of wind direction and velocity, true heading, true airspeed, drift angle, and course (track).

c. Demonstrate use of the CR-3 Computer by applying given wind to a course to determine true heading within ± 2 degrees and groundspeed within ± 2 knots.

6. Demonstrate the application of the CR-3 Computer in the analysis of fuel flow and rate of descent.

a. Know how to solve fuel problems involving conversions between pounds and gallons.

b. Know how to solve fuel rate problems involving fuel flow, fuel quantity, and time.

c. Know how to solve rate of descent problems using the CR-3 Computer.

7. Know the global timekeeping system.

a. Apply standard zone description to convert between Greenwich Mean Time and local zone time.

8. Know the procedures for maintaining a Dead-Reckoning Log.

a. Know dead-reckoning navigation symbols applicable to air navigation chart use.

b. Apply interpolation of given values of variations and deviation from prescribed calibration cards and chart, by converting true heading to magnetic heading and compass heading within a tolerance of ± 1 degree.

9. Know the dead-reckoning (DR) concept of flight planning, inflight analysis, and altered headings to the intended destination.

a. Know how to complete the chart work required for a dead-reckoning navigation flight.

b. Know how to interrelate information from an air navigation chart and log.

10. Know procedures for solving controlled time of arrival problems using a predetermined destination.

a. Demonstrate the use of navigation computer by solving specific time of arrival problems within ± 2 degrees of true heading and ± 2 knots of true airspeed.

11. Know the procedures used to successfully airplot an aircraft's flight path.

 a. Know how to determine the wind direction and velocity using airplot procedures.

 b. Know how to DR out of a fix position by computing track and groundspeed with the CR-3 Computer.

 c. Demonstrate use of all previously introduced navigation equipment by planning a hypothetical flight on a chart using airplot procedures to within ±3 nautical miles of given coordinates.

12. Know the methods used for low-level visual navigation.

 a. Know the advantages and disadvantages of low-level visual navigation.

 b. Know the two types of Lambert Conformal charts used most often for low-level navigation, and describe the characteristics and symbology used with each of them.

 c. Know where descriptions of military training routes can be found, and list the characteristics desirable when determining a low-level mission's route.

 d. Know the procedures for plotting a low-level route to include target/checkpoint symbology, and know the data items contained in the information box of each leg of the route.

13. Know the methods used for electronic navigation.

 a. Know the three main electronic navigation aids used by aviators, and recall the cockpit instruments where the nav-aid information will be presented to the aircrew.

 b. Know the major advantage of TACAN over VOR and ADF electronic nav-aids.

 c. Know how to describe the aircraft's position and course to the nav-aid facility, given the magnetic bearing (radial) of an aircraft from a nav-aid.

 d. Know the two types of enroute charts which portray the airways system, and define the altitudes covered by each of the charts.

 e. Know the general symbology used on the enroute airways charts to include airports, nav-aids, airways, and distance scales.

 f. Know the primary purpose of the "jet log," and list the seven major categories of information contained in the log.

D. *Safety*

1. Know Navy safety programs and precautions including ordnance, workplace and environmental and electrical safety programs.

2. Know classes of fire and agents, equipments, and procedures used to extinguish them.

APPENDIX B

RECOMMENDED PROFESSIONAL READING

The following list of books is recommended to all naval officers in their first three years of service:

Bissel, A. M., D. J. Livingston, and E. J. Oertel. *Shipboard Damage Control.* Annapolis: Naval Institute Press, 1976.

Britton, B. H. *International Law for Seagoing Officers.* Annapolis: Naval Institute Press, 1981.

Byrne, E. *Military Law.* 3rd ed. Annapolis: Naval Institute Press, 1981.

Corse, C. D. *Introduction to Shipboard Weapons.* Annapolis: Naval Institute Press, 1975.

Crenshaw, R. S. *Naval Shiphandling.* 4th ed. Annapolis: Naval Institute Press, 1975.

Day, C. L. *The Art of Knotting and Splicing.* Annapolis: Naval Institute Press, 1986.

Deutermann, P. T. *Ops Officer's Manual.* Annapolis: Naval Institute Press, 1980.

Dodge, D. O., and S. E. Kyriss. *Seamanship.* Annapolis: Naval Institute Press, 1981.

Griffith, S. B. *The Battle for Guadalcanal.* Baltimore: Nautical and Aviation Publishing, 1980.

Gritzen, E. F. *Introduction to Naval Engineering.* Annapolis: Naval Institute Press, 1980.

Henderson, R. *Sail and Power.* Annapolis: Naval Institute Press, 1979.

Hobbs, R. R. *Marine Navigation I and II.* Annapolis: Naval Institute Press, 1981.

Hughes, W. P., Jr. *Fleet Tactics.* Annapolis: Naval Institute Press, 1986.

Jacobsen, K. C. *Watch Officer's Guide.* 11th ed. Annapolis: Naval Institute Press, 1979.

King. R. W., ed. *Naval Engineering and American Seapower.* Baltimore: Nautical and Aviation Publishing, 1989.

Kotsch, W. J. *Weather for the Mariner.* Annapolis: Naval Institute Press, 1983.

Mack, W. P., and A. H. Konetzni. *Command at Sea.* Annapolis: Naval Institute Press, 1982.

Mack, W. P., and R. W. Connell. *Naval Ceremonies, Customs, and Traditions.* Annapolis: Naval Institute Press, 1980.

Maloney, E. S. *Dutton's Navigation and Piloting.* Annapolis: Naval Institute Press, 1985.

Montor, K., et al. *Naval Leadership.* Annapolis: Naval Institute Press, 1987.

Noel, J., and F. Bassett. *Knight's Modern Seamanship.* New York: Van Nostrand Reinhold, 1974.

Operations Analysis Study Group, U.S. Naval Academy. *Naval Operations Analysis.* Annapolis: Naval Institute Press, 1977.

Pemsel, H. *A History of War at Sea.* Annapolis: Naval Institute Press, 1978.

Ruge, F. *The Soviets as Naval Opponents.* Annapolis: Naval Institute Press, 1979.

Seager, R. *Alfred Thayer Mahan: The Man and His Letters.* Annapolis: Naval Institute Press, 1977.

Swartz, O. D. *Service Etiquette.* 4th ed. Annapolis: Naval Institute Press, 1989.

Symonds, C. L. *New Aspects of Naval History.* Annapolis: Naval Institute Press, 1981.

Tate, W. H. *A Mariner's Guide to the Rules of the Road.* Annapolis: Naval Institute Press, 1982.

Winters, D. D. *The Boat Officer's Handbook.* Naval Institute Press, 1981.

Wylie, F. J. *The Use of Radar at Sea.* 5th ed. Annapolis: Naval Institute Press, 1978.

U.S. Government Publications

Read and become familiar with the government publications listed in the bibliography.

Professional Magazines and Journals

U.S. Naval Institute Proceedings
U.S. Naval Institute Naval History
Armed Forces Journal
Navy Times
Defense Science
U.S. Naval War College Review
Marine Corps Gazette
All Hands
Surface Warfare Magazine
Fathom Magazine
Approach Magazine
Aviation Review
Tailhook Magazine
Aviation Week

APPENDIX C

RECOMMENDED READING IN LIBERAL ARTS

The following reading list indicates the range of areas covered in a typical American college liberal arts curriculum. At the end is a selection of titles from the group of "Fifty Great Books" studied at St. John's College, a leading liberal arts school. The officer who wishes to benefit from a liberal arts education should read the books on these lists—or other books in the same general area—within three years. Other readings in English and world literature should be pursued as time permits in years following.

Political Science/Political Philosophy/ Foreign Affairs

Aristotle. *Politics.* Chicago: University of Chicago Press, 1984.

Bickel, A. M. *The Morality of Consent.* New Haven: Yale University Press, 1975.

Current, R. *The Political Thought of Abraham Lincoln.* New York: Macmillan, 1985.

de Tocqueville, A. *Democracy in America.* New York: Alfred A. Knopf, 1985.

Henkin, L. *Foreign Affairs and the Constitution.* New York: Norton, 1975.

The Life and Selected Writings of Thomas Jefferson. New York: Modern Library, 1944.

Locke, J. *Two Treatises of Government.* New York: New American Library, 1960.

Machiavelli. *The Prince.* New York: Penguin Books, 1975.

Madison, J., et al. *The Federalist Papers.* New York: Penguin Books, 1987.

Marx, K., and F. Engels.*The Communist Manifesto.* New York: Norton, 1988.

Milosz, C. *The Captive Mind.* New York: Vintage Books, 1981.

Plato. *The Republic.* New York: E. P. Dutton, 1957.

Revel, J. F. *How Democracies Perish.* New York: Harper and Row, 1983.

Rousseau, J. *The Social Contract and Discourse on the Origins of Inequality.* New York: Washington Square Press, 1967.

Shipler, D. K. *Russia.* New York: Penguin Books, 1984.

Strauss, L., and J. Cropsey. *History of Political Philosophy.* 3d ed. Chicago: University of Chicago Press, 1987.

Will, G. F. *Statecraft as Soulcraft.* New York: Simon & Schuster, 1983.

You may want to substitute current reading for some of the foregoing books. Reading in news magazines such as *U.S. News and World Report* and either *Time* or *Newsweek* is valuable. Comprehensive examinations given for a master's degree in international affairs at George Washington University frequently derive almost 50 percent of their examination material from these periodicals.

Psychology/Philosophy/Religion

Bourke, V. J., ed. *The Pocket Aquinas.* New York: Washington Square Press, 1960.

Burr, J. R., and M. Goldinger, eds. *Philosophy* and *Contemporary Issues.* 5th ed. New York: Macmillan, 1976.

Butterfield, H. *Christianity and History.* New York: Scribner, 1950.

Durant, Will. *The Story of Philosophy.* New York: Simon and Schuster, 1960.

Epictetus, *The Enchiridion.* Indianapolis: Bobbs-Merrill Educational Publishing, 1955.

Meerlow, J. A. M. *The Rape of the Mind.* New York: Grosset and Dunlap, 1961.

Mill, J. S. *On Liberty.* New York: Norton, 1975.

Russell, B. *History of Western Philosophy.* New York: Simon and Schuster, 1972.

Saint Augustine. *Confessions.* New York: Penguin Books, 1974.

Temple, W. *Nature, Mind, and God.* London: Macmillan, 1960.

Tillich, Paul. *The Dynamics of Faith.* New York: Harper and Row, 1957.

Cultural Anthropology

Bloom, A. *The Closing of the American Mind.* New York: Simon and Schuster, 1987.

Campbell, J. *The Hero with a Thousand Faces.* Princeton: Princeton University Press, 1973.

Frazer, J. G. *The Golden Bough.* New York: Macmillan, 1985.

Wilson, E. O. *On Human Nature.* Cambridge: Harvard University Press, 1978.

History

Durant, W. *The Lessons of History.* New York: Simon and Schuster, 1968.

Kennedy, P. *The Rise and Fall of the Great Powers.* New York: Random House, 1989.

Mahan, A. T. *The Influence of Sea Power Upon History.* New York: Little, Brown & Co., 1890.

Morison, S. E. *John Paul Jones.* Boston: Little, Brown and Co., 1959.

Potter, E. B., ed. Annapolis: Naval Institute Press, 1981. *Sea Power.* Englewood Cliffs: Prentice-Hall, 1960.

Thucydides. *The Peloponnesian War.* New York: Penguin Books, 1954.

Tuchman, B. *A Distant Mirror.* New York: Knopf, 1978.

Economics

Samuelson, P., and W. Nordhaus. *Economics.* 13th ed. New York: McGraw-Hill, 1989.

Silk, L. *Economics in Plain English.* New York: Simon and Schuster, 1978.

Smith, A. *The Wealth of Nations.* New York: Penguin Books, 1982.

Sowell, T. *Marxism: Philosophy and Economics.* New York: Morrow, 1986.

English Literature

Ahern, D., and R. Shenk, eds. *Literature in the Education of the Military Professional.* U.S. Government Printing Office: 1984.

Allison, A. W., et al., eds. *The Norton Anthology of Poetry.* New York: Norton, 1975.

Dickens, C. *A Tale of Two Cities.* New York: Bantam Books, 1984.

Homer. *The Odyssey.* New York: Penguin Books, 1988.

Joyce, J. *A Portrait of the Artist as a Young Man.* New York: Penguin Books, 1968.

Melvillle, H. *Billy Budd, Sailor.* Chicago: University of Chicago Press, 1962.

Milton. *Paradise Lost.* New York: The Modern Library, 1969.

Orwell, G. "Politics and the English Language." *The Orwell Reader.* New York: Harcourt, Brace, 1956.

Proust, M. *Swann's Way.* New York: The Modern Library, 1956.

Shakespeare, W. *Richard the Second.* New York: Washington Square Press, 1988.

Sophocles. *Three Tragedies.* Chicago: University of Chicago Press, 1954.

Strunk, W., and E. B. White. *The Elements of Style.* 3rd ed. New York: Macmillan, 1979.

Thoreau, H. D. *Walden.* New York: Bantam Books, 1962.

The foregoing list is only a sampling. Additional works by these and other authors should be read as time permits.

The following titles are taken from the list of Great Books studied at St. John's College:

Thucydides. *The Peloponnesian War.*

Herodotus. *History.*

Marcus Aurelius. *Meditations.*

Epictetus. *Discourses.*

Augustine. *Confessions.*

Machiavelli. *The Prince; Discourses.*

Montaigne. *Essays.*

Galileo. *Two New Sciences.*

Descartes. *Discourses on Method, etc.*

Locke. *Essay Concerning Human Understanding.*

Newton. *Principia.*

Hume. *Treatise of Human Nature.*

de Tocqueville. *Democracy in America.*
Darwin. *Origin of the Species.*
Hegel. *Introduction to the History of Philosophy.*
Nietzsche. *Birth of Tragedy* and *Thus Spake Zarathustra.*
Freud. *General Introduction to Psychoanalysis.*
Heisenberg. *The Physical Principles of the Quantum Theory.*

APPENDIX D

Code of Conduct

Executive Order 10631 of 17 August 1955 established the Code of Conduct for military men and women. After the experience of prisoners of war in Vietnam, article 4 was modified by Executive Order 12017 in November 1977.

Article 1. I am an American fighting man. I serve in the forces which guard my country and our way of life. I am prepared to give my life in their defense.

Article 2. I will never surrender of my own free will. If in command I will never surrender the members of my command while they have the means to resist.

Article 3. If I am captured I will continue to resist by all means available. I will make every effort to escape and aid others to escape. I will accept neither parole nor special favors from the enemy.

Article 4. If I become a prisoner of war, I will keep faith with my fellow prisoners. I will give no information or take part in any action which might be harmful to my comrades. If I am senior, I will take command. If not, I will obey the lawful orders of those appointed over me and will back them up in every way.

Article 5. When questioned, should I become a prisoner of war, I am required to give name, rank, service number, and date of birth. I will evade answering further questions to the utmost of my ability. I will make no oral or written statements disloyal to my country or its allies or harmful to their cause.

Article 6. I will never forget that I am an American fighting man, responsible for my actions, and dedicated to the principles which made my country free. I will trust in my God and the United States of America.

APPENDIX E

MILITARY LAW

In this appendix you will find a condensed version of the essentials of military law. For more detailed information on rules of evidence, elements of offenses, and detailed methods of conducting legal proceedings, consult the *MCM*, the *Manual of the Judge Advocate General*, and the various legal publications in your ship's office or shore station legal office. A handy personal reference, *Military Law*, will answer most of your questions. You will also find the following publications helpful: *Military Law in a Nutshell*, the *Military Justice Handbook*: *Trial Guide*, and the *Basic Military Justice Handbook*.

Every naval officer should know the fundamentals of military law and naval discipline. An officer may have to act as prosecuting attorney if he or she is ordered to act as trial counsel in a special court-martial. An officer may be detailed or requested to act as defense counsel for an enlisted person who is to be tried by court-martial, although travel teams made up of legal officers from the legal review centers are usually available. An officer may have to perform the dual duties of judge and jury if he or she is ordered as senior member of a special court-martial and no legal officer is available. If ordered to conduct a formal pretrial investigation, which always precedes a general court-martial, an officer may perform duties similar to those of a civilian grand jury.

Military law is the body of rules prescribed by competent authority for the government of the armed forces. There are two general sources of military laws, codified and supplemental. The sources of codified or statutory military law include the Constitution, statutes enacted by the Congress, and international law. The sources of supplemental or interpretive law include decisions of the courts; decisions of the president, the secretary of defense, and the secretary of the Navy; opinions of the attorney general and the judge advocate of the Navy; and service usages.

Uniform Code of Military Justice. As a result of the unification of the armed forces and a need for the revision of the Articles of War and the Articles for the Government of the Navy, on 5 May 1950 Public Law 506 of the Eighty-first Congress established the UCMJ. This act unified the systems of military law and justice then in effect in the services and made the new UCMJ applicable to all services, including the Coast Guard. The code was amended significantly in 1965. A joint committee of the services prepared a new manual giving basic instructions for the administration of military justice. Called the *Manual for Courts-Martial*, it was signed into law by the president in 1951. A major revision was completed in 1969 and another in 1984. The Navy subsequently issued the *Manual of the Judge Advocate General.*

UCMJ Art. 137 specifies that certain of its articles be carefully explained to all enlisted persons when they enter active duty, complete six months' active duty, and reenlist; a complete text of the UCMJ is to be made available upon request to any person on active duty. Pertinent articles cover such subjects as persons subject to UCMJ, jurisdiction, apprehension, punishments authorized to be inflicted by various courts and command authorities, detailing and duties of trial counsel and defense counsel, and punitive measures.

Reciprocal jurisdiction is provided for in Art. 17(a), which states: "Each armed force shall have court-martial jurisdiction over all persons subject to this code." Exercise of this jurisdiction is in accordance with regulations prescribed by the president and will usually be restricted to cases where it is not feasible to bring the accused before a court-martial of the same service.

Court of Military Appeals. This court was established in the Department of Defense and is composed of three civilian judges, who are appointed for terms of fifteen years and have the same qualifications as other federal judges. Cases subject to review by this court include all those in which the sentence, as affirmed by a service court of review (Navy–Marine Corps Court of Military Review), affects a general or flag officer or involves the death sentence; all those subject to a service's board of review and forwarded by that service's judge advocate general to the court for further review; and all cases subject to a court of review in which a petition for review by the accused has been granted by the court. The Court of Military Appeals has authority only to disapprove the findings and sentence, dismiss a case, or order a rehearing.

Sentences involving the death penalty or a general or flag

officer must be approved by the president. Sentences dismissing an officer, cadet, or midshipman must be approved by the secretary of the Navy. Dishonorable or bad-conduct discharges or a sentence of one year's confinement or more are not executed until affirmed by a court of review or by the Court of Military Appeals.

Nonjudicial Punishment (NJP). When an enlisted person is reported for an offense, the report slip is routed to an officer of the command for preliminary inquiry or investigation to determine if the reported misconduct was actually committed by the person on report and if it is an offense under UCMJ. All information concerning the reported misconduct, including the investigating officer's charge sheet (NAVMILPERS Form 1626/7), is assembled and presented to the executive officer. He or she reviews the material, conducts a screening mast, and presents the case, if warranted, to the CO, who must decide whether to hear the case at mast, dismiss the case, request further investigation, or refer the case directly to a higher forum. The accused, except those attached to or embarked in ships, have the right to refuse NJP. A common misconception is that a service member can demand a court-martial. This is not true. He or she can refuse NJP, in which case the CO must decide what step to take.

Conduct of Captain's Mast. Mast should be conducted with dignity in a suitable location. The chief master-at-arms or another senior petty officer is detailed to maintain order and to ensure that proper military etiquette is observed. Mast is no longer held before the mainmast as it was in the days of sail, but rather in a designated area suitable to accommodate the number of persons involved. A lectern is provided for the CO. The division officer of each accused person should be informed of all details of the charge and should be prepared to testify to the record and reputation of the accused. The accused should be instructed about procedure at mast and should be advised to present a neat and military appearance. Request mast is held for members of the crew who ask for it and meritorious mast is held to acknowledge good conduct. These masts should be held separately from disciplinary mast or at least before it. The principals are assembled at least fifteen minutes before mast. An officer, usually the legal officer, warns the accused and any witnesses who may be suspects of their rights under UCMJ Art. 31. Those at mast usually face the lectern in one or more ranks three paces in front of it. Witnesses fall in on the left side of the lectern and division officers and officer witnesses fall in on the right side. The chief master-at-arms then advises the executive officer that mast is ready and the CO is subsequently informed. As the CO reaches the mast area, the chief master-at-arms gives the order, "Mast reports salute." After the CO returns the salute, the cases are called. The chief master-at-arms calls each person forward by name. The accused takes position one pace in front of the lectern and uncovers. The CO then considers the report of preliminary investigation and asks witnesses appropriate questions to establish as clearly as possible the nature of the offense. After all witnesses against the accused have been heard, the CO asks the accused if he or she desires to make any statement or to present any matters in defense, mitigation, or extenuation. The accused can interrogate witnesses standing against him or her. The CO, at this stage of the proceedings, should see that the case is fairly heard. After all the evidence has been presented, the CO asks the accused's division officer questions concerning the person's record, reputation, and performance of duty.

After completing these steps, the CO announces a decision. He or she may dismiss the charges; excuse the offense with or without a warning; determine guilt and impose NJP under UCMJ Art. 15; refer the case to a summary or special court-martial or recommend such trial to a superior; order a formal pretrial investigation if the offense appears serious enough to warrant recommendation for trial by general court-martial; or postpone action pending further investigation.

Upon the completion of the last case, the chief master-at-arms orders the mast reports to salute. The CO returns the salute, retires, and mast is piped down.

If the CO has imposed NJP, those punished are advised of their rights to appeal under the provisions of UCMJ Art. 15. Appeals to the CO must be made in writing to his or her immediate superior within a reasonable time, usually within five days after imposition of punishment.

The CO writes the disposition of each case on the mast punishment book or has someone else make such an entry and then initials the page.

Subsequent to the imposition of NJP, the executive officer or someone under his or her direction ensures that all necessary steps are taken to execute punishments not suspended. Other officers record punishments in the log or station journal and see that proper service-record entries are made.

The Navy Department advocates the use of NJP in every possible case where the ends of justice and naval discipline may be attained by its use. Mast proceedings are brief and direct, and most importantly, the punishment is prompt. NJP is not a conviction and cannot be used as such in a subsequent trial (although it may be used as a matter of aggravation).

Summary Courts-Martial. The function of the summary court-martial is to exercise justice promptly for relatively minor offenses. Any person subject to UCMJ, except officers, cadets, and midshipmen, may be tried by summary court-martial. A summary court-martial is composed of one commissioned officer, as a matter of policy a lieutenant in the Navy or a captain in the Marine Corps or higher. A summary court-martial may be convened by any officer having authority to convene a general or special court-martial or by the CO or officer-in-charge of any command when empowered by the secretary of the Navy. To date no one has been so empowered.

In cases where only one officer is attached to a vessel or station, the CO hears and determines all summary court-martial cases brought before him or her. No order appointing the court need be issued. When more than one officer is present in a command, a subordinate officer is appointed summary court-martial, and a written appointing order is issued. The summary court-martial officer is not sworn; he or she performs under the sanction of oath of office.

A reporter is not ordinarily appointed, but the convening authority may order any person under his or her command to perform such duty. The appointing order for a reporter need not be in writing and need not be shown in the trial record.

The examination of witnesses, who testify under oath, is conducted by the summary court-martial officer. If the convening officer is the accuser of the person to be tried, he or she may forward the charges and specifications to superior authority with a recommendation that the court be tried by the senior. Failure to do so will not invalidate the trial, but it is advisable to follow the forwarding procedure (UCMJ Art. 246).

An enlisted person brought before a summary court-martial for trial must signify willingness to be tried by such a court by signing a statement to that effect on the appropriate block on page 4 of the charge sheet. If the accused objects, he or she may be ordered to trial by a higher court. Enlisted persons do not ordinarily object to trial by a summary court-martial because its range of punishment is more restricted than that of other courts-martial (and it does not carry a federal conviction).

It is the duty of the summary court-martial officer to advise the accused of his or her rights and to inform the accused of the general nature of the charges, who appointed the court, the name of the accuser, and the maximum sentence the court can pass. For punishments authorized see UCMJ Art. 20, *MCM* Chap. 25, and *MCM* para. 16b.

In case of acquittal, the accused is informed by the summary court-martial officer. In case of conviction, the findings and sentence are announced to the accused during the trial. A summary of the trial is entered in the ship's log, an entry is made in the service record, and the record of the trial and a summary of the evidence required are forwarded to the convening authority for review (see *MCM* para. 79e)

Special Courts-Martial.   Any person who may convene a general court-martial—the CO of a ship or station, the CO of a detached squadron, battalion, or corresponding unit, and officers in charge of a Navy or Coast Guard command when authorized by their secretaries—may order a special court-martial for officers, petty officers, or enlisted persons under their command for the trial of offenses not deemed serious enough to be tried by a general court-martial. A special court-martial is composed of any number of members but not less than three. The defense counsel must be a lawyer certified under UCMJ Art. 27b; the prosecutor may or may not be so certified. Board members must be commissioned or warrant officers—or if requested by the accused, enlisted persons—of the same service as the accused. Officers and enlisted persons may be ordered temporarily to the command of the convening authority for court-martial duty.

The officer of highest rank on the court is the president, the others are members. There are two types of courts, one with a military judge and one without. When no judge is appointed, the senior member must make judicial rulings. This is rare. If no military judge presides over the court, the sentence that may be passed is limited. The accused may elect trial by military judge only. When a service member is acting as jurist, he or she will have to rule on interlocutory questions and challenges. The trial counsel acts as prosecuting attorney, and the defense counsel acts as defense attorney for the accused.

If an enlisted person requests enlisted members in writing, that person may not be tried by a special court-martial unless its membership includes enlisted persons in a number comprising at least one-third of the court, unless eligible enlisted persons cannot be obtained because of physical conditions or military exigencies. Enlisted persons shall not be members of the same company, air squadron, ship's company, or corresponding unit. When enlisted members cannot be obtained, the court may be convened and the trial held without them, but the convening authority must explain the reasons in detail in a written statement appended to the record. Whenever possible, the senior member should be an officer of a rank not below that equivalent to a lieutenant in the Navy, and no member of the court should be junior to the accused. For punishments see UCMJ Art. 19 and *MCM* paras. 15b, 125–27.

General Courts-Martial. A general court-martial is the highest tribunal in naval law. It is convened for the trial of commissioned officers, warrant officers, petty officers, and enlisted persons. General courts-martial may pass the sentences of death, dismissal, dishonorable discharge, total forfeitures, confinement, and hard labor for periods up to life, and any other punishment any other court is authorized to inflict. General courts-martial may be convened by the president, the secretary of the Navy, the commander in chief of a fleet, the CO of a naval station or of a larger command beyond the continental limits of the United States, and any CO authorized by the president and the secretary of the Navy.

A general court-martial is composed of not less than five commissioned officers or warrant officers, enlisted persons if an enlisted accused has requested them in writing, and a military judge. The accused may also submit a written request to be tried by a military judge alone. (As in a special court-martial, an accused enlisted person has a right to trial by a general court composed of at least one-third enlisted persons.) The *MCM* requires that the president shall have rank at least equivalent to that of a lieutenant in the Navy, but the Navy Department has long maintained a policy that he or she should be a senior line officer. In detailing officers for the trial of a staff or Marine Corps officer, if possible at least one-third of the court should be officers of the same corps as the accused. For trial of an officer, all members except the military judge should be senior to the accused. When an officer of the Regular Navy is tried, it is customary for a majority of members to be of the Regular Navy.

The military judge of a general court-martial is appointed by the convening authority. He or she must be a member of the bar of a federal court or of the highest court of a state and certified to be qualified for duty as military judge by the judge advocate general of the service of which he or she is a member. No person shall act as a military judge when he or she is the accuser or witness for the prosecution or has acted as investigating officer.

Except when reviewing the form of the findings and sentencing, the military judge may consult with members of the court only in the presence of the accused, trial counsel, and defense counsel. The judge does not vote.

Investigation of Charges. The responsibilities of convening authorities, such as investigating charges, informing the accused of the charges, and examining witnesses in the presence of the accused and the counsel, are discussed in detail in *MCM* paras. 31–35. With respect to the convening authority's responsibility for such investigations, the *MCM* states:

> He will make, or cause to be made, a preliminary inquiry into the charges or the suspected offenses sufficient to enable him to make an intelligent disposition of them. This inquiry is usually informal. It may be conducted by the commander or by a member of his command. It may consist only of an examination of the charges and the summary of expected evidence which accompanies them; in other cases it may involve the interview of witnesses, the search of barracks, quarters, or other places, or the collection of documentary evidence. . . . It is not the function of the person making the inquiry merely to prepare a case against the accused. He should collect and examine all evidence that is essential to a determination of the guilt or innocence of the accused, as well as evidence in mitigation or extenuation. (*MCM* 32b).

UCMJ Art. 32 states that no charge shall be referred to a general court-martial for trial until a thorough and impartial investigation of the subject matter of the offense has been conducted prior to the time the accused is charged with the offense; the accused must be present at such an investigation and afforded an opportunity for representation, cross-examination, and presentation of evidence on his or her own behalf. Under certain rare conditions, a court of inquiry or an investigation will suffice as a formal pretrial investigation (see UCMJ Art. 32).

Arrest, Restriction, and Confinement. The various forms of NJP a CO may administer to commissioned and warrant officers are given in UCMJ Art. 15.

As an administrative action, but not as punishment, an officer or any other person subject to UCMJ, when charged with an offense under UCMJ, may be order into arrest or confinement as circumstances require. In lieu of arrest, administrative restriction may be imposed, requiring the accused to remain within a specified area at fixed times. Administrative restriction must be distinguished from NJP restriction, since it is not imposed as a punishment but as a measure to facilitate investigation. It does not carry with it the suspension from duty that may be imposed as part of mast restriction. Administrative restriction is also to be distinguished from arrest: a person under administrative restriction will participate in all military duties and activities, while a person under arrest does not perform full military duty (see UCMJ Art. 10 and *MCM* 20b).

As a rule, a service member may be confined when the convening authority has cause to believe the individual committed a crime; when the individual is likely to be absent from court-martial or is a danger to others in the command; and when lesser forms of restraint have been considered and found wanting. An individual may not be confined because he or she is a nuisance.

Any officer placed under arrest or restriction must confine activities to the areas assigned under disciplinary action. The officer cannot visit the CO or other superior officer unless sent for in a written request.

An officer placed under arrest or restriction aboard ship should not be confined to his or her room or deprived of the proper use of any part of the ship to which he or she was entitled before arrest. If also suspended from duty, the officer may not visit the bridge or quarterdeck unless the safety of the ship requires it. Confinement at a shore station must not be unduly rigorous.

Navy Regulations Art. 1411 states: "Persons in confinement shall be in the custody of a master-at-arms or other person designated by the commanding officer. They shall not be subject to cruel or unusual treatment. They shall be visited as necessary, but at least once every four hours, to ascertain their condition, and to care, as may be appropriate, for their needs."

The use of irons on anyone in the naval service is forbidden, except where it is absolutely necessary with violent prisoners. At no time may their use be inflicted as a punishment. The CO must report immediately by letter to the secretary of the Navy any circumstances requiring the use of irons on a prisoner.

Courts of Inquiry and Investigations. Courts of inquiry and investigations are conducted primarily for fact-finding. Unless directed by the convening authority to express opinions or make recommendations, they should confine themselves to compiling facts.

The proceedings of inquiries and investigations do not constitute a trial. Detailed instructions concerning courts of inquiry and investigations are contained in the *Manual of the Judge Advocate General* chaps. 2, 3, 4, 5, and 6.

Court of Inquiry. UCMJ Art. 135 states:

a. Courts of inquiry to investigate any matter may be convened by any person authorized to convene a general court-martial or by any other person designated by a Secretary of a Department for that purpose whether or not the persons involved have requested such an inquiry.

b. A court of inquiry shall consist of three or more officers. For each court of inquiry the convening authority shall also appoint counsel for the court.

c. Any person subject to this Code whose conduct is subject to inquiry shall be designated as a party. Any person subject to this Code or employed by the Department of Defense who has a direct interest in the subject of inquiry shall have the right to be designated as a party upon request to the court. Any person designated as a party shall be given due notice and shall have the right to be present, to be represented by counsel, to cross-examine witnesses, and to introduce evidence.

d. Members of a court of inquiry may be challenged by a party, but only for cause stated to the court.

e. The members, counsel, the reporter, and interpreters of courts of inquiry shall take an oath or affirmation to faithfully perform their duties.

f. Witnesses may be summoned to appear and testify and be examined before courts of inquiry as provided for courts-martial.

g. Courts of inquiry shall make findings of fact but shall not express opinions or make recommendations unless required to do so by the convening authority.

h. Each court of inquiry shall keep a record of its proceedings, which shall be authenticated by the signatures of the president and counsel for the court and forwarded to the convening authority. In case the record cannot be authenticated by the president, it shall be signed by a member in lieu of the president; and in case the record cannot be authenticated by the counsel for the court, it shall be signed by a member in lieu of the counsel.

Investigations. There are two types of investigations: those where a hearing is required and those where a hearing is not required. Formal investigations are those that may be directed by the appointing officer to take testimony of witnesses under oath and to record their findings verbatim. Investigations where a hearing is not required usually do not take testimony under oath or record summaries of testimony. These investigations consist of one or more officers. (See *Manual of the Judge Advocate General* para. 0512.) A counsel may be appointed for the investigation where a hearing is requested.

Investigations are conducted on accidents and incidents involving military equipment, property, and personnel as well as for suspected violations of UCMJ or governing regulations. Investigation should start as early as possible so that facts will still be fresh in the minds of witnesses.

Chapter 9 of the manual sets out certain criteria that must be met when specific types of incidents—aircraft accidents, flooding, grounding, ship collisions, explosions, and the like—are involved. If injury occurs, a line of duty/misconduct determination is also required, and Chapter 8 of the manual should be consulted.

BIBLIOGRAPHY

Albrecht, A. *Weyer's Warships of the World*. Annapolis: Naval Institute Press, 1980.

Byrne, E. *Military Law*. 3rd ed. Annapolis: Naval Institute Press, 1981.

Collins, J. M. *Grand Strategy*. Annapolis: Naval Institute Press, 1973.

Crenshaw, R. S. *Naval Shiphandling*. Annapolis: Naval Institute Press, 1975.

Deutermann, P. T. *The Ops Officer's Manual*. Annapolis: Naval Institute Press, 1980.

Felger, D. G. *Engineering for the Officer of the Deck*. Annapolis: Naval Institute Press, 1979.

Hunter, W. J. *Challenge: A Professional Anthology*. Annapolis: Naval Institute Press, 1970.

Jacobsen, K. C. *Watch Officer's Guide*. Annapolis: Naval Institute Press, 1930.

Jane, F. T. *Jane's Fighting Ships*. New York: Arco Publishing House. Annual.

Joliff, J. V., and H. E. Robertson. *Naval Engineer's Guide*. Annapolis: U.S. Naval Institute, 1970.

Kotsch, W. J. and R. Henderson. *Heavy Weather Guide*. Annapolis: Naval Institute Press, 1984.

Kotsch, W. J. *Weather for the Mariner*. Annapolis: Naval Institute Press, 1983.

Mack, W. P., and A. H. Konetzni. *Command at Sea*. Annapolis: Naval Institute Press, 1982.

Mack, W. P., and R. Connell. *Naval Ceremonies, Customs, and Traditions*. Annapolis: Naval Institute Press, 1980.

Montor, K., et al. *Naval Leadership*. Annapolis: Naval Institute Press, 1987.

Noel, J. V., and J. Stauridis. *Division Officer's Guide*. Annapolis: Naval Institute Press, 1989.

Noel, J., and F. Bassett. *Knight's Modern Seamanship.* New York: Van Nostrand Reinhold, 1974.

Roskill, R. N. *The Art of Leadership.* London: Collins, 1964.

Winters, D. D. *The Boat Officer's Handbook.* Annapolis: Naval Institute Press, 1981.

Wolfe, M., et al. *Naval Leadership.* Annapolis: U.S. Naval Institute, 1959.

U.S. Government Publications

Basic Military Justice Handbook, 1982.

Department of the Navy Correspondence Manual.

Laws of Naval Warfare, NWP 10–2.

Manual of the Judge Advocate General.

Marine Corps Drill and Ceremonies Manual.

Military Justice Handbook; Trial Guide.

Naval Military Personnel Command Manual.

Navy Guide for Retired Personnel and Their Families, NMPC 15891D.

Organization of the U.S. Navy, NWP 2.

Personnel Management, NAVEDTRA 10848E.

Statement to the Congress, Marine Corps (Annually).

Soviet Military Power; An Assessment of the Threat (Annually), Department of Defense.

Standard Organization and Regulations, U.S. Navy.

Strategic Concepts of the U.S. Navy, NWP 1.

The Maritime Strategy, U.S. Naval Institute supplement to the January 1986 issue of the Naval Institute *Proceedings.*

Understanding Soviet Naval Developments, 5th ed., Office of the Chief of Naval Operations.

Unrestricted Line Officer's Career Planning Guidebook, NMPC 15297A.

Useful Information for the Newly Commissioned Officer, NAVEDTRA 10802AC.

U.S. Navy Regulations.

INDEX

ABOUT THE AUTHORS

Vice Admiral William P. Mack retired in 1975 after forty-two years of service. He served in battleships, destroyers, and amphibians and culminated his sea service with command of the Seventh Fleet during the height of the 1972 North Vietnamese offensive. Ashore he served in a number of personnel billets and as naval aide to the secretary of the navy, deputy assistant secretary of defense for personnel, and finally as superintendent of the Naval Academy. He has written several books on naval subjects and three novels.

Rear Admiral Thomas D. Paulsen served in a variety of billets in surface ships and is currently commander of a cruiser-destroyer flotilla. He served as head of the professional development department at the Naval Academy and as administrative assistant to the chief of naval operations. Admiral Paulsen also coauthored the ninth edition of the Naval Officer's Guide.

The **Naval Institute Press** is the book-publishing arm of the U.S. Naval Institute, a private, nonprofit professional society for members of the sea services and civilians who share an interest in naval and maritime affairs. Established in 1873 at the U.S. Naval Academy in Annapolis, Maryland, where its offices remain today, the Naval Institute has more than 100,000 members worldwide.

Members of the Naval Institute receive the influential monthly magazine *Proceedings* and discounts on fine nautical prints, ship and aircraft photos, and subscriptions to the quarterly *Naval History* magazine. They also have access to the transcripts of the Institute's Oral History Program and get discounted admission to any of the Institute-sponsored seminars regularly offered around the country.

The Naval Institute's book-publishing program, begun in 1898 with basic guides to naval practices, has broadened its scope in recent years to include books of more general interest. Now the Naval Institute Press publishes more than forty new titles each year, ranging from how-to books on boating and navigation to battle histories, biographies, ship and aircraft guides, and novels. Institute members receive discounts on the Press's more than 375 books.

Full-time students are eligible for special half-price membership rates. Life memberships are also available.

For a free catalog describing the Naval Institute Press books currently available, and for further information about U.S. Naval Institute membership, please write to:

Membership & Communications Department
U.S. Naval Institute
118 Maryland Avenue
Annapolis, Maryland 21402-5035

Or call, toll-free, (800) 233-USNI. In Maryland, call (301) 224-3378.

THE NAVAL INSTITUTE PRESS

THE NAVAL OFFICER'S GUIDE
Tenth Edition

Set in Trump Medieval
by JDL Composition Services
Baltimore, Maryland

Printed on 50-lb. Finch Opaque blue-white
and bound in Corvon
by The Maple-Vail Book Manufacturing Group
Binghamton, New York